Navigating Challenges of Object Detection Through Cognitive Computing

Sadique Ahmad
Prince Sultan University, Saudi Arabia

Mansoor Ebrahim
Iqra University, Pakistan

Mohammed El-Affendi
Prince Sultan University, Saudi Arabia

Mohamed Hammad
Prince Sultan University, Saudi Arabia

Vice President of Editorial	Melissa Wagner
Managing Editor of Acquisitions	Mikaela Felty
Managing Editor of Book Development	Jocelynn Hessler
Production Manager	Mike Brehm
Cover Design	Phillip Shickler

Published in the United States of America by
IGI Global Scientific Publishing
701 East Chocolate Avenue
Hershey, PA, 17033, USA
Tel: 717-533-8845
Fax: 717-533-7115
Website: https://www.igi-global.com E-mail: cust@igi-global.com

Copyright © 2025 by IGI Global Scientific Publishing. All rights reserved. No part of this publication may be reproduced, stored or distributed in any form or by any means, electronic or mechanical, including photocopying, without written permission from the publisher.

Product or company names used in this set are for identification purposes only. Inclusion of the names of the products or companies does not indicate a claim of ownership by IGI Global Scientific Publishing of the trademark or registered trademark.

Library of Congress Cataloging-in-Publication Data

LCCN: 2024056692 (CIP Data Pending)
ISBN13: 9798369390573
EISBN13: 9798369390597

British Cataloguing in Publication Data
A Cataloguing in Publication record for this book is available from the British Library.

All work contributed to this book is new, previously-unpublished material.
The views expressed in this book are those of the authors, but not necessarily of the publisher.
This book contains information sourced from authentic and highly regarded references, with reasonable efforts made to ensure the reliability of the data and information presented. The authors, editors, and publisher believe the information in this book to be accurate and true as of the date of publication. Every effort has been made to trace and credit the copyright holders of all materials included. However, the authors, editors, and publisher cannot assume responsibility for the validity of all materials or the consequences of their use. Should any copyright material be found unacknowledged, please inform the publisher so that corrections may be made in future reprints.

Table of Contents

Preface.. xii

Chapter 1
Cognitive Computing Approaches for IoT, Healthcare, Big Data, and
Cybersecurity: A Review 1
> *Mohamed Hammad, Prince Sultan University, Saudi Arabia*
> *Sadique Ahmad, Prince Sultan University, Saudi Arabia*

Chapter 2
Natural Language Processing Techniques for Social Media Sentiment Analysis 33
> *Mohamed Hammad, Prince Sultan University, Saudi Arabia*
> *Wesam Ahmed, Faculty of Computers and Artificial Intelligence,*
> *Hurghada University, Egypt*

Chapter 3
CNN-Based Face Detection Focusing on Diverse Visual Variations 63
> *Faiza Latif Abbasi, Iqra University, Pakistan*
> *Mansoor Ebrahim, Iqra University, Pakistan*
> *Abdul Ahad Abro, Iqra University, Pakistan*
> *Syed Muhammad Daniyal, Iqra University, Pakistan*
> *Ilyas Younus, Iqra University, Pakistan*

Chapter 4
Deep Learning Algorithms for Object Detection in Smart Environments 97
> *D. Dhanya, Artificial Intelligence and Data Science, Mar Ephraem*
>   *College of Engineering and Technology, Kanyakuma, India*
> *R. Rajitha Jasmine, Department of Information Technology, R.M.K.*
>   *Engineering College, Kavaraipettai, India*
> *M. L. Sworna Kokila, CT, SC, Faculty of Engineering and Technology,*
>   *SRM Institute of Science and Technology, Chennai, India*
> *M. Sakthivel, Velammal College of Engineering and Technology,*
>   *Madurai, India*
> *N. Divya, Civil Engineering, Prince Shri Venkateshwara Padmavathy*
>   *Engineering College, Chennai, India*
> *S. Boopathi, Mechanical Engineering, MEC, Namakkal, UAE*

Chapter 5
A Study on Integration of Deep Learning With IoT for Smart Engineering
Solutions 125

    Pydikalva Padmavathi, Electrical and Electronics Engineering,
        Srinivasa Ramanujan Institute of Technology, India
    V. Thrimurthulu, Department of Computer Science Engineering, MLR
        Institute of Technology, Hyderabad, India
    J. S. S. L. Bharani, Department of S.R.K.R. Engineering College,
        Bhimavaram, India
    Vemuri Sailaja, Department of Electronics and Communication and
        Engineering, Pragati Engineering College, Surampalem, India
    Nellore Manoj Kumar, Saveetha School of Engineering,Saveetha
        Institute of Medical and Technical Sciences, Thandal, India
    S. Boopathi, Mechancial Engineering, MEC, Namakkal, India

Chapter 6
Exploring Sentiment Through Cognitive Computing on Social Media
Content 159

    Saifullah Jan, City University of Science and Information Technology,
        Peshawar, Pakistan
    Aiman, City University of Science and Information Technology,
        Peshawar, Pakistan

Chapter 7
Object Detection Algorithm and Challenges 181

    Lubna Aziz, Iqra University, Karachi, Pakistan
    Mansoor Ebrahim, Iqra University, Karachi, Pakistan

Chapter 8
Speech Emotion Recognition-Based Music Recommender 233

    Yasir Hafeez, The University of Nottingham Malaysia, Malaysia
    Syed Hasan Adil, AI Society of Pakistan, Pakistan
    Mansoor Ebrahim, Iqra University, Karachi, Pakistan
    Mirzan Izzfitri Bin Mahadir, The University of Nottingham Malaysia,
        Malaysia

Chapter 9
Smart Processing Line for Automobile Sector Based on Computer Vision 263
> *Muhammad Atif Saeed, Shaheed Zulfikar Ali Bhutto Institute of Science*
> *and Technology, Pakistan*
> *Faraz Junejo, Shaheed Zulfikar Ali Bhutto Institute of Science and*
> *Technology, Pakistan*
> *Imran Amin, Shaheed Zulfikar Ali Bhutto Institute of Science and*
> *Technology, Pakistan*
> *Irfan Khan Tanoli, Universidade da Beira Interior, Portugal*

Compilation of References 291

About the Contributors 335

Index 339

Detailed Table of Contents

Preface... xii

Chapter 1
Cognitive Computing Approaches for IoT, Healthcare, Big Data, and
Cybersecurity: A Review 1
    Mohamed Hammad, Prince Sultan University, Saudi Arabia
    Sadique Ahmad, Prince Sultan University, Saudi Arabia

Cognitive computing has become a crucial technique in contemporary computing because it can solve complex problems that traditional computing systems cannot and because it enables machines to perform tasks that were previously only possible for humans. This chapter provides a comprehensive review of cognitive computing approaches for four critical domains: the Internet of Things (IoT), healthcare, big data, and cybersecurity. The chapter begins by introducing cognitive computing and its potential applications in each of these fields. The section then provides an overview of the current status of research and development in cognitive computing, highlighting key technologies and trends. The chapter then analyses the specific challenges and opportunities presented by each domain, such as data privacy, security, and scalability issues. The chapter concludes with a discussion of the advantages and limitations of cognitive computing in each domain, as well as suggestions for future research and development.

Chapter 2
Natural Language Processing Techniques for Social Media Sentiment Analysis 33
    Mohamed Hammad, Prince Sultan University, Saudi Arabia
    Wesam Ahmed, Faculty of Computers and Artificial Intelligence,
        Hurghada University, Egypt

This Chapter presents a comprehensive examination of Natural Language Processing [NLP] techniques for sentiment analysis in social media contexts, addressing the unique challenges and opportunities presented by user-generated content on social platforms. We trace the evolution of sentiment analysis from early lexicon-based approaches through modern transformer architectures, highlighting the technological advancements that have revolutionized our ability to understand and analyze social media sentiment. The Chapter provides detailed insights into advanced NLP techniques, preprocessing methodologies, and architectural considerations for implementing robust sentiment analysis systems. We also explore evaluation frameworks and metrics for assessing system performance, along with crucial implementation considerations for real-world applications. The Chapter concludes with an examination of emerging trends and future directions, including privacy-preserving techniques and ethical considerations in sentiment analysis.

Chapter 3
CNN-Based Face Detection Focusing on Diverse Visual Variations 63
Faiza Latif Abbasi, Iqra University, Pakistan
Mansoor Ebrahim, Iqra University, Pakistan
Abdul Ahad Abro, Iqra University, Pakistan
Syed Muhammad Daniyal, Iqra University, Pakistan
Ilyas Younus, Iqra University, Pakistan

Facial recognition and emotion detection have become indispensable in modern civilization, affecting a wide range of businesses like banking, social media, education, and commerce. This chapter provides a thorough investigation of emotion recognition from facial expressions, focussing on three important aspects of the process: pre-processing, feature extraction, and classification. With an emphasis on deep learning algorithms that leverage visual facial data, the chapter looks at a variety of cutting-edge and conventional approaches to better understand human emotions. With an emphasis on recent advancements in emotion recognition, comparative results from existing methodologies are shown. The findings show how crucial automated emotion recognition is to some industries and offer useful data regarding the efficacy of various approaches.

Chapter 4
Deep Learning Algorithms for Object Detection in Smart Environments 97
D. Dhanya, Artificial Intelligence and Data Science, Mar Ephraem
College of Engineering and Technology, Kanyakuma, India
R. Rajitha Jasmine, Department of Information Technology, R.M.K.
Engineering College, Kavaraipettai, India
M. L. Sworna Kokila, CT, SC, Faculty of Engineering and Technology,
SRM Institute of Science and Technology, Chennai, India
M. Sakthivel, Velammal College of Engineering and Technology,
Madurai, India
N. Divya, Civil Engineering, Prince Shri Venkateshwara Padmavathy
Engineering College, Chennai, India
S. Boopathi, Mechanical Engineering, MEC, Namakkal, UAE

This chapter has presented the deep learning algorithms in smart environments for object detection purpose; it has, however, come to bode to broader introspect towards more enhanced automation and intelligence. These include advanced architectures of CNN, Region-based CNN, and YOLO which have accomplished their efficiencies in pursuance both for real-time object identification and their subsequent tracking.

These offer high accuracy and multiple applications in the smart home, smart city and Industrial IoT, leveraging large datasets and complex computational power. Discussion The discussion addresses challenges in computing complexity, energy efficiency, and model scalability in resource-impoverished environments. Therefore, important case studies and practical examples would describe the ways in which these alleys can be combined with sensor networks and IoT systems, especially the opportunity to revolutionize areas such as security, automation, and adaptable resource management.

Chapter 5

A Study on Integration of Deep Learning With IoT for Smart Engineering
Solutions 125

> *Pydikalva Padmavathi, Electrical and Electronics Engineering,*
> *Srinivasa Ramanujan Institute of Technology, India*
> *V. Thrimurthulu, Department of Computer Science Engineering, MLR*
> *Institute of Technology, Hyderabad, India*
> *J. S. S. L. Bharani, Department of S.R.K.R. Engineering College,*
> *Bhimavaram, India*
> *Vemuri Sailaja, Department of Electronics and Communication and*
> *Engineering, Pragati Engineering College, Surampalem, India*
> *Nellore Manoj Kumar, Saveetha School of Engineering,Saveetha*
> *Institute of Medical and Technical Sciences, Thandal, India*
> *S. Boopathi, Mechancial Engineering, MEC, Namakkal, India*

The integration of Deep Learning with IoT technology is a significant advancement in the field of artificial intelligence. The chapter explores the integration of IoT architectures and deep learning frameworks, discussing important strategies for data collection, processing techniques, and deep learning model development, focusing on edge and cloud computing. The chapter showcases practical applications in smart engineering, including predictive maintenance, smart manufacturing, energy management, and environmental monitoring. Real-world case studies are presented to demonstrate the application of these technologies and address common challenges and solutions. The chapter predicts future trends in IoT and deep learning, highlighting emerging technologies and potential advancements in smart engineering, promising enhanced efficiency, predictive capabilities, and sustainability.

Chapter 6
Exploring Sentiment Through Cognitive Computing on Social Media
Content 159

Saifullah Jan, City University of Science and Information Technology,
Peshawar, Pakistan
Aiman, City University of Science and Information Technology,
Peshawar, Pakistan

The Covid-19 epidemic is regarded as the most serious concern of our day. It has an impact on many parts of our life, including schooling. As a result, practically every country's education system now requires distance study. Some people found it easy to accept this method, while others thought it was insufficient. In the context of the COVID-19 disruptions of education, especially distance learning, there is the need to leverage cognitive intelligence to determine their social, developmental, and emotional effects on students and educators. Cognitive intelligence, through sentiment analysis, provides the ability to process, learn, and adapt based on user-generated content, enabling policymakers to gain actionable insights into public sentiment. This study utilizes cognitive intelligence principles to assess the efficacy of distance learning using sentiment analysis on a dataset of 202,700 tweets shared during global lockdowns.

Chapter 7
Object Detection Algorithm and Challenges 181
Lubna Aziz, Iqra University, Karachi, Pakistan
Mansoor Ebrahim, Iqra University, Karachi, Pakistan

Object detection, a core task in computer vision, involves identifying and localizing objects in images or videos. Recent deep learning advances have significantly improved accuracy and speed. This chapter explores traditional two-stage methods and modern one-stage techniques. The chapter begins by tracing the history of deep learning and its pivotal role in advancing object detection, followed by a discussion of performance metrics used to evaluate detection accuracy and inference time. A detailed examination of the YOLO series, from its inception to the latest iteration, YOLOv8, highlights the architectural innovations and contributions of each version. Additionally, the chapter addresses the significance of backbone networks and benchmark datasets in driving research progress. Key challenges in the field, including scale and class imbalance, are also analyzed. The chapter concludes by identifying recent trends and future research directions, offering a comprehensive resource for understanding the current state and potential applications of object detection technologies.

Chapter 8
Speech Emotion Recognition-Based Music Recommender 233
Yasir Hafeez, The University of Nottingham Malaysia, Malaysia
Syed Hasan Adil, AI Society of Pakistan, Pakistan
Mansoor Ebrahim, Iqra University, Karachi, Pakistan
Mirzan Izzfitri Bin Mahadir, The University of Nottingham Malaysia,
Malaysia

The objective of this chapter is to provide details implementation of a research project; song recommendations based on speech emotions through Speech Emotion Recognition (SER). This involves developing a Speech Emotion Recognition model utilizing neural network algorithms or deep learning techniques. The selected algorithms include a Convolutional Neural Network (CNN), a Long Short-Term Memory (LSTM) network, a Dense Neural Network (DNN), and a custom hybrid algorithm combining CNN and LSTM. A PyQT5 application framework was implemented to facilitate song recommendations. Users can record their voices, which are processed to predict emotions, and then songs are recommended using the Spotify API, showcasing how SER can enhance personalized content delivery.

Chapter 9
Smart Processing Line for Automobile Sector Based on Computer Vision 263
Muhammad Atif Saeed, Shaheed Zulfikar Ali Bhutto Institute of Science
and Technology, Pakistan
Faraz Junejo, Shaheed Zulfikar Ali Bhutto Institute of Science and
Technology, Pakistan
Imran Amin, Shaheed Zulfikar Ali Bhutto Institute of Science and
Technology, Pakistan
Irfan Khan Tanoli, Universidade da Beira Interior, Portugal

The paper discusses the need for Industrial Automation in Pakistan's automobile and manufacturing industrial sectors. And what are the reasons which hold up this idea factors are controlling its implementation. The work proposes a Smart Painting Machine, a parts painting robot that can be placed in the production line of automobile and manufacturing industries to paint various geometrical parts simultaneously. The factors that stop Pakistani Industries from adopting Industrial Automation are initial high capital investment and maintenance of the machine, efficiency, and productivity, and painting various geometrical parts on the same machine with one program. Also, the machine targets reducing human health risks by promoting automatic painting and welding. The painting mechanism of the machine is a CNC mechanism including a 3-axis (X, Y, and Z) and the program is based on Image Processing which identifies the part geometry and painting real-time, which eradicates the issue of having multiple programs to paint a variety of geometrical parts at a particular time.

Compilation of References 291

About the Contributors 335

Index 339

Preface

The rapid evolution of artificial intelligence and machine learning has ushered in a new era of technological advancements, enabling computers to process, analyze, and interpret complex data with human-like cognition. Object detection, a critical component of computer vision, has witnessed remarkable progress, driven by the integration of deep learning and cognitive computing. As industries increasingly rely on intelligent automation, object detection techniques have found applications in diverse fields such as healthcare, security, smart cities, and autonomous vehicles. However, despite these advances, several challenges persist, necessitating continuous research and innovation.

This book, Navigating Challenges of Object Detection Through Cognitive Computing, provides an in-depth exploration of contemporary developments and challenges in object detection, leveraging cognitive computing principles. The chapters in this book highlight cutting-edge techniques, methodologies, and applications that drive progress in this domain. From deep learning approaches to real-world applications, each chapter offers valuable insights into the current state and future trajectory of object detection technologies. The book also delves into crucial areas such as sentiment analysis, natural language processing, IoT integration, and smart automation, offering a holistic view of how cognitive computing is transforming various industries.

With contributions from esteemed researchers and experts worldwide, this book presents a comprehensive collection of studies, reviews, and case studies that address both theoretical and practical aspects of object detection. The authors bring forward novel frameworks, experimental results, and emerging trends that shape the field, making this volume a valuable resource for researchers, academics, and industry professionals alike. By bridging the gap between theory and application, this book serves as a guide for those seeking to navigate the complexities of object detection in modern computational environments.

CHAPTER OVERVIEWS

Chapter 1: Cognitive Computing Approaches for IoT, Healthcare, Big Data, and Cybersecurity

This chapter provides a comprehensive review of cognitive computing techniques applied to key domains such as the Internet of Things (IoT), healthcare, big data, and cybersecurity. It explores the current state of research, challenges like data privacy and scalability, and potential future directions in these fields. The chapter concludes with a discussion on the advantages and limitations of cognitive computing in these domains.

Chapter 2: Natural Language Processing Techniques for Social Media Sentiment Analysis

This chapter examines various Natural Language Processing (NLP) techniques used for sentiment analysis on social media. It covers the evolution of sentiment analysis from early lexicon-based approaches to modern deep learning models such as transformers. The chapter provides insights into preprocessing techniques, evaluation metrics, and implementation considerations, while also addressing ethical concerns and future trends in sentiment analysis.

Chapter 3: Deep Learning for Emotion Recognition from Facial Expressions

Focusing on emotion recognition from facial expressions, this chapter discusses pre-processing, feature extraction, and classification techniques. It highlights the use of deep learning algorithms for facial emotion recognition, comparing traditional methods with recent advancements. The chapter emphasizes the growing significance of automated emotion recognition in industries such as banking, education, and commerce.

Chapter 4: Deep Learning Algorithms for Object Detection in Smart Environments

This chapter explores deep learning-based object detection methods, including CNN, Region-based CNN, and YOLO architectures. It addresses their applications in smart homes, smart cities, and industrial IoT, emphasizing their effectiveness in real-time object tracking. The discussion also highlights challenges related to computational complexity, energy efficiency, and scalability, supported by real-world case studies.

Chapter 5: Integration of Deep Learning with IoT for Smart Engineering Solutions

The chapter examines how deep learning models are integrated with IoT to enhance smart engineering applications. It discusses data collection strategies, edge and cloud computing techniques, and practical applications such as predictive maintenance and energy management. The chapter also presents case studies illustrating real-world implementations and explores future trends in this interdisciplinary domain.

Chapter 6: Sentiment Analysis Using Cognitive Computing for Social Media Content

This chapter applies sentiment analysis techniques to assess the impact of COVID-19 on education, particularly distance learning. Using cognitive computing principles, the study analyzes social media data to understand public sentiment regarding remote education. The findings offer insights into the social and emotional effects of online learning on students and educators.

Chapter 7: Object Detection Algorithms and Challenges

This chapter provides an overview of traditional and modern object detection methods, including two-stage and one-stage deep learning approaches. It covers the evolution of YOLO models, backbone network architectures, and benchmark datasets. Additionally, it discusses key challenges such as scale and class imbalance, offering insights into the latest trends and future research directions in object detection.

Chapter 8: Speech Emotion Recognition-Based Music Recommender

This chapter presents a speech emotion recognition (SER) system that recommends music based on detected emotions. It details the implementation of deep learning models such as CNN, LSTM, and hybrid architectures for emotion detection from speech. The chapter also describes the development of a PyQT5-based application that integrates with the Spotify API to provide personalized music recommendations.

Chapter 9: Smart Processing Line for the Automobile Sector Using Computer Vision

Focusing on industrial automation, this chapter discusses the development of a smart painting robot for the automobile sector. Using computer vision techniques, the system identifies part geometries in real-time and automates the painting process. The chapter highlights the benefits of industrial automation, including reduced human health risks and improved efficiency, while addressing challenges such as high initial investment and maintenance costs.

We extend our gratitude to all the contributors, whose extensive research and dedication have made this book possible. Their collective expertise has enriched the discourse on object detection, offering readers a deeper understanding of its challenges and solutions. We also appreciate the support of our academic institutions and colleagues, whose encouragement has been instrumental in bringing this project to fruition. Special thanks go to the reviewers and editorial team for their meticulous efforts in refining the content and ensuring the highest quality of scholarship.

As object detection technologies continue to evolve, we hope this book serves as a foundational reference for researchers, engineers, and practitioners. The interdisciplinary nature of cognitive computing ensures that the insights presented herein will contribute to advancements across multiple domains. By fostering further innovation and collaboration, we aspire to pave the way for more robust, efficient, and intelligent object detection systems that address real-world challenges effectively.

Finally, we invite readers to explore the various chapters and engage with the diverse perspectives offered in this volume. We encourage continued research and discussions that push the boundaries of cognitive computing and object detection, ultimately driving technological progress for the betterment of society.

Sadique Ahmad

Prince Sultan University, Saudi Arabia

Mansoor Ebrahim

Iqra University, Pakistan

Mohammed ELAffendi

Prince Sultan University, Saudi Arabia

Mohamed Hammad

Prince Sultan University, Saudi Arabia

Chapter 1
Cognitive Computing Approaches for IoT, Healthcare, Big Data, and Cybersecurity:
A Review

Mohamed Hammad
https://orcid.org/0000-0002-6506-3083
Prince Sultan University, Saudi Arabia

Sadique Ahmad
Prince Sultan University, Saudi Arabia

ABSTRACT

Cognitive computing has become a crucial technique in contemporary computing because it can solve complex problems that traditional computing systems cannot and because it enables machines to perform tasks that were previously only possible for humans. This chapter provides a comprehensive review of cognitive computing approaches for four critical domains: the Internet of Things (IoT), healthcare, big data, and cybersecurity. The chapter begins by introducing cognitive computing and its potential applications in each of these fields. The section then provides an overview of the current status of research and development in cognitive computing, highlighting key technologies and trends. The chapter then analyses the specific challenges and opportunities presented by each domain, such as data privacy, security, and scalability issues. The chapter concludes with a discussion of the advantages and limitations of cognitive computing in each domain, as well as suggestions for future research and development.

DOI: 10.4018/979-8-3693-9057-3.ch001

Copyright © 2025, IGI Global Scientific Publishing. Copying or distributing in print or electronic forms without written permission of IGI Global Scientific Publishing is prohibited.

1- INTRODUCTION

Cognitive computing has revolutionized the manner in which contemporary computing systems address complex problems and tasks that were previously infeasible to accomplish using conventional computing methods (Sreedevi et al., 2022). Figure 1 depicts the structure of cognitive computing. Perception, cognition, and action are the three major components of cognitive computation, as illustrated in the Figure. The component of perception comprises data acquisition and pre-processing, which entails the collection and preparation of data from various sources. The cognition component consists of data analysis, machine learning, and natural language processing duties that enable the system to comprehend and reason about the data (Cambria & White, 2014). The action component involves the execution of appropriate actions, such as making decisions or generating recommendations, based on the insights obtained from the data (Wang, Kung, & Byrd, 2018). The feedback loop between the action and perception components enables the system to continually enhance its performance through learning (Feng, Setoodeh, & Haykin, 2017).

Figure 1. A framework of the cyclical nature of cognitive computation

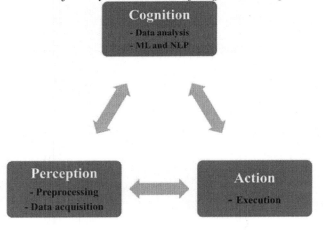

Cognitive computing's prospective applications are vast, with significant impacts across multiple domains, such as IoT (Hammad et al., 2022)(Hammad, Iliyasu, Elgendy, & Abd El-Latif, 2022)(Abd El-Rahiem & Hammad, 2022), healthcare (Hammad et al., 2022)(Hammad et al., 2022)(Salankar et al., 2022)(El-Latif, Chelloug, Alabdulhafith, & Hammad, 2023)(Patro et al., 2023), big data (Abd-El-Atty, Iliyasu, Alanezi, & Abd El-Latif, 2021)(Hammad et al., 2021)(Gupta, Kar, Baabdullah, & Al-Khowaiter, 2018), and cybersecurity (Abbas et al., 2021)(Abbas et al., 2021)(Raghavan, Gudivada, Govindaraju, & Rao, 2016)(Chen et al., 2019)

(Chen, Wang, Mehrotra, Leung, & Humar, 2019). This chapter of a book provides a comprehensive overview of cognitive computing approaches in these four essential domains. Cognitive computing can be used to make meaning of the vast amounts of data generated by sensors, devices, and other connected objects in the context of IoT. By analyzing this data in real-time, cognitive computing systems are able to recognize patterns and trends and make predictions that can be used to optimize performance, reduce downtime, and increase overall efficiency. Cognitive computing has the potential to revolutionize the diagnosis and treatment of diseases by medical professionals. Cognitive computing systems can provide more accurate diagnoses and individualized treatments by analyzing patient data, such as medical histories, genetic information, and real-time sensor data. This can result in improved patient outcomes and more effective utilization of healthcare resources. Another area where cognitive computing can have a significant impact is big data. Traditional computational systems are struggling to keep up as the volume, velocity, and variety of data continue to increase. Cognitive computing systems can aid in the management and analysis of large, complex datasets, yielding insights that would be difficult or impossible to obtain using conventional techniques. Reviewing cognitive computing strategies in IoT, healthcare, big data, and cybersecurity is essential for multiple reasons.

- **Firstly**, these areas are rapidly growing and evolving, and there is a need for innovative solutions to address the complex problems and challenges they present. Cognitive computing offers the potential to revolutionize these fields by providing intelligent, adaptive, and context-aware systems that can process large amounts of data, learn from experience, and make informed decisions.
- **Secondly**, the application of cognitive computing in these areas has the potential to improve the efficiency, effectiveness, and quality of services and systems. For example, in healthcare, cognitive computing can help medical professionals to make more accurate diagnoses, develop more personalized treatment plans, and improve patient outcomes. In big data, cognitive computing can help to analyze and interpret large and complex datasets, identifying patterns, trends, and insights that can inform decision-making and drive innovation. In cybersecurity, cognitive computing can enhance the detection and prevention of cyber threats by providing real-time threat analysis, automated incident response, and intelligent risk management.
- **Thirdly**, reviewing cognitive computing approaches in these areas can help to identify gaps and challenges in the current state of the art and guide future research and development. By understanding the strengths and limitations of existing approaches, researchers and practitioners can develop more effective

and innovative solutions that address the specific needs and requirements of each domain.

The Chapter begins with an overview of cognitive computing and its prospective applications in each discipline. The section then provides an overview of the most recent research and development in cognitive computing, with an emphasis on key technologies and trends. In-depth discussion of the specific challenges and opportunities presented by each domain, including data privacy, security, and scalability issues. In addition, the chapter provides an analysis of the benefits and limitations of cognitive computing in each domain, highlighting its potential to drive substantial improvements in productivity, precision, and cost-effectiveness. The Chapter concludes by identifying critical areas for future cognitive computing research and development in IoT, healthcare, big data, and cybersecurity.

2- COGNITIVE COMPUTING APPROACHES FOR IoT

The Internet of Things (IoT) is a paradigm that can be used in a wide variety of contexts to enable the communication of distributed machines (Ateya, Mahmoud, Zaghloul, Soliman, & Muthanna, 2022) (Bushelenkov et al., 2023). It supports machine-machine communications (M2M), which enables full interactions between machines. IoT is the third wave of the Internet that has many applications in all life fields, especially with the achieved advances in sensory manufacturing. With the release of fifth-generation cellular (5G) and the announcement of the requirements of sixth-generation cellular (6G) (Ateya et al., 2022) (Sedik et al., 2021). IoT networks are expected to support novel applications with new ultimate requirements. These requirements include dense deployment, ultra-high availability of the network, ultra-high data reliability, and support of ultra-low latency (Ateya, Muthanna, Koucheryavy, Maleh, & El-Latif, 2023)(Elgendy, Meshoul, & Hammad, 2023)(Zhang et al., 2020).

This puts many constraints on the design of such networks that can be resolved by introducing novel network architectures, protocols, technologies, and methods. Distributed edge computing (e.g., fog computing) (Yousefpour et al., 2019) (Ren, Zhang, He, Zhang, & Li, 2019), artificial intelligence (AI) (Xu et al., 2020)(Calo, Touna, Verma, & Cullen, 2017), network virtualization (Chowdhury & Boutaba, 2009) (Chowdhury & Boutaba, 2010), and network softwarization (Wang, Yang, Cheng, Han, & Yang, 2016) (Shamsan & Faridi, 2019) are the most critical technologies deployed recently for IoT networks. Computing technology has come a long way in the past decade moving through three main evolutions: fog computing, edge computing, and edge intelligence computing. Edge intelligence is the recent paradigm that implements AI algorithms at the edge unit to turn it smart. Deploying edge intelligence to IoT networks achieves many benefits, including data reduction, core network congestion reduction, providing novel services, and achieving higher reliability and availability.

Cognitive computing is a recent computing paradigm that seeks to solve complex problems and analyze data by simulating human behavior (Chen, Herrera, & Hwang, 2018). It provides an efficient way for managing massive IoT data in ways that meets the applications' requirements. Cognitive systems improve their performance through practice and exposure to new information. Cognitive computing is making rapid strides toward creating technology to aid in answering complicated problems through data mining (Chen, Han, & Yu, 1996) (Roiger, 2017), pattern recognition (Prakash, Patro, Hammad, Tadeusiewicz, & Pławiak, 2022) (Sakr, Pławiak, Tadeusiewicz, & Hammad, 2022), and natural language processing (Hirschberg & Manning, 2015) (Chopra, Prashar, & Sain, 2013). By processing large amounts of data and providing answers to issues that people may have when making judgments, cognitive computers serve as a kind of cognitive prosthesis. Figure 2 presents the main layers of IoT network structure with cognitive computing enabled at the edge layer. The cognitive computing approaches for IoT networks can be implemented at the edge layer with multilevel structure (i.e., fog computing with multiple access edge computing) as presented in Figure 3.

Figure 2. General structure of cognitive computing based IoT network

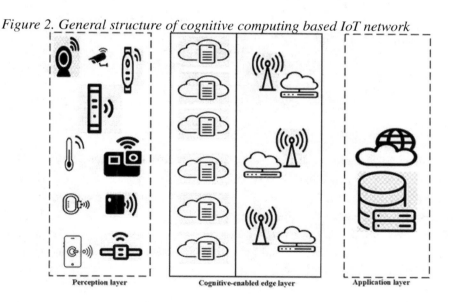

Cognitive computing can be used to support many IoT applications that can be summarized as follows.

Healthcare applications • (Hammad et al., 2022)(Hammad et al., 2022) (Salankar et al., 2022) (El-Latif, Chelloug, Alabdulhafith, & Hammad, 2023) (Patro et al., 2023): Internet of medical devices deploy massive smart wearable devices that generate data input that can aid with advice for healthcare programs. It also provides stress management programs, which can have a significant negative effect on one's health. Cognitive computing provides novel methods for such uses, and they can be scaled up when the demand arises in the future. This provides efficient support for fitness trainers and medical practitioners while also facilitating reliable health tracking.

Figure 3. Edge computing model with cognitive computing

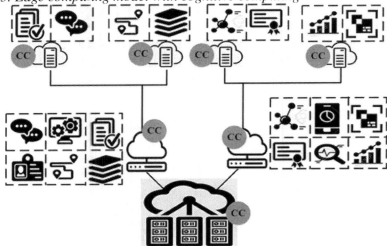

Smart city applications (Zhang et al., 2017) (Eckhoff & Wagner, 2017): IoT is a main enabler of smart cities that can be deployed to achieve various benefits to urban areas. However, the massive data results from smart cities puts many constraints on the design of IoT networks for smart city applications. Cognitive computing is a key solution to manage such massive data and provides the required reliability. Cognitive computing can be deployed for various IoT-based smart city applications that can be summarized as follows.

- *Smart homes*: Smart homes are houses embedded with IoT technologies that allow residents to remotely monitor and manage their home's climate, security, and energy use. Smartphones and other networked devices can often be used to manage smart home equipment.

- *Smart transportation*: Connected and automated driving, and automated adaptive traffic control are all examples of "smart transportation" that rely on the IoT for their management of the transportation network. Improving a country's transportation network requires planning for the construction of new roads, maintenance of existing ones, and the introduction of new technologies. In order to improve transportation systems, we need primarily a network of sensors, microchips, or other communication devices. Such a system requires ultra-high reliability and flexibility, since it is critical for human life. This can be achieved by introducing cognitive computing. One of the most popular IoT-based smart transportation systems now in use is the intelligent transport system (ITS). It uses the IoT to provide commuters with data that helps them pick the best route, the best time to go, the best speed to drive at, and the best settings for traffic lights.

By 2030, completely automated and connected vehicles will have revolutionized the transportation industry. In this scenario, just passengers and not the driver is present, hence the vehicle's sensing and driving functions are automated. When fully automated driving becomes a reality, many technologies will need to work together.

- *Smart public services*: Public services cover areas like public safety and environmental monitoring. Protecting residents and their property, effectively managing emergencies, and keeping the peace are the top priorities in public safety. Measurements of air pollution, the concentration of allergenic pollen or radiation, the discovery of forest fires, and the quantification of harmful emissions from sources like factories all fall under the umbrella of environmental monitoring. IoT-based technologies, dedicated sensors, intelligent cameras, GPS, and other wireless technologies are employed for real-time tracking, monitoring, and localizing to improve public service management.
- *Smart metering*: The meter may report the customer's energy, water, and gas usage in real time to the utility company. It is now possible to send meter readings to the utility company without physically being present at the site.
- *Smart grid*: The smart grid has been proposed to manage electrical energy usage and help existing grid systems. The increased efficacy, efficiency, dependability, stability, and security it provides helps older equipment keep up with the expanding demand for electrical power.
- **Industrial applications (De Chiffre, Carmignato, Kruth, Schmitt, & Weckenmann, 2014):** This domain comprises IoT applications used to improve efficiency, predominantly in the manufacturing, logistics, agricultural

and breeding, and supply chain management industries. This results in the current paradigm of industrial IoT (IIoT), which is the foundation of industry 4.0. Such applications include those listed below.

A. Smart manufacturing: IoT technology enables the monitoring of industries and the collection of as much data as possible during the manufacturing, assembly, testing, and inspection processes.
B. Intelligent logistics: Intelligent logistics ensures that products are transported efficiently and at a lower cost to manufacturers and logistics service providers. It simplifies store inventory control operations by providing accurate inventory data and monitoring products along their delivery route. An optimized route system can help logistics service providers reduce their operational costs and petroleum consumption.

- **Agricultural applications (Weiss, Jacob, & Duveiller, 2020):** Smart farming is a method for increasing the efficacy of agricultural systems by converting and realigning them using techniques such as sensors, M2M communication, geographic mapping, and intelligent network systems. Modern IoT-based technologies in agriculture, such as fermentation and manure control, have made food processing more efficient in terms of water and energy conservation, resource utilization, and waste reduction. Moreover, the use of IoT-based applications has resulted in an increase in agricultural output.

Cognitive computing is a game-changer in the agricultural sector since it represents a significant step forward in helping farmers with everything from crop production and analysis to monitoring and sales. Many countries' rural areas desperately need cognitive systems equipped with personal assistants who can communicate in the local language. Farmers need more accessible options for gathering the necessary information and learning about the state of the market. The most up-to-date farming methods and techniques must be used. Slow uptake of modern farming technology is a major factor in the relatively small number of people who choose farming as a career.

Deploying cognitive computing for IoT networks should meets the following characteristics (Chen et al., 2019)(Wan, Gu, & Ni, 2020):

Self-learning: Cognitive computing schemes able to learn with little to no explicit programming. The cognitive method modifies itself by considering information from its surroundings, interacting with other creatures, and experiencing events. The deployed cognitive computing scheme for IoT networks should be able to self-learning without constraints in an unsupervised approach rather than supervised.

Self-management: Cognitive computing schemes should be able to self-manage IoT networks. This is an important issue for real-time critical IoT applications, including healthcare and industrial applications.

Dependability: The IoT network topology must facilitate individual authentication of billions of distinct devices employing diverse modern communications across multiple administrative disciplines in order to provide security dependability and privacy. Additionally, reliable energy-efficient channels must be designed to assure dependability. Cognitive computing is one way to support IoT network dependability.

Fault tolerance: IoT devices are delicate and prone to errors; thus, the possibility of numerous fault occurrences increases. Cognitive computing schemes should be able to recover these defects, or at least hide them. The majority of IoT applications deliver output in the form of events in response to some triggered action. Therefore, it is possible to become confused while trying to discriminate between an incorrect state and a trigger event. Cognitive schemes should be able to detect and solve such situations.

Scalable: scalability is an important issue with the network algorithms and methods, especially that are developed for next-generation networks. Since IoT is being used in so many places, it is crucial that the system be able to dynamically add or remove mobile devices. Thus, cognitive computing schemes deployed for IoT networks should provide a high level of scalability.

Reliability: The IoT area network is recommended for many applications because it provides reliable data transmission. End-to-end reliability requires a measure to assure the high reliability of data transmission in the IoT area network (Feng, Setoodeh, & Haykin, 2017). To satisfy the requirements of the next generation of networks (NGN), including fifth-generation cellular (5G), IoT networks must offer ultra-high reliability for most of their services. cognitive schemes should be able to meet the ultra-high reliability demands.

3- COGNITIVE COMPUTING APPROACHES FOR HEALTHCARE

There have been a number of persistent challenges in the healthcare industry over the years. These challenges include the complexity of healthcare systems, the scarcity of healthcare professionals, the rising cost of healthcare, and the increasing demand for personalized care. There is a need for more innovative approaches to address these issues, as traditional healthcare systems have struggled to address them. The incorporation of cognitive computing technologies into healthcare is a potential remedy to these problems. Cognitive computing, a subfield of artificial intelligence (AI), has made significant progress in the healthcare sector. Utilizing machine learning algorithms, natural language processing, and data analytics to enable machines to simulate human thought and behavior. By incorporating cognitive computing into healthcare, it is feasible to address some of the industry's most pressing problems (Sreedevi et al., 2022)(Cambria & White, 2014)(Wang, Kung, & Byrd, 2018).

In this context, it is crucial to discuss the challenges in healthcare and the potential benefits of cognitive computing in depth. Understanding these challenges and advantages is essential for appreciating the impact of cognitive computing in healthcare and fostering innovation in the field. Cognitive computing has the potential to revolutionize the diagnosis, treatment, and prevention of disease in healthcare. In this section, we will explore the numerous cognitive computing approaches for the healthcare industry. Figure 4 is a block diagram of a typical cognitive computing approach for healthcare, illustrating the system's components and interactions.

Figure 4. Block diagram of a typical cognitive computing approach for healthcare

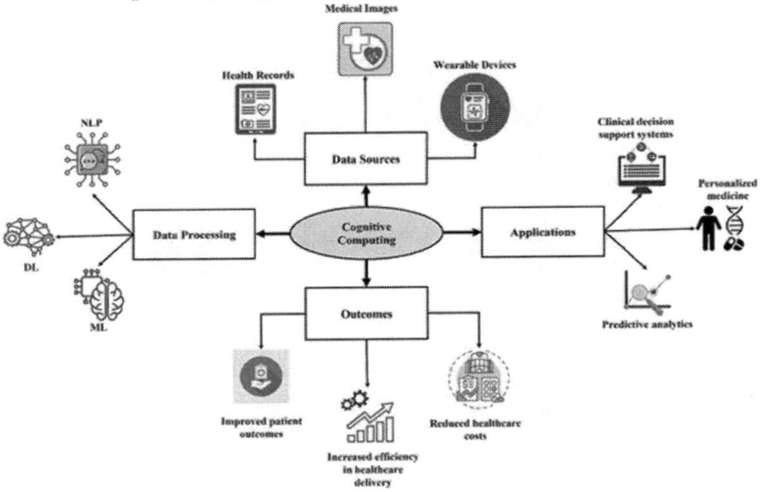

The most common cognitive computing approaches for healthcare are as follows:

1. Clinical Decision Support Systems (CDSS)

CDSS are computerized systems that aid in the diagnosis and treatment decisions made by medical professionals. They are intended to incorporate patient-specific information, clinical knowledge, and evidence-based recommendations to provide individualized recommendations. By providing clinicians with real-time guidance, CDSS can help reduce medical errors, enhance clinical outcomes, and boost efficiency. These systems can also monitor the health status of patients and notify medical personnel of potential problems before they become critical (Velickovski et al., 2014).

2. Natural Language Processing (NLP)

NLP is a subset of AI that allows computers to comprehend and manipulate human language. NLP can be used to extract and analyze unstructured data from electronic health records (EHRs), clinical notes, and other medical documents in the healthcare industry. This data can then be utilized to generate insights that can guide clinical decision-making. Additionally, NLP can be used to create chatbots and virtual assistants that can assist patients in navigating healthcare services (Kang, Cai, Tan, Huang, & Liu, 2020).

3. Predictive Analytics

Utilizing statistical algorithms and machine learning techniques, predictive analytics identifies patterns and trends in data through data analysis and pattern recognition. In healthcare, predictive analytics can be used to identify patients who are at a high risk of developing particular diseases or conditions. This may enable medical professionals to intervene early and prevent the onset of the disease. Optimizing treatment plans and predicting patient outcomes are additional applications of predictive analytics (Mishra & Silakari, 2012).

4. Image Analysis

Utilizing computer algorithms to analyze medical images such as X-rays, CT scans, and MRIs is image analysis. This can aid medical professionals in identifying patterns and anomalies that may be challenging to detect visually. Additionally, image analysis can be utilized to monitor disease progression and treatment efficacy (Sakr et al., 2022).

5. Robotics

Robots can perform a variety of duties in healthcare, including surgery, medication delivery, and patient monitoring. For instance, surgical robotics can aid surgeons in performing complex procedures with greater precision and accuracy. Additionally, robots can be used to automate repetitive duties, allowing healthcare professionals to focus on more intricate patient care (Webb, 2000).

6. Computer Vision

Computer vision is a subfield of artificial intelligence that enables machines to interpret and comprehend visual data from their environment. Computer vision can be utilized to analyze medical images, such as X-rays, CT scans, and MRIs, to aid radiologists in detecting and diagnosing diseases. Computer vision can also be used to monitor patients in real-time, detecting changes in their physical condition and notifying clinicians when intervention is required (Rosenfeld, 1988).

Challenges in Healthcare:

- *Data Complexity*: Healthcare data is frequently complex and heterogeneous, making it difficult to extract insightful information. There is an abundance of difficult-to-interpret unstructured data, such as clinical notes, radiology images, and genomics data.
- Privacy and Security Concerns: Healthcare information is sensitive, and privacy and security are significant industry concerns. Compliance with regulations such as HIPAA (Health Insurance Portability and Accountability Act) is essential, and any security violations can result in severe repercussions.
- Cost and Resource Constraints Healthcare organizations face cost and resource constraints, which can hinder their ability to invest in innovative technologies. Investments in hardware, software, and personnel are necessary for the implementation of cognitive computing.
- Lack of Standardization: Because healthcare data is frequently not standardized, it is difficult to compare and analyze information across various systems and locations.
- Legal and Ethical Considerations The application of cognitive computing in healthcare raises legal and ethical concerns regarding data privacy, informed consent, and liability.

Potential Benefits of Cognitive Computing in Healthcare:

- Improved Diagnosis: By analyzing patient data such as medical history, symptoms, and lab results, cognitive computing can assist healthcare providers in diagnosing diseases more precisely. This can lead to improved treatment outcomes and earlier diagnoses.
- Personalized Medicine: Cognitive computing can analyze vast quantities of data to create personalized treatment plans for patients based on their medical history, genetic information, and other factors.
- Enhanced Clinical Decision-Making: Cognitive computing can provide healthcare professionals with real-time insights and recommendations to aid their decision-making processes, resulting in improved patient outcomes.

- Enhanced Patient Engagement Cognitive computing can provide patients with more personalized and engaging experiences by interacting with them using natural language processing and other technologies.
- Cost Savings: Cognitive computing can reduce healthcare costs by automating administrative tasks, enhancing efficiency, and minimizing errors.
- Enhanced Accessibility: Cognitive computing can make healthcare more accessible to marginalized populations by enhancing diagnostic and treatment options, particularly in remote or rural areas.

4- COGNITIVE COMPUTING APPROACHES FOR BIG DATA

The development of human-centered systems and numerous types of machines has exponentially increased the significance of cognitive computing (Jain et al., 2022)(Hu & Zhang, 2022). Cognitive computing is integral to the effective operation of human-centered systems. With the aid of cognitive computing, these intelligent systems can perform in-depth observation and investigation while making effective decisions as shown in Figure 5. In addition, big data analytics demonstrates that cognitive computing plays a crucial role in the processing of large data volumes. Big data and cognitive computing are highly intertwined due to their shared interests, which include efficient human-centered smart models, the analysis of human emotions, smart systems for healthcare and fraud detection, and data science for business intelligence (Anand, Sindhwani, & Juneja, 2022)(Zhang et al., 2022) (Kleyko et al., 2023).

The velocity characteristic of big data indicates how rapidly data are generated and prepared for intelligent decision-making. Big data consists of structured and unstructured data in addition to semi-structured data, necessitating cognitive-based observation. Human-centered intelligence is required to observe and interpret such large data sets in order to obtain insights (Kumar, Soh, & Ismail, 2022). There are a variety of fields in which these insights can play a crucial role, such as predictive modelling in healthcare, market campaigns, autonomous cars, remote sensing, etc. Customers are always responsible for leveraging big data insights to improve customer experience and sales. Therefore, cognitive computing can provide organizations with valuable customer insights in such circumstances. Therefore, they can use it to refine their marketing strategies and increase customer engagement.

Big data presents many unexplored challenges, but we always discuss the diversity of data and the 5v's of big data. These 5vs are the primary obstacles that must be assessed first. Additionally, diversity is an essential factor that is frequently overlooked. In addition, Volume is the foundation of big data, which has a direct impact on the available computing capacity (Ma & Sun, 2020). Next, velocity influences computing capacity because it indicates the rate at which data is generated and transmitted to the analyst. It is a crucial feature for large organizations that require rapid data processing. Consequently, companies with big data will have a constant flow of data (Vassakis, Petrakis, & Kopanakis, 2018), including information from browsers, computers, networks, customer service, smartphones, and various social media platforms. Therefore, in each of these sections, we require a cognitive approach to analyze massive amounts of data in order to gain meaningful insights. For instance, healthcare organizations employ numerous machines to monitor patients and acquire data that requires intelligent processing. In such circumstances, cognitive approaches cannot be neglected (Lytras et al., 2020).

Variety reflects the numerous data sources that generate data, whereas veracity indicates the data's quality. It illustrates that Data may contain redundant and absent values. Therefore, such a vast quantity of data can pose a significant problem that can result in overfitting or underfitting. In the medical field, for instance, incomplete information regarding the medication a patient should take can imperil the patient's life. The final V in the 5 Vs of big data is value, which demonstrates the predictive value of insights from big data. This feature requires a distinct vision from the beginning of the data analysis phase and feature set selection.

Figure 5. Mutual Interest of cognitive computing and big data

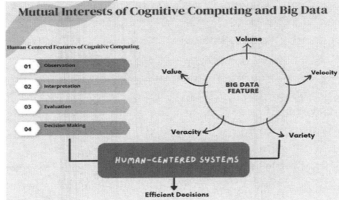

5- COGNITIVE COMPUTING APPROACHES FOR CYBERSECURITY

5.1 Classification of Computing Approaches in Cybersecurity domain

Cognitive computing technologies used in cybersecurity can be classified into three distinct domains, namely machine learning, natural language processing, and artificial intelligence (Georgescu, 2020)(Lauriola, Lavelli, & Aiolli, 2022).

Machine Learning: Machine learning algorithms can be trained on vast amounts of data to recognize patterns and anomalies in network traffic or system behavior. Examples include:

- Using anomaly detection to identify unusual network activity that may indicate a potential cyber-attack.
- Applying machine learning algorithms to detect malware in files and emails based on their behavior and characteristics.
- Using machine learning to predict which users or devices are most likely to be targeted in a cyber-attack based on their past behavior.

Natural Language Processing (NLP): NLP techniques can be used to analyze text data and identify potential threats in emails, social media posts, or other online content. Examples include:

- Analyzing social media feeds to detect early warning signs of cyber-attacks, such as mentions of specific malware or hacking groups.
- Using sentiment analysis to detect negative sentiment in employee emails or chat logs that may indicate insider threats.
- Identifying key entities mentioned in text data, such as specific IP addresses or domain names, to quickly identify potential threats.

Artificial Intelligence (AI): AI can be used to automate various aspects of cybersecurity, from threat detection to incident response. Examples include:

- Using chatbots or virtual assistants to provide instant support to employees who may have been affected by a cyber-attack.
- Developing AI-powered security systems that can automatically detect and mitigate cyber threats in real-time.
- Using expert systems to guide incident response teams through the process of investigating and resolving a security breach.

5.2 Weakness and limitation of Cognitive computing in cyber security

While cognitive computing technologies can offer several benefits for cyber-security, they also have some limitations and weaknesses that need to be carefully considered and managed to ensure their effectiveness and reliability in practice. Here are some of the key ones:

- Lack of transparency: One of the major challenges of cognitive computing technologies is the lack of transparency in the decision-making process. This can make it difficult to understand how a system arrived at a particular conclusion or recommendation, which may be problematic in critical situations (von Eschenbach, 2021).
- Complexity: Cognitive computing systems can be highly complex and difficult to develop and implement. This can make it costly and time-consuming to deploy and may require specialized expertise and resources (Gann & Salter, 2000).
- Bias: Cognitive computing systems are only as unbiased as the data they are trained on. If the data used to train a system is biased in any way, the system may produce biased results or recommendations, which can have serious consequences in a cybersecurity context (Lin, Hung, & Huang, 2021).
- Adversarial attacks: Adversaries can attempt to deceive cognitive computing systems by feeding them misleading or manipulated data. This can result in false positives or false negatives, which can lead to inaccurate threat assessments or ineffective security measures (Almeshekah & Spafford, 2014).
- Dependence on data quality: The accuracy and effectiveness of cognitive computing systems are heavily dependent on the quality and relevance of the data used to train them. Poor-quality or irrelevant data can result in inaccurate results or false positives, which can be costly or damaging in a cybersecurity context (Li, Goh, & Jin, 2020).
- Limited ability to adapt: While cognitive computing systems can learn and evolve over time, they may have limited ability to adapt to new and emerging threats or to respond to unforeseen circumstances. This can make it difficult to stay ahead of rapidly evolving threats and to maintain an effective security posture over time (Avital & Te'Eni, 2009)(Rahim et al., 2023)(Ahmad et al., 2018)(Ahmad et al., 2022)(Anwar et al., 2024)(Ahmad, Li, Eddine, & Khan, 2018)(Ahmad et al., 2020)(Ahmad et al., 2021)(Ahmad, Li, Amin, & Khan, 2018)(Ahmad et al., 2015)(Ahmad & Adnan, 2015)(Abd El-Latif et al., 2023)(Arif et al., 2024)(Ahmad et al., 2023)(Ahmad et al., 2022)(Ahmad

et al., 2018)(Ahmad et al., 2017)(Arshad et al., 2024)(Ahmad et al., 2023) (Khuda, Ahmed, & Ateya, 2024)(Khuda et al., 2024)(Akhtar et al., 2022).

6- COMPARATIVE ANALYSIS OF COGNITIVE COMPUTING APPROACHES

Cognitive computing approaches have been applied in various fields such as IoT, healthcare, big data, and cybersecurity. While the basic principles of cognitive computing are similar across all these domains, there are some unique challenges and considerations that need to be taken into account in each field. In this section, we will compare and contrast the cognitive computing approaches for IoT, healthcare, big data, and cybersecurity in-depth and present the comparison in a table form.

1. IoT:

The Internet of Things (IoT) is a network of physical objects, devices, vehicles, buildings, and other items that are embedded with sensors, software, and connectivity to collect and exchange data. Cognitive computing can be applied to IoT to enhance the ability to process and analyze the massive amount of data generated by IoT devices. Cognitive computing can help in identifying patterns, making predictions, and automating decision-making processes in IoT systems.

Challenges in applying cognitive computing to IoT:

- Real-time data processing: IoT generates a massive amount of data in real-time, which requires efficient and real-time data processing capabilities.
- Edge computing: IoT devices are often deployed in remote locations with limited connectivity, which requires the ability to perform data processing and analysis at the edge of the network.
- Security and privacy: IoT devices are vulnerable to security threats, and cognitive computing systems must be designed with security and privacy in mind.

    Potential benefits of applying cognitive computing to IoT:

- Improved operational efficiency: Cognitive computing can help in automating decision-making processes, reducing manual intervention, and improving operational efficiency.
- Enhanced decision-making: Cognitive computing can help in identifying patterns, predicting future events, and providing actionable insights to support decision-making processes.

- Better customer experience: Cognitive computing can help in personalizing customer experiences by analyzing customer behavior and preferences.

2. Healthcare:

Cognitive computing can be applied to healthcare to improve patient care, optimize resource utilization, and enhance clinical decision-making. Cognitive computing can help in analyzing large amounts of patient data, identifying patterns, predicting outcomes, and recommending treatment options.

Challenges in applying cognitive computing to healthcare:

- Data quality and interoperability: Healthcare data is often stored in multiple systems in different formats, making it difficult to integrate and analyze.
- Regulatory compliance: Healthcare is heavily regulated, and cognitive computing systems must be designed with regulatory compliance in mind.
- Ethical considerations: Cognitive computing systems must be designed to ensure patient privacy and avoid bias in decision-making processes.

Potential benefits of applying cognitive computing to healthcare:

- Improved patient outcomes: Cognitive computing can help in identifying patterns, predicting outcomes, and recommending treatment options, which can lead to improved patient outcomes.
- Cost reduction: Cognitive computing can help in optimizing resource utilization, reducing unnecessary procedures and tests, and minimizing errors, which can lead to cost reduction.
- Enhanced clinical decision-making: Cognitive computing can provide healthcare providers with real-time insights, which can enhance clinical decision-making processes.

3. Big data:

Big data refers to the large and complex data sets that cannot be processed by traditional data processing tools. Cognitive computing can be applied to big data to enhance the ability to analyze and extract insights from large data sets.

Challenges in applying cognitive computing to big data:

- Data quality and integration: Big data is often stored in multiple systems in different formats, making it difficult to integrate and analyze.

- Data privacy and security: Big data contains sensitive information, and cognitive computing systems must be designed to ensure data privacy and security.
- Scalability: Cognitive computing systems must be designed to handle the massive amounts of data generated by big data systems.

Potential benefits of applying cognitive computing to big data:

1. Improved decision-making: Cognitive computing systems can help organizations make better decisions by analyzing large amounts of data and identifying patterns and insights that might not be apparent to humans. This can lead to more informed and accurate decision-making, which can result in better business outcomes.
2. Cost savings: By automating certain processes and tasks, cognitive computing systems can help organizations reduce costs associated with manual labor and other resources. For example, cognitive computing can be used to automate customer service inquiries, reducing the need for human customer service representatives.
3. Faster analysis: Cognitive computing systems can process vast amounts of data at a much faster rate than humans can. This can be particularly useful in industries such as finance, where rapid analysis of large amounts of data is essential for making investment decisions.
4. Personalization: Cognitive computing systems can be used to personalize experiences for customers by analyzing their data and preferences. This can lead to more effective marketing campaigns and higher customer satisfaction.

The table below compares the cognitive computing approaches for IoT, healthcare, big data, and cybersecurity based on their goals, challenges, and potential benefits.

Table 1. **Comparison between the cognitive computing approaches for IoT, healthcare, big data, and cybersecurity based on their goals, challenges, and potential benefits**

Criteria	IoT	Healthcare	Big Data	Cybersecurity
Definition	IoT refers to the network of physical devices, vehicles, home appliances, and other items embedded with sensors, software, actuators, and connectivity, which enables these objects to connect and exchange data.	Healthcare cognitive computing uses artificial intelligence technologies to assist in medical decision-making and provide more personalized care to patients.	Big Data refers to the large and complex data sets that cannot be processed by traditional data processing tools. Cognitive computing can help manage and analyze this data.	Cognitive computing can help cybersecurity by identifying patterns and anomalies in data that may indicate a security threat, and by using natural language processing to understand and respond to cybersecurity incidents.
Key Technologies	Sensors, actuators, connectivity, cloud computing, AI/ML, big data analytics	AI/ML, natural language processing, big data analytics, predictive analytics, electronic health records (EHRs)	Big data analytics, AI/ML, natural language processing, data mining, pattern recognition, predictive analytics	AI/ML, natural language processing, big data analytics, predictive analytics, anomaly detection, threat intelligence
Applications	Smart homes, smart cities, industrial IoT, agriculture, healthcare monitoring	Medical decision-making, personalized treatment, disease diagnosis, patient monitoring	Customer analytics, fraud detection, risk management, supply chain optimization, social media analytics	Threat intelligence, security monitoring, incident response, anomaly detection, access management
Challenges	Security, privacy, lack of interoperability, data overload, standards, connectivity	Data privacy, ethical considerations, lack of standardization, interoperability, regulatory compliance, data quality	Data quality, data overload, complexity, security, privacy, lack of standards	Complexity of threats, security of AI systems, shortage of skilled personnel, lack of standardization, data quality
Benefits	Improved efficiency, reduced costs, increased automation, real-time insights	Personalized treatment, improved patient outcomes, reduced medical errors, enhanced diagnosis and treatment planning	Better decision-making, increased efficiency, improved risk management, enhanced customer experience	Enhanced threat detection, improved incident response, increased efficiency, better risk management

The implications for future research and development in cognitive computing can be summarized as follows:

1. Further advancement in cognitive computing techniques: To make cognitive computing approaches more effective, future research needs to focus on developing new techniques and algorithms that can handle increasingly complex and diverse data.
2. More comprehensive data sets: As cognitive computing approaches rely on data, future research should concentrate on creating more comprehensive data sets that are representative of the different domains.
3. Interdisciplinary collaboration: To address the challenges in these domains effectively, interdisciplinary collaboration is essential. Future research should focus on fostering collaboration among researchers from different fields, including computer science, data science, healthcare, and cybersecurity.
4. Ethics and privacy concerns: Cognitive computing approaches raise ethical and privacy concerns, and future research should focus on addressing these concerns. Researchers need to develop ethical guidelines and best practices for the use of cognitive computing approaches in these domains.
5. Standardization: There is a need for standardization in terms of the tools, techniques, and algorithms used in cognitive computing approaches. Standardization will facilitate the comparison of different approaches and enable the development of more efficient and effective techniques.
6. Real-world applications: Cognitive computing approaches have significant potential in these domains, and future research should focus on developing and testing real-world applications to demonstrate their effectiveness in addressing real-world challenges.

7- CONCLUSION

The emergence of cognitive computing has transformed the modern computing systems, enabling machines to perform tasks that were previously only possible by humans. This chapter presents a comprehensive review of cognitive computing approaches in four significant areas, namely IoT, healthcare, big data, and cybersecurity. The review emphasizes the potential of cognitive computing in each domain by processing large and complex datasets, learning from experience, and making informed decisions. By doing so, it can provide intelligent insights and context-aware solutions, improving efficiency, accuracy, and cost-effectiveness.

The review also highlights the importance of understanding the specific challenges and opportunities presented by each domain. The issues related to data privacy, security, and scalability are of utmost importance, and it is essential to address them while implementing cognitive computing solutions. The practical implications of this review for researchers and practitioners in these domains are numerous. Firstly, there is a need for innovative solutions to address the complex problems and challenges presented by these areas. Secondly, cognitive computing has the potential to revolutionize these fields by providing intelligent, adaptive, and context-aware systems. Lastly, the review identifies key areas for future research and development, emphasizing the need for effective and innovative solutions that address the specific needs and requirements of each domain.

Despite providing a comprehensive overview of cognitive computing approaches for IoT, healthcare, big data, and cybersecurity, there are some limitations to this study. For instance, the review does not cover all the possible applications of cognitive computing, and some areas may require further research. Additionally, the review did not focus on the ethical and social implications of cognitive computing. Future research should address these limitations and examine the ethical and social implications of cognitive computing in each domain.

REFERENCES

Abbas, K., Tawalbeh, L. A. A., Rafiq, A., Muthanna, A., Elgendy, I. A., & Abd El-Latif, A. A. (2021). Convergence of blockchain and IoT for secure transportation systems in smart cities. *Security and Communication Networks*, *2021*, 1–13. DOI: 10.1155/2021/5597679

Abbas, K., Tawalbeh, L. A. A., Rafiq, A., Muthanna, A., Elgendy, I. A., & Abd El-Latif, A. A. (2021). Convergence of blockchain and IoT for secure transportation systems in smart cities. *Security and Communication Networks*, *2021*, 1–13. DOI: 10.1155/2021/5597679

Abd-El-Atty, B., Iliyasu, A. M., Alanezi, A., & Abd El-latif, A. A. (2021). Optical image encryption based on quantum walks. *Optics and Lasers in Engineering*, *138*, 106403. DOI: 10.1016/j.optlaseng.2020.106403

Abd El-Latif, A. A., Maleh, Y., El-Affendi, M. A., & Ahmad, S. (Eds.). (2023). *Cybersecurity Management in Education Technologies: Risks and Countermeasures for Advancements in E-learning*. CRC Press. DOI: 10.1201/9781003369042

. Abd El-Rahiem, B., & Hammad, M. (2022). A multi-fusion IoT authentication system based on internal deep fusion of ECG signals. *Security and Privacy Preserving for IoT and 5G Networks: Techniques, Challenges, and New Directions*, 53-79.

Ahmad, S., & Adnan, A. (2015, July). Machine learning based cognitive skills calculations for different emotional conditions. In *2015 IEEE 14th International Conference on Cognitive Informatics & Cognitive Computing (ICCI* CC)* (pp. 162-168). IEEE. DOI: 10.1109/ICCI-CC.2015.7259381

Ahmad, S., Adnan, A., Khan, G., & Mehmood, N. (2015). Emotions, age, and gender based cognitive skills calculations. *International Journal of Computer Theory and Engineering*, *7*(1), 76–80. DOI: 10.7763/IJCTE.2015.V7.934

Ahmad, S., Anwar, M. S., Ebrahim, M., Khan, W., Raza, K., Adil, S. H., & Amin, A. (2020). Deep network for the iterative estimations of students' cognitive skills. *IEEE Access : Practical Innovations, Open Solutions*, *8*, 103100–103113. DOI: 10.1109/ACCESS.2020.2999064

Ahmad, S., Anwar, M. S., Khan, M. A., Shahzad, M., Ebrahim, M., & Memon, I. (2021, November). Deep Frustration Severity Network for the Prediction of Declined Students' Cognitive Skills. In *2021 4th international conference on Computing & Information Sciences (ICCIS)* (pp. 1-6). IEEE.

Ahmad, S., Aoun, N. B., Ali, G., El-Affendi, M. A., & Anwar, M. S. (2023). Multi-Clustered Mathematical Model for Student Cognitive Skills Prediction Optimization. *IEEE Access : Practical Innovations, Open Solutions, 11*, 65371–65381. DOI: 10.1109/ACCESS.2023.3285612

Ahmad, S., Ben Aoun, N., Affendi, M. A. E., Anwar, M. S., Abbas, S., & Latif, A. A. A. E. (2022). Optimization of Students' Performance Prediction through an Iterative Model of Frustration Severity. *Computational Intelligence and Neuroscience, 2022*(1), 3183492. DOI: 10.1155/2022/3183492 PMID: 36017453

Ahmad, S., El-Affendi, M. A., Anwar, M. S., & Iqbal, R. (2022). Potential future directions in optimization of students' performance prediction system. *Computational Intelligence and Neuroscience, 2022*(1), 6864955. DOI: 10.1155/2022/6864955 PMID: 35619762

Ahmad, S., Li, K., Amin, A., Anwar, M. S., & Khan, W. (2018). A multilayer prediction approach for the student cognitive skills measurement. *IEEE Access : Practical Innovations, Open Solutions, 6*, 57470–57484. DOI: 10.1109/ACCESS.2018.2873608

Ahmad, S., Li, K., Amin, A., & Faheem, M. Y. (2018, July). Simulation of student skills: The novel technique based on quantization of cognitive skills outcomes. In *2018 IEEE 17th International Conference on Cognitive Informatics & Cognitive Computing (ICCI* CC)* (pp. 97-102). IEEE.

Ahmad, S., Li, K., Amin, A., & Khan, S. (2018). A novel technique for the evaluation of posterior probabilities of student cognitive skills. *IEEE Access : Practical Innovations, Open Solutions, 6*, 53153–53167. DOI: 10.1109/ACCESS.2018.2870877

Ahmad, S., Li, K., Eddine, H. A. I., & Khan, M. I. (2018). A biologically inspired cognitive skills measurement approach. *Biologically inspired cognitive architectures, 24*, 35-46.

Ahmad, S., Li, K., Li, Y., Qureshi, H., & Khan, S. (2017, July). Formulation of Cognitive Skills: A theoretical model based on psychological and neurosciences studies. In *2017 IEEE 16th International Conference on Cognitive Informatics & Cognitive Computing (ICCI* CC)* (pp. 167-174). IEEE. DOI: 10.1109/ICCI-CC.2017.8109746

Ahmad, T., Ahmad, S., Rahim, A., & Shah, N. (2023). Development of a Novel Deep Convolutional Neural Network Model for Early Detection of Brain Stroke Using CT Scan Images. In *Recent Advancements in Multimedia Data Processing and Security: Issues, Challenges, and Techniques* (pp. 197-229). IGI Global. DOI: 10.4018/978-1-6684-7216-3.ch010

Akhtar, S., Ali, A., Ahmad, S., Khan, M. I., Shah, S., & Hassan, F. (2022). The prevalence of foot ulcers in diabetic patients in Pakistan: A systematic review and meta-analysis. *Frontiers in Public Health, 10*, 1017201. DOI: 10.3389/fpubh.2022.1017201 PMID: 36388315

Almeshekah, M. H., & Spafford, E. H. (2014, September). Planning and integrating deception into computer security defenses. In *Proceedings of the 2014 New Security Paradigms Workshop* (pp. 127-138). DOI: 10.1145/2683467.2683482

Anand, R., Sindhwani, N., & Juneja, S. (2022). *"Cognitive Internet of Things, Its Applications, and Its Challenges: A Survey." Harnessing the Internet of Things (IoT) for a Hyper-Connected Smart World.* Apple Academic Press. DOI: 10.1201/9781003277347-5

Anwar, M. S., Choi, A., Ahmad, S., Aurangzeb, K., Laghari, A. A., Gadekallu, T. R., & Hines, A. (2024). A Moving Metaverse: QoE challenges and standards requirements for immersive media consumption in autonomous vehicles. *Applied Soft Computing, 159*, 111577. DOI: 10.1016/j.asoc.2024.111577

Arif, F., Khan, N. A., ul Haq, Q. M., Asim, M., & Ahmad, S. (2024). An SDN-AI-Based Approach for Detecting Anomalies in Imbalance Data within a Network of Smart Medical Devices. *IEEE Consumer Electronics Magazine.*

Arshad, M., Khan, B., Ahmad, S., & Asim, M. (2024). Predicting Age and Gender in Author Profiling: A Multi-Feature Exploration. *Computers, Materials & Continua, 79*(2), 3333–3353. DOI: 10.32604/cmc.2024.049254

Ateya, A. A., Mahmoud, M., Zaghloul, A., Soliman, N. F., & Muthanna, A. (2022). Empowering the Internet of Things Using Light Communication and Distributed Edge Computing. *Electronics (Basel), 11*(9), 1511. DOI: 10.3390/electronics11091511

Ateya, A. A., Muthanna, A., Koucheryavy, A., Maleh, Y., & El-Latif, A. A. A. (2023). Energy efficient offloading scheme for MEC-based augmented reality system. *Cluster Computing, 26*(1), 1–18. DOI: 10.1007/s10586-022-03914-7

Ateya, A. A., Soliman, N. F., Alkanhel, R., Alhussan, A. A., Muthanna, A., & Koucheryavy, A. (2022). Lightweight Deep Learning-Based Model for Traffic Prediction in Fog-Enabled Dense Deployed IoT Networks. *Journal of Electrical Engineering & Technology,* ●●●, 1–11.

Avital, M., & Te'Eni, D. (2009). From generative fit to generative capacity: Exploring an emerging dimension of information systems design and task performance. *Information Systems Journal, 19*(4), 345–367. DOI: 10.1111/j.1365-2575.2007.00291.x

Bushelenkov, S., Paramonov, A., Muthanna, A., El-Latif, A. A. A., Koucheryavy, A., Alfarraj, O., Pławiak, P., & Ateya, A. A. (2023). Multi-Story Building Model for Efficient IoT Network Design. *Mathematics*, *11*(6), 1403. DOI: 10.3390/math11061403

Calo, S. B., Touna, M., Verma, D. C., & Cullen, A. (2017, December). Edge computing architecture for applying AI to IoT. In 2017 IEEE International Conference on Big Data (Big Data) (pp. 3012-3016). IEEE. DOI: 10.1109/BigData.2017.8258272

Cambria, E., & White, B. (2014). Jumping NLP curves: A review of natural language processing research. *IEEE Computational Intelligence Magazine*, *9*(2), 48–57. DOI: 10.1109/MCI.2014.2307227

Chen, M., Herrera, F., & Hwang, K. (2018). Cognitive computing: Architecture, technologies and intelligent applications. *IEEE Access : Practical Innovations, Open Solutions*, *6*, 19774–19783. DOI: 10.1109/ACCESS.2018.2791469

Chen, M., Li, W., Fortino, G., Hao, Y., Hu, L., & Humar, I. (2019). A dynamic service migration mechanism in edge cognitive computing. *ACM Transactions on Internet Technology*, *19*(2), 1–15. DOI: 10.1145/3239565

Chen, M., Li, W., Fortino, G., Hao, Y., Hu, L., & Humar, I. (2019). A dynamic service migration mechanism in edge cognitive computing. *ACM Transactions on Internet Technology*, *19*(2), 1–15. DOI: 10.1145/3239565

Chen, M., Wang, H., Mehrotra, S., Leung, V. C., & Humar, I. (2019). Intelligent networks assisted by cognitive computing and machine learning. *IEEE Network*, *33*(3), 6–8. DOI: 10.1109/MNET.2019.8726065

Chen, M. S., Han, J., & Yu, P. S. (1996). Data mining: An overview from a database perspective. *IEEE Transactions on Knowledge and Data Engineering*, *8*(6), 866–883. DOI: 10.1109/69.553155

. Chopra, A., Prashar, A., & Sain, C. (2013). Natural language processing. International journal of technology enhancements and emerging engineering research, 1(4), 131-134.

Chowdhury, N. M. K., & Boutaba, R. (2009). Network virtualization: State of the art and research challenges. *IEEE Communications Magazine*, *47*(7), 20–26. DOI: 10.1109/MCOM.2009.5183468

Chowdhury, N. M. K., & Boutaba, R. (2010). A survey of network virtualization. *Computer Networks*, *54*(5), 862–876. DOI: 10.1016/j.comnet.2009.10.017

De Chiffre, L., Carmignato, S., Kruth, J. P., Schmitt, R., & Weckenmann, A. (2014). Industrial applications of computed tomography. *CIRP Annals*, *63*(2), 655–677. DOI: 10.1016/j.cirp.2014.05.011

Eckhoff, D., & Wagner, I. (2017). Privacy in the smart city—Applications, technologies, challenges, and solutions. *IEEE Communications Surveys and Tutorials*, *20*(1), 489–516. DOI: 10.1109/COMST.2017.2748998

El-Latif, A. A. A., Chelloug, S. A., Alabdulhafith, M., & Hammad, M. (2023). Accurate Detection of Alzheimer's Disease Using Lightweight Deep Learning Model on MRI Data. *Diagnostics (Basel)*, *13*(7), 1216. DOI: 10.3390/diagnostics13071216 PMID: 37046434

Elgendy, I. A., Meshoul, S., & Hammad, M. (2023). Joint Task Offloading, Resource Allocation, and Load-Balancing Optimization in Multi-UAV-Aided MEC Systems. *Applied Sciences (Basel, Switzerland)*, *13*(4), 2625. DOI: 10.3390/app13042625

Feng, S., Setoodeh, P., & Haykin, S. (2017). Smart home: Cognitive interactive people-centric Internet of Things. *IEEE Communications Magazine*, *55*(2), 34–39. DOI: 10.1109/MCOM.2017.1600682CM

Gann, D. M., & Salter, A. J. (2000). Innovation in project-based, service-enhanced firms: The construction of complex products and systems. *Research Policy*, *29*(7-8), 955–972. DOI: 10.1016/S0048-7333(00)00114-1

Georgescu, T. M. (2020). Natural language processing model for automatic analysis of cybersecurity-related documents. *Symmetry*, *12*(3), 354. DOI: 10.3390/sym12030354

Gupta, S., Kar, A. K., Baabdullah, A., & Al-Khowaiter, W. A. (2018). Big data with cognitive computing: A review for the future. *International Journal of Information Management*, *42*, 78–89. DOI: 10.1016/j.ijinfomgt.2018.06.005

Hammad, M., Abd El-Latif, A. A., Hussain, A., Abd El-Samie, F. E., Gupta, B. B., Ugail, H., & Sedik, A. (2022). Deep learning models for arrhythmia detection in IoT healthcare applications. *Computers & Electrical Engineering*, *100*, 108011. DOI: 10.1016/j.compeleceng.2022.108011

Hammad, M., Bakrey, M., Bakhiet, A., Tadeusiewicz, R., Abd El-Latif, A. A., & Pławiak, P. (2022). A novel end-to-end deep learning approach for cancer detection based on microscopic medical images. *Biocybernetics and Biomedical Engineering*, *42*(3), 737–748. DOI: 10.1016/j.bbe.2022.05.009

Hammad, M., Iliyasu, A. M., Elgendy, I. A., & Abd El-Latif, A. A. (2022). End-to-end data authentication deep learning model for securing IoT configurations. *Hum. Cent. Comput. Inf. Sci*, *12*(4).

Hammad, M., Kandala, R. N., Abdelatey, A., Abdar, M., Zomorodi-Moghadam, M., San Tan, R., & Pławiak, P. (2021). Automated detection of Shockable ECG signals: A Review. *Information Sciences, 571*, 580–604. DOI: 10.1016/j.ins.2021.05.035

Hammad, M., Tawalbeh, L. A., Iliyasu, A. M., Sedik, A., Abd El-Samie, F. E., Alkinani, M. H., & Abd El-Latif, A. A. (2022). Efficient multimodal deep-learning-based COVID-19 diagnostic system for noisy and corrupted images. *Journal of King Saud University. Science, 34*(3), 101898. DOI: 10.1016/j.jksus.2022.101898 PMID: 35185304

Hirschberg, J., & Manning, C. D. (2015). Advances in natural language processing. *Science, 349*(6245), 261–266. DOI: 10.1126/science.aaa8685 PMID: 26185244

Hu, B., & Zhang, Z. (2022). Evaluation of Big Data Analytics and cognitive computing in smart health systems. *Journal of Commercial Biotechnology, 27*(2), 2. DOI: 10.5912/jcb1088

Jain, D. K., Boyapati, P., Venkatesh, J., & Prakash, M. (2022). An intelligent cognitive-inspired computing with big data analytics framework for sentiment analysis and classification. *Information Processing & Management, 59*(1), 102758.

Kang, Y., Cai, Z., Tan, C. W., Huang, Q., & Liu, H. (2020). Natural language processing (NLP) in management research: A literature review. *Journal of Management Analytics, 7*(2), 139–172. DOI: 10.1080/23270012.2020.1756939

Khuda, I. E., Aftab, A., Hasan, S., Ikram, S., Ahmad, S., Ateya, A. A., & Asim, M. (2024). Trends of Social Anxiety in University Students of Pakistan Post-COVID-19 Lockdown: A Healthcare Analytics Perspective. *Information (Basel), 15*(7), 373. DOI: 10.3390/info15070373

Khuda, I. E., Ahmed, S., & Ateya, A. A. (2024). STEM-Based Bayesian Computational Leaning Model-BCLM for Effective Learning of Bayesian Statistics. *IEEE Access : Practical Innovations, Open Solutions, 12*, 91217–91228. DOI: 10.1109/ACCESS.2024.3420731

Kleyko, D., Rachkovskij, D., Osipov, E., & Rahimi, A. (2023). A survey on hyper-dimensional computing aka vector symbolic architectures, part ii: Applications, cognitive models, and challenges. *ACM Computing Surveys, 55*(9), 1–52. DOI: 10.1145/3558000

Kumar, H., Soh, P. J., & Ismail, M. A. (2022). Big data streaming platforms: A review. *Iraqi Journal for Computer Science and Mathematics, 3*(2), 95–100. DOI: 10.52866/ijcsm.2022.02.01.010

Lauriola, I., Lavelli, A., & Aiolli, F. (2022). An introduction to deep learning in natural language processing: Models, techniques, and tools. *Neurocomputing*, *470*, 443–456. DOI: 10.1016/j.neucom.2021.05.103

Li, L., Goh, T. T., & Jin, D. (2020). How textual quality of online reviews affect classification performance: A case of deep learning sentiment analysis. *Neural Computing & Applications*, *32*(9), 4387–4415. DOI: 10.1007/s00521-018-3865-7

Lin, Y. T., Hung, T. W., & Huang, L. T. L. (2021). Engineering equity: How AI can help reduce the harm of implicit bias. *Philosophy & Technology*, *34*(S1, Suppl 1), 65–90. DOI: 10.1007/s13347-020-00406-7

Lytras, M., Visvizi, A., Zhang, X., & Aljohani, N. R. (2020). Cognitive computing, Big Data Analytics and data driven industrial marketing. *Industrial Marketing Management*, *90*, 663–666. DOI: 10.1016/j.indmarman.2020.03.024

Ma, L., & Sun, B. (2020). Machine learning and AI in marketing–Connecting computing power to human insights. *International Journal of Research in Marketing*, *37*(3), 481–504. DOI: 10.1016/j.ijresmar.2020.04.005

Mishra, N., & Silakari, S. (2012). Predictive analytics: A survey, trends, applications, oppurtunities & challenges. *International Journal of Computer Science and Information Technologies*, *3*(3), 4434–4438.

Patro, K. K., Prakash, A. J., Neelapu, B. C., Tadeusiewicz, R., Acharya, U. R., Hammad, M., & Pławiak, P. (2023). Application of Kronecker convolutions in deep learning technique for automated detection of kidney stones with coronal CT images. *Information Sciences*, *640*, 119005. DOI: 10.1016/j.ins.2023.119005

Prakash, A. J., Patro, K. K., Hammad, M., Tadeusiewicz, R., & Pławiak, P. (2022). BAED: A secured biometric authentication system using ECG signal based on deep learning techniques. *Biocybernetics and Biomedical Engineering*, *42*(4), 1081–1093. DOI: 10.1016/j.bbe.2022.08.004

Raghavan, V. V., Gudivada, V. N., Govindaraju, V., & Rao, C. R. (2016). *Cognitive computing: Theory and applications*. Elsevier.

Rahim, A., Zhong, Y., Ahmad, T., Ahmad, S., Pławiak, P., & Hammad, M. (2023). Enhancing smart home security: Anomaly detection and face recognition in smart home IoT devices using logit-boosted CNN models. *Sensors (Basel)*, *23*(15), 6979. DOI: 10.3390/s23156979 PMID: 37571762

Ren, J., Zhang, D., He, S., Zhang, Y., & Li, T. (2019). A survey on end-edge-cloud orchestrated network computing paradigms: Transparent computing, mobile edge computing, fog computing, and cloudlet. *ACM Computing Surveys, 52*(6), 1–36. DOI: 10.1145/3362031

. Roiger, R. J. (2017). Data mining: a tutorial-based primer.

Rosenfeld, A. (1988). Computer vision: Basic principles. *Proceedings of the IEEE, 76*(8), 863–868. DOI: 10.1109/5.5961

Sakr, A. S., Pławiak, P., Tadeusiewicz, R., & Hammad, M. (2022). Cancelable ECG biometric based on combination of deep transfer learning with DNA and amino acid approaches for human authentication. *Information Sciences, 585*, 127–143. DOI: 10.1016/j.ins.2021.11.066

Sakr, A. S., Soliman, N. F., Al-Gaashani, M. S., Pławiak, P., Ateya, A. A., & Hammad, M. (2022). An efficient deep learning approach for colon cancer detection. *Applied Sciences (Basel, Switzerland), 12*(17), 8450. DOI: 10.3390/app12178450

Salankar, N., Qaisar, S. M., Pławiak, P., Tadeusiewicz, R., & Hammad, M. (2022). EEG based alcoholism detection by oscillatory modes decomposition second order difference plots and machine learning. *Biocybernetics and Biomedical Engineering, 42*(1), 173–186. DOI: 10.1016/j.bbe.2021.12.009

Sedik, A., Hammad, M., Abd El-Latif, A. A., El-Banby, G. M., Khalaf, A. A., Abd El-Samie, F. E., & Iliyasu, A. M. (2021). Deep learning modalities for biometric alteration detection in 5G networks-based secure smart cities. *IEEE Access: Practical Innovations, Open Solutions, 9*, 94780–94788. DOI: 10.1109/ACCESS.2021.3088341

Shamsan, A. H., & Faridi, A. R. (2019, March). Network softwarization for IoT: A survey. In 2019 6th International Conference on Computing for Sustainable Global Development (INDIACom) (pp. 1163-1168). IEEE.

Sreedevi, A. G., Harshitha, T. N., Sugumaran, V., & Shankar, P. (2022). Application of cognitive computing in healthcare, cybersecurity, big data and IoT: A literature review. *Information Processing & Management, 59*(2), 102888.

Sreedevi, A. G., Nitya Harshitha, T., Sugumaran, V., & Shankar, P. (2022). Vijayan Sugumaran, and P. Shankar. "Application of cognitive computing in healthcare, cybersecurity, big data and IoT: A literature review.". *Information Processing & Management, 59*(2), 102888. DOI: 10.1016/j.ipm.2022.102888

Vassakis, K., Petrakis, E., & Kopanakis, I. (2018). Big data analytics: applications, prospects and challenges. Mobile big data: A roadmap from models to technologies, 3-20.

Velickovski, F., Ceccaroni, L., Roca, J., Burgos, F., Galdiz, J. B., Marina, N., & Lluch-Ariet, M. (2014). Clinical Decision Support Systems (CDSS) for preventive management of COPD patients. *Journal of Translational Medicine, 12*(Suppl 2), 1–10. DOI: 10.1186/1479-5876-12-S2-S9 PMID: 25471545

von Eschenbach, W. J. (2021). Transparency and the black box problem: Why we do not trust AI. *Philosophy & Technology, 34*(4), 1607–1622. DOI: 10.1007/s13347-021-00477-0

Wan, S., Gu, Z., & Ni, Q. (2020). Cognitive computing and wireless communications on the edge for healthcare service robots. *Computer Communications, 149*, 99–106. DOI: 10.1016/j.comcom.2019.10.012

Wang, F. Y., Yang, L., Cheng, X., Han, S., & Yang, J. (2016). Network softwarization and parallel networks: Beyond software-defined networks. *IEEE Network, 30*(4), 60–65. DOI: 10.1109/MNET.2016.7513865

Wang, Y., Kung, L., & Byrd, T. A. (2018). Big data analytics: Understanding its capabilities and potential benefits for healthcare organizations. *Technological Forecasting and Social Change, 126*, 3–13. DOI: 10.1016/j.techfore.2015.12.019

Webb, B. (2000). What does robotics offer animal behaviour? *Animal Behaviour, 60*(5), 545–558. DOI: 10.1006/anbe.2000.1514 PMID: 11082225

Weiss, M., Jacob, F., & Duveiller, G. (2020). Remote sensing for agricultural applications: A meta-review. *Remote Sensing of Environment, 236*, 111402. DOI: 10.1016/j.rse.2019.111402

Xu, Z., Liu, W., Huang, J., Yang, C., Lu, J., & Tan, H. (2020). Artificial intelligence for securing IoT services in edge computing: A survey. *Security and Communication Networks, 2020*, 1–13. DOI: 10.1155/2020/8872586

Yousefpour, A., Fung, C., Nguyen, T., Kadiyala, K., Jalali, F., Niakanlahiji, A., Kong, J., & Jue, J. P. (2019). All one needs to know about fog computing and related edge computing paradigms: A complete survey. *Journal of Systems Architecture, 98*, 289–330. DOI: 10.1016/j.sysarc.2019.02.009

Zhang, K., Ni, J., Yang, K., Liang, X., Ren, J., & Shen, X. S. (2017). Security and privacy in smart city applications: Challenges and solutions. *IEEE Communications Magazine, 55*(1), 122–129. DOI: 10.1109/MCOM.2017.1600267CM

Zhang, W. Z., Elgendy, I. A., Hammad, M., Iliyasu, A. M., Du, X., Guizani, M., & Abd El-Latif, A. A. (2020). Secure and optimized load balancing for multitier IoT and edge-cloud computing systems. *IEEE Internet of Things Journal, 8*(10), 8119–8132. DOI: 10.1109/JIOT.2020.3042433

Zhang, Y., Wu, C., Qiao, C., Sadek, A., & Hulme, K. F. (2022). A cognitive computational model of driver warning response performance in connected vehicle systems. *IEEE Transactions on Intelligent Transportation Systems, 23*(9), 14790–14805. DOI: 10.1109/TITS.2021.3134058

Chapter 2
Natural Language Processing Techniques for Social Media Sentiment Analysis

Mohamed Hammad
https://orcid.org/0000-0002-6506-3083
Prince Sultan University, Saudi Arabia

Wesam Ahmed
https://orcid.org/0009-0008-5675-5724
Faculty of Computers and Artificial Intelligence, Hurghada University, Egypt

ABSTRACT

This Chapter presents a comprehensive examination of Natural Language Processing [NLP] techniques for sentiment analysis in social media contexts, addressing the unique challenges and opportunities presented by user-generated content on social platforms. We trace the evolution of sentiment analysis from early lexicon-based approaches through modern transformer architectures, highlighting the technological advancements that have revolutionized our ability to understand and analyze social media sentiment. The Chapter provides detailed insights into advanced NLP techniques, preprocessing methodologies, and architectural considerations for implementing robust sentiment analysis systems. We also explore evaluation frameworks and metrics for assessing system performance, along with crucial implementation considerations for real-world applications. The Chapter concludes with an examination of emerging trends and future directions, including privacy-preserving techniques and ethical considerations in sentiment analysis.

DOI: 10.4018/979-8-3693-9057-3.ch002

Copyright © 2025, IGI Global Scientific Publishing. Copying or distributing in print or electronic forms without written permission of IGI Global Scientific Publishing is prohibited.

1. INTRODUCTION

The advent of social media platforms has fundamentally transformed the landscape of human communication and expression, generating unprecedented volumes of user-generated content that present both extraordinary opportunities and unique challenges for sentiment analysis (Popescu & Vaľko, 2023). This chapter provides a comprehensive exploration of Natural Language Processing [NLP] techniques essential for extracting and analyzing sentiment from social media data, with particular emphasis on addressing the distinctive characteristics of social media text (Khan et al., 2016).

As illustrated in Figure 1, the evolution of sentiment analysis in social media contexts represents a fascinating journey through four distinct technological eras, each bringing significant advancements in our ability to understand and analyze social media sentiment. In the early 2000s, researchers primarily relied on lexicon-based approaches, which involved carefully curated dictionaries of words and their associated sentiment values (Yousif et al., 2019). These dictionaries, often containing thousands of pre-labeled terms, formed the backbone of early sentiment analysis systems. While these methods were groundbreaking for their time, they faced significant limitations when confronted with the informal and dynamic nature of social media communication. The rigid nature of lexicon-based approaches made it difficult to capture context-dependent meanings, handle neologisms, and interpret informal expressions that are prevalent in social media discourse.

The period between 2010 and 2015 marked a significant paradigm shift towards machine learning approaches (Deng & Li, 2013) (Chang et al., 2014)(Poria et al., 2014)(Medhat et al., 2014)(Montoyo et al., 2012)(Stieglitz et al., 2014). This era saw researchers leveraging supervised learning techniques to capture more nuanced sentiment expressions. The revolution in methodology enabled systems to learn from labeled examples and adapt to the evolving language patterns characteristic of social media platforms. Machine learning models, particularly Support Vector Machines [SVMs] and Random Forests, demonstrated superior ability to handle the variability in social media text by learning from large datasets of annotated content (Hartmann et al., 2019)(Airlangga, 2024)(Ahmed et al., 2023). This period also saw the development of sophisticated feature engineering techniques that could capture both linguistic and social media-specific features.

Figure 1. Evolution of Sentiment Analysis Approaches

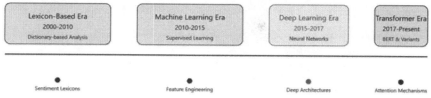

The deep learning transformation, beginning around 2015, brought unprecedented capabilities to sentiment analysis systems, as shown in Figure 2. Neural networks demonstrated remarkable ability to capture complex linguistic patterns and contextual nuances that had previously proven challenging for traditional approaches (Goldberg, 2017)(Monroe et al., 2017)(Nadeau, 2015)(Zhang et al., 2016)(Hurwitz et al., 2015)(Prusa & Khoshgoftaar, 2017)(Xun et al., 2016). This era saw the emergence of various neural architectures, including Convolutional Neural Networks [CNNs] for capturing local patterns and Recurrent Neural Networks [RNNs] for processing sequential information. These models could automatically learn hierarchical representations from raw text, reducing the need for manual feature engineering while improving performance on complex sentiment analysis tasks.

The introduction of transformer architecture in 2017, particularly with models like BERT and its variants, represented another quantum leap in the field's capabilities (Mukesh et al., 2024)(Nieminen, 2023)(Canchila et al., 2024)(Lin et al., 2022) (Yıldırım & Asgari-Chenaghlu, 2024)(Tripathy et al., 2021)(Semary et al., 2023) (Semary et al., 2024)(Hammad et al., 2025)

(Ahmed et al., 2025). These models revolutionized sentiment analysis through their innovative attention mechanisms, which could process context bidirectionally and handle long-range dependencies. This capability proved especially valuable for social media content, where meaning often depends heavily on context and reference. Transformer models could effectively capture the relationships between words across long distances in text, understand contextual word usage, and handle the informal nature of social media communication more effectively than previous approaches.

Figure 2. Modern Sentiment Analysis Architecture

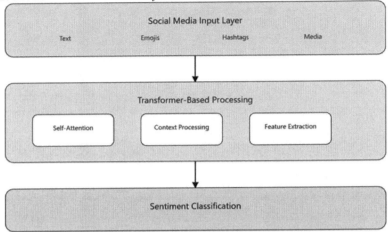

The modern sentiment analysis landscape has evolved into a sophisticated ecosystem that combines multiple technological approaches to address the unique challenges of social media content (Toivonen et al., 2019)(Ilieva & McPhearson, 2018). Contemporary systems must handle not only traditional text but also emojis, hashtags, multimedia content, and platform-specific features. They must process content in real-time, adapt to rapidly evolving language patterns, and provide accurate sentiment analysis across multiple languages and cultural contexts.

This chapter is organized into *eight* sections, starting with Section 2, which examines the unique Characteristics of social media Text. Section 3 outlines the Preprocessing Pipeline for social media Text, detailing essential steps such as normalization. Section 4 explores Advanced NLP Techniques for Sentiment Analysis, highlighting deep learning architecture like CNNs, RNNs, and transformers. Section 5 presents an Evaluation Framework, discussing metrics and methodologies to assess performance effectively. Section 6 focuses on Implementation Considerations. Section 7 explores Future Directions and Emerging Trends. Finally, Section 8 concludes with a summary of key insights, emphasizing progress and identifying opportunities for future research and innovation in sentiment analysis for social media.

2. CHARACTERISTICS OF SOCIAL MEDIA TEXT

Social media text embodies a dynamic and evolving linguistic environment shaped by the unique demands and affordances of digital platforms (Costa, 2018) (Androutsopoulos, 2011). Unlike traditional written communication, social media text reflects a blend of creativity, brevity, and informality, driven by character constraints, platform conventions, and the desire for rapid interaction. This linguistic evolution is marked by distinctive morphological, syntactic, and semantic features that deviate from conventional norms while introducing new patterns of meaning and expression. At the same time, analyzing social media text poses significant technical challenges, including text normalization, noise management, and context resolution, as these texts are often laden with non-standard language, multimodal elements, and high context dependency. Understanding the characteristics of social media text requires an exploration of its linguistic innovations alongside the computational hurdles that arise in processing this rich yet complex form of digital communication.

2.1. Linguistic Features

The linguistic landscape of social media presents a fascinating tapestry of language evolution and adaptation (Khabibullaevna, 2023)(Abdullayev, 2023). At the morphological level, social media users frequently engage in creative word formation processes that challenge traditional linguistic analysis (Onyedum, 2012). As illustrated in Figure 3, these linguistic features operate across multiple interconnected layers, each contributing to the complex meaning-making process in social media communication.

Morphological innovations manifest through various character manipulations, where users employ strategies like letter repetition ["sooooo excited", "yaaaaas"], deliberate misspellings ["boi", "smol"], and creative abbreviations ["tbh", "imo"]. As shown in the morphological layer of Figure 3, these modifications serve a dual purpose of emotional amplification and efficient communication, with users leveraging techniques like capitalization, strategic spacing, and mixed case to convey intensity and emotion that would typically be expressed through vocal intonation in spoken language.

Figure 3. Social Media Text Analysis Layers and Relationships

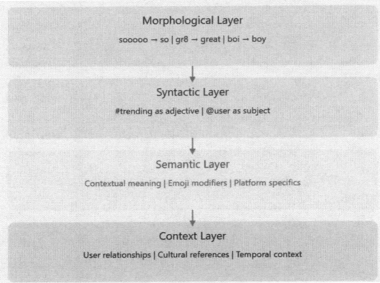

Platform-specific adaptations have given rise to a unique linguistic environment where character limitations spawn innovative shortenings and efficient information packaging techniques (Moshagen et al., n.d.). These adaptations have evolved beyond mere space-saving devices to become integral elements of social media's linguistic identity, creating a rich layer of meaning that often requires insider knowledge to fully comprehend.

Syntactic patterns in social media text reflect a significant departure from conventional grammar rules, creating an emergent grammatical system that follows its own internal logic (Eisenlauer, 2013). As depicted in the syntactic layer of Figure 1, the integration of platform-specific elements such as hashtags and @mentions has fundamentally altered traditional sentence structures, with these elements now functioning as legitimate grammatical units. For instance, hashtags frequently serve as adjectives or thematic markers, while @mentions can function as subjects or objects within sentences. This evolution represents not just a modification of existing grammar, but the emergence of a new syntactic framework specifically adapted to digital communication.

The semantic landscape of social media communication presents particularly complex challenges, characterized by rapid evolution and high context-dependency (Mishra et al., 2025). As illustrated in the semantic layer of Figure 3, words and phrases frequently undergo meaning shifts, acquiring platform-specific definitions that may differ significantly from their traditional usage. This semantic fluidity is further complicated by the multi-modal nature of social media communication, where meaning is constructed through the interplay of text, emoji, and media elements. The temporal dimension of semantic evolution is especially pronounced in social media, with meanings rapidly shifting in response to meme culture and viral trends.

2.2. Technical Challenges

The technical challenges in processing social media text are deeply intertwined with the linguistic features shown in Figure 3. Text normalization presents intricate challenges that require sophisticated solutions (Shukla et al., 2023). The fundamental difficulty lies in distinguishing between intentional linguistic variations that carry meaning and unintentional errors that require correction. This process must carefully balance the standardization of text for analysis while preserving the unique semantic intent behind stylistic choices. The dynamic nature of social media language further complicates this task, as normalization rules must constantly evolve to keep pace with emerging linguistic patterns and platform-specific conventions.

Noise management represents another critical challenge in social media text analysis (Gasco et al., 2019). The high volume of spam, automated content, and irrelevant information necessitates robust filtering mechanisms that can identify and remove noise while preserving important contextual cues. This challenge extends beyond simple text filtering to encompass multi-modal noise across various content types, including hashtags, mentions, and embedded media. The increasing sophistication of automated content generators adds another layer of complexity to this task, requiring advanced techniques to distinguish between human and bot-generated content.

Context resolution, represented in the deepest layer of Figure 3, stands as perhaps the most complex challenge in social media text analysis. Understanding sentiment and meaning often requires synthesizing multiple contextual layers, including temporal context, conversation threading, cultural references, and user relationship dynamics (Clavel & Callejas, 2015). This complexity is particularly evident in the detection of sarcasm and irony, where meaning often inverts based on subtle contextual cues. The challenge extends beyond individual posts to encompass broader conversational contexts, platform-specific cultural norms, and the intricate web of user relationships that influence how sentiment is expressed and interpreted.

3. PREPROCESSING PIPELINE FOR SOCIAL MEDIA TEXT

Preprocessing social media text is a critical step in preparing data for sentiment analysis, as it addresses the unique and often challenging characteristics of user-generated content (Xu et al., 2022). Unlike traditional text, social media posts are informal, unstructured, and rich in creative expressions, such as emojis, hashtags, URLs, and platform-specific jargon. The preprocessing pipeline must therefore strike a delicate balance between cleaning noisy data and preserving sentiment-relevant information. This section outlines a systematic approach to preprocessing, encompassing text cleaning and normalization as well as feature engineering, with the aim of transforming raw social media content into a structured format suitable for advanced NLP techniques. By effectively addressing the complexities of social media text, this pipeline lays the foundation for accurate and robust sentiment analysis.

3.1. Text Cleaning and Normalization

The preprocessing pipeline for social media text requires a sophisticated and nuanced approach that goes beyond traditional text processing methods (George & Baskar, 2024). One of the foundational steps in this pipeline is URL processing. URLs embedded in social media text often provide context or reference external content relevant to the sentiment being expressed. Advanced systems extract metadata, anchor text, or summary information from these links rather than simply removing them, as illustrated in Figure 4.

Figure 4. Handling embedded links by either removing or extracting relevant metadata for sentiment analysis

Original Text: "Check out this link: https://example.com!"

Processed Text: "Check out this link: [URL]"

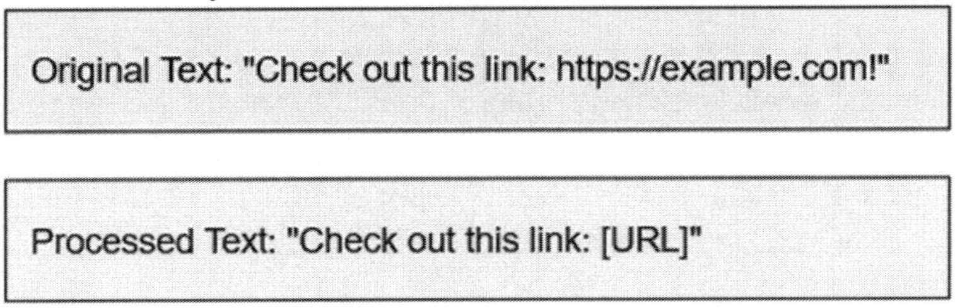

Special character handling is another critical component. Social media text frequently contains emojis, emoticons, hashtags, and various Unicode symbols that convey significant sentiment. For instance, emojis such as [crying with laughter] or [heart] carry emotional context. Modern preprocessing systems normalize these symbols into a standard format while preserving their sentimental value, as demonstrated in Figure 5. Unicode normalization ensures that all special characters are processed uniformly, and domain-specific rules address how emoticons or hashtags contribute to sentiment analysis.

Figure 5. Preserving semantic information from emojis, emoticons, and Unicode symbols

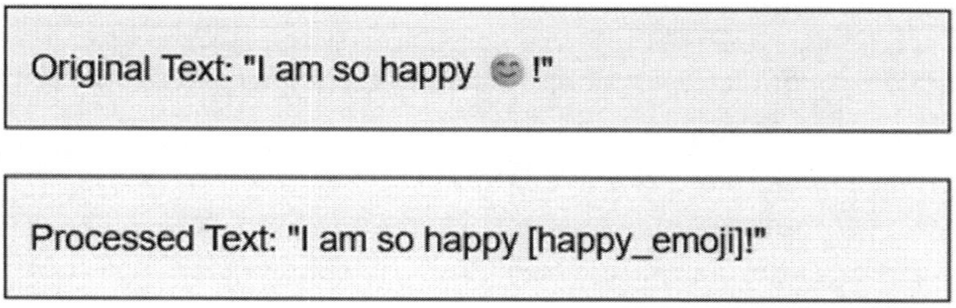

Original Text: "I am so happy 😊!"

Processed Text: "I am so happy [happy_emoji]!"

Whitespace normalization, though seemingly straightforward, demands a nuanced approach in social media contexts. Users often utilize creative spacing for emphasis, such as "so much fun," which carries stylistic intent. Naive normalization could strip away these meaningful patterns. Advanced systems employ algorithms to distinguish between intentional spacing [for emphasis] and random noise, preserving the former while standardizing the latter. Figure 6 provides a detailed visual representation of this process.

Figure 6. Distinguishing intentional spacing patterns from noise to ensure accurate text processing

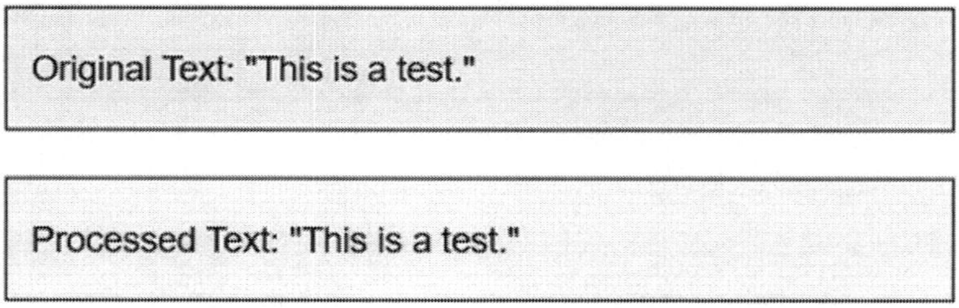

Original Text: "This is a test."

Processed Text: "This is a test."

3.2. Feature Engineering

Feature engineering for social media sentiment analysis requires a tailored approach to account for platform-specific characteristics and the creative use of language (Khanday et al., 2024). Traditional lexical features, such as word frequency and sentiment lexicons, must be adapted to capture the nuances of informal language, creative spelling, and abbreviations prevalent in social media text. Advanced systems employ n-gram generation techniques that incorporate token-level insights (Jeong & Lee, 2024), enabling them to capture colloquial phrases like "can't even" or "on fleek," as shown in Figure 7.

Syntactic feature extraction presents unique challenges. Social media posts often deviate from conventional grammar, incorporating incomplete sentences, creative punctuation, or platform-specific conventions like hashtags [#] and mentions [@]. To address this, modern preprocessing systems use robust dependency parsing algorithms tailored for non-standard text. These algorithms extract meaningful syntactic structures despite the lack of traditional grammatical rules. Figure 8 illustrates how syntactic relationships are identified and preserved.

Figure 7. Capturing linguistic patterns and platform-specific expressions for feature engineering

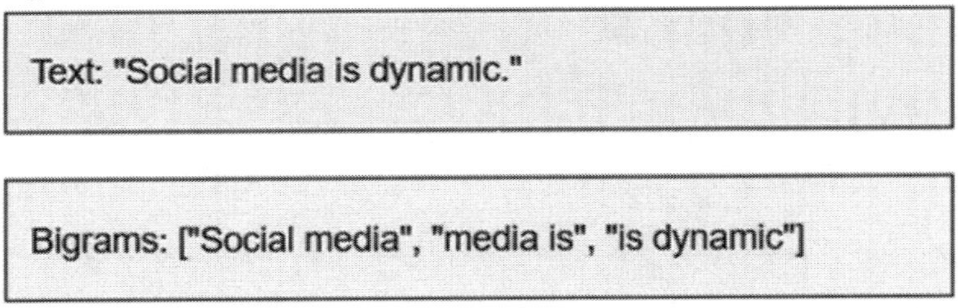

Text: "Social media is dynamic."

Bigrams: ["Social media", "media is", "is dynamic"]

Figure 8. Robust parsing of social media text, accounting for non-standard grammatical rules

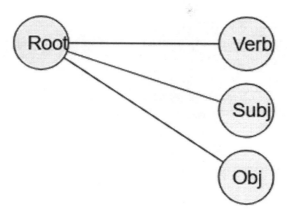

By combining advanced text cleaning, normalization techniques, and robust feature engineering strategies, the preprocessing pipeline ensures that social media text is accurately prepared for downstream sentiment analysis. This comprehensive approach lays the foundation for effective and context-aware sentiment modeling.

4. ADVANCED NLP TECHNIQUES FOR SENTIMENT ANALYSIS

Advanced NLP techniques have revolutionized sentiment analysis, particularly in the context of social media (Beigi et al., 2016)(Sharma et al., 2024). These techniques address the challenges posed by unstructured data, multimodal content, and platform-specific nuances. Modern systems leverage deep learning architectures, contextual analysis frameworks, and cross-platform integration to capture nuanced sentiment signals from diverse data sources. This section explores these cutting-edge techniques, focusing on their design, functionality, and transformative impact on sentiment analysis in social media contexts.

4.1. Deep Learning Architectures

The implementation of deep learning architectures for social media sentiment analysis represents a significant advancement in the field's capabilities (Beigi et al., 2016)(Sharma et al., 2024)(Yadav & Vishwakarma, 2020)(Araque et al., 2017)(Dang et al., 2020)(Feisheng, 2024). As illustrated in Figure 9, modern sentiment analysis systems employ a sophisticated multi-layer architecture that processes social media content through successive stages of refinement. This architectural approach, comprising input processing, core processing, and analysis layers, enables systems to capture both the explicit and implicit sentiment signals present in social media communications.

Transformer-based models have emerged as particularly powerful tools for social media sentiment analysis, offering unprecedented capabilities in handling context and long-range dependencies (Kumar et al., 2025)(Abdullah & Ahmet, 2022). The success of these models lies in their sophisticated attention mechanisms, which enable them to weigh different parts of the input text differently based on their relevance to sentiment expression. As shown in Figure 10, the embedding model architecture incorporates multiple specialized components designed specifically for social media content, including emoji-aware attention mechanisms and platform-specific feature processors.

Figure 9. Social media sentiment analysis architecture

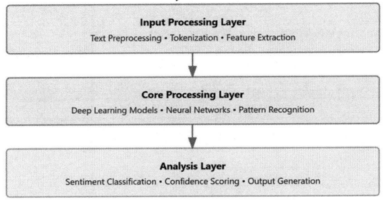

The attention mechanisms employed in modern sentiment analysis systems have evolved significantly to address the unique characteristics of social media content (George & Baskar, 2024)(Maheswari & Priya, 2024)(Nithya et al., 2023). Traditional attention mechanisms, while effective for standard text, have been enhanced with specialized components that can process the multi-modal nature of social media posts (Qian et al., 2022)(Suman et al., 2022)

(Subbaiah et al., 2024). These systems now incorporate sophisticated methods for aligning text with accompanying images, videos, and other media types, ensuring that sentiment analysis captures the full spectrum of expression across different modalities.

Figure 10. Embedding model architecture with attention mechanisms

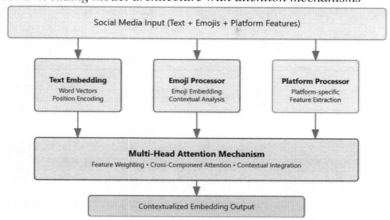

4.2. Contextual Analysis Framework

The contextual analysis framework, depicted in Figure 3, illustrates the complex interplay between different types of contexts in social media sentiment analysis. At the center of this framework lies the social media post, surrounded by four key contextual dimensions: temporal, user, social, and platform contexts. Each of these dimensions contributes crucial information to the overall sentiment interpretation process.

Temporal context processing represents a particularly challenging aspect of social media sentiment analysis (Maynard et al., 2017)(Al-Tameemi et al., 2024). Social media expressions often carry temporal dependencies that can significantly impact their interpretation. For instance, the sentiment associated with certain hashtags or phrases may evolve rapidly in response to ongoing events or changing social dynamics. Advanced systems employ sophisticated time-series analysis techniques to track these temporal patterns and adjust sentiment interpretations accordingly.

4.3. Cross-Platform Integration

Cross-platform integration in sentiment analysis requires careful consideration of platform-specific features and conventions (Novielli et al., 2020)(Naeem, 2019). As detailed in Table 1, different social media platforms exhibit distinct characteristics that can significantly impact sentimental expression and interpretation.

Table 1. Platform-Specific Characteristics and Their Impact on Sentiment Analysis

Platform	Characteristic Features	Sentiment Impact	Analysis Adaptations
Twitter	Character limits, hashtags	Condensed expression	Specialized tokenization
Facebook	Extended text, reactions	Multi-modal sentiment	Reaction integration
Instagram	Image-text combinations	Visual context dependency	Multi-modal analysis
LinkedIn	Professional context	Formal expression	Domain adaptation
TikTok	Video-text integration	Dynamic sentiment	Temporal analysis

The integration of these platform-specific features requires sophisticated normalization strategies that can preserve platform-specific sentiment indicators while enabling cross-platform analysis. Advanced systems employ dedicated normalization pipelines for each platform, followed by a standardization layer that enables consistent cross-platform sentiment analysis.

5. EVALUATION FRAMEWORK

The evaluation of sentiment analysis systems in social media contexts presents unique challenges that demand sophisticated and multi-faceted assessment approaches (Liu, 2010). Traditional evaluation frameworks, while valuable, often fail to capture the complex dynamics of social media communications, including temporal variations, platform-specific nuances, and multi-modal content interactions. This section explores a comprehensive evaluation framework that addresses these challenges, incorporating both established metrics and innovative assessment techniques specifically designed for social media sentiment analysis.

5.1. Comprehensive Metrics

The evaluation of sentiment analysis systems requires a sophisticated framework that can capture performance across multiple dimensions. As illustrated in Figure 11, the evaluation metrics framework encompasses both traditional classification metrics and specialized measures designed specifically for social media sentiment analysis. This comprehensive approach enables detailed assessment of system performance across different aspects of sentiment analysis. The foundation of sentiment analysis evaluation begins with traditional classification metrics, but these must be carefully adapted to account for the unique characteristics of social media content. Accuracy measurements in social media contexts must consider the inherent ambiguity and subjectivity of sentiment expressions, often requiring sophisticated weighting schemes that account for inter-annotator agreement levels and confidence scores.

Precision and recall metrics are enhanced through contextual weighting mechanisms that assign greater importance to challenging cases, such as sarcasm detection and implicit sentiment expression.

Figure 11. Evaluation Metrics Framework

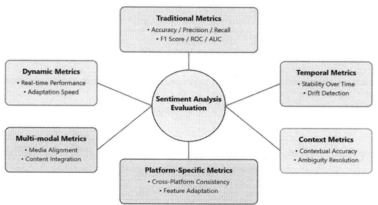

Traditional evaluation metrics, including accuracy, precision, recall, and F1 score, provide a foundation for performance assessment. However, these metrics must be supplemented with specialized measures that can capture the unique challenges of social media sentiment analysis. As shown in Table 2, these specialized metrics address various aspects of system performance. Temporal stability metrics evaluate a system's consistency across different time periods, accounting for evolving language patterns and shifting sentiment contexts. These metrics employ sophisticated time-series analysis techniques to detect and quantify temporal drift in system performance, enabling the identification of models that maintain robust performance despite temporal variations in language and sentiment expression patterns.

Context sensitivity metrics represent another crucial dimension of evaluation, measuring a system's ability to accurately interpret sentiment in various contextual settings. These metrics employ context-weighted scoring mechanisms that consider factors such as conversation threads, user relationships, and historical interactions. The evaluation framework incorporates sophisticated context modeling techniques that can distinguish between different types of contextual dependencies and assess their impact on sentiment interpretation accuracy.

Cross-platform evaluation presents particular challenges that require specialized metrics and methodologies. These metrics assess a system's ability to maintain consistent performance across different social media platforms while accurately handling platform-specific features. The evaluation framework employs cross-validation techniques that specifically target platform adaptation capabilities, measuring how well systems can transfer learning between platforms while preserving sentiment interpretation accuracy.

Table 2. Advanced Evaluation Metrics for Social Media Sentiment Analysis

Metric Category	Description	Calculation Method	Application Context
Temporal Stability	Consistency over time	Variance analysis	Trend analysis
Context Sensitivity	Contextual accuracy	Context-weighted scoring	Ambiguity resolution
Cross-Platform	Platform independence	Cross-validation	Platform adaptation
Multi-modal	Multi-media alignment	Modal correlation	Rich media analysis

5.2. Benchmarking Methodology

The benchmarking methodology for social media sentiment analysis systems must account for the dynamic nature of social media content. This requires careful consideration of dataset composition, temporal coverage, and platform representation. Advanced benchmarking frameworks employ stratified sampling techniques to ensure comprehensive coverage of different content types, sentiment expressions, and platform-specific features.

The methodology incorporates both static and dynamic evaluation components. Static evaluation components utilize strategically designed test cases that probe specific system capabilities. These test sets are constructed through sophisticated sampling techniques that ensure comprehensive coverage of edge cases, challenging scenarios, and common patterns. The methodology employs stratified sampling approaches that maintain representative distributions of different content types while deliberately including challenging cases that test system robustness.

Dynamic evaluation components address the real-time nature of social media communication by assessing system performance on streaming data. This approach employs continuous monitoring frameworks that track performance metrics over time, enabling the detection of performance degradation and adaptation capabilities. The dynamic evaluation framework incorporates feedback loops that enable systematic assessment of system learning and adaptation capabilities in response to evolving social media patterns.

The benchmarking process implements rigorous validation protocols that ensure evaluation reliability and reproducibility. These protocols include standardized data preprocessing pipelines, controlled testing environments, and systematic documentation of evaluation parameters and conditions. The methodology also incorporates stress testing components that assess system performance under various load conditions and content patterns, providing insights into scalability and robustness.

6. IMPLEMENTATION CONSIDERATIONS

The successful deployment of sentiment analysis systems in social media environments requires a sophisticated understanding of both technical architecture and performance optimization strategies (Fatima et al., 2022)(Ali et al., 2022)(Gonçalves et al., 2021)(Verma et al., 2023). Modern social media platforms generate massive volumes of data at unprecedented velocities, while users expect real-time insights and responses. This section explores the critical considerations in implementing robust, scalable, and efficient sentiment analysis systems, focusing on architectural design patterns, processing optimizations, and performance tuning strategies that enable these systems to meet the demanding requirements of social media applications.

6.1. System Architecture Design

The implementation of social media sentiment analysis systems requires careful consideration of scalability and real-time processing capabilities. Modern architecture, as depicted in Figure 12, employs distributed processing frameworks that can handle the massive volume and velocity of social media data. The architecture implements a sophisticated microservices approach, where each component operates as an independent service with its own scaling capabilities. The data ingestion layer employs advanced stream processing techniques, utilizing technologies like Apache Kafka or Amazon Kinesis for handling high-velocity data streams. This layer implements sophisticated backpressure mechanisms and rate limiting strategies to ensure system stability under varying load conditions.

Figure 12. System architecture: Social media sentiment analysis

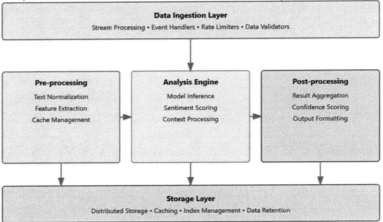

Real-time processing capabilities are achieved through a combination of event-driven architecture and sophisticated caching strategies. As shown in Figure 13, the system employs a multi-level caching architecture that optimizes both processing speed and resource utilization.

Figure 13. Multi-level caching architecture

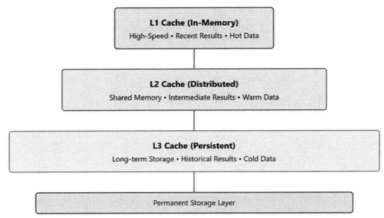

6.2. Performance Optimization

The optimization of sentiment analysis systems for social media content requires careful attention to both computational efficiency and accuracy. Table 3 presents a comprehensive overview of various optimization strategies and their impact on system performance.

Table 3. Optimization Strategies and Performance Impact

Strategy	Implementation Approach	Performance Impact	Resource Requirements
Batch Processing	Aggregated analysis	Increased throughput	Higher memory usage
Incremental Updates	Progressive refinement	Reduced latency	Moderate CPU load
Caching	Multi-level caching	Improved response time	Additional storage
Model Compression	Quantization techniques	Reduced resource usage	Lower accuracy trade-off
Distributed Processing	Load balancing	Enhanced scalability	Infrastructure complexity

7. FUTURE DIRECTIONS AND EMERGING TRENDS

The landscape of social media sentiment analysis is undergoing rapid transformation, driven by technological advancements, evolving user expectations, and increasing awareness of ethical considerations. As social media platforms continue to evolve and user interactions become increasingly complex, the field faces both exciting opportunities and significant challenges. This section explores emerging trends, technical innovations, and crucial ethical considerations that are shaping the future of social media sentiment analysis, highlighting key developments that promise to revolutionize how we understand and analyze social media sentiment.

7.1. Technical Advancements

The field of social media sentiment analysis continues to evolve rapidly, with several promising directions for future research and development. Advanced neural architectures are emerging that can better handle the multi-modal nature of social media content. These systems, illustrated in Figure 14, incorporate sophisticated fusion mechanisms that can process text, images, videos, and audio in a unified framework, providing more comprehensive sentiment analysis capabilities.

Privacy-preserving sentiment analysis represents another crucial area of development. As concerns about user privacy continue to grow, researchers are developing innovative techniques for performing sentiment analysis while maintaining user anonymity. These approaches include federated learning systems that can train sentiment analysis models without centralizing user data, and differential privacy mechanisms that provide formal privacy guarantees while maintaining analytical accuracy.

Figure 14. Advanced multi-modal fusion architecture

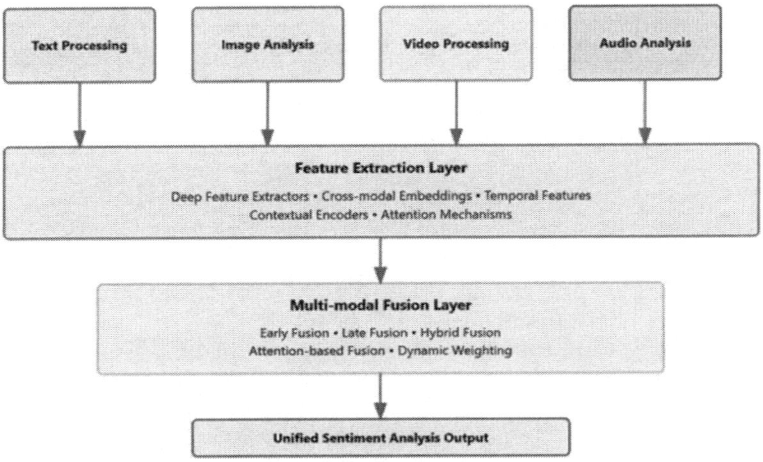

The multi-modal fusion architecture represents a significant advancement in sentiment analysis technology. Each modality processor employs specialized neural networks optimized for their specific data type. The text processing module utilizes advanced transformer architectures with enhanced contextual understanding capabilities. Image analysis incorporates vision transformers and neural architectures specifically designed for social media imagery, including meme analysis and visual sentiment detection. Video processing employs sophisticated spatio-temporal networks that can capture both motion dynamics and temporal sentiment evolution. Audio analysis includes advanced speech processing and emotional tone detection.

Privacy-preserving sentiment analysis has emerged as a crucial area of development, driven by increasing concerns about user privacy and data protection regulations. Researchers are developing innovative techniques that maintain analytical capabilities while ensuring user privacy. These approaches include:

- **Federated Learning Systems**: These distributed learning frameworks enable model training across decentralized devices while keeping user data local. Advanced protocols ensure model convergence while maintaining data privacy, implementing sophisticated aggregation mechanisms that prevent model inversion attacks.
- **Differential Privacy Mechanisms**: These mathematical frameworks provide formal privacy guarantees while preserving analytical accuracy. The implementation includes adaptive noise injection techniques, privacy budget optimization, and advanced composition theorems for multiple queries.

7.2. Ethical Considerations

Bias mitigation in sentiment analysis systems has become a critical focus area, requiring sophisticated approaches to ensure fair and equitable analysis. Modern systems implement multi-faceted debiasing strategies that operate at various levels. Data-level debiasing involves sophisticated sampling and augmentation techniques that address representation imbalances. Model-level debiasing incorporates adversarial training approaches and fairness constraints directly into the learning objective. Output-level debiasing employs post-processing techniques that adjust model predictions to ensure demographic parity while maintaining accuracy.

Transparency and explainability have evolved beyond simple attributes to encompass comprehensive interpretation frameworks. Modern approaches implement:

- Hierarchical Explanation Systems: These provide multiple levels of interpretation, from high-level sentiment drivers to detailed feature contributions.
- Counterfactual Explanations: Generate alternative scenarios that help users understand what changes would lead to different sentiment predictions.
- Interactive Visualization Tools: Enable users to explore sentiment analysis results through dynamic, interactive interfaces that reveal the underlying decision processes.

The future of social media sentiment analysis will likely see continued innovation in these areas, with increasing emphasis on responsible AI practices and user-centric design. Emerging research directions include:

- Cross-cultural Sentiment Understanding: Developing models that can accurately interpret sentiment across different cultural contexts and languages.
- Temporal Sentiment Evolution: Advanced frameworks for tracking and analyzing how sentiments evolve over time and across different social contexts.

- Multi-stakeholder Considerations: Balancing the needs and interests of different stakeholders while maintaining system effectiveness and ethical compliance.

8. CONCLUSION

This chapter presented a comprehensive examination of NLP techniques for social media sentiment analysis. We have explored the unique challenges presented by social media text, detailed the sophisticated preprocessing pipelines required for effective analysis, and examined advanced deep learning architectures designed specifically for this domain. The evaluation frameworks and implementation considerations discussed provide a foundation for developing robust sentiment analysis systems capable of handling the complexity of social media content.

The field continues to evolve rapidly, with emerging technologies and approaches promising even more sophisticated sentiment analysis capabilities. As social media platforms continue to evolve and new forms of expression emerge, sentiment analysis systems must adapt and improve to maintain their effectiveness. The future directions and ethical considerations discussed highlight the ongoing challenges and opportunities in this dynamic field.

REFERENCES

Abdullah, T., & Ahmet, A. (2022). Deep learning in sentiment analysis: Recent architectures. *ACM Computing Surveys*, *55*(8), 1–37. DOI: 10.1145/3548772

Abdullayev, S. (2023). The evolving landscape of translation. *Philological issues are in the eyes of young researchers, 1*[1].

Ahmad, P. N., Guo, J., AboElenein, N. M., Haq, Q. M. U., Ahmad, S., Algarni, A. D., & Ateya, A. (1827). A. (2025). Hierarchical graph-based integration network for propaganda detection in textual news articles on social media. *Scientific Reports*, *15*(1).

Ahmed, M. T., Antar, A. H., Rahman, M., Islam, A. Z. M. T., Das, D., & Rashed, M. G. (2023). Social media cyberbullying detection on political violence from Bangla texts using machine learning algorithm. *Journal of Intelligent Learning Systems and Applications*, *15*(4), 108–122. DOI: 10.4236/jilsa.2023.154008

Ahmed, W., Semary, N. A., Amin, K., & Hammad, M. (2025). Hyperparameter Optimization of Machine Learning Models Using Grid Search for Twitter Sentiment Analysis. In *Humanizing Technology With Emotional Intelligence* [pp. 419-432]. IGI Global Scientific Publishing.

Airlangga, G. (2024). Comparative Analysis of Machine Learning Models for Real-Time Disaster Tweet Classification: Enhancing Emergency Response with Social Media Analytics. *Brilliance: Research of Artificial Intelligence*, *4*(1), 25–31. DOI: 10.47709/brilliance.v4i1.3669

Al-Tameemi, I. K. S., Feizi-Derakhshi, M. R., Pashazadeh, S., & Asadpour, M. (2024). A comprehensive review of visual–textual sentiment analysis from social media networks. *Journal of Computational Social Science*, *7*(3), 2767–2838. DOI: 10.1007/s42001-024-00326-y

Ali, K. M., Ahmed Khan, T., Ali, S. M., Aziz, A., Khan, S. A., & Ahmad, S. (2024). An Exhaustive Comparative Study of Machine Learning Algorithms for Natural Language Processing Applications. *Engineering Proceedings*, *76*(1), 79.

Androutsopoulos, J. (2011). Language change and digital media: A review of conceptions and evidence. *Standard languages and language standards in a changing. Europe, 1*, 145–159.

Araque, O., Corcuera-Platas, I., Sánchez-Rada, J. F., & Iglesias, C. A. (2017). Enhancing deep learning sentiment analysis with ensemble techniques in social applications. *Expert Systems with Applications*, *77*, 236–246. DOI: 10.1016/j. eswa.2017.02.002

Arshad, M., Khan, B., Ahmad, S., & Asim, M. (2024). Predicting Age and Gender in Author Profiling: AMulti-Feature Exploration. *Computers, Materials & Continua*, *79*(2).

Beigi, G., Hu, X., Maciejewski, R., & Liu, H. (2016). An overview of sentiment analysis in social media and its applications in disaster relief. *Sentiment analysis and ontology engineering: An environment of computational intelligence*, 313-340.

Canchila, S., Meneses-Eraso, C., Casanoves-Boix, J., Cortés-Pellicer, P., & Castelló-Sirvent, F. (2024). Natural language processing: An overview of models, transformers and applied practices. *Computer Science and Information Systems*, *21*(00), 31–31. DOI: 10.2298/CSIS230217031C

Chang, R. M., Kauffman, R. J., & Kwon, Y. (2014). Understanding the paradigm shift to computational social science in the presence of big data. *Decision Support Systems*, *63*, 67–80. DOI: 10.1016/j.dss.2013.08.008

Clavel, C., & Callejas, Z. (2015). Sentiment analysis: From opinion mining to human-agent interaction. *IEEE Transactions on Affective Computing*, *7*(1), 74–93. DOI: 10.1109/TAFFC.2015.2444846

Costa, E. (2018). Affordances-in-practice: An ethnographic critique of social media logic and context collapse. *New Media & Society*, *20*(10), 3641–3656. DOI: 10.1177/1461444818756290 PMID: 30581356

Dang, N. C., Moreno-García, M. N., & De la Prieta, F. (2020). Sentiment analysis based on deep learning: A comparative study. *Electronics (Basel)*, *9*(3), 483. DOI: 10.3390/electronics9030483

Deng, L., & Li, X. (2013). Machine learning paradigms for speech recognition: An overview. *IEEE Transactions on Audio, Speech, and Language Processing*, *21*(5), 1060–1089. DOI: 10.1109/TASL.2013.2244083

Eisenlauer, V. (2013). A critical hypertext analysis of social media. *A Critical Hypertext Analysis of Social Media*, 1-256.

Fatima, R., Samad Shaikh, N., Riaz, A., Ahmad, S., El-Affendi, M. A., Alyamani, K. A., & Latif, R. M. A. (2022). A natural language processing (NLP) evaluation on COVID-19 rumour dataset using deep learning techniques. *Computational Intelligence and Neuroscience*, *2022*(1), 6561622.

Feisheng, L. [2024, April]. Systematic Review of Sentiment Analysis: Insights Through CNN-LSTM Networks. In *2024 5th International Conference on Industrial Engineering and Artificial Intelligence [IEAI]* [pp. 102-109]. IEEE.

Gasco, L., Clavel, C., Asensio, C., & de Arcas, G. (2019). Beyond sound level monitoring: Exploitation of social media to gather citizens subjective response to noise. *The Science of the Total Environment*, *658*, 69–79. DOI: 10.1016/j.scitotenv.2018.12.071 PMID: 30572215

George, A. S., & Baskar, T. (2024). Leveraging Big Data and Sentiment Analysis for Actionable Insights: A Review of Data Mining Approaches for Social Media. *Partners Universal International Innovation Journal*, *2*(4), 39–59.

George, A. S., & Baskar, T. (2024). Leveraging Big Data and Sentiment Analysis for Actionable Insights: A Review of Data Mining Approaches for Social Media. *Partners Universal International Innovation Journal*, *2*(4), 39–59.

Goldberg, Y. (2017). *Neural network methods in natural language processing.* Morgan & Claypool Publishers. DOI: 10.1007/978-3-031-02165-7

Hammad, M., Semary, N. A., Amin, K., & Ahmed, W. (2025). Techniques and Approaches for Sentiment Analysis in Social Media. In *Humanizing Technology With Emotional Intelligence* [pp. 403-418]. IGI Global Scientific Publishing.

Hartmann, J., Huppertz, J., Schamp, C., & Heitmann, M. (2019). Comparing automated text classification methods. *International Journal of Research in Marketing*, *36*(1), 20–38. DOI: 10.1016/j.ijresmar.2018.09.009

Hurwitz, J., Kaufman, M., Bowles, A., Nugent, A., Kobielus, J. G., & Kowolenko, M. D. (2015). *Cognitive computing and big data analytics* [Vol. 288]. Wiley.

Ilieva, R. T., & McPhearson, T. (2018). Social-media data for urban sustainability. *Nature Sustainability*, *1*(10), 553–565. DOI: 10.1038/s41893-018-0153-6

Jeong, B., & Lee, K. J. (2024). NLP-based Recommendation Approach for Diverse Service Generation. *IEEE Access : Practical Innovations, Open Solutions*, *12*, 14260–14274. DOI: 10.1109/ACCESS.2024.3355546

Khabibullaevna, N. A. (2023). Unveiling the labyrinth of internet phraseology: navigating the linguistic landscape of the digital era. *qo 'qon universiteti xabarnomasi, 7*, 78-81.

Khan, M. T., Durrani, M., Ali, A., Inayat, I., Khalid, S., & Khan, K. H. (2016). Sentiment analysis and the complex natural language. *Complex Adaptive Systems Modeling*, *4*(1), 1–19. DOI: 10.1186/s40294-016-0016-9

Khanday, A. M. U. D., Wani, M. A., Rabani, S. T., Khan, Q. R., & Abd El-Latif, A. A. (2024). HAPI: An efficient Hybrid Feature Engineering-based Approach for Propaganda Identification in social media. *PLoS One*, *19*(7), e0302583. DOI: 10.1371/journal.pone.0302583 PMID: 38985703

Khuda, I. E., Ahmed, S., & Ateya, A. A. (2024). STEM-Based Bayesian Computational Leaning Model-BCLM for Effective Learning of Bayesian Statistics. *IEEE Access : Practical Innovations, Open Solutions.*

Kumar, M., Khan, L., & Chang, H. T. (2025). Evolving techniques in sentiment analysis: A comprehensive review. *PeerJ. Computer Science*, *11*, e2592. DOI: 10.7717/peerj-cs.2592 PMID: 39957863

Lin, J., Nogueira, R., & Yates, A. (2022). *Pretrained transformers for text ranking: Bert and beyond.* Springer Nature. DOI: 10.1007/978-3-031-02181-7

Liu, B. (2010). Sentiment analysis: A multi-faceted problem. *IEEE Intelligent Systems*, *25*(3), 76–80. DOI: 10.1109/MIS.2022.3145503

Maheswari, V. U., & Priya, R. (2024). Optimized deep learning framework for analyzing offensive content on social media with bilstm and dual attention mechanisms. In *Computer Science Engineering* [pp. 360-370]. CRC Press.

Maynard, D., Roberts, I., Greenwood, M. A., Rout, D., & Bontcheva, K. (2017). A framework for real-time semantic social media analysis. *Journal of Web Semantics*, *44*, 75–88. DOI: 10.1016/j.websem.2017.05.002

Medhat, W., Hassan, A., & Korashy, H. (2014). Sentiment analysis algorithms and applications: A survey. *Ain Shams Engineering Journal*, *5*(4), 1093–1113. DOI: 10.1016/j.asej.2014.04.011

Mishra, A. K., Raghuvanshi, C. S., Soni, H. K., & Goswami, P. (2025). Analytics of Text and Social Media for Challenges of Hateful and Offensive Speech Detection. In *Text and Social Media Analytics for Fake News and Hate Speech Detection* [pp. 75-91]. Chapman and Hall/CRC.

Monroe, W., Hawkins, R. X., Goodman, N. D., & Potts, C. (2017). Colors in context: A pragmatic neural model for grounded language understanding. *Transactions of the Association for Computational Linguistics*, *5*, 325–338. DOI: 10.1162/tacl_a_00064

Montoyo, A., Martínez-Barco, P., & Balahur, A. (2012). Subjectivity and sentiment analysis: An overview of the current state of the area and envisaged developments. *Decision Support Systems*, *53*(4), 675–679. DOI: 10.1016/j.dss.2012.05.022

Moshagen, S. N., Pirinen, F., Antonsen, L., Gaup, B., Mikkelsen, I., Trosterud, T., ... & Hiovain-Asikainen, K. The GiellaLT infrastructure: A multilingual infrastructure for rule-based NLP1. *Rule-Based Language Technology*, 70.

Mukesh, K., Jayaprakash, S. L., & Kumar, R. P. (2024). QViLa: Quantum Infused Vision-Language Model for Enhanced Multimodal Understanding. *SN Computer Science*, *5*(8), 1–12. DOI: 10.1007/s42979-024-03398-9

Nadeau, S. E. (2015). Neural Network Mechanisms of Adult Language. In *Routledge handbook of communication disorders* [pp. 22-33]. Routledge.

Naeem, M. (2019). Uncovering the role of social media and cross-platform applications as tools for knowledge sharing. *VINE Journal of Information and Knowledge Management Systems*, *49*(3), 257–276. DOI: 10.1108/VJIKMS-01-2019-0001

Nieminen, M. (2023). The Transformer Model and Its Impact on the Field of Natural Language Processing.

Nithya, S., Presskila, X. A., Sakthivel, B., Krishnan, R. S., Narayanan, K. L., & Sundararajan, S. (2023, September). Enhancing Sentiment Analysis of Twitter Data Using Recurrent Neural Networks with Attention Mechanism. In 2023 4th International Conference on Smart Electronics and Communication (ICOSEC) (pp. 1348-1354). IEEE.

Novielli, N., Calefato, F., Dongiovanni, D., Girardi, D., & Lanubile, F. (2020, June). Can we use se-specific sentiment analysis tools in a cross-platform setting? In *Proceedings of the 17th International Conference on Mining Software Repositories* (pp. 158-168).

Onyedum, A. (2012). *Social media Neologisms: A morpho-semantic analysis*. University of Lagos.

Popescu, A., & Vaľko, M. (2023). Social Media Sentiment Analysis in the Age of Big Data: Understanding User Behavior and Predicting Trends. *International Journal of Business Intelligence and Big Data Analytics*, *6*(1), 31–39.

Poria, S., Cambria, E., Winterstein, G., & Huang, G. B. (2014). Sentic patterns: Dependency-based rules for concept-level sentiment analysis. *Knowledge-Based Systems*, *69*, 45–63. DOI: 10.1016/j.knosys.2014.05.005

Prusa, J. D., & Khoshgoftaar, T. M. (2017). Improving deep neural network design with new text data representations. *Journal of Big Data*, *4*(1), 1–16. DOI: 10.1186/s40537-017-0065-8

Qian, Y., Xu, W., Liu, X., Ling, H., Jiang, Y., Chai, Y., & Liu, Y. (2022). Popularity prediction for marketer-generated content: A text-guided attention neural network for multi-modal feature fusion. *Information Processing & Management*, *59*(4), 102984. DOI: 10.1016/j.ipm.2022.102984

Sánchez-Rada, J. F., & Iglesias, C. A. (2019). Social context in sentiment analysis: Formal definition, overview of current trends and framework for comparison. *Information Fusion*, *52*, 344–356. DOI: 10.1016/j.inffus.2019.05.003

Semary, N., Ahmed, W., Amin, K., Pławiak, P., & Hammad, M. (2024). Enhancing machine learning-based sentiment analysis through feature extraction techniques. *PLoS One*, *19*(2), e0294968.

Semary, N. A., Ahmed, W., Amin, K., Pławiak, P., & Hammad, M. (2023). Improving sentiment classification using a RoBERTa-based hybrid model. *Frontiers in Human Neuroscience*, *17*, 1292010. DOI: 10.3389/fnhum.2023.1292010 PMID: 38130432

Sharma, N. A., Ali, A. S., & Kabir, M. A. (2024). A review of sentiment analysis: Tasks, applications, and deep learning techniques. *International Journal of Data Science and Analytics*, •••, 1–38. DOI: 10.1007/s41060-024-00594-x

Shukla, K., Vashishtha, E., Sandhu, M., & Choubey, P. R. (2023). *Natural Language Processing: Unlocking the Power of Text and Speech Data*. Xoffencerpublication.

Stieglitz, S., Dang-Xuan, L., Bruns, A., & Neuberger, C. (2014). Social media analytics: An interdisciplinary approach and its implications for information systems. *Business & Information Systems Engineering*, *6*(2), 89–96. DOI: 10.1007/s12599-014-0315-7

Subbaiah, B., Murugesan, K., Saravanan, P., & Marudhamuthu, K. (2024). An efficient multimodal sentiment analysis in social media using hybrid optimal multi-scale residual attention network. *Artificial Intelligence Review*, *57*(2), 34. DOI: 10.1007/s10462-023-10645-7

Suman, C., Chaudhary, R. S., Saha, S., & Bhattacharyya, P. (2022). An attention based multi-modal gender identification system for social media users. *Multimedia Tools and Applications*, *81*(19), 1–23. DOI: 10.1007/s11042-021-11256-6

Toivonen, T., Heikinheimo, V., Fink, C., Hausmann, A., Hiippala, T., Järv, O., Tenkanen, H., & Di Minin, E. (2019). Social media data for conservation science: A methodological overview. *Biological Conservation*, *233*, 298–315. DOI: 10.1016/j.biocon.2019.01.023

Tripathy, J. K., Sethuraman, S. C., Cruz, M. V., Namburu, A., Mangalraj, P., & Vijayakumar, V. (2021). Comprehensive analysis of embeddings and pre-training in NLP. *Computer Science Review*, *42*, 100433. DOI: 10.1016/j.cosrev.2021.100433

Xu, Q. A., Chang, V., & Jayne, C. (2022). A systematic review of social media-based sentiment analysis: Emerging trends and challenges. *Decision Analytics Journal*, *3*, 100073. DOI: 10.1016/j.dajour.2022.100073

Xun, G., Jia, X., Gopalakrishnan, V., & Zhang, A. (2016). A survey on context learning. *IEEE Transactions on Knowledge and Data Engineering*, *29*(1), 38–56. DOI: 10.1109/TKDE.2016.2614508

Yadav, A., & Vishwakarma, D. K. (2020). Sentiment analysis using deep learning architectures: A review. *Artificial Intelligence Review*, *53*(6), 4335–4385. DOI: 10.1007/s10462-019-09794-5

Yıldırım, S., & Asgari-Chenaghlu, M. (2024). *Mastering Transformers: The Journey from BERT to Large Language Models and Stable Diffusion*. Packt Publishing Ltd.

Yousif, A., Niu, Z., Tarus, J. K., & Ahmad, A. (2019). A survey on sentiment analysis of scientific citations. *Artificial Intelligence Review*, *52*(3), 1805–1838. DOI: 10.1007/s10462-017-9597-8

Yousuf, W. B., Talha, U., Abro, A. A., Ahmad, S., Daniyal, S. M., Ahmad, N., & Ateya, A. A. (2024). Novel Prognostic Methods for System Degradation Using LSTM. *IEEE Access : Practical Innovations, Open Solutions*.

Zhang, Q., Gong, Y., Wu, J., Huang, H., & Huang, X. (2016, October). Retweet prediction with attention-based deep neural network. In *Proceedings of the 25th ACM international on conference on information and knowledge management* (pp. 75-84).

Chapter 3
CNN–Based Face Detection Focusing on Diverse Visual Variations

Faiza Latif Abbasi

Iqra University, Pakistan

Mansoor Ebrahim

https://orcid.org/0000-0002-2000-8398

Iqra University, Pakistan

Abdul Ahad Abro

https://orcid.org/0000-0002-3591-9231

Iqra University, Pakistan

Syed Muhammad Daniyal

Iqra University, Pakistan

Ilyas Younus

Iqra University, Pakistan

ABSTRACT

Facial recognition and emotion detection have become indispensable in modern civilization, affecting a wide range of businesses like banking, social media, education, and commerce. This chapter provides a thorough investigation of emotion recognition from facial expressions, focussing on three important aspects of the process: pre-processing, feature extraction, and classification. With an emphasis on deep learning algorithms that leverage visual facial data, the chapter looks at a variety of cutting-edge and conventional approaches to better understand human emotions. With an emphasis on recent advancements in emotion recognition, com-

DOI: 10.4018/979-8-3693-9057-3.ch003

parative results from existing methodologies are shown. The findings show how crucial automated emotion recognition is to some industries and offer useful data regarding the efficacy of various approaches.

1. INTRODUCTION

In recent years, researchers have focused a lot of their research on determining students' moods and behaviors in the classroom. Several approaches to these problems have been put forth, and they have produced promising results, along with the development of advanced computer vision techniques and computational power. When creating intelligent tutoring and adaptive learning systems, it is essential to determine each student's degree of participation in the classroom. Student involvement is connected with the outcomes that are expected of students in both regular classroom settings and online learning contexts. According to some studies, engagement detection creates opportunities for better learning and teaching, including the ability to modify a lesson like a skilled teacher would and receive real-time feedback on how engaged an audience is. Educational managers or monitors can even use it to launch focused interventions. The most popular approach for identifying students' engagement in a classroom setting uses several facial expression recognition (FER) techniques (Sattar et al., 2022). Another automated engagement technique uses physiological and neurological sensors, such as EEG, blood pressure, heart rate, or galvanic skin reaction, to gauge the degree of arousal or attention among students (Apicella et al., 2022). These ideas employed the elements of cognitive engagement to identify SE, but they are ineffective in the actual classroom setting because of their high cost and scalability problems. At the moment, deep learning and computer vision techniques are the sole tools used by academics to study behavioral and emotional engagement (Bustos-López et al., 2022). Using computer vision techniques, it is possible to identify whether or not students are participating in the lecture by looking at their apparent or emotional behavior. Numerous studies on facial expression detection have been carried out to investigate how students interact with the online learning environment (e-learning) (Karimah & Hasegawa, 2022). FER consists of many phases, such as classification, feature extraction, and face detection. These systems' primary benefit is that they assess interest levels covertly, focusing students' attention on the engagement assessment procedure itself. In this chapter, the main focus is on the detailed examination of the overall framework, and performance (power management, speed, computational complexity), along with the advantages, disadvantages, and implementation of Facial Expression Recognition. After a brief introduction, section 2 will present the historical background. Section 3 will discuss current trends and developments. Section 4 provides a literature review;

Section 5 provides facial expression recognition using different algorithms, while Section 6 discusses the Proposed methodology and 7 will present the dataset and Section 8 will discuss the Comparative analysis of Face Emotion and Recognition techniques. Finally, Section 9 will demonstrate comparative analysis 8 provide results and discussion and Section 10 will represent the Conclusion and future work.

2. HISTORICAL BACKGROUND

Over the past few decades, considerable improvements in computer vision, machine learning, and artificial intelligence have propelled advancements in facial expression recognition (FER). The development of this field has witnessed important turning points and notable changes in approaches, technologies, and applications, which are briefly discussed below.

Researchers such as Paul Ekman, who created the Facial Action Coding System (FACS) and classified six primary emotions into happiness, sorrow, anger, fear, surprise, and disgust placed a foundation of work in the early years, of the 1970s and 1980s. FACS was an essential technique for facial expression analysis since it divided facial motions into action units (Daniyal et al., 2024). These early models' main objective was to locate and quantify key facial landmarks, like the mouth, nose, and eyes, as well as their relative motions.

In the 1990s, machine learning methods for FER started to take shape. HMMs, or hidden Markov models, are statistical models that academics have begun to use to detect temporal patterns in facial expressions. Another significant development was the introduction of Active Appearance Models (AAMs), which combined shape and texture data to more accurately represent facial changes (Kopalidis et al., 2024). Facial expression tracking and recognition were made possible by AAMs by the application of a statistical model to face pictures. In the 2000s, significant advancements were made in feature extraction and categorization methods. Real-time face detection was revolutionized by boosting algorithms like the Viola-Jones face detection algorithm, which used a cascade of fundamental features and boosting approaches (Khan, 2022). This invention laid the groundwork for practical FER uses. In addition, Support Vector machines (SVMs) became a popular method for facial expression categorization because of their performance in high-dimensional feature spaces. Researchers employed a range of manually generated characteristics, such as Gabor filters and Local Binary Patterns (LBP), to describe the textures and structures of faces.

A major change in FER was brought about by the advent of deep learning in the 2010s. Convolutional Neural Networks (CNNs) have become the most common architecture in FER since Alex Net's 2012 achievement demonstrated the potential of deep learning (Gupta & Kumar, 2023). CNNs perform more reliably and precisely than previous methods because they directly learn hierarchical features from raw images. To build deep FER models, especially for facial expression recognition, researchers began utilizing large-scale datasets and transfer learning strategies. Recurrent neural networks (RNNs) and long short-term memory (LSTM) networks were used to capture temporal dynamics in video sequences, which further enhanced the ability to identify expressions across time.

In the 2020s, advances in modern FER methodologies and applications have progressed. By incorporating attention mechanisms and transformer models which have become increasingly prominent in natural language processing into FER, interpretability, and concentration on relevant facial regions have been enhanced. FER systems have been developed in response to the increasing prominence of ethical concerns like as privacy, bias, and fairness. Their goal is to be more open and inclusive.

3. CURRENT TRENDS AND DEVELOPMENT

Computer vision was completely transformed by the development of convolutional neural networks, or CNNs. Computer vision applications including segmentation, object identification, and picture recognition have been tackled with a variety of CNN models. CNNs are widely used due to their ability to automatically extract features from images. The convolutional layers use a variety of filters, and methods like pooling are used to lower dimensionality and boost resistance to fluctuations. The quick development of technology has led to the employment of several techniques for emotion recognition at various points in time. In the beginning, conventional feature extraction-based techniques were applied, such as LBP, HOG, NMF, K-NN, Random Forest, and SVM. While manual feature engineering was laborious and ineffective for complex picture categorization, these strategies worked well for certain jobs. (Chen, 2023)

A number of the shortcomings of conventional machine learning techniques were solved by the inclusion of deep learning techniques including CNNs, generative adversarial networks (GANs), transfer learning, and recurrent neural networks (RNNs). In order to further enhance the performance of deep learning techniques, additional attention mechanisms were included. In picture identification and classification, deep learning techniques performed better than typical machine learning techniques. Even with their advantages, long-range relationships and contextual information in data are still difficult for attention mechanisms included in deep learning techniques to manage. (Abdulhussien & Saud, 2022) Many of the shortcomings of conventional FER methods were overcome by the development of deep learning techniques, especially CNNs. CNNs were quite successful at recognizing emotions because they could extract features automatically from unprocessed picture input. Additionally, they demonstrated a superior ability to manage problems such as obscured faces or low-quality photos, which are prevalent in practical uses.

CNNs have so outperformed conventional techniques in terms of accuracy and scalability. Furthermore, new developments in FER have led to the creation of hybrid approaches, which combine conventional feature extraction techniques with deep learning techniques to further enhance performance. By combining the robustness of hand-crafted features with the self-learning capabilities of CNNs, these hybrid models seek to take advantage of the best aspects of both approaches to produce more accurate and dependable emotion identification systems. It is anticipated that as technology develops, the discipline of FER will adopt ever-more complex models and methodologies, expanding the realm of real-time emotion detection and analysis (Abdulhussien & Saud, 2022a).

4. LITERATURE REVIEW

In the research paper (Abdulhussien & Saud, 2022b), the author presented a novel approach to face detection using a cascade architecture of convolutional neural networks (CNNs). The model used in this paper focuses on addressing the challenge of large visual variations in face detection by efficiently processing input images at different resolutions. The cascade design ensures the rejection of non-face regions at low resolution, followed by detailed processing of challenging regions at higher resolution for accurate detection. Additionally, calibration nets were introduced in the cascade to enhance detection speed and improve bounding quality. The CNN-based face detector demonstrates robustness to diverse visual variations and outperforms several other methods. The author has also deliberated upon the speed and efficiency of the face detector, indicating its ability to process a variety of images. The impressive detection speed and competitive performance of the proposed model position the CNN cascade as a promising solution for real-world face detection applications.

The authors in the research paper (Sriman et al., 2021) have proposed a quicker face detection method based on discriminative complete features (DCFs) which are extracted by using convolutional neural networks (CNN). The research in this paper is significant from the point of view that the authors have thoroughly discussed the issue of computational complexity in different face detection methods. The aim is basically to improve the efficiency of face detection by directly performing it on complete feature maps using DCFs. Experimental results on popular face identification datasets show enhanced performance and efficiency over conventional approaches that rely on multi-scale feature extraction, demonstrating the effectiveness and utility of the proposed face detection strategy. By contrasting it with alternative face detection techniques, the author has verified the methodology. The comparison is based on performance indicators, such as Receiver Operating Characteristic (ROC) and Precision-Recall (PR) curves. The ROC curves provide information on the trade-off between true positive rate and false positive rate, while the PR curves show how the approaches' precision and recall are related. The ROC curves demonstrate that the recommended strategy outperforms the other methods. The comparison shows that the proposed method outperforms most existing algorithms in terms of efficiency and accuracy for face detection.

The paper in (Arabian et al., 2021) has presented a traditional approach for detecting emotions through Facial Emotion Recognition using the Convolutional Neural Networks (FERC) algorithm. A conventional method for identifying emotions through Facial Emotion Recognition with the Convolutional Neural Networks (FERC) algorithm has been described in the study (Arabian et al., 2021). The primary objective of the suggested model is to precisely recognize five common facial expressions happiness, sorrow, anger, surprise, and disgust—by leveraging the capabilities of Convolutional Neural Networks (CNN) and supervised learning. The approach uses a two-level CNN framework. The first level concentrates on extracting the primary expressional vector (EV), a 24-value vector produced by tracking pertinent facial points and directly linked to changes in expression, from the background using traditional CNN network modules. The extraction of face feature vectors for emotion recognition is the main objective of the framework's second section. The suggested method achieved an amazing accuracy of up to 96% in emotion identification after being trained and tested on a sizable dataset of more than 750,000 photos from diverse sources.

The Faster R-CNN technique is tested in the research paper in (Ikram et al., 2023) using a sizable face database to determine its efficacy in face detection and to verify the model's adaptability and application across various datasets. According to the conclusions and outcomes covered in this work, the Faster R-CNN model has demonstrated improved performance in reliably and effectively detecting faces, as evidenced by its more than satisfactory results on several face detection standards. The Faster R-CNN model outperforms the others in face detection tasks, according to the paper's comparison of its model with CNN object detection models and a few other high-performing metrics. Its computational complexity is higher than others, though.

In the study paper in (Onyema et al., 2021), the topic of face identification is investigated using Convolutional Neural Networks (CNN) to improve recognition accuracy and speed of execution. The study emphasizes that in order to improve identification rates and execution efficiency, deep learning approaches must be used with traditional methodologies. It also provides a thorough approach to accurate face detection with CNN. The outcomes and suggestions show how effectively the suggested RFDCNN technique manages face recognition in a variety of datasets. CNN's efficacy in facial recognition is demonstrated by the increased recognition rates obtained by the approach proposed in this study. Furthermore, by combining deep learning approaches with conventional methods like downsampling and Gabor feature extraction, the study offers some advancements in face detection.

In (Sikha & Bharath, 2022), a deep and effective transfer learning algorithm is used to analyze student participation in a classroom context. Based on attributes that were retrieved, data from 45 students in 32 films from an offline classroom setting were analyzed to classify the students' behavior into engaged and non-engaged states. This study's primary goals were to calculate students' emotional states and examine engagement trends according to time stamps and gender. Annotating the frames into engaged and non-engaged states based on student behavior in the gathered movies is the first step in the feature extraction process. Transfer learning using the VGG16 model expanded with extra layers comes next. In order to accurately classify student engagement states, the model is then trained on annotated frames, and its performance is evaluated on unseen data.

To assess the effectiveness and performance of the suggested model, it has also been contrasted with alternative transfer learning methods, including AlexNet, InceptionV3, GoogleNet, Xception, MobileNet, and SqueezeNet. All things considered, the method has proven useful in cutting down on computation time without sacrificing accuracy, which makes it a useful and effective tool for evaluating student participation in real-time in classroom settings.

The majority of the research in (Pabba & Kumar, 2022) focuses on the use of FER in emotional computing and education. The Computer Expression Recognition Toolbox (CERT) is used in the study to monitor facial expressions associated with learning outcomes, frustration, and engagement. The research's primary strength is its novel method for determining students' affective involvement states in real-time. Through the analysis of the intensity and frequency of key facial movements that can improve the learning experience and boost students' emotional well-being, the researchers can properly anticipate student engagement and annoyance levels. Additionally, the study offers a thorough summary of the body of research on FER in educational settings. The results gain confidence from the validation of the CERT tool by comparison with hand annotations, which also shows that automated facial expression tracking in educational research is dependable. The very small sample size of the dataset, which needs to be increased to increase the generalisability of the findings, is one possible drawback of the study.

A thorough investigation on the automatic identification of student engagement is provided in (Ge et al., 2022), addressing issues such as restricted facial expressiveness and a tendency to tilt the head downward during writing assignments, which provide particular difficulties. To get above these obstacles, the researchers examined facial features taken from the movies and used video-based detection as a route for engagement detection. Different involvement levels, such as engaged, supposedly engaged, and not engaged, are matched to the recognized emotions. Emotions such as enjoyment, surprise, and neutrality are examples of engaged emotions; on the other hand, melancholy, wrath, and fear may be signs of lesser degrees of engagement. Based on the associated emotion weights and expected emotion probabilities, an engagement index (EI) is computed for every student. Higher values in the Engagement Index (EI) indicate higher levels of engagement. The student's involvement state is classified as engaged or disengaged based on the computed EI. Based on pupils' EI scores, a threshold can be set to determine whether or not they are engaged.

5. FACIAL EXPRESSION RECOGNITION USING DIFFERENT ALGORITHMS

Facial expression recognition is the process of identifying and classifying the emotional state of a person based on their facial expressions. It is a field of computer vision and pattern recognition that aims to detect and analyze human facial expressions automatically. The complete process involves data collection, Facial expression recognition, Implementation of algorithms for continuous facial expression analysis, and engagement assessment. Various phases involved in FER are face detection, feature extraction, classification, and recognition as shown in Figure 1. Identifying and categorizing an individual's emotional state from their facial expressions is the main goal of the field of facial expression recognition (FER), which is a significant area of computer vision and pattern recognition. Happiness, sadness, rage, surprise, and other emotions can all be automatically detected by FER systems through the analysis of facial movements and features. Face detection, feature extraction, categorization, and identification are some of the crucial steps in the procedure. Using methods like convolutional neural networks (CNNs) or the Haar cascade classifier, the system first recognizes the face in an image or video. Key facial landmarks, such as the mouth, nose, and eyes, are identified using feature extraction techniques once the face has been detected. These landmarks are essential for emotion analysis. In this stage, CNNs and other contemporary deep learning models are crucial in automatically identifying the crucial characteristics required for categorization.

The next step is to classify the expressions into predetermined emotion categories after the characteristics have been retrieved. This is the situation in which deeper learning techniques or machine learning algorithms like Support Vector Machines (SVM) are used. Large datasets with a variety of labeled facial expressions are used to train these models, which enables them to effectively classify and generalize expressions. The algorithm uses the classified features to identify the emotion in the final phase, recognition. This procedure is very helpful for real-time applications where emotions are dynamically tracked, such as continuous video monitoring.

FER has made progress, however there are still a number of issues. The accuracy of recognition can be hampered by variations in facial expressions caused by cultural differences, obstruction by devices such as glasses or masks, changes in illumination, or changes in face orientation. Robust techniques and a variety of datasets are necessary to solve these problems. Training these systems to identify facial expressions in a variety of settings and demographics depends heavily on data collecting. Furthermore, emotions must be continually analyzed over time in real-time FER systems. This is frequently accomplished by sophisticated algorithms like Long Short-Term Memory (LSTM) models or Recurrent Neural Networks (RNNs), which can evaluate emotional engagement in dynamic environments.

FER finds wide-ranging applications in the fields of marketing, security, healthcare, and human-computer interaction (HCI). FER makes it possible for systems to respond to users' emotions in HCI, resulting in more individualized and organic interactions. FER can be used in the medical field to track patients' emotional well-being, which can help with the diagnosis and management of disorders including depression and anxiety. Businesses utilize FER in marketing to assess how consumers respond to ads or products. Furthermore, FER systems in security can assist in identifying questionable actions or psychological discomfort. Overall, FER is developing thanks to advances in deep learning and machine learning, despite obstacles to overcome. This creates new opportunities for emotion-aware devices. There are different techniques to analyze facial expressions, which are covered in detail in the subsequent paragraphs.

Figure 1. Various Stages in Face Emotion Recognition

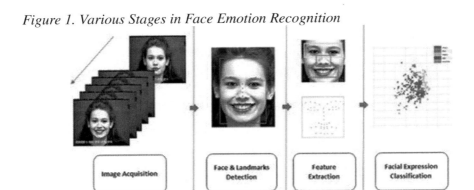

5.1. Viola-Jones Method

In Research Paper (Mohibullah et al., 2022), the famous object detection algorithm was developed by Paul Viola and Michael Jones in 2001 and has been used for Facial feature detection as shown in Figure 2. The Viola-Jones algorithm is best known for its real-time processing capabilities, high detection rates, simplicity, and low computational power requirements compared to some other deep learning-based algorithms. The research paper aims to evaluate the Viola-Jones algorithm through different tests to identify its strengths, limitations, and influencing factors. By conducting these tests, the authors have ascertained the algorithm's performance, limitations, and potential solutions for enhancing its accuracy, reducing detection time, or improving training efficiency. Four main concepts were employed in the implementation of the V-J algorithm one of which is the Haar-like features, which characterize facial features through a set of rectangular blocks that are related to Haar wavelets and include edge, line, and centrally surrounded elements. The difference between pixel values in white and black rectangles is utilized to calculate the feature value. Next are the integral images which are used to proficiently calculate the number of pixels over a pre-defined rectangular area which helps in enabling quick computation of Haar-like features. The study goes on to address Adaptive Boosting (AdaBoost), a crucial component of the Viola-Jones system that is well-known for its face recognition abilities. Typically, each iteration involves training a weak classifier, evaluating its performance, and adjusting the weights as needed. Samples that are wrongly categorized are allotted a larger weight, which forces the algorithm to concentrate more on the difficult samples in subsequent rounds. This iterative process is continued until the required degree of precision is achieved or a prearranged number of iterations is completed. Overall review of the paper centers around identifying facial highlights in pictures, like eyes, nose, and mouth, even in complex foundations. The proposed calculation consolidates different methods to find and dissect these facial highlights precisely. The paper plans to improve face recognition precision and productivity, with possible applications in PC vision and picture examination. The study also presents several limitations of the Viola-Jones algorithm, which include long training times, challenges in feature selection, binary classification restrictions, and susceptibility to false-positive detections. According to (Balovsyak et al., 2024), Eye location utilizing the Viola-Jones strategy gives a dependable approach to tracking down eyeballs in different photos. It attempts to increment eye recognition precision and productivity by consolidating corner focuses and the Viola-Jones strategy. The methodology is versatile to issues like lighting problems, looks, and the presence of scenes. It can perceive eyeballs in both front-facing and profile facial photographs, with low computational intricacy yet extraordinary precision and speed. The outcomes beat other recently revealed strategies, making this a possible procedure for different true applications. In (Thilagavathi et al., 2021), a technique for recognizing faces from live pictures utilizing the Viola-Jones calculation and Adaboost calculation is introduced. This calculation is used to identify faces in the entire picture, while the Adaboost calculation is utilized to remove the facial district. The exploration likewise examines the viability of face discovery on static information bases and live photographs with different foundations and lighting conditions. By and large, the technique tries to limit Figureuring time while keeping up with great location exactness, making it quicker than prior strategies.

Figure 2. Voila-Jones Method for Object Detection

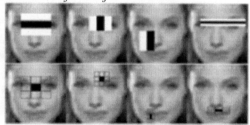

5.2. Histogram of Oriented Gradients

In computer vision and image processing, the Histogram of Oriented Gradients is an element descriptor method for object recognition. Its fundamental goal is to catch an item's shape by counting the occasions of a slope's direction in the unambiguous region of a picture and making histograms in light of the angles' magnitude and direction. To deliver a dependable portrayal of facial features, the strategy involves various essential stages and philosophies. The input picture is preprocessed to upgrade its quality and make it reasonable for highlight extraction followed by estimation of slopes histogram. The inclination directions are then accumulated into histograms over little spatial locales called cells. Every cell's histogram addresses the nearby direction data, and these histograms are consolidated into an element vector for the whole picture fix. In (Chen et al., 2021), the application of HOG features is explored for robust face recognition as shown in Figure 3. The authors have presented a different approach to utilizing HOG descriptors in the face recognition domain in order to address challenges such as occlusions, pose variations, and changes in illumination. The research paper has also discussed three main contributions in the field of face recognition using HOG features. In the first, HOG descriptors are extracted from a regular grid to compensate for errors in facial feature detection (Hung, 2021). This approach basically aims to improve the robustness of the face recognition system by providing an even sampling of facial features. Secondly, the HOG descriptors are fused at different scales to capture essential information so that the system can better adapt to variations in facial appearance, leading to improved recognition performance. In the end, the research emphasizes the importance of dimensionality reduction in the HOG representation. Dimensionality reduction helps avoid overfitting by lowering noise and improving computing performance, particularly when handling overlapping cells during feature extraction. In a research work (Saurav et al., 2023), bitmap-based HoG techniques, namely bHoG and bbHoG, are used to speed up face detection. The performance is then compared with the conventional HoG method. The paper's discussions and conclusions indicate that bitmap-based HoG techniques greatly decreased the burden related to HoG classifiers. By encoding only the pixels or blocks included in the reference image, extraneous background pixels were removed from the processing, resulting in a reduction of the burden. By reducing noise and enhancing computational efficiency, dimensionality reduction helps prevent overfitting, especially when managing overlapping cells during feature extraction. Bitmap-based HoG methods, specifically bHoG and bbHoG, are employed in a study (Saurav et al., 2023) to expedite face detection. Next, a comparison is made between the performance and the traditional HoG approach. The discussions and conclusions in the research show that bitmap-based HoG approaches significantly reduced the HoG classifier burden. The processing load was decreased by eliminating unnecessary background pixels by encoding just the pixels or blocks included in the reference image.

The utilization of complex elements like Histogram of Oriented Gradients (HoG) to further develop face identification accuracy and diminish computational burden is investigated in (Hussein et al., 2022). The authors present HOG alterations in light of bitmaps, which diminish closer view pixels and increment effectiveness. Using three particular bitmap designs and applying these ways to deal with face ID, the review shows an extensive decrease in responsibility in contrast with customary HOG with irrelevant execution influence. In light of everything, this work has handled the issues related to computational hardships in face ID and given a few serviceable fixes to speed up.

The author in (Tripathi & Jalal, 2021) has explored the utilization of HOG descriptors in uncontrolled settings. The review centers around how appropriate HOG descriptors are to oversee changes in lighting and articulation, as opposed to traditional methodologies that rely upon layered decrease or standardization steps. The examination features the capability of HOG descriptors to beat regular strategies in face acknowledgment frameworks, even in somewhat controlled conditions, by contrasting the presentation of HOG matched and different distance classifiers against the notable Eigenfaces method. Some of the advantages of using HOG are that it is simple to implement and therefore, computationally efficient. It gives great execution as far as catching fundamental facial elements for appearance acknowledgment. A few limits are that it might struggle with huge varieties of facial postures and outrageous articulations. It catches neighborhood inclination data however could miss worldwide settings without extra handling steps. HOG-based face detectors are also robust to changes in lighting, posture, and facial expressions. According to the search results, HOG-based face identification has a 92% detection rate, which translates into good accuracy.

The papers on Face Expression Recognition in (27) have mainly discussed Local Binary Patterns (LBP) and Gabor features for face recognition utilizing appearance-based statistical techniques, mainly focusing on Principal Component Analysis (PCA). The study delves into the implementation of PCA for dimensionality reduction and recognition in face recognition technology, showcasing promising results across various databases and scenarios. The use of PCA basically projects images into a region where the orthogonal dimensions capture variance among the images. Subsequently, eigenvectors for the covariance matrix are determined which aids in reducing the dimensionality of the data, making it a valuable statistical technique for face recognition. Among different challenges, one addressed in the study is pose variation, where the position of the face in the image varies. This variation can impact the accuracy of face recognition systems, making it essential to develop robust techniques that can handle pose changes effectively. Another challenge that has been discussed in detail is poor image quality which can introduce noise and distortions, affecting the performance of face recognition algorithms.

Figure 3. HOG for Face Recognition

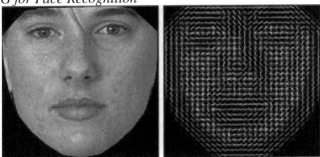

5.3. Gabor Features

Gabor features are commonly employed in image processing for feature extraction because they can successfully capture both spatial and frequency information. They are employed to preprocess face photos to extract relevant information required for facial expression recognition. Gabor channels can break down pictures in many scales and directions simultaneously. This trademark empowers them to effectively catch complex examples and surfaces in picture information.

The paper (Zhou et al., 2024) describes the framework for facial expression recognition from images using local Gabor filters and a combination of Principal Component Analysis (PCA) and Linear Discriminant Analysis (LDA) as shown in Figure 4. The study explores different methods and frameworks to improve the accuracy of facial expression recognition systems. Initially starting with the application of face detection algorithms to locate and extract the facial regions, the study progresses towards feature extraction from faces by using Gabor filters. These are applied to capture texture and spatial information from the facial region in order to represent the unique characteristics of facial expressions. The results thus obtained are then mapped into two different approaches namely Principal Component Analysis (PCA) and Linear Discriminant Analysis (LDA). PCA is basically utilized for dimensionality reduction and feature extraction, while LDA helps in maximizing the class separability for enhanced classification of images. After the extraction of features, a classification algorithm like the weighted neighbor approach, is employed to categorize the facial expressions into different classes (e.g., anger, surprise, happiness, neutral). The classification of emotions utilizes the extracted features and the discriminative power of the feature subspace to accurately recognize and differentiate between various facial expressions.

Gabor filters are commonly employed in image processing for feature extraction because they can successfully capture both spatial and frequency information. They are applied to preprocessed face photos to extract relevant information required for facial expression recognition. Gabor channels can break down pictures in many scales and directions simultaneously. This trademark empowers them to effectively catch complex examples and surfaces in picture information more. Gabor channels are particularly valuable for edge identification and surface investigation assignments. They can work on the edges and surface limits of pictures, making them valuable for highlight extraction in undertakings like face emotion identification. In (Al-Dabagh et al., 2024), the author has described a method that combines local transitional patterns with the Gabor wavelet transform to enhance the accuracy of face emotion detection. Utilizing textural features and spatial changes through the use of Gabor filters and local transitional patterns in face images, this hybrid approach can very much boost the system's capacity to identify and distinguish between distinct facial emotions. The system can accurately recognize emotions by employing this composite feature representation to identify even minute differences in facial expressions. A more complete examination of facial characteristics can be made possible by the combination of Gabor filtering and local transitional pattern coding, which helps in retrieving relevant data and hence more correctly differentiates between various expressions.

Figure 4. Gabor Feature Extraction

5.4. Local binary patterns

Local Binary Patterns (LBP) is a texture descriptor that is widely used in computer vision and image processing applications, including facial feature extraction and face recognition. It looks at the power of a center pixel to that of its encompassing pixels to catch nearby surface examples. It encodes surface data with twofold examples, which are then histogram med to give an element vector that portrays the picture's surface. LBP is powerful at catching textural varieties in looks and is strong for changes in brightening. Different explores did utilizing LBP are talked about in the ensuing sections. As discussed above, in (Al-Dabagh et al., 2024) the LBP technique is applied to the Gabor-filtered pictures acquired from the face districts of interest as shown in Figure 5. The Gabor-filtered pictures are separated into blocks, with each block addressing a limited locale of the face, like the eyes and lips. This division permits the extraction of surface elements well-defined for facial locales. Inside each block, the LBP operator is applied to register values for the pixels in that block. The administrator then, at that point, looks at the force of a focal pixel with adjoining pixels to create a double example that encodes the nearby surface data. By consolidating the Gabor sifting for spatial recurrence data and the LBP technique for surface portrayal, the framework improves its capacity to precisely perceive looks by catching both underlying and textural highlights of the face.

In (Sfärlea et al., 2024), the author has proposed a multi-scale featured local binary pattern (MSFLBP) method which is a better version of the traditional

LBP approach. The model has shown better results in terms of accuracy and efficiency. The proposed model achieved an accuracy of 99.12% for the Extended Cohn–Kanade (CK+) dataset and 89.08% for the Karolinska Directed Emotional Faces (KDEF) dataset which points towards a significant improvement in accuracy compared to traditional LBP methods. Additionally, by precisely extracting frequency information from facial photos, the MSFLBP approach makes it possible to analyze facial expressions in greater detail and comprehensively. Complicatency issues are resolved as the procedure of obtaining neighboring pixel relations at various scales is reduced, making implementation simpler and processing times quicker. Utilizing this model also has the benefit of requiring less data storage than other approaches while maintaining high accuracy levels, which makes it a workable option for applications with constrained storage. The MSFLBP method is a useful strategy for face expression recognition systems because it provides a number of advantages, such as enhanced efficiency, accuracy, and frequency extraction capacity; it also reduces complexity and improves prediction performance and storage efficiency.

The author of (Reddy & Nithya, 2024) has mostly covered the application of Principal Component Analysis (PCA) in conjunction with several classification strategies to reduce dimensionality. The study primarily looks at the effectiveness of Support Vector Machines (SVM), One-dimensional PCA, Two-dimensional PCA, and KNN for facial recognition tasks. The complexities of kNN and SVM as facial recognition classification techniques are also covered in detail in the paper. kNN employs data proximity to make classification decisions, whereas SVM uses the optimum hyperplane to maximize class margin. Throughout the paper, emphasis is placed on how important these classification methods are when combined with PCA to provide accurate and efficient facial recognition. Furthermore, the study investigates the use of kernel techniques in support vector machines (SVM) to address non-linear separability issues in the feature space, thereby enhancing the classification performance of the facial recognition system. The primary goal of the study was to use kernel functions to increase the classification algorithms' discriminative power in complex facial recognition scenarios.

Due to their reliance on simple highlights or descriptors, the standard methodologies described in the aforementioned studies may have trouble capturing nuanced and subtle differences in face impressions. This obstacle may lead to a reduction in the accuracy of identifying different emotions. In order to meet these challenges, the Extended Local Binary Pattern (LBP) strategy is depicted in (Wen et al., 2024), which overcomes the limitations by using two LBP arrangements with two kernel matrices to compute the focal pixel of every cell at various scales. This multi-scale approach considers catching surface data at different degrees of detail, improving the component extraction process. In addition, when joined with a Support Vector Machine (SVM), the proposed multi-scale featured LBP approach beats conventional LBP-based approaches as far as exactness by applying two rotational parts and using two open datasets, accordingly increasing the representation of facial elements. The paper has presented numerous key differences compared to traditional approaches in facial emotion recognition. The main difference involves a combination of global features extracted using the Haar wavelet method and local features extracted using the Gabor wavelet method. This resulted in the enhancement of the discriminative power of the system compared to using a single type of feature extraction method. Additionally, the model uses Nonlinear Principal Component Analysis (NLPCA) rather than conventional Principal Component Analysis (PCA) for dimensionality reduction. Because it can identify both linear and nonlinear correlations in the data, NLPCA outperforms the old method and produces a more thorough feature representation. In addition, the model classifies and recognizes six primary emotions using a Support Vector Machine (SVM) as the classifier. Strong Vector Machines (SVM) are renowned for their ability to manage intricate classification jobs and high-dimensional data, offering a sturdy structure for identifying emotions. Ultimately, the model outperformed the current techniques in terms of recognition rates when tested on the Extended Cohn-Kanade dataset.

Figure 5. LBP for Face Recognition

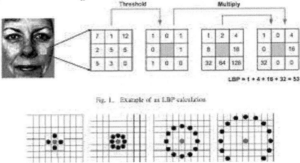

6. PROPOSED METHODOLOGY

6.1. Convolutional Neural Network

Recently, convolutional neural networks (CNNs) have gained popularity as facial expression identification methods because of their efficacious handling of the intricacies associated with distinguishing faces from various images. As Figure. 6 illustrates, Convolutional Neural Networks (CNNs) have transformed computer vision, especially face identification, by automatically and successfully extracting spatial characteristics from input images. The architecture of CNNs, which consists of several layers intended to gradually extract increasingly sophisticated characteristics from raw image input, makes them very skilled at processing visual data. There are a few distinct types of layers used commonly in CNNs such as convolutional layer, pooling layer, ReLu (Rectified Linear Units) layer, fully connected layer, and loss layer.

Figure 6. CNN for Face Expression Recognition

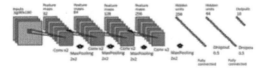

The fundamental component of a CNN-based algorithm is the convolutional layer, which, depending on the approach, can be applied one or more times. A convolution layer's main function is to extract features from the input picture and the model here uses using 3*3 size on the convolutional layer. One type of non-linear down-sampling is the pooling layer. Max-pooling layers and average-pooling layers are the two types of pooling layers that are most commonly used. The maximum/average value from each sub-region is output after the input photos are divided into a set of non-overlapping N by N rectangles (N can be any divisor of the image size). Images are better highlighted by max-pooling as the model is using 2*2 max pooling. ReLU, which comes after the convolutional layer but before max pooling, is one of the most often used forms of nonlinearity in neural networks. It applies zero to all of the feature map's negative pixel values. Usually, it comes after the convolutional layer. When fully connected layers are applied at the conclusion of the network, they accept an input volume that is the result of the preceding procedure and produce an N-dimensional vector, where N is the total number of classes the program had to choose. It's among the least expensive methods for picking up non-linear combinations of these characteristics.

7. DATA COELECTION

Datasets play a very important role in model training and selecting a dataset that provides accurate and sufficient information is one of the important conditions for training a sufficiently satisfactory quality model. For data collection, to gather a diverse dataset of facial images representing different expressional states. Popular datasets, which are known as the best datasets for emotion recognition, include AffectNet, and Jaffe datasets as shown in Figure 7 and 8 (Li et al., 2024). The most widely used datasets for facial expression recognition (FER) are JAFFE (Japanese Female Facial Expression Database) and AffectNet. One of the biggest datasets for emotion detection is called AffectNet, which has over a million face photos labeled with seven distinct emotion categories—happiness, sorrow, surprise, fear, anger, disgust, and neutral—for facial image analysis. Valence-arousal annotations, which offer continuous assessments of emotion intensity, are another feature of AffectNet. The dataset's size and diversity make it especially useful for training deep learning models. It has a wide variety of photos that have been gathered from the internet, depicting different ages, races, and environmental settings. Because of this variety, models trained on AffectNet are better equipped to handle the intricacies of detecting emotions in the real world, which include changing facial angles, changing lighting conditions, and spontaneous expressions (Li et al., 2024).

JAFFE, on the other hand, is a more condensed and targeted dataset that includes 213 pictures of the expressions on the faces of ten Japanese female models. Each picture depicts a neutral look together with one of the six fundamental emotions: happiness, sadness, surprise, anger, fear, and disgust. Because of its excellent, hand-annotated photos, JAFFE is still regarded as a highly valued dataset in the academic world despite its reduced size. The controlled environment and accurate labelling of the dataset make it perfect for usage in scenarios where high accuracy in identifying subtle emotional expressions is required, as well as for evaluating FER models. Nevertheless, JAFFE's capacity to assist models in generalizing across more diverse populations is constrained by its emphasis on a particular demographic subset.

The performance and generalization of the model are significantly influenced by the dataset selection in FER. Although JAFFE offers a controlled environment to assist in fine-tuning models for certain tasks, AffectNet's broad and diverse dataset helps increase a model's robustness in real-world applications. Building fair emotion detection systems requires ensuring that models do not get biased towards particular age groups, genders, or ethnicities. This is ensured by using a varied dataset. More extensive datasets that record emotional expressions in a range of contexts, age groups, and cultural backgrounds will be developed in the future as part of the FER dataset development. This will improve FER systems' resilience even more and enable them to function well in a variety of real-world situations.

Figure 7. AffectNet Dataset

Figure 8. Jaffe Dataset

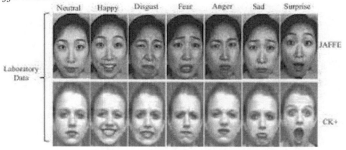

8. COMPARATIVE ANALYSIS OF FACE EMOTION USING DIFFERENT ALGORITHMS

In order to implement the most appropriate algorithm as per the requirements, it is essential to know about the strengths and limitations of each method. The criteria on which the different FER techniques are being evaluated are described below.

a) *Accuracy:* Accuracy is basically the ability of any FER technique to correctly identify faces from a given image. High accuracy is important for many practical applications where false positives/negatives can result in significant errors. Factors that influence accuracy include quality anthe d diversity of training data, the ability of the concerned method to capture relevant features, and sturdiness to variations such as lighting, pose, and occlusions (Bhavani & Karthikeyan, 2024).

Complexity: Complexity defines the intricacy of a particular algorithm and specifies how many processes/parameters would be utilized in an algorithm for the intended work. The degree of complexity has a direct impact on interpretability, computational resources required for training and inference, and ease of implementation. Higher precision is achievable with more intricate algorithms, but on the other hand, they would require more work and computing • (Singh et al., 2024).

a) *Computational Efficiency:* It is essentially a measure of the amount of memory, processing power, and time needed to compute the resources needed to train and execute a model. Effective algorithms are more suited for real-time applications since they can process images more quickly and with fewer resources. Efficiency can be expressed as a function of memory utilization, processing time, and the requirement for specialized hardware, such as GPUs. Computational efficiency is directly impacted by the hardware being utilized, the complexity of an algorithm, and how it is implemented (Rangayya & Patil, 2024).

Robustness: The robustness of any technique is the capacity to maintain a standard performance despite variations encountered in input conditions, such as changes in lighting, posture, occlusions, and noise. Thus, a strong algorithm can detect faces correctly in a variety of situations without suffering from a noticeable drop in performance. A common method for assessing a model's robustness is to test it on several datasets and track any changes in accuracy. The variety and caliber of training data, augmentation strategies, and an algorithm's innate capacity for generalization are some of the variables that affect resilience • (Thatere et al., 2024).

Scalability: Scalability is the ability of a method to handle more complex or larger models without observing a discernible drop in performance. It shows how well an algorithm works with larger datasets or more complicated computing jobs. Scalability is defined by how well the model performs when trained and assessed on larger datasets or when its complexity is increased (Wu et al., 2024). Scalability is influenced by the algorithm's underlying architecture, the effectiveness of data handling and processing, and the computation's capacity to be done in parallel (Hosni et al., 2018) (Anwar et al., 2018)(Hosni et al., 2019)(Anwar et al., 2024) (Ahmad et al., 2022) (Akhtar et al., 2022) (Ahmad et al., 2018) (Abdullah et al., 2022) (Anwar et al., 2023) (Akhtar et al., 2022) (Abdullah et al., 2022)(Ahmad et al., 2020)(Anwar et al., 2019) (Rahim et al., 2024) (Khan et al., 2020). While less scalable techniques might find it difficult to retain accuracy and efficiency as data volumes or complexity increase, scalable algorithms, like CNNs, can profit greatly from additional data and processing resources, enhancing performance as they scale (Khan et al., 2024).

Facial Expression Recognition (FER) approaches provide many solutions, each with pros and cons of its own. While some methods, such as Convolutional Neural Networks (CNNs), automatically extract and learn features from facial photos, they can be computationally demanding and require huge training datasets. Nevertheless, CNNs are known for their high accuracy (Irshad et al., 2024). On the other hand, while more straightforward and quick, conventional techniques like Support Vector Machines (SVMs) and Local Binary Patterns (LBP) might not function as well on more complicated or real-world data. A comparative analysis of the techniques discussed above is summarized in Table 1 below:

Table 1. Comparative analysis of FER techniques

Parameter	Viola Jones	HOG	Gabor Features	LBP	CNN
Accuracy	Good	Good for controlled environments	High for texture representation	Good for texture and pattern recognition	Very high, robust to variations
Complexity	Low	Moderate	High	Low to Moder ate	High
Computational Efficiency	High	Moderate	Low	High	Low to Moderate
Robustness	Moderate, struggles with pose and lighting variations	Moderate, less effective with lighting and occlusions	High, robust to lighting and geometric changes	Moderate, robust to mono-tonic lighting changes	Very high, robust to pose, lighting, and occlusions
Scalability	Limited	Moderate	Moderate	High	High

9. RESULTS AND DISCUSSION

The experimental results of different techniques for the validation set and the test set are summarized in Tables 4 and 5, respectively. It can be seen from the results that the proposed model outperforms all baseline models on the validation and test sets in every evaluation criterion, proving the effectiveness of initializing a proposed recognition model on simple facial expression data. The advantages of employing deep learning to recognize the proposed are demonstrated by the fact that all deep learning models give low results as compared to the proposed model and proposed models perform better than other methods.

Table 2. Experimental Results

Tech	Accuracy	F1	AUC
HOG/ SVM	67	75	65
VGG	68	71	68
Proposed	95	97	93

The confusion matrices for the HOG+SVM, VGG Net, and CNN models are illustrated in Tables 3, 4, and 5. The tables indicate the proportions of projected classes compared to actual classes, allowing for an analysis of accuracy by class. It's noteworthy to see that deep models outperform the HOG+SVM model in terms of recognizing disengaged samples. Disengaged samples exhibit a more diverse range of body postures and facial expressions than engaged ones. Because of their complex architecture, deep learning models are better at catching these broader variances. The VGGnet model, which has a more complicated architecture than the CNN model, can also detect disengaged samples with more accuracy. Since the proposed model was trained on fundamental facial expression data, it is the most successful technique for recognizing disengaged samples, reaching 95%accuracy.

Table 3. Confusion matrix of HOG+SVM

Predicted		Engaged	Disengaged
Actual	Engaged	92	8
	Disengaged	66	34

The model accurately predicted 92 out of 100 "Engaged" persons in the HOG+SVM confusion matrix (true positives), which means that 92% of the cases were properly classified as engaging. But it also incorrectly labeled eight engaged people as "Disengaged" (false negatives), demonstrating that the model failed to recognize involvement in these instances. The model frequently overestimated involvement when it came to identifying "Disengaged" people, mistakenly classifying 66 out of 100 disengaged cases as "Engaged" (false positives). Positively, 34 "Disengaged" people (true negatives) were accurately recognized by the model; but, a large number of false positives indicates a flaw in the disengagement detection process.

Overall, engagement was detected more accurately by the HOG+SVM model than disengagement. The "Disengaged" class has a significant amount of false positives, suggesting that the model has difficulty correctly categorizing disengagement, which frequently results in overpredictions of engagement. This implies that the model has a bias in favor of predicting engagement, which can be problematic in situations where identifying disengagement is just as critical or perhaps more so.

Table 4. Confusion matrix of CNN

Predicted			
		Engaged	Disengaged
Actual	Engaged	95	5
	Disengaged	97	3

The model performed well in identifying engagement in the CNN confusion matrix, properly classifying 95 out of 100 "Engaged" persons (true positives). It missed a small percentage of engaged people, with only 5 false negative mistakes. Nevertheless, CNN had a great deal of difficulty identifying "Disengaged" people. Only three disengaged people were accurately identified (true negatives), while 97 disengaged people were mistakenly labeled as "Engaged" (false positives). This shows that although CNN is very good at identifying engagement, it is very bad at identifying disengagement. Due to an imbalance in the training data or a model design that is more sensitive to identifying positive emotional states, the large frequency of false positives indicates that the model is unduly optimistic in predicting engagement. Because of this, the CNN is a bad option for applications where accurately detecting disengagement is essential.

Table 5. Confusion matrix VGG NET

Predicted		Engaged	Disengaged
Actual	Engaged	89	11
	Disengaged	52	48

The model performed somewhat worse in detecting engagement than the CNN and HOG+SVM models, accurately classifying 89 out of 100 "Engaged" persons (true positives) in the confusion matrix, while incorrectly classifying 11 engaged individuals as disengaged (false negatives). On the other hand, the VGG Net outperformed the two models in identifying disengagement. It misclassified 52 disengaged people as engaged (false positives) and accurately identified 48 disengaged people (true negatives).

The VGG Net performs more equitably in terms of identifying involvement and disengagement. Its accuracy in classifying engagement is marginally lower than CNN's, but it does a much better job of identifying disengaged people with fewer false positives. Because of this equilibrium, the VGG Net is a more flexible model, particularly when correct recognition of both involvement and disengagement is required.

The proposed model outperforms better than VGG Net, HOG+SVM technique. The proposed model gives an accuracy of 95% as shown in Figure 9. It is evident from a comparison of the three models that each has advantages and disadvantages. There are a lot of false positives for the "Disengaged" class as a result of HOG+SVM and CNN's greater accuracy in recognizing engagement but their considerable difficulties with disengagement. For applications where both states are equally critical, however, the VGG Net is the ideal option due to its more balanced performance. All of the models, meanwhile, may use some work, especially in identifying disengaged people, which is important for applications like tracking emotional states or attention in environments like customer service, healthcare, or education. Using more balanced datasets or investigating different designs that can more effectively capture disengagement may be necessary to improve these models.

Figure 9. Accuracy of the Proposed Model

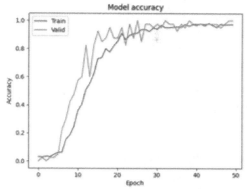

10. CONCLUSION FUTURE WORK

Even though FER has advanced significantly in recent years, there are still a number of issues that need to be resolved, such as the need for more diverse datasets, increased resistance to hostile attacks, and enhanced low-resolution picture handling. Particularly encouraging are the potential benefits of multimodal fusion and cloud computing for improving the precision and effectiveness of FER. These issues can be resolved to make FER systems more reliable, accurate, and useful across a variety of sectors, including marketing, healthcare, autonomous driving, and security. Facial Expression Recognition techniques are reviewed and analyzed in detail in this chapter, along with comparative studies, current trends, problems, and future directions in the field. It highlights the promise of multimodal fusion, which combines speech, physiological, and visual data to improve the accuracy of emotion identification. Robust datasets and flexible models are needed to address age, gender, and cultural variances in facial expressions. The ultimate goal is to create equitable and all-encompassing emotion identification systems for robotics and marketing applications. The study also covers the necessity of sophisticated algorithms for better face recognition from low-resolution photos and the significance of varied training datasets for increased resilience under various circumstances. It also addresses the vulnerability of deep neural networks to spoofing attacks and outlines recent efforts to strengthen these systems. Finally, the chapter looks into how cloud computing might be used in FER particularly in autonomous driving to improve safety and real-time emotional monitoring.

REFERENCES

Abdullah, F. B., Iqbal, R., Ahmad, S., El-Affendi, M. A., & Abdullah, M. (2022). An empirical analysis of sustainable energy security for energy policy recommendations. *Sustainability*, *14*(10), 6099.

Abdullah, F. B., Iqbal, R., Ahmad, S., El-Affendi, M. A., & Kumar, P. (2022). Optimization of multidimensional energy security: An index based assessment. *Energies*, *15*(11), 3929.

Ahmad, S., Anwar, M. S., Ebrahim, M., Khan, W., Raza, K., Adil, S. H., & Amin, A. (2020). Deep network for the iterative estimations of students' cognitive skills. *IEEE Access : Practical Innovations, Open Solutions*, *8*, 103100–103113. DOI: 10.1109/ACCESS.2020.2999064

Ahmad, S., El-Affendi, M. A., Anwar, M. S., & Iqbal, R. (2022). Potential future directions in optimization of students' performance prediction system. *Computational Intelligence and Neuroscience*, *2022*(1), 6864955.

Ahmad, S., Li, K., Eddine, H. A. I., & Khan, M. I. (2018). A biologically inspired cognitive skills measurement approach. Biologically inspired cognitive architectures, 24, 35-46.

Akhtar, S., Ali, A., Ahmad, S., Khan, M. I., Shah, S., & Hassan, F. (2022). The prevalence of foot ulcers in diabetic patients in Pakistan: A systematic review and meta-analysis. *Frontiers in Public Health*, *10*, 1017201. DOI: 10.3389/fpubh.2022.1017201 PMID: 36388315

Akhtar, S., Ramzan, M., Shah, S., Ahmad, I., Khan, M. I., Ahmad, S., & Qureshi, H. (2022). Forecasting exchange rate of Pakistan using time series analysis. *Mathematical Problems in Engineering*, *2022*(1), 9108580.

Al-Dabagh, M. Z. N., Hussein, H. I., Raheem, S. A., Ahmed, M. I., & Othman, N. A. (2024). Enhancing Face Recognition for Security Systems: An Approach Using Gabor Wavelet, t-SNE, and SVM. In *ITM Web of Conferences* (Vol. 64, p. 01008). EDP Sciences.

Anwar, M. S.. (2023). *"Immersive learning and AR/VR-based education: cybersecurity measures and risk management." Cybersecurity Management in Education Technologies*. CRC Press. DOI: 10.1201/9781003369042-1

Anwar, M. S., Choi, A., Ahmad, S., Aurangzeb, K., Laghari, A. A., Gadekallu, T. R., & Hines, A. (2024). A Moving Metaverse: QoE challenges and standards requirements for immersive media consumption in autonomous vehicles. *Applied Soft Computing*, *159*, 111577. DOI: 10.1016/j.asoc.2024.111577

Anwar, M. S., Wang, J., Ullah, A., Khan, W., Ahmad, S., & Li, Z. (2019, December). Impact of stalling on QoE for 360-degree virtual reality videos. In *2019 IEEE International Conference on Signal, Information and Data Processing (ICSIDP)* (pp. 1-6). IEEE.

Anwar, M. S., Wang, J., Ullah, A., Khan, W., Li, Z., & Ahmad, S. (2018, October). User profile analysis for enhancing QoE of 360 panoramic video in virtual reality environment. In *2018 International Conference on Virtual Reality and Visualization (ICVRV)* (pp. 106-111). IEEE.

Apicella, A., Arpaia, P., Frosolone, M., Improta, G., Moccaldi, N., & Pollastro, A. (2022). Eeg-based measurement system for monitoring student engagement in learning 4.0. *Scientific Reports*, *12*(1), 12. DOI: 10.1038/s41598-022-09578-y PMID: 35393470

Arabian, H., Wagner-Hartl, V., & Moeller, K. (2021). Traditional versus neural network classification methods for facial emotion recognition. *Current Directions in Biomedical Engineering*, *7*(2), 203–206. DOI: 10.1515/cdbme-2021-2052

Balovsyak, S., Derevyanchuk, O., Kovalchuk, V., Kravchenko, H., & Kozhokar, M. (2024). Face Mask Recognition by the Viola-Jones Method Using Fuzzy Logic. *International Journal of Image* [IJIGSP]. *Graphics and Signal Processing*, *16*(3), 39–51. DOI: 10.5815/ijigsp.2024.03.04

Bhavani, S. A., & Karthikeyan, C. (2024). Robust 3D face recognition in unconstrained environment using distance based ternary search siamese network. *Multimedia Tools and Applications*, *83*(17), 51925–51953. DOI: 10.1007/s11042-023-17545-6

Chen, Q. (2023). *Summary of research on facial expression recognition*. Highlights in Science, Engineering and Technology. DOI: 10.54097/hset.v44i.7200

Chen, T., Gao, T., Li, S., Zhang, X., Cao, J., Yao, D., & Li, Y. (2021). A novel face recognition method based on fusion of LBP and HOG. *IET Image Processing*, *15*(14), 3559–3572. DOI: 10.1049/ipr2.12192

Daniyal, S. M., Masood, A., Ebrahim, M., Adil, S. H., & Raza, K. (2024). An Improved Face Recognition Method Based on Convolutional Neural Network. *Journal of Independent Studies and Research Computing*, *22*(1), 103–110. DOI: 10.31645/JISRC.24.22.1.10

Dina, M. (2022). Abdulhussien and Laith Jasim Saud. Evaluation study of face detection by viola-jones algorithm. *International Journal of Health Sciences.*

Dina, M. (2022). Abdulhussien and Laith Jasim Saud. Evaluation study of face detection by viola-jones algorithm. *International Journal of Health Sciences.*

Ge, H., Zhu, Z., Dai, Y., Wang, B., & Wu, X. (2022). Facial expression recognition based on deep learning. *Computer Methods and Programs in Biomedicine, 215,* 106621. DOI: 10.1016/j.cmpb.2022.106621 PMID: 35164903

Gupta, R., & Kumar, S. (2023). Facial expression recognition using deep learning. *International Journal of Computer Vision.*

Hosni, A. I. E., Li, K., & Ahmad, S. (2019, December). DARIM: Dynamic approach for rumor influence minimization in online social networks. In *International Conference on Neural Information Processing* (pp. 619-630). Cham: Springer International Publishing.

Hosni, A. I. E., Li, K., Ding, C., & Ahmed, S. (2018, November). Least cost rumor influence minimization in multiplex social networks. In *International Conference on Neural Information Processing* (pp. 93-105). Cham: Springer International Publishing.

Hung, B. T. (2021). Face recognition using hybrid HOG-CNN approach. In *Research in Intelligent and Computing in Engineering: Select Proceedings of RICE 2020* (pp. 715-723). Springer Singapore. DOI: 10.1007/978-981-15-7527-3_67

Hussein, H. I., Dino, H. I., Mstafa, R. J., & Hassan, M. M. (2022). Person-independent facial expression recognition based on the fusion of HOG descriptor and cuttlefish algorithm. *Multimedia Tools and Applications, 81*(8), 11563–11586. DOI: 10.1007/s11042-022-12438-6

Ikram, S., Ahmad, H., Mahmood, N., Faisal, C. M. N., Abbas, Q., Qureshi, I., & Hussain, A. (2023). C. M. Nadeem Faisal, Qaisar Abbas, Imran Qureshi, and Ayyaz Hussain. Recognition of student engagement state in a classroom environment using a deep and efficient transfer learning algorithm. *Applied Sciences (Basel, Switzerland), 13*(15), 8637. DOI: 10.3390/app13158637

Irshad, M. H., Ebrahim, M., Abro, A. A., Raza, K., & Adil, S. H. (2024). Detecting Shadows in Computer Vision: A MATLAB-Based Approach. *The Asian Bulletin of Big Data Management, 4*(1). *Science,* ●●●, 4.

Karimah, S. N., & Hasegawa, S. (2022). Automatic engagement estimation in smart education/learning settings: A systematic review of engagement definitions, datasets, and methods. *Smart Learning Environments, 9*(1), 31.

Khan, A. R. (2022). Facial emotion recognition using conventional machine learning and deep learning methods: Current achievements, analysis and remaining challenges. *Information (Basel)*, *13*(6), 268.

Khan, S., Vohra, S., Siddique, S. A., Abro, A. A., & Ebrahim, M. (2024, January). A Computer Vision-Based Vehicle Detection System Leveraging Deep Learning. In *2024 IEEE 1st Karachi Section Humanitarian Technology Conference (KHI-HTC)* (pp. 1-7). IEEE. DOI: 10.1109/KHI-HTC60760.2024.10482163

Khan, S., Zhang, Z., Zhu, L., Rahim, M. A., Ahmad, S., & Chen, R. (2020). SCM: Secure and accountable TLS certificate management. *International Journal of Communication Systems*, *33*(15), e4503.

Kopalidis, T., Solachidis, V., Vretos, N., & Daras, P. (2024). Advances in facial expression recognition: A survey of methods, benchmarks, models, and datasets. *Information (Basel)*, *15*(3), 135. DOI: 10.3390/info15030135

Li, H., Luo, Y., Gu, T., & Chang, L. (2024). BFFN: A novel balanced feature fusion network for fair facial expression recognition. *Engineering Applications of Artificial Intelligence*, *138*, 109277. DOI: 10.1016/j.engappai.2024.109277

Maritza Bustos-Lo'pez. (2022). Nicandro Cruz-Ram'ırez, Alejandro Guerra-Herna'ndez, Laura Nely Sa'nchez-Morales, Nancy Aracely Cruz-Ramos, and Giner Alor- Herna'ndez. Wearables for engagement detection in learning environments: A review. *Biosensors (Basel)*, ●●●, 12.

Mehrabinezhad, A., Teshnehlab, M., & Sharifi, A. (2024). A comparative study to examine principal component analysis and kernel principal component analysis-based weighting layer for convolutional neural networks. *Computer Methods in Biomechanics and Biomedical Engineering. Imaging & Visualization*, *12*(1), 2379526. DOI: 10.1080/21681163.2024.2379526

Mohibullah, M., Ahammad, M. K., Muzammel, C. S., Hosen, M. S., & Islam, M. R. (2022). Face Detection and Recognition from Real Time Video or Recoded Video using Haar Features with Viola Jones Algorithm and Eigenface Approach with PCA. *International Journal of Research Publications*, *93*(1), 122–133. DOI: 10.47119/IJRP100931120222769

Onyema, E. M., Shukla, P. K., Dalal, S., Mathur, M. N., Zakariah, M., & Tiwari, B. (2021). Enhancement of patient facial recognition through deep learning algorithm: ConvNet. *Journal of Healthcare Engineering*, *2021*(1), 5196000. DOI: 10.1155/2021/5196000 PMID: 34912534

Pabba, C., & Kumar, P. (2022). An intelligent system for monitoring students' engagement in large classroom teaching through facial expression recognition. *Expert Systems: International Journal of Knowledge Engineering and Neural Networks*, *39*(1), e12839. DOI: 10.1111/exsy.12839

Rahim, M., Amin, F., Tag Eldin, E. M., Khalifa, A. E. W., & Ahmad, S. (2024). p, q-Spherical fuzzy sets and their aggregation operators with application to third-party logistic provider selection. *Journal of Intelligent & Fuzzy Systems*, *46*(1), 505–528.

Rangayya, V., Virupakshappa, , & Patil, N. (2024). Improved face recognition method using SVM-MRF with KTBD based KCM segmentation approach. *International Journal of System Assurance Engineering and Management*, *15*(1), 1–12. DOI: 10.1007/s13198-021-01483-3

Reddy, P., & Nithya, R. (2024, May). Comparative analysis of detection rate in real-time novel facial recognition using k-nearest neighbor algorithm with linear discriminant analysis algorithm. In *AIP Conference Proceedings* (Vol. 2853, No. 1). AIP Publishing. DOI: 10.1063/5.0203740

Sattar, T., Ullah, M. I., & Ahmad, B. (2022). The role of stakeholders participation, goal directness and learning context in determining student academic performance: Student engagement as a mediator. *Frontiers in Psychology*, *13*, 13. DOI: 10.3389/fpsyg.2022.875174 PMID: 35928408

Saurav, S., Saini, R., & Singh, S. (2023). Fast facial expression recognition using boosted histogram of oriented gradient (BHOG) features. *Pattern Analysis & Applications*, *26*(1), 381–402. DOI: 10.1007/s10044-022-01112-0

Sfärlea, A., Buhl, C., Lukas, L., & Schulte-Körne, G. (2024). Superior facial emotion recognition in adolescents with anorexia nervosa–A replication study. *European Eating Disorders Review*, *32*(5), 943–951. DOI: 10.1002/erv.3103 PMID: 38733271

Sikha, O. K., & Bharath, B. (2022). VGG16-random Fourier hybrid model for masked face recognition. *Soft Computing*, *26*(22), 12795–12810. DOI: 10.1007/s00500-022-07289-0 PMID: 35844262

Singh, P., Kansal, M., Singh, R., Kumar, S., & Sen, C. (2024). A Hybrid Approach based on Haar Cascade, Softmax, and CNN for Human Face Recognition: A HYBRID APPROACH FOR HUMAN FACE RECOGNITION. [JSIR]. *Journal of Scientific and Industrial Research*, *83*(4), 414–423.

Sriman, K. P., Kumar, P. R., Naveen, A., & Kumar, R. S. (2021, March). Comparison of Paul Viola–Michael Jones algorithm and HOG algorithm for face detection. []. IOP Publishing.]. *IOP Conference Series. Materials Science and Engineering*, *1084*(1), 012014.

Thatere, A., Meshram, A., Verma, P., & Jirapure, A. (2024, March). Face Recognition under Occlusion: An efficient Handcrafted Feature & SVM based Approach. In *2024 IEEE International Conference on Interdisciplinary Approaches in Technology and Management for Social Innovation (IATMSI)* (Vol. 2, pp. 1-5). IEEE. DOI: 10.1109/IATMSI60426.2024.10502484

Thilagavathi, B., Suthendran, K., & Srujanraju, K. (2021). Evaluating the AdaBoost algorithm for biometric-based face recognition. In *Data Engineering and Communication Technology* [Springer Singapore.]. *Proceedings of ICDECT, 2020*, 669–678.

Tripathi, R. K., & Jalal, A. S. (2021, May). A Local Descriptor for Age Invariant Face Recognition under Uncontrolled Environment. In *2021 2nd International Conference on Secure Cyber Computing and Communications (ICSCCC)* (pp. 513-517). IEEE. DOI: 10.1109/ICSCCC51823.2021.9478154

Wen, K. C. S., Markom, M. A., Tan, E. S. M. M., Adom, A. H., & Markom, A. M. (2024, February). Multi faces recognition using deep learning approach. In *AIP Conference Proceedings* (Vol. 2898, No. 1). AIP Publishing. DOI: 10.1063/5.0192131

Wu, D., Qiang, J., Hong, W., Du, H., Yang, H., Zhu, H., Pan, H., Shen, Z., & Chen, S. (2024). Artificial intelligence facial recognition system for diagnosis of endocrine and metabolic syndromes based on a facial image database. *Diabetes & Metabolic Syndrome*, *18*(4), 103003. DOI: 10.1016/j.dsx.2024.103003 PMID: 38615568

Zhou, J., Zhang, Q., Zeng, S., Zhang, B., & Fang, L. (2024). Latent linear discriminant analysis for feature extraction via isometric structural learning. *Pattern Recognition*, *149*, 110218. DOI: 10.1016/j.patcog.2023.110218

Chapter 4
Deep Learning Algorithms for Object Detection in Smart Environments

D. Dhanya

Artificial Intelligence and Data Science, Mar Ephraem College of Engineering and Technology, Kanyakuma, India

R. Rajitha Jasmine

Department of Information Technology, R.M.K. Engineering College, Kavaraipettai, India

M. L. Sworna Kokila

CT, SC, Faculty of Engineering and Technology, SRM Institute of Science and Technology, Chennai, India

M. Sakthivel

Velammal College of Engineering and Technology, Madurai, India

N. Divya

Civil Engineering, Prince Shri Venkateshwara Padmavathy Engineering College, Chennai, India

S. Boopathi

https://orcid.org/0009-0008-4621-0034

Mechanical Engineering, MEC, Namakkal, UAE

ABSTRACT

This chapter has presented the deep learning algorithms in smart environments for object detection purpose; it has, however, come to bode to broader introspect towards more enhanced automation and intelligence. These include advanced architectures of CNN, Region-based CNN, and YOLO which have accomplished their efficiencies in pursuance both for real-time object identification and their subsequent tracking. These offer high accuracy and multiple applications in the smart home, smart city and Industrial IoT, leveraging large datasets and complex computational power. Discussion The discussion addresses challenges in computing complexity, energy

DOI: 10.4018/979-8-3693-9057-3.ch004

Copyright © 2025, IGI Global Scientific Publishing. Copying or distributing in print or electronic forms without written permission of IGI Global Scientific Publishing is prohibited.

efficiency, and model scalability in resource-impoverished environments. Therefore, important case studies and practical examples would describe the ways in which these alleys can be combined with sensor networks and IoT systems, especially the opportunity to revolutionize areas such as security, automation, and adaptable resource management.

INTRODUCTION

Deep learning technologies have spurred a sea change in object detection within the ambit of intelligent environments. This type of environment is characterized by the incorporation of IoT devices, a very advanced sensor network, and AI. It achieves better automation, better operation efficiency, and responsiveness. Object detection is one of the important parts of computer vision and contributes much to such systems because it allows machines to sense, understand, and interact with their surroundings. The functions can detect objects and interpret a pattern of anomalies in a complex environment. Deep learning-based object detection is rapidly revolutionizing many businesses, especially in smart cities, smart homes, smart manufacturing, smart health service providers, and security(Zhao et al., 2019).

Deep learning is a subarea of machine learning that utilizes artificial neural networks to mimic the characteristics of the human brain's operating mechanism and, therefore, enables the model to learn in large sets of data and make predictions or informative decisions. This approach has outreached more traditional techniques in aspects of precision, speed, and flexibility in object detection. This new horizon opened by shifting from traditional feature-centric techniques like HOG and SIFT to holistic deep learning methodology has topped the frameworks developed for the task of object detection. These algorithms rely on hierarchical feature extraction, spatial relationships, and data-informed learning processes for accurate object identification(Wu et al., 2020).

Intelligent environments pose challenges and opportunities in object detection. With regard to the variety of objects, variations in environmental conditions, and requirements for real-time processing, robust and flexible solutions are needed. For instance, in a smart city, object detection algorithms used in traffic management systems to detect vehicles, pedestrians, and road signs promote smooth flow of traffic and improves safety. Similarly, in smart homes, these algorithms are put inside surveillance cameras and automation for home systems to detect intruders, monitor activities, or identify familiar faces. Industrial quality control, assembly line automated, and hazard detection will be enhanced with object detection on Industrial IoT(Pathak et al., 2018).

Of the top deep learning-based object detection techniques, CNNs stand out because they can automatically extract hierarchical features from raw image data. Through the stacking of several layers of convolution, pooling, and fully connected operations, the CNNs learn to recognize edges and textures, shapes, and higher-level patterns, making them very effective for tasks concerning image classification and object detection. Region-based CNNs or R-CNNs improve the same with a focus of a region of interest in an image and can localize objects with relatively good precision. Fast R-CNN and Faster R-CNN have improved both speed and accuracy of detection but without the computational constraints the previous versions had(Y. Xiao et al., 2020).

Another groundbreaking method was YOLO, because it changed the game of real-time object detection by having an end-to-end single stage. It is different from other methods, which made the detection process occur in steps; however, YOLO predicts bounding boxes and class probabilities directly from an input image in a single pass. This makes it most suited to applications requiring a response when immediate, like driverless cars, drones, and real-time surveillance networks. Because of its proper balance between speed and accuracy, YOLO finds perfect usage in scenarios requiring low latency(L. Liu et al., 2020). Deep learning-based object detection systems experience a lot of challenges in intelligent environments. The main challenge is that these algorithms carry very high computational complexity; they demand much processing power and memory. That has been a limitation on their usage in edge devices and IoT systems with resource-limited deployments. Another is on energy efficiency, particularly when deployed in battery-powered applications, in remote locations, or in mobile applications. All these are being addressed with research on lightweight architectures, quantization techniques, and hardware acceleration. Two major concerns are scalability and generalization, since a model may behave differently for some other new environment or on some objects that it has never seen before, even after it is trained on some particular dataset(Jiao et al., 2019).

Along with other sensory input functionalities such as temperature, motion and sound data, IoT and sensor networks are expected to be one of the potent candidates in accommodating object detection algorithms for creating intelligent smart systems. The case of the smart factory is informative; in the case of a smart factory, the vibrations sensors input can easily be combined with visual object detection for prediction of equipment failure. This particular pair of technologies does not only improve the functionality of systems, but provides new avenues of innovation applications(Tang et al., 2017).

Besides, it is real case studies and implementations that portray deep learning power in detecting objects. The intelligent surveillance by an object-detecting algorithm at the security end is able at least to detect some suspicious behaviors, find faces as well as predict threats. Similar algorithms in drone and robotic systems allow them to map and survey the crops in search for pests and resource allocation for maximum-impact strategies. Intelligent shelving systems and cashier-less stores in the retail business are adopting object detection tech for tracing level of inventories, theft avoidance, and more experience enhancement to the customers. Examples can well showcase the adaptability and applicability of deep learning in resolving different issues across several industries. It will be future trends that will shape how object detection in smart environments is set. The future is going to solve the related bottlenecks of latency and bandwidth through edge computing, and the 5G network, thus facilitating real-time processing at the device level(Y. Liu et al., 2021).

The development of more efficient deep learning models, such as transformers and self-supervised learning algorithms, is expected to improve accuracy and decrease training data requirements. Ethical concerns like data confidentiality, equality, and openness may impact the adoption and governance of deep learning algorithms, which are increasingly integral to object detection in intelligent environments. They allow machines to sense and interact ever so differently with their environment to be realized in terms of unparalleled automation, effectiveness, and cognitive capability(Jiang et al., 2019). Future developments in this discipline will have to overcome current challenges while seizing all the new opportunities toward the fullest realization of these technologies' potential. Sustained innovation and cross-disciplinary collaboration will enable deep-learning-based object detection to impact progressively responsive, adaptive, and sustainable intelligent environments in a future that we can only imagine.

Objectives

This chapter seeks to review how much further the deep learning algorithms can be enhanced for object detection in smart environments and possible analyses of such integrations with IoT systems for practical uses. In this way, it aims at a more advanced architecture, I mean CNNs R-CNNs, and YOLO in relative to the efficiency of the real-time recognition and tracking. This would also involve discussions on such issues as the computational complexity, energy utilization and the ability to scale up systems to work under a constrained environment. This final part will contain key illustrations, which, in case if applied, can raise that innovation Smart systems will encompass in such areas as security, automation, and adaptive resource management.

DEEP LEARNING FOR OBJECT DETECTION

Object recognition has been significantly advanced by deep learning, making it possible to accomplish high-speed and highly accurate levels of detection and classification of objects in images or video feed. Autoencoding reflects the human neural network structure, and utilizing multiple layers, deep learning is ideal for analyzing large data sets to identify objects. Compared to conventional techniques where extracting features and representational forms was done manually and where the methods cannot be easily switched with other commonly used types of models, deep learning methods construct the features and representations that perform well in various tasks(Schneider et al., 2018). This capability has been critical in pushing the envelope in areas such as security and automation, as well as Agents in smart environments managing resources. The figure 1 illustrates the concepts of deep learning for object detection.

Figure 1. Concepts of Deep Learning for Object Detection

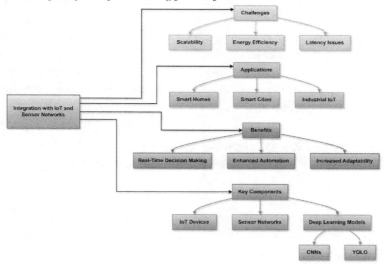

Algorithms that would help to process and analyze the images in question are at the heart of deep learning approach to object detection. The starting point for most object detection algorithms remains Convolutional Neural Networks (CNNs). CNNs are composed of convolutional layers that filter for spatial hierarchies of images, pooling that down samples the elements and the fully connected layer for classification. The structural organization of CNNs enables them to initialize and extract low-level output prows such as edges and textures before complex forms of shapes and objects. This architecture has been extremely useful in recognizing images or classifying them for that matter and thus stands out as a major tool in the object detection framework.

Proposing a step beyond CNNs, Region-based Convolutional Neural Networks (R-CNNs) marked changes in object detection by integrating the use of object proposal boxes. Although R-CNNs can analyze an image in a more unified manner compared to selective search, instead of scanning the image in a very meticulous fashion, the R-CNNs first forecast few Regions of Interest (ROIs) and then run a CNN to classify them. Other adaptations include a Fast R-CNN and even the faster R-CNN, this enhanced this approach because it solved computational issues and incorporated the use of region proposal networks (RPNs) to the procedure. Specifically, the Faster R-CNN reduced the detection time greatly and made the variation near real-time.

One more significant algorithm of object detection in the field of deep learning is YOLO (You Only Look Once). Unlike R-CNNs which analyze images through several stages, YOLO utilizes a single neural network for the forecast of bounding boxes and category probabilities. By creating an end-to-end real solution YOLO is able to deliver real-time accurate results, as the above images depict. This is so because, apart from dividing an image into a grid and predicting the number of bounding boxes and their associated class probabilities per cell, YOLO has a solution well suited to dynamic environments. Subsequently, improvements like better detection accuracy in YOLOv3 & YOLOv4, special attention towards recognizing small objects, and better scalability led to YOLO as the favorite for applications that need speed, for instance, surveillance and robotics.

The implementation of deep learning algorithms in smart environment has dynamism in various fields. In smart homes, such models support higher level features including recognizing objects in a house, observing activities as well as improving security systems. For instance, CNNs and YOLO can be used to alert of intruders or to monitor pets walking or wandering around the house, for security and comfort. In smart cities, object detection is employed in controlling traffic, in monitoring pedestrians and even in the management of waste, making for enhanced resource optimization in the design of the smart city. Consequently, the industrial IoT systems include the deep learning to control the quality and to detect the faults of the equipment as well as to identify the position of objects for optimization of the workflow.

However, deep learning algorithms for object detection also encounter some difficulties, as follows. One of the main challenges of deep learning is the complexity of operations since deep models training is a computationally intensive process. This is a bit of a drawback especially when it comes to deploying them, in environment where resources are limited like in edge devices and system on chip.

Another major consideration is energy efficiency especially when devices in IoT are limited in battery power. To overcome these limitations, several studies are going on on lightweight architectures together with model compression.

Model scalability is another hurdle, especially in scenarios involving diverse and dynamic data. Adapting deep learning models to handle variations in object size, lighting conditions, and occlusions requires robust training and fine-tuning. Transfer learning and data augmentation have emerged as effective solutions, enabling models to generalize better across different datasets. Additionally, the integration of sensor data with visual information is a promising avenue for enhancing detection accuracy and contextual understanding in smart environments.

When discussing details of deep learning algorithms for object detection, the subjects are described with the help of examples and examples of use. For example, using YOLO in traffic surveillance systems optimize on real time identification of cars, people, and traffic signs to enhance safety and address traffic congesting. In industrial applications, CNN based systems are used for automatic detection of defects in manufacturing lines hence promoting quality products while minimizing wastage. Likewise, in agricultural IoT structures, object detection mode recognizes pests and crop health conditions and supports farmers in precision farming methods for higher crop yield and reduced wastage.

Thus, deep learning has become the tool that has had an impact on the object detection of smart environments. Recognizing that CNNs, R-CNNs, and YOLO serve as the basic algorithms for efficient and reliable detect are the key element that make so many potential applications feasible from smart homes all the way to industrial automation. There are still significant problems to which solutions remain unknown, such as computational complexity, energy efficiency, and scalability concerns; however, as researchers and developers proceed with increasing advances, the opportunities for building more robust and scalable systems only improve. Using deep learning with physical sensors and IoT platforms, object detection has the potential to cvlalaly transform intelligent and autonomous spaces of the future.

Figure 2. Architecture and functionality of Convolutional Neural Networks (CNNs)

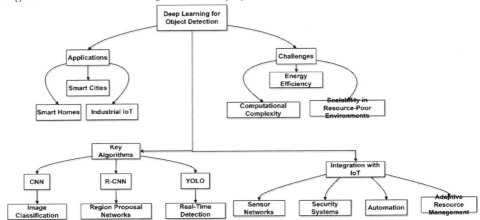

CONVOLUTIONAL NEURAL NETWORKS (CNNS)

Architecture and Functionality

They are also called deep learning neural networks and broadly categorised under the perspective of deep learning models that mimic the biological neural structure in the human visual cortex termed the Convolutional Neural Network or CNN. The core process in the CNNs is convolution – a mathematical calculation which reveals spatial pyramids and features from the input data. CNNs have more than one layer to form a strong pattern in the data, and each layer is programmed to learn elevated level of abstraction in order to differentiate between the data(Nguyen et al., 2020; B. Xiao & Kang, 2021). The figure 2 depicts the architecture and functionality of Convolutional Neural Networks (CNNs).

The major signs of CNNs are the convolutional layer, the pooling layer, and fully connected layers, activation functions. This layer, the convolutional layer extracts feature through application of filters (also known as kernels) and comes up with feature maps which are important attributes of images for instance edges, texture and shapes. These feature maps are then fed down through the pooling layers such as before max pooling where it actually reduces dimension but also retains important features making it computational and less likely to over-fit.

Activation functions such as ReLU (Rectified Linear Unit) apply non-linear transformations, and thus let the model capture complex relationships. The output layers of the mapping on the last three fully connected layers are designed to map the extracted features to the output of the network; it maybe a classifier label, a regression value or an object detection. The training process then begins back propagation of error through the network; the changing in weights and bias of the filters. The final step of the training process — repeated optimization resulting from utilizing the SGD or Adam algorithm improves the network's predictive accuracy.

There are the current typical CNN architectures including AlexNet, VGGNet, ResNet, and DenseNet which bring out some changes in their architecture to give and improved performance. For instance, ResNet correctly solves the vanishing gradient problems with skip connections, and DenseNet optimizes feature reuse by dense connections. All these advances have made CNNs versatile to different uses more so in smart settings.

Applications in Smart Environments

CNNs have established themselves as the key enablers to realize intelligence and automation in smart environments. Their precision when interpreting data from visual models also makes them invaluable in smart home, city and industrial IoT applications(Patil et al., 2022).

Smart Homes: CNNs also have important applications in improving security, comfort, and energy management systems of smart homes. With Cameras, and sensors, CNNs facilitate real-time facial recognition; thus, users can be provided with tailored experiences and security can be easily escalated. For example, examining smart doorbell systems, it was determined that the CNN-based models successfully recognize people to sort them as family members, visitors or potential intruders. In addition, they enable activity recognition, alerting the homeowners to actions that are suspicious that may pose a threat or danger at the compound such as falls or fire outbreaks.

Smart Cities: The use of CNNs in smart city management advances informs the general management and dynamics of cities. Traffic surveillance has CNNs for the identification of automobiles, pedestrians and bike riders for enhancing the traffic fluidity. Through video tracking, CNNs help in crime analysis and equally help prevent undesirable incidents in the society. Further, the CNN-powered systems help in tracking waste disposed off, air quality index, and the resource utilization for making sustainable cities.

Industrial IoT: In industrial applications, CNN incorporates innovation and safety in allowing better monitoring and predictive maintenance. In dangerous settings including oil platforms or chemical factories, CNNs with interfaces that include drones or robots, can detect potential threats including equipment breakdowns or toxic fumes and alert the human crew without exposing them to harm. Healthcare and Assisted Living: In areas such as patient monitoring, disease diagnosis, and telemedicine, smart healthcare environments find uses of CNNs. CNNs are used for interpretation of medical imaging data, including X-ray and MRI scans to identify such things as tumors or fractures. In assisted living facilities, CNN-based systems monitor the behavior and function of the residents thus mitigating risks that are likely to harm them while giving information that can be used to make specific recommendations on the kind of care to offer a certain resident.

Autonomous Vehicles: CNNs are extensively used in autonomous vehicles for real-time perception as well as decision making. Using input from cameras and LiDAR sensors, CNNs detect traffic signs, road lanes, and obstacles as well as pedestrians to drive safely. It also works with smart traffic systems to help manage the movements of vehicles to avoid common calamities and increase productivity.

Retail and Consumer Behavior Analysis: In the retail area, CNNs successfully manage intelligent shopping environments with the help of cameras installed inside stores. Through tracking the motion and facial expressions, CNNs assist retailers in learning consumers' behaviors and preferences about store designs. Automated checkout systems also incorporate CNNs to detect and count bought items and also minimize the payment procedures.

Challenges and Future Directions

Although CNNs present different opportunities, the application of CNNs in smart environments has some limitations. This is even more so when it is free in resource-limited settings such as in the IoT devices and edge computing platforms. Solutions to tackle all these are in the form of model size reduction strategies like pruning, quantization and knowledge distillation among others(Tong et al., 2020; Wang & others, 2016).

Another important factor is energy which becomes a concern of worry especially when the processes are on continuous form. However, a point of concern arises regarding the problem of manufacturing specialized hardware accelerators, including GPUs and TPUs, and the design of efficient power-hungry algorithms. The challenge of scalability is still seen since CNNs used learn different environments and also different data conditions. Domain adaptation can be used as a potential means of improving model's generalization.

In conclusion, CNNs have dramatically transformed the way of integrating the intelligence to smart environments toward continuous identification of objects together with a precise analysis in real time. So, the possibilities of the CNNs' application increase proportionally to the development of deep learning and computational hardware. The sensitization of issues such as mathematical complexity, energy and scalability, CNNs have added tremendous value to the advancement of smart environments.

Figure 3. Region-Based CNNs (R-CNNs)- Detection and Localization

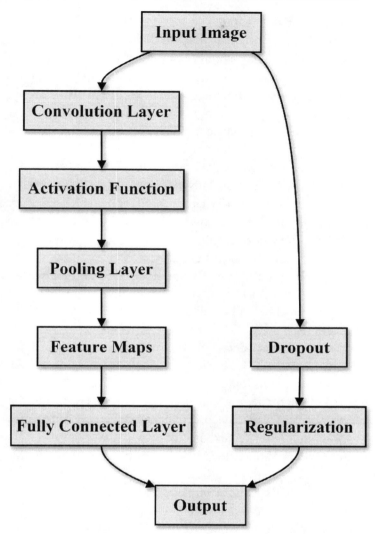

REGION-BASED CNNS (R-CNNS)

Detection and Localization

Region-Based Convolutional Neural Networks (R-CNNs) are highly effective in object detection and localization as a dramatically improved system with integration of various deep learning techniques. The R-CNN framework operates in three key stages: region proposal generation, feature extraction and classification. First, the selective search is used to produce a number of region proposals that could be genuine bounding boxes around any object. These proposals are to minimize the heavy computation involved when the entire image is scanned, by directing the search toward more promising areas only(Ghasemi et al., 2022; Jiao et al., 2021). Once these proposals are generated, what is passed through a Convolutional Neural Network (CNN) are the proposal regions which are able to extract deep features, reflecting spatial and semantic distribution of the objects within the proposals. These features are then forwarded to a classification layer where an SVM, among other techniques can be used to classify the object type and the regression layer refines the bounding box coordinates to offer precise location of the object. The figure 3 depicts the detection and localization of Region-Based CNNs (R-CNNs) in various applications.

Thanks to R-CNNs, object detection woke up due to the use of conventional CNNs such as AlexNet or VGG for feature extraction. By merging transfer learning, the large-scale datasets such as ImageNet could be effectively used with boosting up the generalization of the model for the various object classes. In addition, R-CNN presented the way of fine-tuning deep networks for the object detection task and copaves the way for integrating feature extraction with the main detection goal. This paradigm not only enhanced the detection accuracy but also laid a platform for later development of models under region-based object detection category.

Although the R-CNN was quite accurate, there were three issues that were common with the model: computational complexity. Due to the pre-set restriction of processing each region proposal through a deep CNN, this caused a lot of duplication and time waste. For example, a single image could generate thousands of region proposals – each of which requires the computation of its features – as in the case of R-CNN making the latter infeasible for real-time use. To counter this, changes in subsequent models, namely Fast R-CNN and Faster R-CNN included features like shared computations on convolutional operations and incorporated RPNs into the overall system which tremendously cut down computational load but at the same time may enhance detection precision.

Advantages and Limitations

One of the main elements of strength for the R-CNNs is that they offer relatively high levels of accuracy for object detection and localization. Unlike traditional scanning methods that can be exhaustive, where R-CNNs draw an object's basic box, the approach ensures the noise of scanning the full image does not contribute to the model's computation, instead, it tightly directs the computation to areas of possible objects only. From an application point of view, the ability of CNNs to capture the deep features of an image enables R-CNNs to work supportably, offered that they are able to spot more complex patterns and hierarchies in the datasets, and therefore to classify objects more effectively across datasets that can be quite diverse and testing(Li et al., 2022). Moreover, the feature of R-CNN that consists of proposal generation, feature extraction, and classification allows for further modifications as well as optimizing of the selected elements. Researchers can substitute or extend some of the module components or even apply more accurate architectures such as improved CNN for features extraction, or evolutional algorithms for more effective proposals creation. In this approach, there are also some drawbacks of the R-CNNs that are notable as follows. However, the main weakness of the initial R-CNN approach is its segmentation in terms of computational complexity because each proposal conducts its own feature extraction. This redundancy serves not only to slow down processing time but also to require significant amounts of memory and computations.

The other drawback of R-CNNs is that they are prone to overfitting, given the training of a few samples and rarely balanced datasets. The fine-tuning process helps in improving the performance of the model although gets sensitive to produce a model that memorizes a training data pattern rather that learning to recognize features. Moreover, the initial R-CNN framework lacks the ability to handle the multi-scale object detection where objects of different sizes can be of the same image. Hence, while later versions like the Faster R-CNN raised it by focusing on feature pyramids through the multi-scale learning process, the traditional R-CNN model does not possess this capacity.

However, as we shall see in the subsequent sections, the computationally and energy expensive nature of R-CNNs becomes a major issue in platforms with limited resources such as mobile or embedded systems. The requirement for subtle GPUs or characteristic hardware accelerators to offer real-time execution reduces the applicability of R-CNNs to edge computing. Thus, along with R-CNNs, boosters should be used in sensor networks and IoT systems to increase their integration effectiveness and communication rates. Some challenges for instance, latency, bandwidth, and energy must be solved to make available the smart use of R-CNNs in smart environments.

The recurrence of convolutional networks has spurred rapid development and implementation of object detection. Adding to the foundational concept of R-CNN, people contributed the Fast R-CNN and Faster R-CNN, also utilizing innovations such as RoI pooling and end-to-end trainable Region Proposal Network. Such improvements not only increased the speed and accuracy of the detection but also expand the possibility of using R-CNN-based methods in real-time and in large scale scenarios.

Thus, the R-CNNs are the significant advancement in the field of object detection and localization, because it uses the strong features of the deep learning and region-based approach to yield high accurate detection and localization schemes in various applications. Although the original R-CNN model had some issues such as computational complexity and scalability, its concept has led to successive models that overcome these limitations to contribute to development in areas of auto-mobile systems, security cameras, and smart environments. In future as the research contributes to develop and expand the R-CNN methodologies, implementation of such methods into upcoming concepts like edge computing and smart sensing systems will lead to unprecedented enhancements in the field of intelligent automation and adaptive resource management.

Figure 4. YOLO (You Only Look Once)- Concept

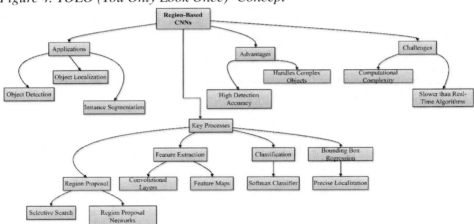

YOLO (YOU ONLY LOOK ONCE)

YOLO is the state-of-the-art deep learning algorithm that has revolutionized the domain of real-time object detection by providing excellent speed and accuracy. Unlike other conventional techniques of object detection, which are based on a two-stage approach—namely, region of interest identification followed by classification—YOLO is based on a unified, end-to-end framework. This novel framework allows for class probability and bounding box prediction in one shot, thus making possible fast and efficient object detection(Jiao et al., 2019; Zaidi et al., 2022). The algorithm breaks up the input image into a grid structure; each cell in the grid is assigned to detect and localize objects within its boundary. This distinctive approach highly reduces computation requirements and thus makes YOLO a suitable candidate for applications involving real time in various intelligent environments. One of the most significant advantages of YOLO is the fact that it processes images at high frame rates without reducing the accuracy in the process. For example, latter versions of the algorithm like YOLOv4 and YOLOv5 are able to detect multiple objects in complex scenes in milliseconds. Such a possibility positions YOLO at the top of the list for applications that require real-time responses, such as self-driving cars, video surveillance systems, and augmented reality. In terms of self-driving vehicles, YOLO would quickly detect road signs, pedestrians, and other surrounding vehicles in order to navigate more safely and efficiently. Similarly, in video surveillance systems, YOLO helps monitor live feeds and analyze the same to identify suspicious activities or unauthorized access, thereby enhancing security measures. The concept of YOLO (You Only Look Once) is illustrated in Figure 4.

The YOLO for real-time object detection capability is extended into many more domains such as industrial automation, healthcare, and retail. In the industrial world, YOLO helps track assembly lines, ensuring that defective products are identified and removed in time. It reduces operational downtime and enhances the overall efficiency. In the healthcare sector, YOLO can be used for medical imaging to detect anomalies such as tumors in the X-rays or MRIs, thus allowing for early-stage diagnosis and treatment. In the retail industry, system deployment can be done using object detection with YOLO for inventory management, where a count of objects on racks is automatically tracked to regulate stock levels and minimize the wastage.

The utility of YOLO continues to be demonstrated by its integration with IoT ecosystems. By integrating YOLO with IoT-enabled sensor networks, smart systems are able to achieve higher levels of automation and intelligence. For instance, in smart cities, the YOLO algorithm can be used in the management of traffic by monitoring real-time video feeds to identify congestion, accidents, or violations. This information can then be relayed back to the traffic control systems to optimize the flow of traffic and reduce delays. Similarly, in smart houses, YOLO-capable cameras can recognize and follow individuals, therefore allowing personalized automation like modifying lighting or temperature according to the presence of specific house occupants.

Even though it has several positive attributes, its practical deployment on real-world problems is difficult. One significant challenge for real-time processing of high-resolution images or videos is computational complexity. While modern GPUs and edge devices somewhat mitigate this limitation, environments that come with limited resources, such as low-power IoT-based devices, are pretty challenging for effective execution of YOLO. To respond to this problem, researchers are looking into streamlined variants of the algorithm, like Tiny-YOLO, which present a compromise between precision and computational demands. The other thing that could be done to enhance the deployment of YOLO on edge devices is through model quantization and pruning methods. An important issue would be energy efficiency, particularly for continuous operation applications such as surveillance or wildlife observation. Since YOLO incurs high computation, its energy consumption goes up. For battery-powered devices, this would become a limiting factor. To address this, there is a quest towards developing energy-efficient hardware accelerators and algorithmic optimizations. For example, the use of hardware-based devices such as tensor processing units (TPUs), field-programmable gate arrays (FPGAs), and other designs can be used to curtail energy consumption without incurring a loss in performance. Therefore, these innovations are very important for ensuring sustainability in YOLO-based systems in various applications.

Scalability of models is a key factor, especially when working with YOLO within large IoT networks or intelligent environments. With the increasing number of connected devices, managing and synchronizing YOLO-driven object detection models throughout the network can be a big challenge. The integration of cloud-based solutions with edge computing provides a viable solution by distributing the computational demands. For instance, edge devices can accomplish preliminary object detection while complex analyses are performed by the cloud servers. The hybrid model therefore brings about a balance between computational efficiency and scalability, which makes YOLO work perfectly within large systems. The case studies presented in the paper will illustrate the applicability of YOLO in smart environments. In the case of a smart city, YOLO was implemented together with IoT-based cameras at traffic intersections for monitoring and controlling urban traffic. The system identified and classified vehicles, detected traffic infractions, and transmitted instant information to the management centers. This project reduced congestion and increased the safety of roadways. Another case was the usage of YOLO in an intelligent agriculture project that tracked and monitored the livestock by using aerial images captured from drones. The analysis of the animals' movement and activity patterns enabled the farmers to secure their welfare and ensure proper resource utilization.

In the security domain, the YOLO algorithm has been integrated into high-end surveillance systems to enhance the detection of threats. A notable example of this use is in airport security, where YOLO scans live video feeds for banned items or suspicious activities. The real-time detection capabilities of the algorithm enable quick responses to potential threats, thus minimizing risks and ensuring the safety of passengers. Similarly, the YOLO architecture has been used in public places such as stadiums and malls to monitor crowd behavior and prevent events like stampedes or illegal entry. Finally, the real-time object detection capabilities of YOLO have made it a revolutionary tool in intelligent environments. It can combine the speed and accuracy with flexibility, making it suitable for applications in various domains, from autonomous transport to healthcare, retail, and smart urban environments. But these have to be addressed for the full potential to be unlocked: computational complexity, energy efficiency, and scalability of models. With advancements in hardware and algorithm development, YOLO will be used further in automation and intelligence in a multitude of areas. As the technology advances, its integration with IoT systems and sensor networks will further expand its impact, paving the way for smarter, more connected environments.

Figure 5. Challenges in Object Detection

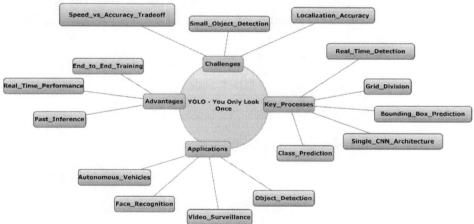

CHALLENGES IN OBJECT DETECTION

Many of the significant challenges related to the application of deep learning algorithms for object detection appear concerning the computational complexity, energy efficiency, and scalability. Computational complexity is considered a major challenge because deep architectures such as CNNs, R-CNNs, and YOLO inherently involve high computational complexity. The use of such models requires large computational power to carry out real-time object detection, primarily in complex scenes with many objects or high-resolution video images. The enormous size of these models and the need to process high-dimensional data make it computationally demanding to perform real-time inferences in resource-constrained environments. In addition, these models require memory-intensive resources for storing parameters, intermediate results, and batch processing, which put a big load on the computational resources(Deng et al., 2020; Jiang et al., 2019). The figure 5 outlines the challenges in object detection.

Another critical challenge is energy efficiency, especially in battery-powered devices and edge computing scenarios where the power consumption needs to be optimized. Deep learning models, especially those related to complex object detection, tend to be very resource-intensive, which can easily translate to higher energy consumption. This becomes problematic in IoT devices where there is a need to save as much energy as possible for the devices to survive and continue operating for as long as possible. In sophisticated methodologies for object detection, algorithms optimized in terms of energy consumption and hardware accelerators are required to achieve energy efficiency without compromising the performance level. However, the issue becomes very serious in practical applications, especially considering battery life and thermal management.

Scalability is equally important for object detection models, especially when deployed across multiple domains, such as smart homes, cities, industrial IoT, and autonomous vehicles. However, with the quantity of objects and environments, maintaining performance becomes problematic. Scalability issues then arise when object detection models are used in distributed systems, where latency, communication overhead, and resource availability need to be balanced. Moreover, practical applications often require models to handle different types of data, environments, and sensor configurations, which adds further complexity to scalability. A major challenge in the successful deployment of these technologies is ensuring that object detection systems can adapt efficiently to varying levels of complexity and function across different scenarios.

Overall, overcoming computational complexity, optimizing energy usage, and ensuring scalability are significant challenges toward the development of deep learning in object detection, mainly in smart environments and IoT systems, in which management of resources is very vital and performance is paramount.

INTEGRATION WITH IOT AND SENSOR NETWORKS

Figure 6. Integration with IoT and Sensor Networks

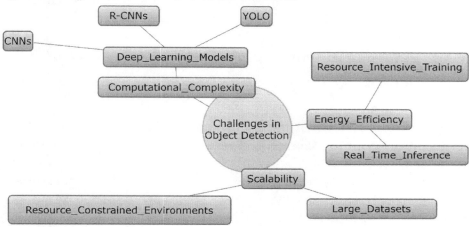

This integration of object detection technologies with IoT and sensor networks has dramatically transformed several sectors-from smart homes and cities to industrial IoT applications. Deep architectures, such as CNNs and YOLO (You Only Look Once), enable informed real-time decision-making for such systems, thereby boosting automation and responsiveness(Masita et al., 2020; Pal et al., 2021). The figure 6 demonstrates the integration of IoT and sensor networks.

Smart Homes and Cities

In smart homes and cities, the confluence of IoT and object detection enables a seamless and responsive environment for residents and authorities. Smart homes employ a large number of sensors, ranging from cameras to motion detectors and environmental sensors, which monitor and control aspects of the living space. Object detection therefore plays a pivotal role in enabling intelligent interactions within the environment. For example, security systems can use object detection to differentiate between occupants, intruders, and pets, triggering appropriate responses such as alerts or automatic lock systems. Additionally, in smart home systems, appliances like refrigerators, lighting, and climate control can adjust themselves based on real-time object detection, optimizing energy use and enhancing user experience(Deng et al., 2020; Jiang et al., 2019).

In smart cities, object detection integrated with IoT networks supports urban planning, traffic management, and public safety. Video surveillance systems can process live feeds to detect anomalies such as accidents, crowd formations, or unauthorized activities, providing timely insights for city management. Likewise, traffic management systems utilize object detection to monitor vehicles and optimize traffic flow, thereby reducing congestion and improving commuter satisfaction. Connecting multiple sensor networks, including cameras, environmental monitors, and vehicular sensors, will allow a smart city to create a connected ecosystem that can leverage data-driven decisions to improve the quality of life in the community.

Industrial IoT Systems

Object detection coupled with sensor networks enhances industrial IoT (IIoT) systems' efficiency in operational performance, predictive maintenance, and safety in industrial environments. Industrial facilities depend on real-time information obtained from a range of sensors, including temperature, vibration, and pressure gauges, to oversee machinery and production processes. The integration of object detection technology allows these systems to identify equipment degradation, irregularities, or hazardous situations, thereby promoting timely intervention and minimizing operational interruptions. For example, in a manufacturing setting, object detection can detect faulty components or variations from established operating parameters, enhancing quality assurance and decreasing production waste(Boopathi, 2024; K. S. et al., 2024; KAV et al., 2023).

Scalability in deep learning models helps industrial IoT systems cope with large amounts of sensor data generated in real time. Object detection excels particularly in the area of predictive maintenance: sensors and cameras work together to predict failures based on historical data and real-time monitoring. Maintenance costs go down, and equipment lasts longer, all of which adds up to the bottom line for overall efficiency of operations. Besides, object detection in automation systems used in industrial environments helps regulate workflows and improve supply chain operations to increase the efficiency of production lines and reduce resource waste.

In a nutshell, object detection integration with IoT and sensor networks holds much promise to transform smart homes, cities, and industrial IoT systems. Real-time data processing will make the intelligent systems even better for security, efficiency, and user experience in creating more connected and adaptive environments. Scalable and energy-efficient object detection models continue to be developed for such integrations in addressing diverse and evolving needs across both consumer and industrial markets.

CASE STUDIES AND PRACTICAL APPLICATIONS

Security Systems

Object detection-based security systems that integrate with IoT and sensor networks can drastically enhance safety in many different applications. A case example is smart home security where cameras classify between occupants, intruders, and pets based on deep learning object detection algorithms. In a home environment, a smart security system can detect unusual movements or unauthorized entry, which may trigger alarms or send instant alerts to homeowners through mobile applications. This integration technology not only allows for advance monitoring but also reduces false alarms since it can distinguish between several types of motion, such as animals or shadows, rather than human intrusion(Agrawal et al., 2023; Karthik et al., 2023; Maguluri et al., 2023). Object detection through smart city surveillance systems in urban areas contributes to public safety by monitoring hotspots and possibly dangerous situations. Real-time video feed evaluation helps authorities identify unauthorized activities, incidents, or emergencies and therefore allows timely intervention. For example, facial recognition technologies and object tracking systems are used during major public events to monitor crowd management and safety standards and, therefore, allow security personnel to respond accordingly to any unexpected events.

Adaptive Resource Management

Adaptive resource management is another practical application of IIoT systems where object detection plays a key role. For example, manufacturing facilities employ real-time data from sensor networks and object detection algorithms to optimize resource allocation. Such systems continuously monitor the machinery and production lines to predict resource needs and adjust accordingly. For example, in the manufacturing plant, wear and tear on machinery can be detected through visual inspections and sensor readings, which may activate predictive maintenance strategies to avoid expensive breakdowns. In addition, this technology is applied in smart grid monitoring, in which object detection networks analyze data from smart meters, sensors, and other IoT devices to efficiently distribute energy.

For instance, object detection algorithms that find patterns in energy consumption will help utilities optimize their distribution and prevent overloads, while in agriculture, it will be possible to handle resources in precision farming properly by checking crop health, locating pest infestations, and improving irrigation schedules, meaning the best possible allocation of resources. In total, the case studies show how integrating object detection with IoT and sensor networks revolutionizes security and adaptive resource management in several different industries. From personal and public safety to operational efficiency, these technologies prove the power of intelligent systems to give smarter, more responsive, and sustainable solutions.

FUTURE TRENDS AND DEVELOPMENTS

Object detection is a field of present and future interest due to the constant developments in the improvement and enhancement of deep learning processes and the continually growing need for enhanced, more efficient, and adaptive detection systems. Several trends and development are seen to be on the horizon across technology advancement in object detection ensuing future improvements on model performance and real-world application of object detection across different domains(Hema et al., 2023; K. S. et al., 2024; Syamala et al., 2023).

Advanced Machine Learning Processes

Among the issues that are being actively worked in the context of object detection is the search for new architectures and methods for deep learning, which can surpass existing ones. CNN has been almost the standard architecture for most of the object detection systems; however, lately, Vision Transformer and others based on the attention mechanism are gaining popularity. Vision Transformers have been specifically presented to be capable of capturing the long-range dependencies and effectiveness when it comes to large-scale data regimes, which makes them useful in a variety of object detection tasks. Modern models are being incorporated into real time detection systems improving the accuracy while maintaining better detection rates in low powered hardware systems. Another new trend is the application of any of the deep learning methods in conjunction with other features, for instance, coupling object detecting with NLP for context recognition. This has been widely seen in these newer, multimodal models which not only enable the system to detect the object of interest but also interpret data around it, thus making them better placed to operate in larger environments. For instance, combining the data analyzed through video with sounds can enhance the ability of systems to discern between similar objects with more ease when there is noise. Also, the improvements in methods of semi-supervised and few-shot learning are allowing to decrease the dependence on large annotated datasets, which are commonly necessary for training high-accuracy object detectors. These approaches are more beneficial in environments with limited budget or money and or for tasks where data labeling is costly or lengthy. Real-time decision making, where models can make decisions instantly, is a regularly emerging practice; a technique such as self-supervised learning uses data without labels and related tasks to enhance the model's overall performance(Mohanraj et al., 2024; Sonia et al., 2024; Sundar et al., 2024).

Enhancing Model Performance

While using object detection system spread trough smart spaces, IoT, and industrial automation, the focus on increasing the model performance in terms of accuracy, speed, and scalability emerges. To this end, researchers are paying a great deal of attention to fine-tuning both the hardware and software technologies. Among them there are model quantization and pruning, which nowadays are on spotlight because they try to decrease a computational load and still provide high accuracy. Specific accelerators that enhance relevant devices include GPUs, TPUs, and ASICs, guaranteeing their proper deployment in existing edge computations. This is true whereby energy efficiency is still a key factor of concern particularly for cases where battery powered is used or else where systems are placed in relays distant from control centers. Future developments are pointing to energy optimized models that will afford operation in energy constrained environments without a commensurate degradation of performance.

Additionally, transfer learning and domain adaptation techniques are now being fine-tuned so as to be applicable on any real world scenario. Thus, some of object detection systems allows fine-tuning of the initial models for targeted tasks or adaptation to different conditions, which makes such systems more flexible and less sensitive to shift in the data distribution. Therefore, the future of object detection may be said to be in the further development of algorithms which would make the detection process more precise, fast, flexible and creative. Starting from the release of new architectures such as Vision Transformers to the efficiency enhancement of models for Real-time, and efficient Resource management these innovations are laying a foundation for a future that enables more intelligent Object detection across different sectors and domains.

CONCLUSION

This chapter presented the effects that can be obtained from deep learning algorithms for the task of intelligent object detection. In particular, the detailed architectures comparison like CNNs, R-CNNs, YOLO showed how the models' indicators for live object recognition and tracking in various environment sectors such as homes, city and industries IoT. Once combined with the sensor networks and IoT systems these models proved more if atomization, intellect and resource integration in various domains such as security and mobility adaptation and smart decision-making areas.

Even so, there are still the open problems, such as computational cost, energy considerations, and large-scale analysis, when it comes to small devices or networks. Emerging challenges are being addressed to the degree that new directions will arise, such as the development of deeper learning methods or more energy-efficient models and techniques. By looking at the cases and use cases, one could say with great certainty that the implementation of object detection into IoT and sensor networks is going to take most of the industries to smarter, sustainable, and efficient systems.

REFERENCES

Agrawal, A. V., Magulur, L. P., Priya, S. G., Kaur, A., Singh, G., & Boopathi, S. (2023). Smart Precision Agriculture Using IoT and WSN. In *Handbook of Research on Data Science and Cybersecurity Innovations in Industry 4.0 Technologies* (pp. 524–541). IGI Global. DOI: 10.4018/978-1-6684-8145-5.ch026

Boopathi, S. (2024). Advancements in Machine Learning and AI for Intelligent Systems in Drone Applications for Smart City Developments. In *Futuristic e-Governance Security With Deep Learning Applications* (pp. 15–45). IGI Global. DOI: 10.4018/978-1-6684-9596-4.ch002

Deng, J., Xuan, X., Wang, W., Li, Z., Yao, H., & Wang, Z. (2020). A review of research on object detection based on deep learning. *Journal of Physics: Conference Series*, *1684*(1), 012028. DOI: 10.1088/1742-6596/1684/1/012028

Ghasemi, Y., Jeong, H., Choi, S. H., Park, K.-B., & Lee, J. Y. (2022). Deep learning-based object detection in augmented reality: A systematic review. *Computers in Industry*, *139*, 103661. DOI: 10.1016/j.compind.2022.103661

Hema, N., Krishnamoorthy, N., Chavan, S. M., Kumar, N., Sabarimuthu, M., & Boopathi, S. (2023). A Study on an Internet of Things (IoT)-Enabled Smart Solar Grid System. In *Handbook of Research on Deep Learning Techniques for Cloud-Based Industrial IoT* (pp. 290–308). IGI Global. DOI: 10.4018/978-1-6684-8098-4.ch017

Jiang, X., Hadid, A., Pang, Y., Granger, E., & Feng, X. (2019). *Deep learning in object detection and recognition.*

Jiao, L., Zhang, F., Liu, F., Yang, S., Li, L., Feng, Z., & Qu, R. (2019). A survey of deep learning-based object detection. *IEEE Access : Practical Innovations, Open Solutions*, *7*, 128837–128868. DOI: 10.1109/ACCESS.2019.2939201

Jiao, L., Zhang, R., Liu, F., Yang, S., Hou, B., Li, L., & Tang, X. (2021). New generation deep learning for video object detection: A survey. *IEEE Transactions on Neural Networks and Learning Systems*, *33*(8), 3195–3215. DOI: 10.1109/TNNLS.2021.3053249 PMID: 33534715

KS. K. K., Isaac, J. S., Pratheep, V. G., Jasmin, M., Kistan, A., & Boopathi, S. (2025). Smart Food Quality Monitoring by Integrating IoT and Deep Learning for Enhanced Safety and Freshness. In Edible Electronics for Smart Technology Solutions (pp. 79-110). IGI Global.

Karthik, S., Hemalatha, R., Aruna, R., Deivakani, M., Reddy, R. V. K., & Boopathi, S. (2023). Study on Healthcare Security System-Integrated Internet of Things (IoT). In *Perspectives and Considerations on the Evolution of Smart Systems* (pp. 342–362). IGI Global.

KAV. R. P., Pandraju, T. K. S., Boopathi, S., Saravanan, P., Rathan, S. K., & Sathish, T. (2023, November). Hybrid Deep Learning Technique for Optimal Wind Mill Speed Estimation. In 2023 7th International Conference on Electronics, Communication and Aerospace Technology (ICECA) (pp. 181-186). IEEE.

Li, Z., Wang, Y., Zhang, N., Zhang, Y., Zhao, Z., Xu, D., Ben, G., & Gao, Y. (2022). Deep learning-based object detection techniques for remote sensing images: A survey. *Remote Sensing (Basel)*, *14*(10), 2385. DOI: 10.3390/rs14102385

Liu, L., Ouyang, W., Wang, X., Fieguth, P., Chen, J., Liu, X., & Pietikäinen, M. (2020). Deep learning for generic object detection: A survey. *International Journal of Computer Vision*, *128*(2), 261–318. DOI: 10.1007/s11263-019-01247-4

Liu, Y., Sun, P., Wergeles, N., & Shang, Y. (2021). A survey and performance evaluation of deep learning methods for small object detection. *Expert Systems with Applications*, *172*, 114602. DOI: 10.1016/j.eswa.2021.114602

Maguluri, L. P., Arularasan, A., & Boopathi, S. (2023). Assessing Security Concerns for AI-Based Drones in Smart Cities. In *Effective AI, Blockchain, and E-Governance Applications for Knowledge Discovery and Management* (pp. 27–47). IGI Global. DOI: 10.4018/978-1-6684-9151-5.ch002

Masita, K. L., Hasan, A. N., & Shongwe, T. (2020). Deep learning in object detection: A review. *2020 International Conference on Artificial Intelligence, Big Data, Computing and Data Communication Systems (icABCD)*, 1–11. DOI: 10.1109/icABCD49160.2020.9183866

Mohanraj, G., Krishna, K. S., Lakshmi, B. S., Vijayalakshmi, A., Pramila, P. V., & Boopathi, S. (2024). Optimizing Trust and Security in Healthcare 4.0: Human Factors in Lightweight Secured IoMT Ecosystems. In *Lightweight Digital Trust Architectures in the Internet of Medical Things (IoMT)* (pp. 52–72). IGI Global. DOI: 10.4018/979-8-3693-2109-6.ch004

Nguyen, N.-D., Do, T., Ngo, T. D., & Le, D.-D. (2020). An evaluation of deep learning methods for small object detection. *Journal of Electrical and Computer Engineering*, *2020*(1), 3189691. DOI: 10.1155/2020/3189691

Pal, S. K., Pramanik, A., Maiti, J., & Mitra, P. (2021). Deep learning in multi-object detection and tracking: State of the art. *Applied Intelligence, 51*(9), 6400–6429. DOI: 10.1007/s10489-021-02293-7

Pathak, A. R., Pandey, M., & Rautaray, S. (2018). Application of deep learning for object detection. *Procedia Computer Science, 132*, 1706–1717. DOI: 10.1016/j.procs.2018.05.144

Patil, S. M., Raut, C. M., Pande, A. P., Yeruva, A. R., & Morwani, H. (2022). An efficient approach for object detection using deep learning. *Journal of Pharmaceutical Negative Results,* ●●●, 563–572. DOI: 10.47750/pnr.2022.13.S09.062

Schneider, S., Taylor, G. W., & Kremer, S. (2018). Deep learning object detection methods for ecological camera trap data. *2018 15th Conference on Computer and Robot Vision (CRV)*, 321–328.

Sonia, R., Gupta, N., Manikandan, K., Hemalatha, R., Kumar, M. J., & Boopathi, S. (2024). Strengthening Security, Privacy, and Trust in Artificial Intelligence Drones for Smart Cities. In *Analyzing and Mitigating Security Risks in Cloud Computing* (pp. 214–242). IGI Global. DOI: 10.4018/979-8-3693-3249-8.ch011

Sundar, R., Srikaanth, P. B., Naik, D. A., Murugan, V. P., Karumudi, M., & Boopathi, S. (2024). Achieving Balance Between Innovation and Security in the Cloud With Artificial Intelligence of Things: Semantic Web Control Models. In *Advances in Web Technologies and Engineering* (pp. 1–26). IGI Global. DOI: 10.4018/979-8-3693-1487-6.ch001

Syamala, M., Komala, C., Pramila, P., Dash, S., Meenakshi, S., & Boopathi, S. (2023). Machine Learning-Integrated IoT-Based Smart Home Energy Management System. In *Handbook of Research on Deep Learning Techniques for Cloud-Based Industrial IoT* (pp. 219–235). IGI Global. DOI: 10.4018/978-1-6684-8098-4.ch013

Tang, C., Feng, Y., Yang, X., Zheng, C., & Zhou, Y. (2017). The object detection based on deep learning. *2017 4th International Conference on Information Science and Control Engineering (ICISCE)*, 723–728.

Tong, K., Wu, Y., & Zhou, F. (2020). Recent advances in small object detection based on deep learning: A review. *Image and Vision Computing, 97*, 103910. DOI: 10.1016/j.imavis.2020.103910

Wang, X. & others. (2016). Deep learning in object recognition, detection, and segmentation. *Foundations and Trends® in Signal Processing, 8*(4), 217–382.

Wu, X., Sahoo, D., & Hoi, S. C. (2020). Recent advances in deep learning for object detection. *Neurocomputing, 396*, 39–64. DOI: 10.1016/j.neucom.2020.01.085

Xiao, B., & Kang, S.-C. (2021). Development of an image data set of construction machines for deep learning object detection. *Journal of Computing in Civil Engineering, 35*(2), 05020005. DOI: 10.1061/(ASCE)CP.1943-5487.0000945

Xiao, Y., Tian, Z., Yu, J., Zhang, Y., Liu, S., Du, S., & Lan, X. (2020). A review of object detection based on deep learning. *Multimedia Tools and Applications, 79*(33-34), 23729–23791. DOI: 10.1007/s11042-020-08976-6

Zaidi, S. S. A., Ansari, M. S., Aslam, A., Kanwal, N., Asghar, M., & Lee, B. (2022). A survey of modern deep learning based object detection models. *Digital Signal Processing, 126*, 103514. DOI: 10.1016/j.dsp.2022.103514

Zhao, Z.-Q., Zheng, P., Xu, S., & Wu, X. (2019). Object detection with deep learning: A review. *IEEE Transactions on Neural Networks and Learning Systems, 30*(11), 3212–3232. DOI: 10.1109/TNNLS.2018.2876865 PMID: 30703038

Chapter 5
A Study on Integration of Deep Learning With IoT for Smart Engineering Solutions

Pydikalva Padmavathi
https://orcid.org/0009-0003-2192-2864

Electrical and Electronics Engineering, Srinivasa Ramanujan Institute of Technology, India

V. Thrimurthulu
https://orcid.org/0000-0002-4115-2241

Department of Computer Science Engineering, MLR Institute of Technology, Hyderabad, India

J. S. S. L. Bharani

Department of S.R.K.R. Engineering College, Bhimavaram, India

Vemuri Sailaja
https://orcid.org/0009-0002-1139-9160

Department of Electronics and Communication and Engineering, Pragati Engineering College, Surampalem, India

Nellore Manoj Kumar
https://orcid.org/0000-0002-1349-800X

Saveetha School of Engineering,Saveetha Institute of Medical and Technical Sciences, Thandal, India

S. Boopathi
https://orcid.org/0009-0008-4621-0034

Mechancial Engineering, MEC, Namakkal, India

ABSTRACT

The integration of Deep Learning with IoT technology is a significant advancement in the field of artificial intelligence. The chapter explores the integration of IoT architectures and deep learning frameworks, discussing important strategies for data collection, processing techniques, and deep learning model development, focusing

DOI: 10.4018/979-8-3693-9057-3.ch005

Copyright © 2025, IGI Global Scientific Publishing. Copying or distributing in print or electronic forms without written permission of IGI Global Scientific Publishing is prohibited.

on edge and cloud computing. The chapter showcases practical applications in smart engineering, including predictive maintenance, smart manufacturing, energy management, and environmental monitoring. Real-world case studies are presented to demonstrate the application of these technologies and address common challenges and solutions. The chapter predicts future trends in IoT and deep learning, highlighting emerging technologies and potential advancements in smart engineering, promising enhanced efficiency, predictive capabilities, and sustainability.

INTRODUCTION

The convergence of Deep Learning (DL) and the Internet of Things (IoT) represents a pivotal shift in the field of engineering, enabling more intelligent and responsive systems. This integration is transforming how data is collected, analyzed, and utilized, leading to smarter and more efficient engineering solutions across various domains. The Internet of Things (IoT) is a network of interconnected devices that communicate and exchange data with one another. These devices, which include sensors, actuators, and embedded systems, collect vast amounts of data from their environments. IoT systems are deployed in numerous applications, such as smart homes, industrial automation, and environmental monitoring(Elhanashi et al., 2023). By gathering real-time data, IoT enables remote monitoring and control, enhances operational efficiency, and facilitates predictive maintenance. The data generated by these IoT devices, however, can be overwhelming in volume and complexity, necessitating advanced analytical techniques to extract meaningful insights.

Deep Learning (DL), a subset of machine learning, involves training neural networks with multiple layers to model complex patterns in data. Unlike traditional machine learning methods that rely heavily on manual feature extraction, deep learning models can automatically learn representations from raw data. This capability makes DL particularly well-suited for handling large-scale, high-dimensional data, such as that produced by IoT systems. By leveraging deep learning, engineers can develop models that recognize patterns, make predictions, and automate decision-making processes with greater accuracy and efficiency(Medhat et al., 2020).

The integration of DL with IoT is transformative because it combines the strengths of both technologies. IoT provides the data, and DL offers advanced analytical capabilities to interpret and act upon this data. This synergy enables the development of smart engineering solutions that are not only more accurate but also more adaptive to changing conditions. For instance, in industrial settings, IoT sensors monitor machinery in real-time, generating data that deep learning algorithms analyze to predict equipment failures before they occur. This predictive maintenance approach reduces downtime and operational costs by addressing issues before they lead to significant problems(Ma et al., 2019).

Architectures and frameworks play a crucial role in this integration. IoT architectures typically involve edge computing, where data processing occurs closer to the source of data generation, and cloud computing, which handles more extensive data processing and storage. Edge computing is advantageous for applications requiring real-time responses, as it reduces latency by processing data locally. Cloud computing, on the other hand, provides the scalability and computational power necessary for training complex deep learning models. The interplay between these architectures is essential for efficiently managing and analyzing IoT data using deep learning techniques(Ma et al., 2019).

Data collection and processing are fundamental aspects of the IoT-DL integration. IoT devices collect data through sensors and transmit it to processing units. This raw data often requires preprocessing to handle issues such as noise, missing values, and inconsistencies. Data preprocessing techniques, including normalization, feature extraction, and data augmentation, prepare the data for deep learning models. Effective preprocessing improves model performance by ensuring that the input data is clean and representative of the real-world scenarios being analyzed(Thakur et al., 2023).

Model development in the context of IoT and deep learning involves selecting appropriate algorithms and architectures for specific applications. Convolutional Neural Networks (CNNs), for example, are commonly used for image and video analysis, while Recurrent Neural Networks (RNNs) and Long Short-Term Memory (LSTM) networks are suited for sequential data, such as time-series data from IoT sensors. The choice of model depends on the nature of the data and the specific problem being addressed. Training these models involves optimizing parameters to achieve the best performance, which can be computationally intensive and requires access to significant processing power(Asharf et al., 2020).

Applications of integrated IoT and deep learning technologies span various domains. In smart manufacturing, for instance, deep learning algorithms analyze data from IoT sensors to optimize production processes, improve quality control, and enhance overall efficiency. Energy management systems use IoT devices to monitor energy consumption in real-time, while deep learning models predict energy demand and optimize the distribution of resources. Environmental monitoring benefits from IoT's ability to collect data on environmental parameters and deep learning's capability to analyze this data for patterns indicating environmental changes or potential hazards. Challenges in integrating DL with IoT include handling the sheer volume of data generated, ensuring data privacy and security, and managing the computational requirements of deep learning models(Dimililer et al., 2021). Addressing these challenges requires advancements in data processing technologies, secure communication protocols, and efficient algorithms.

Future trends in this integration point towards increasingly sophisticated applications and greater automation. Advances in edge computing, improvements in deep learning algorithms, and the proliferation of IoT devices will drive the development of more intelligent and responsive engineering solutions. As technology evolves, the integration of IoT and deep learning will continue to shape the future of smart engineering, offering new possibilities for innovation and efficiency(Dimililer et al., 2021).

Hence, the integration of Deep Learning with the Internet of Things is revolutionizing engineering solutions by enhancing data analysis capabilities and enabling smarter, more adaptive systems. As these technologies continue to advance, their combined potential will drive significant improvements across various engineering fields.

Scope

This chapter examines the integration of Deep Learning (DL) with the Internet of Things (IoT) to enhance smart engineering solutions. It covers the fundamental principles of IoT and DL, explores significant architectures and frameworks, and details integration strategies including data collection, processing, and model development. The scope extends to practical applications such as predictive maintenance, smart manufacturing, energy management, and environmental monitoring, supported by real-world case studies. Additionally, it addresses the challenges faced in this integration and explores future trends, emphasizing the potential advancements and impact on engineering practices.

Objectives

Chapter explores the integration of Deep Learning (DL) and Internet of Things (IoT) technologies in smart engineering solutions. It details architectures and frameworks for combining DL with IoT, including edge and cloud computing. The text also showcases practical applications in predictive maintenance, smart manufacturing, energy management, and environmental monitoring. It also analyzes common challenges and predicts future trends in DL and IoT integration in engineering.

FUNDAMENTALS OF IOT AND DEEP LEARNING

The Internet of Things (IoT) is a network of interconnected devices that communicate and exchange data through the internet. These devices, often equipped with sensors, actuators, and embedded systems, collect and transmit data from their surroundings to central processing units or cloud-based systems for analysis. The primary goal of IoT is to enable seamless connectivity between physical objects and digital systems, facilitating automation and enhanced decision-making(Dawoud et al., 2018). Figure 1 illustrates how IoT devices gather and send data to cloud systems where deep learning models analyze it to generate insights and predictions. The feedback loop shows how model improvements can enhance device performance and functionality.

Figure 1. Integration of IoT with deep learning

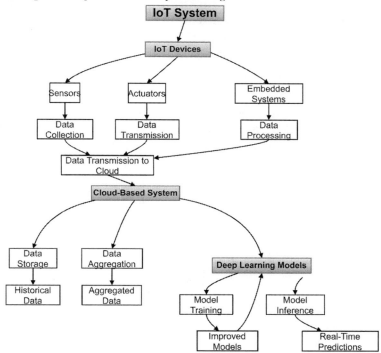

Components of IoT

Sensors and Actuators: Sensors are devices that detect changes in the environment, such as temperature, humidity, motion, or light. Actuators, on the other hand, are devices that take actions based on data received from sensors. Together, they form the input-output mechanism of IoT systems, allowing for real-time monitoring and control(Tsimenidis et al., 2022).

Connectivity: IoT devices rely on various communication protocols and networks to transmit data. Common connectivity options include Wi-Fi, Bluetooth, Zigbee, LoRa, and cellular networks. The choice of connectivity depends on factors such as range, data rate, and power consumption.

Edge and Cloud Computing: Edge computing involves processing data locally on the IoT device or nearby edge servers, which reduces latency and bandwidth usage. Cloud computing, in contrast, involves processing and storing data in remote data centers. This combination allows for efficient data management and analysis, balancing real-time processing needs with long-term storage and computational power.

Data Management and Analytics: Once data is collected and transmitted, it must be processed and analyzed to extract meaningful insights. Data management involves storage, retrieval, and organization of data, while analytics entails using statistical and machine learning techniques to interpret data and generate actionable information.

User Interfaces: User interfaces, such as dashboards and mobile applications, provide users with access to IoT data and control over IoT devices. These interfaces are crucial for monitoring system performance and making informed decisions based on the data collected.

Core Concepts of Deep Learning

Deep Learning (DL) is a subset of machine learning that utilizes neural networks with multiple layers to model complex patterns in data. Unlike traditional machine learning methods, which rely on manual feature extraction, deep learning models learn representations from raw data through a process known as automatic feature learning(Lakshmanna et al., 2022).

Neural Networks: Neural networks are the foundation of deep learning. They consist of interconnected layers of nodes (neurons) that process data through weighted connections. Each layer extracts features from the input data, with deeper layers capturing more abstract representations. Common types of neural networks include feedforward networks, convolutional neural networks (CNNs), and recurrent neural networks (RNNs).

Training and Optimization: Training a deep learning model involves adjusting the weights of the network through a process called backpropagation. During training, the model makes predictions on the input data, calculates the error, and updates the weights to minimize this error. Optimization algorithms, such as stochastic gradient descent (SGD) and Adam, are used to improve the efficiency and effectiveness of this training process.

Activation Functions: Activation functions introduce non-linearity into the neural network, allowing it to learn complex patterns. Common activation functions include ReLU (Rectified Linear Unit), Sigmoid, and Tanh. These functions determine whether a neuron should be activated based on the input it receives.

Overfitting and Regularization: Overfitting occurs when a model learns the training data too well, leading to poor generalization on new, unseen data. Regularization techniques, such as dropout, L1/L2 regularization, and data augmentation, help mitigate overfitting by adding constraints or noise to the training process.

Hyperparameters: Hyperparameters are settings that control the training process, such as learning rate, batch size, and the number of layers in the network. Tuning these hyperparameters is crucial for achieving optimal model performance and involves techniques like grid search and random search.

Synergy Between IoT and Deep Learning

The integration of IoT and deep learning creates a powerful synergy that enhances the capabilities of both technologies. IoT systems generate vast amounts of data from interconnected devices, which can be leveraged by deep learning models to extract valuable insights and drive intelligent actions(Thakkar & Lohiya, 2021).

Enhanced Data Analysis: IoT generates high-dimensional, temporal, and spatial data that deep learning models are well-suited to analyze. For example, CNNs can analyze images captured by IoT cameras for object detection, while RNNs and LSTMs can process time-series data from sensors to predict trends or anomalies.

Real-Time Decision Making: By combining IoT's real-time data collection with deep learning's predictive capabilities, systems can make informed decisions quickly. For instance, in smart manufacturing, IoT sensors monitor machinery conditions, and deep learning models predict equipment failures, enabling proactive maintenance.

Automation and Efficiency: The integration allows for automated decision-making based on data-driven insights. In smart homes, IoT devices can adjust lighting, heating, and security systems based on deep learning models' predictions about user behavior and environmental conditions.

Scalability and Adaptability: Deep learning models can scale to handle large volumes of IoT data and adapt to evolving patterns over time. This scalability ensures that IoT systems remain effective as the number of devices and data volume increases.

Hence, the fundamental concepts of IoT and deep learning provide a strong foundation for their integration. IoT's ability to collect and transmit data complements deep learning's capability to analyze and interpret this data, resulting in smarter, more efficient engineering solutions. This synergy opens new possibilities for innovation and application across various domains, from industrial automation to smart cities.

ARCHITECTURES AND FRAMEWORKS

IoT Architectures: Edge and Cloud Computing

The integration of Internet of Things (IoT) with deep learning necessitates a robust and scalable architecture to manage and analyze vast amounts of data effectively. Two primary architectural paradigms in IoT are edge computing and cloud computing, each offering distinct advantages and playing complementary roles in a comprehensive IoT system(Lakshmanna et al., 2022; Thakkar & Lohiya, 2021). The figure 2 illustrates the integration of edge and cloud computing in an IoT architecture.

Figure 2. Integration of edge and cloud computing in an IoT architecture

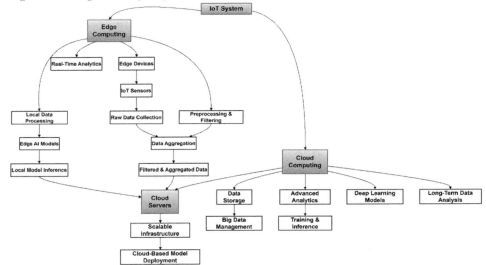

Edge Computing: Edge computing refers to the practice of processing data close to the source of data generation rather than relying solely on centralized cloud servers. This approach involves deploying computing resources at the network edge, which can be within or near IoT devices. Edge computing is crucial for applications requiring real-time processing and low latency.

Key Advantages:

Reduced Latency: By processing data locally, edge computing minimizes the delay between data acquisition and response, which is critical for applications like autonomous vehicles or industrial automation.

Bandwidth Efficiency: Local data processing reduces the amount of data that needs to be transmitted to the cloud, thus conserving bandwidth and reducing network congestion.

Enhanced Security: Edge computing can enhance security by keeping sensitive data closer to the source, limiting exposure to potential threats during transmission.

Architectural Components:

Edge Devices: These include sensors, gateways, and embedded systems equipped with local processing capabilities.

Edge Nodes: Intermediate processing units that aggregate data from multiple edge devices and perform preliminary analysis.

Local Storage and Databases: Local storage solutions to retain data temporarily for immediate processing and decision-making.

Cloud Computing: Cloud computing involves centralized data processing and storage in remote servers managed by cloud service providers. It offers scalable resources and powerful computing capabilities, making it suitable for processing large volumes of data and training complex deep learning models.

Key Advantages:

Scalability: Cloud platforms provide virtually unlimited computing resources, which can be scaled up or down based on demand, making it ideal for handling large datasets and extensive deep learning tasks.

Centralized Management: Centralized storage and processing simplify data management and integration, facilitating more comprehensive analytics and reporting.

Cost-Effectiveness: Pay-as-you-go pricing models offered by cloud providers reduce upfront capital expenditures and allow for cost-effective scaling.

Architectural Components:

Cloud Services: Includes Infrastructure as a Service (IaaS) for computing resources, Platform as a Service (PaaS) for application development, and Software as a Service (SaaS) for end-user applications.

Data Centers: Large-scale facilities housing servers and storage systems that manage and process data.

APIs and Interfaces: Interfaces for integrating cloud services with IoT devices and applications.

Deep Learning Frameworks: TensorFlow, PyTorch, Keras

Deep learning frameworks provide the tools and libraries needed to build, train, and deploy deep learning models. The choice of framework can influence the ease of development, performance, and scalability of machine learning solutions(Tsimenidis et al., 2022).

TensorFlow: Developed by Google, TensorFlow is one of the most widely used deep learning frameworks. It offers a comprehensive ecosystem for developing machine learning models, including tools for model training, evaluation, and deployment. TensorFlow is a versatile neural network architecture that enables custom model creation and modification. It offers distributed computing tools for training large models across multiple GPUs and machines. It seamlessly integrates with other Google services like TensorFlow Extended for production pipelines and TensorFlow Lite for mobile and edge devices.

PyTorch: PyTorch, developed by Facebook's AI Research lab, is known for its dynamic computation graph and user-friendly interface. It is widely favored in research environments due to its ease of use and flexibility. PyTorch is a Python tool that enables the creation of dynamic computational graphs, making it suitable for tasks requiring variable input lengths and structures. Its user-friendly interface and Pythonic nature make it easy for developers to build and test models quickly.

Keras: Keras is an open-source deep learning library that provides a high-level API for building and training neural networks. It was initially developed as a standalone library but has since been integrated into TensorFlow as its default high-level API. Keras is a user-friendly deep learning model creation tool that offers simplicity for both beginners and experts. It supports multiple backends like TensorFlow, Theano, and Microsoft Cognitive Toolkit, allowing users to choose their preferred training method. Keras also provides a range of pretrained models for faster development and experimentation.

Integration Frameworks and Tools

Integrating IoT with deep learning involves using various frameworks and tools to streamline data collection, processing, and analysis. Key integration frameworks and tools include:

- Apache Kafka: Apache Kafka is a distributed event streaming platform that can handle high-throughput data streams. It is often used to ingest and process data from IoT devices in real-time, providing a reliable and scalable solution for data integration.

- Apache Flink: Apache Flink is a stream processing framework that enables real-time data processing and analytics. It is suitable for processing IoT data streams and integrating with deep learning models for real-time predictions.
- NVIDIA CUDA: NVIDIA CUDA (Compute Unified Device Architecture) provides a parallel computing platform and programming model for leveraging GPU capabilities. It accelerates deep learning training and inference, making it essential for handling large-scale IoT data and complex models.
- TensorFlow Serving and ONNX Runtime: TensorFlow Serving is a flexible, high-performance serving system for machine learning models, particularly TensorFlow models. ONNX (Open Neural Network Exchange) Runtime provides a framework-agnostic serving solution for models trained in different deep learning frameworks.
- Docker and Kubernetes: Docker and Kubernetes are essential tools for containerization and orchestration. Docker containers encapsulate applications and their dependencies, ensuring consistent deployment across different environments. Kubernetes orchestrates container deployment, scaling, and management, facilitating efficient deployment of IoT and deep learning solutions.

In summary, the integration of IoT and deep learning involves leveraging edge and cloud computing architectures, utilizing advanced deep learning frameworks like TensorFlow, PyTorch, and Keras, and employing various integration tools to manage and process data efficiently. These components collectively enable the development of intelligent, scalable, and responsive engineering solutions.

DATA COLLECTION AND PROCESSING

IoT Sensor Data Collection

The first step in harnessing the potential of IoT and deep learning is effective data collection. IoT devices are equipped with a variety of sensors designed to capture data from the physical world. These sensors measure different environmental or operational parameters such as temperature, humidity, pressure, motion, and more. Data collection involves not just the sensors themselves but also the systems that gather, transmit, and store this data(Jeevanantham et al., 2022; Reddy et al., 2023).

Sensor Types and Functions

- Environmental Sensors: These include temperature sensors, humidity sensors, and air quality sensors, used to monitor environmental conditions in real-time.
- Motion Sensors: Accelerometers, gyroscopes, and inertial measurement units (IMUs) are used to detect motion and orientation, essential for applications in wearables and autonomous vehicles.
- Optical Sensors: Cameras and image sensors capture visual data, which can be processed using computer vision techniques to detect objects, recognize faces, or monitor activities.
- Proximity Sensors: These sensors measure the presence and distance of objects, commonly used in automated systems and smart infrastructure.

Data Transmission and Communication:

Data collected by sensors is transmitted to central processing units or cloud servers using various communication protocols. The choice of protocol depends on factors such as range, power consumption, and data rate. Common protocols include:

- Wi-Fi: Suitable for high-bandwidth applications but limited by range and power consumption.
- Bluetooth: Ideal for short-range communication with low power requirements.
- Zigbee and LoRa: Used for low-power, long-range communication, often in industrial and agricultural IoT applications.
- Cellular Networks: Provides wide-area coverage, suitable for mobile IoT applications.

Data Preprocessing Techniques

Data preprocessing is crucial for ensuring that the raw data collected from IoT sensors is suitable for analysis and modeling. This step involves cleaning, transforming, and preparing the data to enhance its quality and usability(Agrawal et al., 2023; Venkateswaran et al., 2024). The figure 3 illustrates the various steps involved in preparing IoT sensor data for analysis and modeling.

Figure 3. Steps of IoT sensor data for analysis and modeling

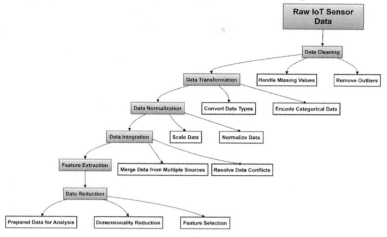

1. **Data Cleaning:** Data cleaning addresses issues such as missing values, outliers, and noise. Techniques include:
    - **Handling Missing Values:** Methods such as imputation (e.g., filling missing values with mean, median, or using predictive models) or deletion (removing records with missing values) are used based on the extent and nature of missing data.
    - **Outlier Detection:** Outliers are extreme values that deviate significantly from the norm. Techniques such as statistical methods (e.g., Z-score) or machine learning algorithms (e.g., Isolation Forest) help identify and handle outliers.
    - **Noise Reduction:** Noise refers to random errors or fluctuations in data. Techniques such as smoothing (e.g., moving average) or filtering (e.g., Kalman filters) are applied to reduce noise.
2. **Data Transformation:** Data transformation involves converting data into a format suitable for analysis. Key techniques include:
    - **Normalization and Scaling:** Normalization (scaling data to a range, e.g., [0,1]) and standardization (transforming data to have zero mean and unit variance) ensure that features are on a comparable scale, improving model performance.
    - **Feature Extraction:** Transforming raw data into meaningful features that capture essential information. For example, converting time-series data into statistical features or applying dimensionality reduction tech-

niques like Principal Component Analysis (PCA) to reduce the number of features while retaining important information.

- **Encoding Categorical Data:** Categorical data, such as labels or categories, are converted into numerical formats using techniques like one-hot encoding or label encoding.

3. **Data Aggregation:** Data aggregation involves combining data from multiple sources or sensors to create a unified dataset. This can include:

- **Temporal Aggregation:** Combining data points collected at different times, such as averaging sensor readings over specific time intervals to smooth out fluctuations.
- **Spatial Aggregation:** Integrating data from sensors distributed across different locations to provide a comprehensive view of a monitored area.

Data Quality and Management

Ensuring high data quality and effective data management is essential for reliable analysis and model performance. Poor-quality data can lead to inaccurate insights and unreliable predictions(Ali et al., 2024; Veeranjaneyulu et al., 2023; Venkata-subramanian et al., 2024).

Data Quality Metrics: Accuracy measures the accuracy of data values, while consistency refers to the uniformity of data across different sources. Completeness ensures all required fields are filled and collected comprehensively, with regular checks and validation processes. Timeliness measures the current and up-to-date data, with real-time or near-real-time data collection and processing ensuring timeliness.

Data Management Practices: Data storage involves selecting suitable storage solutions for structured and unstructured data, such as relational or NoSQL databases, based on data type and usage. Data security involves implementing measures like encryption and secure communication protocols to protect data from unauthorized access. Data governance involves establishing policies for data management, including ownership and compliance with regulations.

Data Integration: Data warehousing and data pipelines are essential for integrating data from diverse sources or sensors into a unified system, enabling easy access and analysis through centralized storage solutions and automated workflows.

Hence, effective data collection and processing are foundational to leveraging IoT and deep learning technologies. Accurate and timely data collection, combined with rigorous preprocessing and robust data management practices, ensures that the data used for analysis is of high quality and suitable for generating actionable insights. These practices are essential for developing intelligent systems and applications that drive innovation and efficiency in various domains.

MODEL DEVELOPMENT AND INTEGRATION

Choosing Deep Learning Models for IoT Data

Selecting the appropriate deep learning model for IoT data depends on the nature of the data, the specific application, and the desired outcomes. Different models are suited for various types of IoT data and tasks, such as classification, regression, or anomaly detection. Here are some common deep learning models and their applications(Hema et al., 2023; Syamala et al., 2023):

Explanation:

- The flowchart begins with identifying the type of task required (classification, regression, or anomaly detection).
- Depending on the task, the type of IoT data (e.g., image, time-series, text, numerical) is considered.
- Based on the data type, suitable deep learning models (like CNN, RNN, LSTM, BERT, Autoencoder, GAN) are suggested.

The Figure 4 representation aids in selecting the suitable deep learning model based on the IoT data and the specific task at hand.

Figure 4. Selection process of deep learning models for IoT data

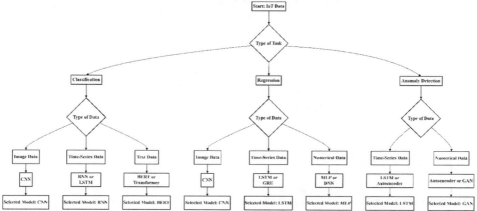

- **Convolutional Neural Networks (CNNs):** CNNs are particularly effective for image and video data, making them ideal for applications involving visual data from IoT cameras or imaging sensors. They excel in tasks such as object detection, image classification, and feature extraction. CNNs enhance image processing by learning spatial hierarchies and patterns, reducing manual feature extraction, and exploiting spatial locality, making them efficient for processing images and videos.

- **Recurrent Neural Networks (RNNs) and Long Short-Term Memory (LSTM) Networks:** RNNs and LSTMs are well-suited for time-series data and sequential data analysis. They are used for tasks such as forecasting, anomaly detection, and pattern recognition in IoT sensor data. RNNs and LSTMs offer important advantages in time-series analysis by capturing temporal dependencies in sequential data and improving performance in tasks with long-term dependencies due to their memory mechanisms.
- **Autoencoders:** Autoencoders are used for data compression and anomaly detection. They are effective for tasks such as feature reduction and detecting anomalies in sensor data. Autoencoders reduce the complexity of IoT data by compressing high-dimensional data into lower-dimensional representations, and can detect anomalies or faults in sensor data by identifying deviations from normal patterns.
- **Transformers:** Transformers have gained popularity for their ability to handle sequential data with self-attention mechanisms. They are useful for tasks requiring context and relationships across long sequences, such as natural language processing and time-series forecasting. Transformers enhance performance in complex sequential tasks by using self-attention to weigh input sequence importance, and their scalability allows them to handle large datasets, making them ideal for complex IoT applications.

Training and Optimization of Models

Training and optimizing deep learning models involve several critical steps to ensure that the models perform well and generalize effectively to new data(Venkateswaran et al., 2024).

1. Training Process:

Data Preparation: Training data must be preprocessed, including normalization, augmentation, and splitting into training, validation, and test sets. Proper data preparation helps in improving model performance and generalization.

Model Architecture: Define the architecture of the deep learning model, including the number of layers, types of layers, and hyperparameters. Model architecture design is crucial for achieving the desired performance.

Loss Function and Optimization Algorithm: Choose an appropriate loss function and optimization algorithm. Common loss functions include cross-entropy loss for classification and mean squared error for regression. Optimization algorithms like Adam or SGD are used to update model weights during training.

2. Hyperparameter Tuning:

Hyperparameter tuning involves adjusting model parameters to optimize performance. Key hyperparameters include:

Learning Rate: The rate at which the model weights are updated during training. A proper learning rate helps in converging to a good solution without overshooting.

Batch Size: The number of samples processed before updating model weights. Smaller batch sizes may lead to more accurate updates but require more training time.

Epochs: The number of times the entire training dataset is passed through the model. More epochs can improve performance but may also lead to overfitting.

3. Regularization Techniques:

Regularization techniques help prevent overfitting and improve model generalization:

Dropout: Randomly drops units from the model during training to prevent overfitting and improve robustness.

L2 Regularization: Adds a penalty to the loss function based on the magnitude of the weights, discouraging overly complex models.

Early Stopping: Monitors model performance on a validation set and stops training when performance plateaus to avoid overfitting.

Model Deployment and Integration with IoT Systems

Once a model is trained and optimized, the next step is deployment and integration with IoT systems to make real-time predictions and insights accessible. The figure 5 illustrates the integration of a trained deep learning model with IoT systems, enabling real-time predictions and insights to be made accessible.

Figure 5. Integration of a trained deep learning model with IoT systems

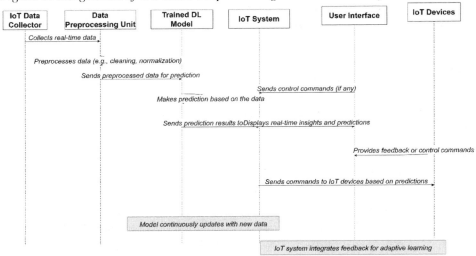

1. Model Deployment:

Edge Deployment: Deploying models on edge devices allows for real-time processing and decision-making. This is crucial for applications requiring low latency, such as autonomous vehicles or industrial automation. Tools like TensorFlow Lite and ONNX Runtime are used to deploy models on resource-constrained devices.

Cloud Deployment: For applications requiring more computational resources or large-scale processing, models can be deployed on cloud platforms. Cloud deployment allows for scaling and managing models with powerful infrastructure. Services like AWS SageMaker, Google AI Platform, and Azure Machine Learning facilitate cloud deployment.

2. Integration with IoT Systems:

APIs and Microservices: Develop APIs and microservices to integrate deep learning models with IoT systems. These interfaces allow for communication between the model and IoT devices, enabling data exchange and model inference.

Data Pipelines: Implement data pipelines to manage the flow of data from IoT sensors to the model and vice versa. Data pipelines ensure that data is processed, transmitted, and utilized efficiently.

Real-time Processing: Implement systems for real-time data processing and model inference. Real-time processing frameworks, such as Apache Kafka and Apache Flink, can handle streaming data and integrate with deep learning models for immediate insights.

3. Monitoring and Maintenance:

Performance Monitoring: Continuously monitor the performance of deployed models to ensure they operate effectively in real-world conditions. Performance metrics and logs help in identifying issues and making necessary adjustments.

Model Updates: Regularly update models to incorporate new data, improve accuracy, and adapt to changing conditions. Automated model retraining and deployment pipelines can streamline this process.

Hence, model development and integration in IoT systems involve selecting suitable deep learning models, training and optimizing them effectively, and deploying them within IoT frameworks. Successful integration requires careful consideration of deployment strategies, real-time processing, and ongoing maintenance to ensure models deliver accurate and actionable insights in practical applications. This holistic approach ensures that deep learning models enhance the functionality and intelligence of IoT systems, driving innovation and efficiency across various domains.

APPLICATIONS IN SMART ENGINEERING

Predictive Maintenance

Predictive maintenance leverages IoT sensors and deep learning models to anticipate equipment failures before they occur, enhancing reliability and reducing downtime in industrial settings. By analyzing data from various sensors—such as temperature, vibration, and pressure—predictive maintenance systems can identify patterns and anomalies indicative of potential failures(S., 2024).

1. Data Collection and Analysis:

Sensors continuously collect data on equipment conditions. Deep learning models analyze this data to detect early signs of wear or malfunction. Techniques like time-series analysis and anomaly detection are used to forecast maintenance needs and optimize scheduling.

2. Benefits:

Reduced Downtime: By predicting failures before they happen, predictive maintenance minimizes unplanned downtime, leading to increased operational efficiency.

Cost Savings: Maintenance can be performed based on actual equipment condition rather than on a fixed schedule, reducing unnecessary maintenance costs and extending the lifespan of machinery.

Enhanced Safety: Predictive maintenance helps in identifying potential safety hazards early, ensuring safer working environments.

3. Real-World Examples:

Manufacturing Plants: Sensors monitor machine health, with models predicting when parts need replacement or servicing, thus avoiding unexpected breakdowns.

Aerospace Industry: Predictive maintenance is used to ensure the reliability of critical components in aircraft, reducing the risk of failures during flights.

Smart Manufacturing

Smart manufacturing integrates IoT and deep learning to create highly automated, efficient, and adaptive production environments. The approach focuses on optimizing production processes, improving quality control, and enhancing flexibility.

1. **Process Optimization: Real-time Monitoring:** IoT sensors provide real-time data on various aspects of the manufacturing process, such as temperature, pressure, and machine speed. Deep learning models analyze this data to identify inefficiencies and optimize operations. **Adaptive Production:** Machine learning algorithms adjust production parameters dynamically based on real-time data, ensuring optimal performance and minimizing waste.
2. **Quality Control: Defect Detection:** Deep learning models analyze images from quality control cameras to identify defects and anomalies in products. This allows for early detection and correction of quality issues, reducing the number of defective products. **Process Improvement:** Data-driven insights enable manufacturers to continuously improve processes and maintain high-quality standards.
3. **Real-World Examples: Automotive Industry:** Smart manufacturing systems use IoT sensors and deep learning to monitor assembly lines, ensuring precise operations and high-quality output. **Electronics Manufacturing:** Quality control systems leverage computer vision and deep learning to detect defects in electronic components, enhancing product reliability.

Energy Management

Energy management systems use IoT and deep learning to optimize energy consumption in buildings, industrial facilities, and smart grids. The goal is to improve energy efficiency, reduce costs, and support sustainability goals(Saravanan et al., 2024; Tirlangi et al., 2024; Ugandar et al., 2023).

1. **Energy Consumption Monitoring: Real-time Data Collection:** IoT sensors collect data on energy usage across different systems and devices. Deep learning models analyze this data to identify patterns and inefficiencies in energy consumption. **Demand Forecasting:** Predictive models forecast energy demand based on historical data and real-time inputs, enabling better energy management and load balancing.
2. **Optimization and Control: Automated Control:** Deep learning algorithms automate the control of HVAC systems, lighting, and other energy-consuming devices based on real-time data, optimizing energy use while maintaining comfort and operational efficiency. **Energy Savings:** By identifying inefficiencies and optimizing energy use, smart energy management systems can lead to significant cost savings and reduced environmental impact.
3. **Real-World Examples: Smart Buildings:** Energy management systems in smart buildings use IoT data and deep learning to control lighting, heating, and cooling, leading to reduced energy consumption and operational costs. **Industrial Facilities:** In manufacturing plants, energy management systems optimize the use of machinery and equipment, improving overall energy efficiency.

Environmental Monitoring

Environmental monitoring systems use IoT sensors and deep learning to track and analyze environmental conditions, contributing to better management and protection of natural resources.

1. **Data Collection and Analysis: Sensor Deployment:** IoT sensors are deployed to monitor air quality, water quality, soil conditions, and other environmental parameters. Deep learning models analyze this data to identify trends, anomalies, and potential issues. **Predictive Analysis:** Models predict environmental changes and potential risks, such as pollution levels or natural disasters, based on historical data and real-time inputs.
2. **Benefits: Improved Response:** Real-time monitoring and predictive analytics enable timely responses to environmental issues, such as pollution events or changes in weather patterns. **Regulatory Compliance:** Environmental monitor-

ing systems help organizations comply with regulations by providing accurate data on environmental conditions and impacts. **Sustainability:** By optimizing resource use and reducing environmental impact, these systems support sustainability initiatives and contribute to environmental protection.

3. **Real-World Examples: Air Quality Monitoring:** Cities use IoT sensors and deep learning to monitor air pollution levels, providing data to inform public health decisions and improve air quality. **Water Quality Management:** Environmental agencies deploy sensors to track water quality in rivers and lakes, using deep learning to detect contamination and ensure safe water supplies.

In summary, the integration of IoT and deep learning in smart engineering applications provides significant benefits across various domains. Predictive maintenance, smart manufacturing, energy management, and environmental monitoring all leverage these technologies to improve efficiency, reduce costs, and enhance overall performance. These advancements drive innovation and contribute to more sustainable and intelligent engineering solutions.

PRACTICAL EXAMPLE

Smart Manufacturing with IoT and Deep Learning

In a modern smart manufacturing facility, IoT and deep learning technologies work together to optimize production processes and enhance operational efficiency(Ali et al., 2024).

Real-Time Monitoring and Data Collection: In a smart factory, various IoT sensors are deployed across production lines to monitor machinery conditions such as temperature, vibration, and pressure. These sensors continuously collect data and transmit it to a central system for analysis.

Predictive Maintenance: Deep learning models analyze the sensor data to predict potential equipment failures. For instance, a deep neural network is trained on historical data from similar machines to identify patterns associated with wear and tear. The model can detect anomalies, such as abnormal vibration patterns, that signal impending failures.

Automated Quality Control: High-resolution cameras equipped with deep learning algorithms inspect products on the assembly line. Convolutional neural networks (CNNs) are used to analyze images and detect defects such as surface imperfections or incorrect assembly. The system can automatically remove defective products from the production line, ensuring high quality and reducing waste.

Process Optimization: The insights gained from data analysis are used to optimize production processes. For example, if the deep learning model identifies that certain machine settings lead to more efficient production or higher quality outputs, these settings are adjusted automatically. This continuous optimization process ensures that production runs at peak efficiency.

Enhanced Decision-Making: The integration of IoT and deep learning provides actionable insights that help managers make informed decisions. Dashboards display real-time data, predictive maintenance alerts, and quality control metrics, enabling proactive management and timely interventions.

In this example, the combination of IoT and deep learning technologies leads to improved equipment reliability, enhanced product quality, and optimized manufacturing processes, demonstrating their practical impact on modern industrial operations.

CHALLENGES AND SOLUTIONS

Data Volume and Complexity

One of the primary challenges in integrating IoT with deep learning is managing the vast volume and complexity of data generated by IoT devices. IoT systems continuously produce large amounts of data from sensors, devices, and applications, which can be overwhelming to process and analyze. The complexity increases with the diversity of data types, such as time-series data, images, and environmental readings, each requiring different processing techniques(Kavitha et al., 2023; Rahamathunnisa et al., 2024; Syamala et al., 2023).

Solutions:

Data Aggregation and Filtering: Implementing data aggregation techniques helps in reducing the volume of data that needs to be processed. Aggregation involves summarizing data from multiple sources into a more manageable format. Data filtering can also be applied to remove irrelevant or redundant information before analysis.

Edge Computing: Deploying edge computing solutions allows for data processing closer to the source of data generation. By performing initial data processing and analysis at the edge, only relevant or summarized data is sent to the central system, reducing the overall data volume and network congestion.

Advanced Data Management Platforms: Leveraging platforms and frameworks designed for handling big data, such as Apache Hadoop or Apache Spark, can help manage and process large datasets efficiently. These platforms offer distributed processing capabilities, allowing for the handling of vast amounts of data.

Privacy and Security Concerns

As IoT devices collect sensitive and personal data, privacy and security become significant concerns. The integration of deep learning models adds another layer of complexity, as models themselves can be vulnerable to attacks, and the data used to train these models may be exposed to unauthorized access.

Solutions:

- **Data Encryption:** Encrypting data both in transit and at rest is crucial for protecting sensitive information from unauthorized access. Advanced encryption techniques ensure that data remains secure even if intercepted or accessed by malicious actors.
- **Access Control and Authentication:** Implementing robust access control measures and authentication protocols helps prevent unauthorized access to IoT devices and data. This includes using multi-factor authentication, role-based access controls, and secure credential management.
- **Privacy-Preserving Techniques:** Techniques such as differential privacy and federated learning can help protect user privacy. Differential privacy adds noise to data to obscure individual entries, while federated learning enables model training across multiple devices without sharing raw data, thus preserving privacy.
- **Regular Security Audits:** Conducting regular security audits and vulnerability assessments helps identify and address potential security weaknesses. Updating and patching systems promptly in response to discovered vulnerabilities is essential for maintaining security.

Computational and Resource Requirements

Deep learning models are computationally intensive and require significant resources for training and inference. The integration with IoT systems exacerbates these requirements, as models need to be deployed across a wide range of devices, including those with limited computational capabilities.

Solutions:

- **Model Optimization:** Techniques such as model pruning, quantization, and knowledge distillation can help reduce the computational requirements of deep learning models. Model pruning involves removing redundant neurons or connections, while quantization reduces the precision of model weights. Knowledge distillation transfers the knowledge from a large model to a smaller, more efficient model.

- **Hardware Acceleration:** Utilizing specialized hardware, such as Graphics Processing Units (GPUs) or Tensor Processing Units (TPUs), can significantly speed up the training and inference processes. Edge devices may also benefit from dedicated accelerators designed for deep learning tasks.
- **Cloud and Edge Hybrid Solutions:** Employing a hybrid approach that combines cloud and edge computing can help manage computational requirements. Complex and resource-intensive tasks can be offloaded to cloud servers, while simpler, real-time processing is handled by edge devices. This approach balances computational loads and optimizes resource usage.

Addressing Integration Challenges

Integrating deep learning models with IoT systems presents several challenges, including compatibility issues, interoperability, and managing the lifecycle of integrated solutions. Ensuring seamless integration between different components and systems is critical for the effective operation of smart engineering solutions.

Solutions:

- **Standardization and Protocols:** Adopting standardized protocols and frameworks for communication and data exchange can improve interoperability between different IoT devices and deep learning systems. Standards such as MQTT (Message Queuing Telemetry Transport) and CoAP (Constrained Application Protocol) facilitate efficient and reliable communication.
- **Modular Design:** Designing systems with modularity in mind allows for easier integration and scalability. Modular components can be updated or replaced independently, reducing the complexity of integrating new technologies or adapting to changing requirements.
- **Lifecycle Management:** Implementing robust lifecycle management practices helps in managing the deployment, maintenance, and updates of integrated systems. Automated deployment tools and configuration management systems can streamline these processes and ensure consistent operation.
- **Integration Platforms:** Leveraging integration platforms and middleware solutions can simplify the process of connecting IoT devices with deep learning models. These platforms provide tools and interfaces for managing data flows, device interactions, and model deployments.

In conclusion, while integrating IoT with deep learning presents several challenges, effective solutions are available to address these issues. By managing data volume and complexity through aggregation and edge computing, ensuring privacy and security with encryption and access controls, optimizing computational resources with model and hardware strategies, and addressing integration challenges through standardization and modular design, organizations can overcome obstacles and harness the full potential of these advanced technologies. These efforts contribute to the development of robust, efficient, and secure smart engineering solutions that drive innovation and enhance operational performance.

FUTURE TRENDS AND DIRECTIONS

Emerging Technologies in IoT and Deep Learning

The convergence of IoT and deep learning continues to evolve, driven by advancements in technology and increasing demands for smarter, more efficient systems(Boopathi, 2023; Karthik et al., 2023; Maheswari et al., 2023). Several emerging technologies are shaping the future of this integration:

5G Connectivity:

The rollout of 5G networks is set to revolutionize IoT and deep learning applications. With significantly higher data transfer speeds, lower latency, and increased connectivity, 5G enables real-time data processing and communication. This advancement supports more responsive and scalable IoT systems, enhancing the performance of deep learning models deployed in various applications, from autonomous vehicles to smart cities.

Edge AI:

Edge AI refers to deploying artificial intelligence algorithms directly on IoT devices or edge servers rather than relying on centralized cloud computing. This trend reduces latency, enhances privacy, and decreases dependency on cloud infrastructure. Edge AI allows for faster decision-making and real-time analytics, which is crucial for applications requiring immediate responses, such as industrial automation and smart surveillance systems.

Federated Learning:

Federated learning is an approach that enables training machine learning models across multiple devices without transferring data to a central server. Instead, models are trained locally on each device and only aggregated updates are sent to the central server. This method enhances privacy, reduces bandwidth usage, and allows for collaborative model improvement without exposing sensitive data. It's particularly useful in scenarios where data privacy is critical, such as healthcare and finance.

Advanced Sensor Technologies:

Innovations in sensor technology, including the development of more accurate, miniaturized, and cost-effective sensors, are expanding the capabilities of IoT systems. These advancements enable more granular and diverse data collection, which enhances the effectiveness of deep learning models. For example, advanced environmental sensors can provide detailed data on air quality, which can be used to train models for better pollution prediction and management.

Predictions for Smart Engineering Solutions

As IoT and deep learning technologies continue to advance, several important trends and predictions are expected to shape the future of smart engineering solutions(S., 2024):

Increased Automation and Autonomy: Future smart engineering solutions will see a significant increase in automation and autonomy. Deep learning models will become more sophisticated, enabling IoT systems to perform complex tasks with minimal human intervention. For instance, autonomous industrial robots will handle intricate manufacturing processes, and smart grids will autonomously manage energy distribution based on real-time data analysis.

Enhanced Personalization: IoT and deep learning will drive greater personalization in various applications. In smart homes, for example, systems will offer highly personalized experiences by learning user preferences and adapting to their habits. Similarly, personalized healthcare solutions will leverage data from wearable devices and deep learning to provide tailored treatment plans and wellness recommendations.

Expansion of Smart Cities: The development of smart cities will accelerate, with IoT and deep learning playing central roles. Cities will integrate a wide range of IoT devices, such as traffic sensors, environmental monitors, and smart infrastructure, to optimize urban management. Deep learning will analyze data from these devices to improve traffic flow, enhance public safety, and manage resources more efficiently.

Advanced Predictive Analytics: Predictive analytics will become more advanced, leveraging deeper insights from IoT data and sophisticated deep learning models. This capability will enable more accurate forecasting and proactive management across various domains, including supply chain management, disaster response, and infrastructure maintenance.

Potential Developments and Innovations

Looking ahead, several potential developments and innovations are poised to further transform the landscape of IoT and deep learning(Boopathi, 2024; Samikannu et al., 2022):

Integration of Quantum Computing: Quantum computing has the potential to revolutionize data processing capabilities, enabling the handling of complex computations that are currently beyond the reach of classical computers. The integration of quantum computing with IoT and deep learning could lead to breakthroughs in data analysis and model training, allowing for more accurate and efficient predictions.

Development of Autonomous IoT Systems: Future innovations may lead to fully autonomous IoT systems that can self-manage and adapt to changing conditions without human intervention. These systems will leverage advanced deep learning models to make real-time decisions and optimize their performance independently, enhancing efficiency and reliability across various applications.

Enhanced Human-Machine Collaboration: The future of IoT and deep learning will likely involve enhanced collaboration between humans and machines. Advanced interfaces and human-centric designs will enable more intuitive interactions with smart systems. For example, natural language processing and augmented reality may be used to create more seamless and interactive experiences for users managing IoT systems.

Focus on Sustainability: Sustainability will become a main focus, with IoT and deep learning technologies being harnessed to address environmental challenges. Innovations will include smarter energy management systems, more efficient waste management, and advanced climate monitoring solutions. These technologies will support global efforts to reduce environmental impact and promote sustainable practices.

In summary, the integration of IoT and deep learning is set to advance rapidly, driven by emerging technologies and innovative solutions. With trends such as 5G connectivity, edge AI, and federated learning paving the way, the future of smart engineering solutions promises increased automation, enhanced personalization, and more efficient management of urban environments. As these technologies continue to evolve, they will enable new possibilities and drive significant progress in various domains, shaping a more intelligent and interconnected world.

CONCLUSION

The integration of IoT and deep learning represents a transformative advancement in smart engineering solutions. By leveraging IoT's extensive data collection capabilities and deep learning's powerful analytical models, industries can achieve unprecedented levels of automation, efficiency, and insight. This convergence enables real-time monitoring, predictive maintenance, automated quality control, and process optimization, driving substantial improvements across various applications.

The chapter has explored the fundamental concepts of IoT and deep learning, their synergy, and the architectures and frameworks that facilitate their integration. It also addressed practical aspects such as data collection, model development, and application scenarios like predictive maintenance and smart manufacturing.

Challenges such as managing data complexity, ensuring privacy and security, and meeting computational demands were discussed, along with potential solutions.

Looking ahead, emerging technologies like 5G, edge AI, and federated learning will further enhance the capabilities and applications of IoT and deep learning. As these technologies continue to evolve, they will unlock new possibilities and drive innovation in smart engineering. The ongoing advancement in these fields promises to deliver more efficient, intelligent, and sustainable solutions, shaping the future of industrial and urban environments.

REFERENCES

Abdullah, F. B., Iqbal, R., Ahmad, S., El-Affendi, M. A., & Abdullah, M. (2022). An empirical analysis of sustainable energy security for energy policy recommendations. *Sustainability*, *14*(10), 6099.

Agrawal, A. V., Magulur, L. P., Priya, S. G., Kaur, A., Singh, G., & Boopathi, S. (2023). Smart Precision Agriculture Using IoT and WSN. In *Handbook of Research on Data Science and Cybersecurity Innovations in Industry 4.0 Technologies* (pp. 524–541). IGI Global. DOI: 10.4018/978-1-6684-8145-5.ch026

Ahmad, S., El-Affendi, M. A., Anwar, M. S., & Iqbal, R. (2022). Potential future directions in optimization of students' performance prediction system. *Computational Intelligence and Neuroscience*, *2022*(1), 6864955.

Ahmad, S., Li, K., Eddine, H. A. I., & Khan, M. I. (2018). A biologically inspired cognitive skills measurement approach. Biologically inspired cognitive architectures, 24, 35-46.

Akhtar, S., Ali, A., Ahmad, S., Khan, M. I., Shah, S., & Hassan, F. (2022). The prevalence of foot ulcers in diabetic patients in Pakistan: A systematic review and meta-analysis. *Frontiers in Public Health*, *10*, 1017201. DOI: 10.3389/fpubh.2022.1017201 PMID: 36388315

Akhtar, S., Ramzan, M., Shah, S., Ahmad, I., Khan, M. I., Ahmad, S., & Qureshi, H. (2022). Forecasting exchange rate of Pakistan using time series analysis. *Mathematical Problems in Engineering*, *2022*(1), 9108580.

Ali, M. N., Senthil, T., Ilakkiya, T., Hasan, D. S., Ganapathy, N. B. S., & Boopathi, S. (2024). IoT's Role in Smart Manufacturing Transformation for Enhanced Household Product Quality. In *Advanced Applications in Osmotic Computing* (pp. 252–289). IGI Global. DOI: 10.4018/979-8-3693-1694-8.ch014

Anwar, M. S.. (2023). *"Immersive learning and AR/VR-based education: cybersecurity measures and risk management." Cybersecurity Management in Education Technologies*. CRC Press. DOI: 10.1201/9781003369042-1

Anwar, M. S., Choi, A., Ahmad, S., Aurangzeb, K., Laghari, A. A., Gadekallu, T. R., & Hines, A. (2024). A Moving Metaverse: QoE challenges and standards requirements for immersive media consumption in autonomous vehicles. *Applied Soft Computing*, *159*, 111577. DOI: 10.1016/j.asoc.2024.111577

Anwar, M. S., Wang, J., Ullah, A., Khan, W., Li, Z., & Ahmad, S. (2018, October). User profile analysis for enhancing QoE of 360 panoramic video in virtual reality environment. In *2018 International Conference on Virtual Reality and Visualization (ICVRV)* (pp. 106-111). IEEE.

Asharf, J., Moustafa, N., Khurshid, H., Debie, E., Haider, W., & Wahab, A. (2020). A review of intrusion detection systems using machine and deep learning in internet of things: Challenges, solutions and future directions. *Electronics (Basel)*, *9*(7), 1177. DOI: 10.3390/electronics9071177

Boopathi, S. (2023). Internet of Things-Integrated Remote Patient Monitoring System: Healthcare Application. In *Dynamics of Swarm Intelligence Health Analysis for the Next Generation* (pp. 137–161). IGI Global. DOI: 10.4018/978-1-6684-6894-4.ch008

Boopathi, S. (2024). Sustainable Development Using IoT and AI Techniques for Water Utilization in Agriculture. In *Sustainable Development in AI, Blockchain, and E-Governance Applications* (pp. 204–228). IGI Global. DOI: 10.4018/979-8-3693-1722-8.ch012

Boopathi, S. (2024). Advancements in Optimizing Smart Energy Systems Through Smart Grid Integration, Machine Learning, and IoT. In Optimization Techniques for Hybrid Power Systems: Renewable Energy, Electric Vehicles, and Smart Grid (pp. 33-61). IGI Global.

Dawoud, A., Shahristani, S., & Raun, C. (2018). Deep learning and software-defined networks: Towards secure IoT architecture. *Internet of Things : Engineering Cyber Physical Human Systems*, *3*, 82–89. DOI: 10.1016/j.iot.2018.09.003

Dimililer, K., Dindar, H., & Al-Turjman, F. (2021). Deep learning, machine learning and internet of things in geophysical engineering applications: An overview. *Microprocessors and Microsystems*, *80*, 103613. DOI: 10.1016/j.micpro.2020.103613

Elhanashi, A., Dini, P., Saponara, S., & Zheng, Q. (2023). Integration of deep learning into the iot: A survey of techniques and challenges for real-world applications. *Electronics (Basel)*, *12*(24), 4925. DOI: 10.3390/electronics12244925

Hema, N., Krishnamoorthy, N., Chavan, S. M., Kumar, N., Sabarimuthu, M., & Boopathi, S. (2023). A Study on an Internet of Things (IoT)-Enabled Smart Solar Grid System. In *Handbook of Research on Deep Learning Techniques for Cloud-Based Industrial IoT* (pp. 290–308). IGI Global. DOI: 10.4018/978-1-6684-8098-4.ch017

Hosni, A. I. E., Li, K., & Ahmad, S. (2019, December). DARIM: Dynamic approach for rumor influence minimization in online social networks. In *International Conference on Neural Information Processing* (pp. 619-630). Cham: Springer International Publishing.

Hosni, A. I. E., Li, K., Ding, C., & Ahmed, S. (2018, November). Least cost rumor influence minimization in multiplex social networks. In *International Conference on Neural Information Processing* (pp. 93-105). Cham: Springer International Publishing.

Jeevanantham, Y. A., Saravanan, A., Vanitha, V., Boopathi, S., & Kumar, D. P. (2022). Implementation of Internet-of Things (IoT) in Soil Irrigation System. *IEEE Explore*, 1–5.

Karthik, S., Hemalatha, R., Aruna, R., Deivakani, M., Reddy, R. V. K., & Boopathi, S. (2023). Study on Healthcare Security System-Integrated Internet of Things (IoT). In *Perspectives and Considerations on the Evolution of Smart Systems* (pp. 342–362). IGI Global.

Kavitha, C., Varalatchoumy, M., Mithuna, H., Bharathi, K., Geethalakshmi, N., & Boopathi, S. (2023). Energy Monitoring and Control in the Smart Grid: Integrated Intelligent IoT and ANFIS. In *Applications of Synthetic Biology in Health, Energy, and Environment* (pp. 290–316). IGI Global.

Lakshmanna, K., Kaluri, R., Gundluru, N., Alzamil, Z. S., Rajput, D. S., Khan, A. A., Haq, M. A., & Alhussen, A. (2022). A review on deep learning techniques for IoT data. *Electronics (Basel)*, *11*(10), 1604. DOI: 10.3390/electronics11101604

Ma, X., Yao, T., Hu, M., Dong, Y., Liu, W., Wang, F., & Liu, J. (2019). A survey on deep learning empowered IoT applications. *IEEE Access : Practical Innovations, Open Solutions*, 7, 181721–181732. DOI: 10.1109/ACCESS.2019.2958962

Maheswari, B. U., Imambi, S. S., Hasan, D., Meenakshi, S., Pratheep, V., & Boopathi, S. (2023). Internet of things and machine learning-integrated smart robotics. In *Global Perspectives on Robotics and Autonomous Systems: Development and Applications* (pp. 240–258). IGI Global. DOI: 10.4018/978-1-6684-7791-5.ch010

Medhat, N., Moussa, S. M., Badr, N. L., & Tolba, M. F. (2020). A framework for continuous regression and integration testing in iot systems based on deep learning and search-based techniques. *IEEE Access : Practical Innovations, Open Solutions*, 8, 215716–215726. DOI: 10.1109/ACCESS.2020.3039931

Rahamathunnisa, U., Sudhakar, K., Padhi, S., Bhattacharya, S., Shashibhushan, G., & Boopathi, S. (2024). Sustainable Energy Generation From Waste Water: IoT Integrated Technologies. In *Adoption and Use of Technology Tools and Services by Economically Disadvantaged Communities: Implications for Growth and Sustainability* (pp. 225–256). IGI Global.

Reddy, M. A., Reddy, B. M., Mukund, C., Venneti, K., Preethi, D., & Boopathi, S. (2023). Social Health Protection During the COVID-Pandemic Using IoT. In *The COVID-19 Pandemic and the Digitalization of Diplomacy* (pp. 204–235). IGI Global. DOI: 10.4018/978-1-7998-8394-4.ch009

Samikannu, R., Koshariya, A. K., Poornima, E., Ramesh, S., Kumar, A., & Boopathi, S. (2022). Sustainable Development in Modern Aquaponics Cultivation Systems Using IoT Technologies. In *Human Agro-Energy Optimization for Business and Industry* (pp. 105–127). IGI Global.

Saravanan, S., Khare, R., Umamaheswari, K., Khare, S., Krishne Gowda, B. S., & Boopathi, S. (2024). AI and ML Adaptive Smart-Grid Energy Management Systems: Exploring Advanced Innovations. In *Principles and Applications in Speed Sensing and Energy Harvesting for Smart Roads* (pp. 166–196). IGI Global. DOI: 10.4018/978-1-6684-9214-7.ch006

Syamala, M., Komala, C., Pramila, P., Dash, S., Meenakshi, S., & Boopathi, S. (2023). Machine Learning-Integrated IoT-Based Smart Home Energy Management System. In *Handbook of Research on Deep Learning Techniques for Cloud-Based Industrial IoT* (pp. 219–235). IGI Global. DOI: 10.4018/978-1-6684-8098-4.ch013

Thakkar, A., & Lohiya, R. (2021). A review on machine learning and deep learning perspectives of IDS for IoT: Recent updates, security issues, and challenges. *Archives of Computational Methods in Engineering*, 28(4), 3211–3243. DOI: 10.1007/s11831-020-09496-0

Thakur, D., Saini, J. K., & Srinivasan, S. (2023). DeepThink IoT: The strength of deep learning in internet of things. *Artificial Intelligence Review*, 56(12), 14663–14730. DOI: 10.1007/s10462-023-10513-4

Tirlangi, S., Teotia, S., Padmapriya, G., Senthil Kumar, S., Dhotre, S., & Boopathi, S. (2024). Cloud Computing and Machine Learning in the Green Power Sector: Data Management and Analysis for Sustainable Energy. In *Developments Towards Next Generation Intelligent Systems for Sustainable Development* (pp. 148–179). IGI Global. DOI: 10.4018/979-8-3693-5643-2.ch006

Tsimenidis, S., Lagkas, T., & Rantos, K. (2022). Deep learning in IoT intrusion detection. *Journal of Network and Systems Management*, *30*(1), 8. DOI: 10.1007/s10922-021-09621-9

Ugandar, R., Rahamathunnisa, U., Sajithra, S., Christiana, M. B. V., Palai, B. K., & Boopathi, S. (2023). Hospital Waste Management Using Internet of Things and Deep Learning: Enhanced Efficiency and Sustainability. In *Applications of Synthetic Biology in Health, Energy, and Environment* (pp. 317–343). IGI Global.

Veeranjaneyulu, R., Boopathi, S., Kumari, R. K., Vidyarthi, A., Isaac, J. S., & Jaiganesh, V. (2023). Air Quality Improvement and Optimisation Using Machine Learning Technique. *IEEE- Explore*, 1–6.

Venkatasubramanian, V., Chitra, M., Sudha, R., Singh, V. P., Jefferson, K., & Boopathi, S. (2024). Examining the Impacts of Course Outcome Analysis in Indian Higher Education: Enhancing Educational Quality. In *Challenges of Globalization and Inclusivity in Academic Research* (pp. 124–145). IGI Global.

Venkateswaran, N., Kiran Kumar, K., Maheswari, K., Kumar Reddy, R. V., & Boopathi, S. (2024). Optimizing IoT Data Aggregation: Hybrid Firefly-Artificial Bee Colony Algorithm for Enhanced Efficiency in Agriculture. *AGRIS On-Line Papers in Economics and Informatics*, *16*(1), 117–130. DOI: 10.7160/aol.2024.160110

Chapter 6
Exploring Sentiment Through Cognitive Computing on Social Media Content

Saifullah Jan
https://orcid.org/0000-0001-9890-6991
City University of Science and Information Technology, Peshawar, Pakistan

Aiman
City University of Science and Information Technology, Peshawar, Pakistan

ABSTRACT

The Covid-19 epidemic is regarded as the most serious concern of our day. It has an impact on many parts of our life, including schooling. As a result, practically every country's education system now requires distance study. Some people found it easy to accept this method, while others thought it was insufficient. In the context of the COVID-19 disruptions of education, especially distance learning, there is the need to leverage cognitive intelligence to determine their social, developmental, and emotional effects on students and educators. Cognitive intelligence, through sentiment analysis, provides the ability to process, learn, and adapt based on user-generated content, enabling policymakers to gain actionable insights into public sentiment. This study utilizes cognitive intelligence principles to assess the efficacy of distance learning using sentiment analysis on a dataset of 202,700 tweets shared during global lockdowns.

DOI: 10.4018/979-8-3693-9057-3.ch006

Copyright © 2025, IGI Global Scientific Publishing. Copying or distributing in print or electronic forms without written permission of IGI Global Scientific Publishing is prohibited.

1. INTRODUCTION

In recent years, the Internet has significantly transformed how individuals express their thoughts and opinions. This shift is most evident across various digital platforms, including blogs, online forums, product review websites, and social media channels. Today, a vast number of people actively use social networking platforms such as Facebook, Twitter, and Google Plus to share their emotions, views, and insights on everyday experiences. The widespread adoption of media has transformed the way individuals, in today's society engage with each other both privately and publicly. These digital communities create spaces where individuals utilize forums to inform and support one another. As a result, social media platforms produce quantities of content filled with emotions including blog posts remarks, evaluations, tweets, and status updates. This information reflects the experiences and perspectives of users. Serves as a significant resource, for public sentiments and emotional reflections (Dwivedi et al., 2021). In light of the COVID 19 disruptions to education, and in particular, the transition to distance learning, research is necessary to understand the social, developmental and affective effects of education on students and educators. Finding ways can shed insights to the improvements that can be made in remote learning methods and help to build more sustainable and resilient future education systems.

Sentiment Analysis aims to understand and ascertain opinions embedded in text data as such providing useful information about people's attitudes towards specific topics. In order to ascertain the overall feel of the populace this method utilizes the analysis of millions of pages of text from various sources including personal blogs, criticism or review portals and social networks. A major challenge in sentiment analysis is Classifying opinionated content – so it involves figuring out whether the opinion expressed is more positive or more negative. This particular problem has been resolved to a large extent in many works through the use of machine learning techniques which provide efficient approaches for sentiment classification (J. Ahmed & M. Ahmed, 2023). Factual data and sentiment data are the two main categories into which online textual information may be broadly divided. Objective information about different entities, subjects, or events is included in factual data (Hussain et al., 2024). On the other hand, sentiment data consists of subjective statements that represent a person's views or convictions toward a specific thing, item, or occasion. Sentiment analysis is the act of identifying and categorizing people's online feelings to ascertain whether they are neutral, negative, or positive in relation to a particular product, issue, or event (Ahmad et al., 2023).

Approximately 111 microblogging systems are thought to be in use today. Users create frequent, short posts on these platforms, which function as social media networks. Twitter is among the most widely recognized microblogging services, enabling users to compose and read messages limited to 148 characters, commonly known as "tweets." These tweets serve as a primary source of raw data for analysis. With the increasing volume of sentiment-related content on social media platforms such as Twitter, Facebook, blogs, and online forums, sentiment analysis has become a significant research focus in the field of computational linguistics (Muliyah et al., 2020).

Textual information retrieval techniques have traditionally focused on the processing, searching, and analysis of objective factual data. However, in addition to factual content, there exists a category of textual data that conveys subjective elements (6) including opinions, sentiments, evaluations, attitudes, and emotions—core aspects of Sentiment Analysis (Hussain et al., 2024) . This Sentiment Analysis presents numerous opportunities for the development of innovative applications, largely driven by the exponential growth of online data from sources such as blogs and social networks (Muliyah et al., 2020)

(Semary et al., 2024). Sentiment Analysis can be utilized to enhance recommendation systems by predicting item recommendations based on the presence of positive or negative sentiments expressed about those items (Semary et al., 2024).

In this regard, this paper presents the comparative analysis of random forest (RF), K-nearest neighbor (KNN), and naïve bayes (NB) machine learning (ML) models on Twitter data. The model comparison is done based on recall, precision, F1 score and accuracy.

One of the main contributions of this work is a thorough sentiment analysis of over 202,700 tweets collected during the COVID-19 epidemic to ascertain public opinion regarding distance education. We are investigating the effectiveness of three machine learning models. Random Forest (RF) Naïve Bayes (NB) and KNN (Neighbor). To determine the most suitable classifier, for analyzing sentiments in a given context. The performance of these models is evaluated using metrics such as recall rate, reliability rate, output accuracy rate and F measure score to obtain an understanding of their capabilities. Furthermore, the results offer insights into perceptions about remote learning which can be leveraged to enhance educational strategies in times of crises, like the current COVID-19 pandemic.

This work is innovative because it applies machine learning and sentiment analysis in a novel way to remote learning during the COVID-19 epidemic. Even while sentiment analysis has been applied extensively in many different fields, our study stands out by examining public opinions regarding distant learning amid a worldwide crisis, which coincided with swift and unheard-of changes in educational systems. Our research offers a deeper knowledge of how public opinion fluctuates across different countries by using a huge Twitter dataset and comparing various machine learning algorithms. This provides important insights into how to improve distant learning practices during comparable events. This study makes a substantial contribution to the domains of computational and educational research since it employs Random Forest (RF) as the most effective model for sentiment classification, demonstrating its resilience when dealing with complicated textual data.

The rest of this paper is organized as Section 2 discusses the literature review, Section 3 presents the methodology, Section 4 presents the results evaluations and discussion, and finally, Section 5 concluded this study.

2. LITERATURE REVIEW

Several techniques have been developed in the last ten years to improve sentiment analysis (SA) with data from social media. An open-source approach was used in 2015 to gather and examine Twitter microblogs, with a particular emphasis on user reviews of Tesco and Asda, two of the biggest retailers in the UK, during the 2014 Christmas season. Using social media data, this approach allowed businesses to assess their competitive positioning and comprehend consumer sentiment (Muliyah et al., 2020). Building on this, SARGS, an optimized method for producing meta-actions more rapidly and efficiently, was released in 2017. Using sentiment analysis data from Twitter, the system was compared to other systems like Apache Spark and Hadoop, showing better performance while managing massive amounts of social data (Ali et al., 2024). The recent progress highlights the increasing focus, on optimizing systems for more accurate sentiment analysis tasks. However advanced sentiment analysis owes much of its evolution to visualization methods. In 2011, re-searchers devised time driven visual sentiment analysis strategies, like topic-oriented analysis, streak analysis and pixel cell centered emotion calendars to handle amounts of Twitter data.

Research into sentiment analysis of customer reviews has explored various techniques to improve accuracy and efficiency in extracting insights from textual data. A study conducted in 2014 emphasized the application of sentiment analysis on customer reviews by implementing key techniques such as pre-processing, adjective extraction, and machine learning algorithms to enhance the quality of sentiment classification (Semary et al., 2024). In 2016, a comparative study evaluated different opinion mining approaches, focusing on both machine learning and lexicon-based methods, particularly applied to Twitter data. The study utilized a range of machine learning models and underscored the im-portance of effective pre-processing techniques for accurate classification of sentiments. This research highlighted the value of opinion classification into positive, negative, and neutral categories, providing insights that can inform product and service enhancements based on customer feedback (Kubara & Kopczewska, 2024). The focus on Twitter as a data source for sentiment analysis has continued to grow, with several studies developing sentiment classifiers aimed at identifying public opinions on various topics. These classifiers leverage a com-bination of machine learning techniques and refined pre-processing steps to achieve reliable sentiment categorization, demonstrating the critical role of sentiment analysis in gathering actionable insights from social media data. This body of work offers a foundation for ongoing advancements in opinion mining and sentiment classification for applications across industries.

The analysis of tweets presents significant challenges, primarily due to the vast volume of tweets generated daily. The use of hashtags in tweets serves multiple functions, adding complexity to the categorization process. The context-dependent nature of hashtags, combined with the presence of slang, acronyms, and emoticons, further complicates the interpretation of sentiment within the constraints of limited character counts (Aiman et al., 2024). A noteworthy approach utilizing the TripAdvisor dataset for evaluation was proposed in (10-15). This method exemplifies the growing interest in sentiment analysis, which can be traced back to foundational studies conducted in 2002 (Ahmad et al., 2018)(Fatima et al., 2022)(Hosni, Li, & Ahmad, 2020)(Anwar et al., 2024)(Anwar et al., 2019)(Ahmad et al., 2020)(Khan et al., 2020)(Abdullah et al., 2022)(Rahim et al., 2024)(Akhtar et al., 2022)(Abdullah et al., 2022)(Anwar et al., 2023)(Ahmad et al., 2018)(Akhtar et al., 2022)(Ahmad et al., 2022)(Anwar et al., 2018). One of these seminal papers emphasized language analysis techniques, while the other focused on the application of machine learning methods for opinion mining (Kovács et al., 2024).

Since then, researchers have increasingly investigated hybrid systems that integrate both language analysis and machine learning methodologies. These hybrid approaches aim to capitalize on the strengths of each technique, facilitating more comprehensive sentiment analysis and enhancing classification accuracy (Arshad et al., 2024). This evolution in sentiment analysis reflects a broader trend toward the development of sophisticated tools that can effectively interpret and analyze public sentiment across various platforms.

In early 2021, the introduction of vaccines provided a sense of relief to many; however, it also ignited significant debates between pro-vaccine and anti-vaccine groups. This study utilizes social media data to investigate public opinion on vaccine hesitancy through sentiment analysis, employing three methodologies: Azure Machine Learning (ML), VADER, and TextBlob. After evaluating five algorithms with different vectorization techniques, the optimal model was identified, which integrated TextBlob, Term Frequency-Inverse Document Frequency (TF-IDF), and Linear Support Vector Classification (LinearSVC). This combination demonstrated high accuracy in classifying sentiment related to vaccine hesitancy (Sun et al., 2024).

In (Sarro et al., 2020) authors used supervised machine learning classifiers; the Random Search method is used to optimize each model's hyperparameters. The SVC model, using BoW and TF-IDF feature extraction, achieves the best performance with classification accuracy reaching 71%. However, due to limited training data, classifiers using the Word2Vec embedding method show lower prediction accuracy. Overall, applying machine learning to sentiment analysis allows for accurate text feature extraction without relying on pre-defined lexicons.

Social media, especially platforms like Twitter, is crucial for data sharing and sentiment analysis (Raees & Fazilat, 2024). Using machine learning algorithms like Support Vector Machine, Naive Bayes, and Long Short-Term Memory, this paper explores Twitter sentiment analysis through a Flask environment. The results, fetched via API calls, classify tweets as positive, negative, or neutral, and are displayed on a webpage with visual comparisons across industries and companies.

Scientists and citizens seek ways to address the effects of COVID-19, with many turning to social media to share experiences. Research by (Ahmad et al., 2018) analyzes Twitter data using sentiment analysis and linguistic techniques, focusing on tweet evolution, sentiment differences in tweets with and without images, and the relationship between tweets, Google searches, and Wikipedia views. The study reveals changes in emotional expression over time and shows how COVID-19-related terms influence tweet impact and user communication during the pandemic.

3. METHODOLOGY

This study aims to perform a comparative analysis of various ML models for Twitter sentiment analysis. This study's complete procedure is shown in Figure 1. A systematic approach is used in the technique for Twitter sentiment analysis in the context of online learning in order to extract insightful information from the Twitter data. To ensure data relevancy, tweets are initially gathered using particular hashtags linked to online education. The data is then cleaned by pre-processing methods such as deleting duplicates, punctuation, hashtags, and links. To prepare the text data for machine learning models, feature extraction approaches like Term Frequency-Inverse Document Frequency (TF-IDF) and vectorization are used. For sentiment classification, four different models NB, KNN, Rf, and lexicon-based analysis are used. Finally, a thorough knowledge of sentiment patterns in the online education conversation on Twitter is provided by the performance of these models, which is assessed using metrics like Accuracy, Precision, and Recall. This technique makes sure that sentiment in online education debates is thoroughly and methodically analyzed, providing insightful information for those involved in education.

Figure 1. Proposed Methodology

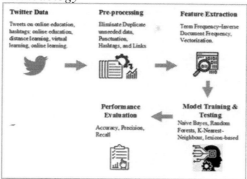

3.1. Tweet Extraction

The dataset, named "distance learning tweets," was sourced from Twitter via a developer account in December 2020, comprising 202,700 tweets and six attributes. Python libraries, including Tweepy, were imported for analysis. To begin, we create a Twitter Developer Account to have access to the Twitter API. Using this API, we gathered tweets on online education that included the hashtags online education, distance learning, virtual learning, and online learning.

3.2. Preprocessing

The first stage in pre-processing is to eliminate duplicate and unneeded data, often known as nameless data. After pre-processing, we were left with 187000 tweets out of a total of 202700 tweets. Stop words, punctuation, hashtags, and links have all been deleted. The dataset was pre-processed using the procedures listed below.

Tweets are broken down into words based on the spaces within words. We removed URLs from tweets as they constitute extraneous information, and we also eliminated common stop words and frequent phrases like "is, the, a," and so forth.

3.3. Sentiment Analysis

After pre-processing, the second stage involves sentiment analysis using the TF-IDF (Term Frequency–Inverse Document Frequency) Vectorizer module. This assigns polarity (positive or negative) and subjectivity (opinion or statement) scores to tweet terms. TextBlob, a Natural Language Processing (NLP) package, was used for this, categorizing sentiments as positive, negative, or neutral based on polarity, as shown in Table 1.

Table 1. Polarity classification

Sentiments	Polarity Values
Positive	$n > 0$
Negative	$n < 0$
Neutral	$n = 0$

3.4. Filtering and Tokenization

Filtering is the process of cleansing raw data. URL linkages (e.g., http://twitter.com), special terms in Twitter (e.g., "RT" which signifies Retweet), and user names in Twitter emoticons are eliminated in this phase.

Sentence segmentation is referred to as tokenization. In this phase, we will tokenize or segment text by dividing it up with spaces and punctuation marks to create a container of words.

3.5. Removal of Stopping Words

Stop words such as "a," "an," "the," "to," "of," "is," "are," and "this" has been deleted in this phase. Finally, we employ lemmatization, a natural language processing approach that aids in the resolution of vocabulary mismatches while preserving the true meaning of words.

3.6. Performance Evaluation Matrix

Any research project's principal purpose is to analyze models. Some typical assessment measures must be taken into account. In this study, assessment measures used are accuracy, recall, F1-score and precision. These measures can be calculated as:

$$Recall = \frac{TP}{TP + FN} \tag{1}$$

$$Precision = \frac{TP}{TP + FP} \tag{2}$$

$$Accuracy = \frac{TP + TN}{TP + TN + FP + FN} \tag{3}$$

$$F1 - Score = \frac{2*Precision*Recall}{Precision + Recall} \qquad (4)$$

Where, the terms TP, FN, TN, and FP refer to the number of true-positive classifications (Kubara & Kopczewska, 2024), false-negative classifications, true-negative classifications, and false-positive classifications, respectively (Aiman et al., 2024).

3.7. Techniques

In this study, various ML methods are employed to determine the most effective sentiment analysis techniques for online education. These models include NB, KNN, RF, and LA.

3.7.1. Naive Bayes

Named after Thomas Bayes, the NB Classifier stands out for its ease of development and superior computing efficiency compared to other machine learning algorithms (Khan et al., 2020). This supervised classifier calculates the likelihood of a dataset being labeled as positive or negative, employing probabilistic methods to learn patterns within classified texts (Hosni, Li, & Ahmad, 2019). It matches document contents with a list of terms to categorize them accurately. The Naive Bayes classifier, often employed for text classification, categorizes documents using a multinomial approach.

The Naïve Bayes (NB) classifier is essentially grounded on Bayes' hypothesis with autonomy suspicions among predictors. NB model is exceptionally easy to fabricate and can be executed for colossal datasets. NB classifier frequently accomplishes well than increasingly refined classification strategies. The back likelihood, P(A|B) is figured from P(A), P(B), and P(B|A) as follows:

$$P(AB) = P(BA) . P(A)/P(B) \qquad (5)$$

where:

- P(A|B) P (A | B) P(A|B) is the posterior probability: the probability of event A occurring given that B is true.
- P(B|A) P (B | A) P(B|A) is the likelihood: the probability of event B occurring given that A is true.
- P(A) is the prior probability: the initial probability of event A occurring, without considering B.
- P(B) is the marginal probability: the total probability of event B occurring, across all possible outcomes of A.

Using Bayesian probability terminology, the above equation can be written as: Posterior = Prior * Likelihood, Posterior is what parameters are likely after observing the data objects, Prior is uncertainty of data object prior, and Likelihood is the probability of falling under a specific category or class, while Evidence is the factor that is the same as for all possible hypothesis being considered. The impact of the estimation of a forecaster (B) on an assumed class (A) is autonomous of the estimations of different predictors. This supposition is called class uncertain independence.

3.7.2. Random Forest

RF is an ensemble learning method that combines multiple decision trees to classify new cases. They use a majority vote from the trees to determine the output class (Hosni et al., 2018). They are user-friendly, making them accessible to both experts and non-experts with minimal programming and statistical knowledge. Randomly select subsets of features for each decision tree in the forest (Anwar et al., 2020). Build decision trees using these subsets, ensuring all sub-samples become leaf nodes. Repeat the process to create multiple decision trees (K) for the final random forest.

The Random Forest algorithm can be described as an ensemble of decision trees (8). The final prediction for a given input x can be expressed as shown in Eq. (6).

$$\hat{y} = \frac{1}{N} \sum_{i=1}^{N} T_i(x) \tag{6}$$

Where:

- N is the number of decision trees.
- Ti(x) is the prediction from the ith tree.

3.7.3. K–Nearest Neighbor

KNN is a simple yet effective non-parametric supervised classification method widely used in various fields. It employs analogy-based classification, comparing unknown data to training data using Euclidean distance. To avoid attribute range bias, values are standardized (Khan et al., 2023). The KNN algorithm assigns the most frequent class among the K-nearest neighbors, with ties resolved by the shortest average distance to the unknown pattern. KNN is categorized by a majority vote of its neighbors, with the case being allocated to the most common class among its nearest K-neighbors (Kubara & Kopczewska, 2024).

The k-NN algorithm predicts the output for a given input x based on the majority class of its k nearest neighbors in the training dataset:

$$\hat{y} = mod(y1, y2, \ldots, yk) \tag{7}$$

Where:

- yi are the labels of the k nearest neighbors of x.

3.7.4. Lexicon-based Approach

The lexicon-based method relies on sentiment words to gauge positive or negative attitudes, using a sentiment lexicon for polarity classification (positive, negative, neutral). It's more straightforward than machine learning approaches (Hosni, Li, & Ahmed, 2018). By employing a sentiment dictionary, we score opinion terms and assess tweet sentiment. Pre-processing involves eliminating duplicates and irrelevant data, leaving 187,000 out of 202,700 tweets after removing stop words, punctuation, hashtags, and links.

For a lexicon-based sentiment analysis model, the prediction can be expressed using Eq. (Kubara & Kopczewska, 2024).

$$\hat{y} = \frac{1}{N} \sum_{i=1}^{N} w_i f(x_i) \tag{8}$$

Where:

- y^ is the predicted sentiment score.
- wi is the weight of the ith word in the lexicon.
- f(xi) is a function that indicates the presence (or absence) of the ith word in the input xxx.
- n is the number of words in the lexicon.

4. METHODOLOGY

To evaluate our results, we split our data into a 60% training set and a 40% test set. We employed ML techniques, including NB, RF, and KNN, to classify the text based on sentiment polarity, and then assessed the outcomes., as illustrated in Figure 1.

Figure 2. Polarity of the Feelings after Categorizing

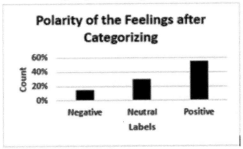

It demonstrates that the majority of individuals have voiced a favorable attitude toward distance education. As illustrated in Figure 4.2, positive tweets account for 55% of all tweets, negative tweets account for 15%, and neutral tweets account for 30%.

On a Twitter dataset, these strategies are tested using four assessment measures: accuracy, precision, recall, and F1-Score. Three algorithms, NB, RF, and KNN, were used to determine which method performs best in sentiment analysis. Figure 2 shows the analysis obtained through precision, F1-Score, and recall.

Figure 3. Sentiment Count

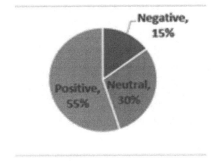

Table 2. Analysis through Precision, F-measure, and Recall

Technique	Precision	F 1 score	Recall
Random Forest	0.94	0.95	0.95
Naïve Bayes	0.87	0.88	0.90
KNN	0.92	0.42	0.27

The findings demonstrate that RF excels over alternative methods, achieving an accuracy rate of 0.92, an F1 score of 0.95, and a recall score of 0.95. In contrast, KNN's results are notably underwhelming. Figure 3 depicts the total outcomes.

The percentage difference presented in Table 2 compares the three models applied to sentiment analysis including NB, KNN, and RF based on their precision, F1 score, and recall. On all the parameters, the performance of RF has been pretty consistent compared to NB and KNN concerning its 8.05% higher precision and 7.95% better F1 score than the NB along with 5.56% higher recall. Compared to KNN, the difference is even starker. The F1 score of RF is 126.19% better and recall is 251.85% better. KNN had performed significantly behind in both of these evaluation measures. The precision of RF compared to KNN is, however relatively modest at 2.17%, inferring that the precision of KNN is close but still not up to par. By comparison, NB proves to be the best in performance with better values in F1 score and recall percentages of 109.52% and 233.33% compared to KNN, which, however, reveals a minor improvement in precision with a 5.75% lower value as compared to NB. Altogether, this analysis verifies that RF is the best model with NB in the second position, whereas KNN's performance is relatively poor, especially in terms of F1 score and recall.

Table 3. Comparative percentage differences

Metric	Model Comparison	RF	NB	KNN
Precision	RF	—	+0.07	+0.02
	NB	-0.07	—	-0.05
	KNN	-0.02	+0.05	—
Recall	RF	—	+0.05	+0.68
	NB	-0.05	—	+0.63
	KNN	-0.68	-0.63	—
F1 Score	RF	—	+0.07	+0.53
	NB	-0.07	—	+0.46
	KNN	-0.53	-0.46	—

The cross-comparison shown in Table 3 explains the differences in performance among the three models: RF, NB, and KNN. As seen across the three main metrics-precision, recall, and F1 score-it shows that RF outperformed NB and KNN without fail. Precision general, this was slightly better compared to NB at 0.07 and KNN at 0.02. For recall, RF beats NB by 0.05 and KNN by a great margin of 0.68, thus indicating its superior capability to detect relevant positive cases. For the F1 score, the RF beats NB by 0.07 and KNN by 0.53, thus indicating RF's prowess over other models with a better balance between precision and recall. NB performs worse than RF, but better than KNN, providing better recall and F1 score values by 0.63 and 0.46, respectively; it also falls a bit short in precision by 0.05. KNN performs worse than all, with the weakest overall performance and most importantly, with extremely poor recall and F1 score values (and 0.68 worse compared to RF) making it an unpopular model for projects that require more precision and recall. Although it has a slight difference in accuracy at 0.02, the fact that KNN fails to hold a high value for the recall makes the overall performance a compromise. In summary, the table indicates that RF is the best balanced and effective model for sentiment analysis followed by NB and, by a large margin, KNN, especially the weakness of recall and F1 score.

Table 4. Cross-comparison of precision, recall, and F1 score

Metric	Model Comparison	RF	NB	KNN
Precision	RF	---	+0.07	+0.02
.	NB	-0.07	---	-0.05
.	KNN	-0.02	+0.05	---
Recall	RF	---	+0.05	+0.68
.	NB	-0.05	---	+0.63
.	KNN	-0.68	-0.63	---
Recall	RF	---	+0.07	+0.53
.	NB	-0.07	---	+0.46
.	KNN	-0.53	-0.46	---

Figure 4. Analysis through Precision, F-measure, and Recall

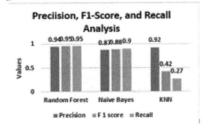

Figure 5. Accuracy Analysis of each Model

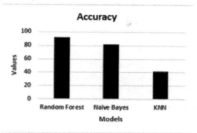

The study employs the "distance learning tweets" dataset, collected via a Twitter developer account, featuring six parameters (content, location, user name, retweet count, favorites) with a total of 202,700 tweets about distance education.

Three ML, namely RF, NB, and KNN, were employed. RF yielded the highest accuracy at 92%, outperforming other methods. Naive Bayes achieved 82% accuracy (Figure 5), while KNN lagged behind at 42% accuracy.

When it comes to conducting sentiment analysis on Twitter, the Random Forest (RF) model shows better results than Naive Bayes (NB) and K-Nearest Neighbors (KNN) thanks to its ensemble structure comprising of multiple decision trees which aggregates results of models to limit overfitting and increase generalization on highly noisy text data. Unlike NB, which assumes (wrongly in cases of text data where words are interdependent) that features are independent, RF learns relationships among features and more complex patterns which enables it to perform better in classifying intricate sentiments. RF is also tolerant to data imbalances, which is a common phenomenon in social networks sentiments because it can perform satisfactorily on majority and minority classes which sufficiently translated into high recall and F1 scores in the study. In comparison with KNN, which is ineffective for high-dimensional text data, RF has the opposite relationship in which high values of precision are balanced with recall to produce good results across all metrics thus making it the best model for the study as shown in Table 5.

Table 5. Comparison of Random Forest, Naive Bayes, and K-Nearest Neighbors

Factor	Random Forest (RF)	Naive Bayes (NB)	K-Nearest Neighbors (KNN)
Model Structure	Ensemble of decision trees, aggregates results for better generalization	Probabilistic classifier assuming feature independence	Non-parametric, distance-based classifier relying on nearest neighbors
Handling Feature Dependency	Captures complex patterns and dependencies among features, improving sentiment classification	Assumes feature independence, limiting ability to capture word dependencies	No specific handling for feature relationships, limiting accuracy in high-dimensional data
Data Imbalance Robustness	Can manage class imbalance effectively, achieving high recall and F1 scores	Sensitive to class imbalance; may misclassify minority classes	Struggles with class imbalance, resulting in lower recall and F1 scores
Handling High Dimensionality	Resilient to high-dimensional text data due to random feature selection at each split	Handles high-dimensional data well but lacks flexibility to capture complex patterns	Sensitive to high dimensionality; performance decreases with text data complexity
Overall Effectiveness	Superior model for sentiment analysis due to high balance between precision and recall	Moderate performance, effective but limited by feature independence assumption	Weakest model in this context, struggling with both accuracy and sensitivity to class balance

5. CONCLUSIONS

Amid the COVID-19 pandemic, our research centered on conducting sentiment analysis and opinion mining on remote education through Twitter data. Our aim was to better understand public sentiments and viewpoints regarding distance learning. We collected a dataset of 202,700 tweets and employed Textblob for sentiment analysis, evaluating aspects like polarity and subjectivity. Our findings revealed that a majority of tweets expressed positivity, with Random Forest (RF) demonstrating superior performance in sentiment analysis compared to NB and K-Nearest Neighbors KNN.

Table 6. presents a concise yet detailed view of the recommendations for future research

Category	Research Recommendations
Dataset Expansion	■ Include tweets in multiple languages for demographic diversity. ■ Collect longitudinal data for sentiment trend analysis.
Preprocessing Refinement	■ Use context-aware stop word removal and semantic summarization. ■ Leverage deep learning-based preprocessing techniques (e.g., sarcasm detection).
Advanced Models	■ Employ transformers (e.g., BERT, RoBERTa) for better context understanding. ■ Combine multiple classifiers using ensemble learning methods.
Sentiment Intensity	■ Extend analysis to measure sentiment intensity levels (e.g., highly positive). ■ Use sentiment scoring for nuanced polarity analysis.

continued on following page

Table 6. Continued

Category	Research Recommendations
Real-time Analysis	▪ Implement pipelines for real-time sentiment tracking. ▪ Develop dashboards to visualize real-time sentiment patterns.
User Demographics	▪ Analyze sentiment variations across user demographics (age, location, profession). ▪ Compare sentiment trends between educators, students, and parents.
Cross- platform Analysis	▪ Extend research to include other platforms (e.g., Facebook, LinkedIn). ▪ Compare sentiment trends across platforms for broader insights.

Future research can use the extended dataset of tweets in more languages alongside longitudinal data for trend analysis with more preprocessing using context aware and deep learning techniques. Classification performance can be improved using advanced models such as transformers (e.g., BERT) or ensemble learning methods. With extension towards measuring intensity levels and polarity nuances and the topic modeling the key themes and trends in online education discussions, sentiment analysis can be used. Data imbalance can be addressed with augmentation or weighted loss functions, and on top of that, it can be used for real-time sentiment tracking and demographic analysis for providing actionable insights. The study can also be cross nationally and compared cross platform for policy impact with assessment of ethical considerations and public transparency.

REFERENCES

Abdullah, F. B., Iqbal, R., Ahmad, S., El-Affendi, M. A., & Abdullah, M. (2022). An empirical analysis of sustainable energy security for energy policy recommendations. *Sustainability*, *14*(10), 6099.

Abdullah, F. B., Iqbal, R., Ahmad, S., El-Affendi, M. A., & Kumar, P. (2022). Optimization of multidimensional energy security: An index based assessment. *Energies*, *15*(11), 3929.

Ahmad, P. N., Liu, Y., Ali, G., Wani, M. A., & ElAffendi, M. (2023). Robust Benchmark for Propagandist Text Detection and Mining High-Quality Data. *Mathematics*, *11*(12), 2668. Advance online publication. DOI: 10.3390/math11122668

Ahmad, S., Anwar, M. S., Ebrahim, M., Khan, W., Raza, K., Adil, S. H., & Amin, A. (2020). Deep network for the iterative estimations of students' cognitive skills. *IEEE Access : Practical Innovations, Open Solutions*, *8*, 103100–103113. DOI: 10.1109/ACCESS.2020.2999064

Ahmad, S., El-Affendi, M. A., Anwar, M. S., & Iqbal, R. (2022). Potential future directions in optimization of students' performance prediction system. *Computational Intelligence and Neuroscience*, *2022*(1), 6864955.

Ahmad, S., Li, K., Amin, A., Anwar, M. S., & Khan, W. (2018). A multilayer prediction approach for the student cognitive skills measurement. *IEEE Access : Practical Innovations, Open Solutions*, *6*, 57470–57484. DOI: 10.1109/ACCESS.2018.2873608

Ahmad, S., Li, K., Eddine, H. A. I., & Khan, M. I. (2018). A biologically inspired cognitive skills measurement approach. Biologically inspired cognitive architectures, 24, 35-46.

Ahmed, J., & Ahmed, M. (2023). Classification, detection and sentiment analysis using machine learning over next generation communication platforms. *Microprocessors and Microsystems*, *98*, 104795. DOI: 10.1016/j.micpro.2023.104795

Aiman, M. (2024). "Predicting Age and Gender in Author Profiling: A Multi-Feature Exploration,". *Computers, Materials & Continua*, *79*(2), 3333–3353. DOI: 10.32604/cmc.2024.049254

Akhtar, S., Ali, A., Ahmad, S., Khan, M. I., Shah, S., & Hassan, F. (2022). The prevalence of foot ulcers in diabetic patients in Pakistan: A systematic review and meta-analysis. *Frontiers in Public Health*, *10*, 1017201. DOI: 10.3389/fpubh.2022.1017201 PMID: 36388315

Akhtar, S., Ramzan, M., Shah, S., Ahmad, I., Khan, M. I., Ahmad, S., & Qureshi, H. (2022). Forecasting exchange rate of Pakistan using time series analysis. *Mathematical Problems in Engineering*, *2022*(1), 9108580.

Ali, S., Kayani, U., & Yousaf, I. (2024). Time-frequency comovements between news sentiments, Non-fungible tokens, and DeFi assets: Evidence from the wavelet analysis. *Applied Economics*, *0*(0), 1–20. DOI: 10.1080/00036846.2024.2405659

Anwar, M. S., Choi, A., Ahmad, S., Aurangzeb, K., Laghari, A. A., Gadekallu, T. R., & Hines, A. (2024). A Moving Metaverse: QoE challenges and standards requirements for immersive media consumption in autonomous vehicles. *Applied Soft Computing*, *159*, 111577. DOI: 10.1016/j.asoc.2024.111577

Anwar, M. S., Ullah, I., Ahmad, S., Choi, A., Ahmad, S., Wang, J., & Aurangzeb, K. (2023). Immersive learning and AR/VR-based education: cybersecurity measures and risk management. In *Cybersecurity management in education technologies* (pp. 1–22). CRC Press.

Anwar, M. S., Wang, J., Ahmad, S., Khan, W., Ullah, A., Shah, M., & Fei, Z. (2020). Impact of the impairment in 360-degree videos on users VR involvement and machine learning-based QoE predictions. *IEEE Access : Practical Innovations, Open Solutions*, *8*, 204585–204596. DOI: 10.1109/ACCESS.2020.3037253

Anwar, M. S., Wang, J., Ullah, A., Khan, W., Ahmad, S., & Li, Z. (2019, December). Impact of stalling on QoE for 360-degree virtual reality videos. In *2019 IEEE International Conference on Signal, Information and Data Processing (ICSIDP)* (pp. 1-6). IEEE.

Anwar, M. S., Wang, J., Ullah, A., Khan, W., Li, Z., & Ahmad, S. (2018, October). User profile analysis for enhancing QoE of 360 panoramic video in virtual reality environment. In *2018 International Conference on Virtual Reality and Visualization (ICVRV)* (pp. 106-111). IEEE.

Arshad, M., Khan, B., Khan, K., Qamar, A. M., & Khan, R. U. (2024). ABMRF: An Ensemble Model for Author Profiling Based on Stylistic Features Using Roman Urdu. *Intelligent Automation & Soft Computing*, *39*(2), 301–317. DOI: 10.32604/iasc.2024.045402

Dwivedi, Y. K., Ismagilova, E., Hughes, D. L., Carlson, J., Filieri, R., Jacobson, J., Jain, V., Karjaluoto, H., Kefi, H., Krishen, A. S., Kumar, V., Rahman, M. M., Raman, R., Rauschnabel, P. A., Rowley, J., Salo, J., Tran, G. A., & Wang, Y. (2021). Setting the future of digital and social media marketing research: Perspectives and research propositions. *International Journal of Information Management*, *59*, 102168. DOI: 10.1016/j.ijinfomgt.2020.102168

Fatima, R., Samad Shaikh, N., Riaz, A., Ahmad, S., El-Affendi, M. A., Alyamani, K. A., & Latif, R. M. A. (2022). A natural language processing (NLP) evaluation on COVID-19 rumour dataset using deep learning techniques. *Computational Intelligence and Neuroscience*, *2022*(1), 6561622.

Hosni, A. I. E., Li, K., & Ahmad, S. (2019, December). DARIM: Dynamic approach for rumor influence minimization in online social networks. In *International Conference on Neural Information Processing* (pp. 619-630). Cham: Springer International Publishing.

Hosni, A. I. E., Li, K., & Ahmad, S. (2020). Analysis of the impact of online social networks addiction on the propagation of rumors. *Physica A*, *542*, 123456. DOI: 10.1016/j.physa.2019.123456

Hosni, A. I. E., Li, K., & Ahmed, S. (2018). HISBmodel: A rumor diffusion model based on human individual and social behaviors in online social networks. In Neural Information Processing: 25th International Conference, ICONIP 2018, Siem Reap, Cambodia, December 13–16, 2018 [Springer International Publishing.]. *Proceedings*, *25*(Part II), 14–27.

Hosni, A. I. E., Li, K., Ding, C., & Ahmed, S. (2018, November). Least cost rumor influence minimization in multiplex social networks. In *International Conference on Neural Information Processing* (pp. 93-105). Cham: Springer International Publishing.

Hussain, T., Yu, L., Asim, M., Ahmed, A., & Wani, M. A. (2024). Enhancing E-Learning Adaptability with Automated Learning Style Identification and Sentiment Analysis: A Hybrid Deep Learning Approach for Smart Education. *Information (Basel)*, *15*(5), 277. Advance online publication. DOI: 10.3390/info15050277

Khan, B., Naseem, R., Muhammad, F., Abbas, G., & Kim, S. (2020). An empirical evaluation of machine learning techniques for chronic kidney disease prophecy. *IEEE Access : Practical Innovations, Open Solutions*, *8*, 55012–55022. DOI: 10.1109/ACCESS.2020.2981689

Khan, M. I., Qureshi, H., Bae, S. J., Khattak, A. A., Anwar, M. S., Ahmad, S., Hassan, F., & Ahmad, S. (2023). Malaria prevalence in Pakistan: A systematic review and meta-analysis (2006–2021). *Heliyon*, *9*(4), 4. DOI: 10.1016/j.heliyon.2023.e15373 PMID: 37123939

Khan, S., Zhang, Z., Zhu, L., Rahim, M. A., Ahmad, S., & Chen, R. (2020). SCM: Secure and accountable TLS certificate management. *International Journal of Communication Systems*, *33*(15), e4503.

Kovács, E. A., Ország, A., Pfeifer, D., & Benczúr, A. (2024). Generalized Naive Bayes. arXiv preprint arXiv:2408.15923.

Kubara, M., & Kopczewska, K. (2024). Akaike information criterion in choosing the optimal k-nearest neighbours of the spatial weight matrix. *Spatial Economic Analysis*, *19*(1), 73–91. DOI: 10.1080/17421772.2023.2176539

Muliyah, T. P., Aminatun, D., Nasution, S. S., Hastomo, T., & Setiana, S. W. S. (2020). No Title No Title No Title. *J. GEEJ*, *7*(2).

Raees, M., & Fazilat, S. (2024). Lexicon-based sentiment analysis on text polarities with evaluation of classification models. arXiv preprint arXiv:2409.12840.

Rahim, M., Amin, F., Tag Eldin, E. M., Khalifa, A. E. W., & Ahmad, S. (2024). p, q-Spherical fuzzy sets and their aggregation operators with application to third-party logistic provider selection. *Journal of Intelligent & Fuzzy Systems*, *46*(1), 505–528.

Sarro, F., Moussa, R., Petrozziello, A., & Harman, M. (2020). Learning from mistakes: Machine learning enhanced human expert effort estimates. *IEEE Transactions on Software Engineering*, *48*(6), 1868–1882. DOI: 10.1109/TSE.2020.3040793

Semary, N. A., Ahmed, W., Amin, K., Pławiak, P., & Hammad, M. (2024, February). Enhancing machine learning-based sentiment analysis through feature extraction techniques. *PLoS One*, *19*(2). Advance online publication. DOI: 10.1371/journal. pone.0294968 PMID: 38354193

Sun, Z., Wang, G., Li, P., Wang, H., Zhang, M., & Liang, X. (2024). An improved random forest based on the classification accuracy and correlation measurement of decision trees. *Expert Systems with Applications*, *237*, 121549. DOI: 10.1016/j. eswa.2023.121549

Chapter 7
Object Detection Algorithm and Challenges

Lubna Aziz
Iqra University, Karachi, Pakistan

Mansoor Ebrahim
https://orcid.org/0000-0002-2000-8398
Iqra University, Karachi, Pakistan

ABSTRACT

Object detection, a core task in computer vision, involves identifying and localizing objects in images or videos. Recent deep learning advances have significantly improved accuracy and speed. This chapter explores traditional two-stage methods and modern one-stage techniques. The chapter begins by tracing the history of deep learning and its pivotal role in advancing object detection, followed by a discussion of performance metrics used to evaluate detection accuracy and inference time. A detailed examination of the YOLO series, from its inception to the latest iteration, YOLOv8, highlights the architectural innovations and contributions of each version. Additionally, the chapter addresses the significance of backbone networks and benchmark datasets in driving research progress. Key challenges in the field, including scale and class imbalance, are also analyzed. The chapter concludes by identifying recent trends and future research directions, offering a comprehensive resource for understanding the current state and potential applications of object detection technologies.

DOI: 10.4018/979-8-3693-9057-3.ch007

Copyright © 2025, IGI Global Scientific Publishing. Copying or distributing in print or electronic forms without written permission of IGI Global Scientific Publishing is prohibited.

1 INTRODUCTION

Object detection, a core task in computer vision, involves identifying and locating specific objects within images (Everingham et al., 2010). This challenging problem has been a focus of research for decades, with significant advancements driven by deep learning techniques (Mark Everingham, Van Gool, Williams, Winn, & Zisserman, 2010; Russakovsky et al., 2015). Object detection is essential for various applications, including scene understanding, activity recognition, segmentation, tracking, and image captioning. Its applications span fields such as consumer electronics, human-computer interaction, robotics, surveillance, content-based image retrieval, and augmented reality. Deep convolutional neural networks (DCNNs) (G. E. Hinton & Salakhutdinov, 2006; LeCun, Bengio, & Hinton, 2015), combined with the increased availability of GPUs, have played a crucial role in improving object detection performance through automated feature learning.

Deep learning has emerged as the leading method for computer vision tasks, including object detection (Girshick, 2015a; Girshick, Donahue, Darrell, & Malik, 2014; K. He, Zhang, Ren, & Sun, 2015; Ren, He, Girshick, & Sun, 2015). Object detection can be classified into two main categories: instance detection and category detection (Grauman & Leibe, 2011; X. Zhang, Yang, Han, Wang, & Gao, 2013). AlexNet (Krizhevsky, Sutskever, & Hinton, 2017), a ground breaking deep convolutional neural network (DCNN), achieved significant success in the ImageNet Large-Scale Visual Recognition Challenge (ILSVRC) (Russakovsky et al., 2015), establishing a new benchmark for image classification. This breakthrough spurred the adoption of deep learning techniques in various computer vision fields, including general object detection.

2 HISTORY OF DEEP LEARNING

To comprehend deep learning-based object recognition, it's crucial to grasp the fundamental concepts of deep learning, especially convolutional neural networks (CNNs). Deep learning, a branch of artificial intelligence, involves training neural networks with multiple layers to learn intricate patterns from data. The history of neural networks dates back to the 1940s when researchers aimed to replicate the problem-solving abilities of the human brain (Pitts & McCulloch, 1947). While deep learning gained momentum in the late 1980s and 1990s with the development of backpropagation (Rumelhart, Hinton, & Williams, 1988), its popularity declined in the early 2000s due to computational constraints, limited data, and inferior performance compared to other machine learning approaches.

A resurgence of interest in deep learning occurred in 2006, driven by remarkable achievements in speech recognition (G. Hinton et al., 2012). Several factors contributed to this revival:

1. **Abundant Annotated Data:** The availability of extensive labeled datasets, such as ImageNet (J. Deng et al., 2009), has been instrumental in training deep learning models.
2. **Enhanced Hardware:** The development of powerful parallel computing systems, like GPU clusters and TPUs, has significantly accelerated deep learning training.
3. **Innovative Architectures and Training Techniques:** Advanced architectures and training strategies, including Auto-Encoders (L. Deng et al., 2010),, Restricted Boltzmann Machines, dropout regularization, data augmentation, and batch normalization, have addressed challenges like overfitting and computational efficiency.
4. **Landmark Network Architectures:** Architectures such as AlexNet (Krizhevsky, Sutskever, & Hinton, 2012), GoogleNet (Szegedy et al., 2015), VGG (Simonyan & Zisserman, 2014), Overfeat (Sermanet et al., 2013), and ResNet (K. He, Zhang, Ren, & Sun, 2016) have revolutionized deep learning, enabling new levels of performance.

These advancements collectively paved the way for deep learning's remarkable success in various domains, including object recognition.

Convolutional Neural Networks: A Foundation for Deep Learning

Convolutional neural networks (CNNs) are fundamental to deep learning, utilizing a 3D matrix structure with three color channels (RGB) to represent features. This structure, called a feature map, creates a multi-channel image with distinct pixel values signifying specific features. In a CNN layer, each neuron is connected to neighboring neurons in the previous layer.

Filter and pooling operations are essential for extracting robust features (Krizhevsky et al., 2012; Maxime Oquab, Leon Bottou, Ivan Laptev, & Josef Sivic, 2014; Maxime Oquab, Léon Bottou, Ivan Laptev, & Josef Sivic, 2014). Filter transformations are applied to the convolution matrix to determine the associated neuron field estimates. Non-linear activation functions, such as Sigmoid or ReLU (Wadley, 1952), are then used to calculate the final output. Pooling operations, including average, global, L2, max, and local contrast normalization (Kavukcuoglu, Ranzato, Fergus, & LeCun, 2009), enhance feature robustness.

To tackle diverse visual tasks, CNNs integrate convolutional and pooling layers with fully connected layers, establishing a hierarchical feature representation through supervised learning. The output layer utilizes a suitable activation function to calculate the conditional probability of each neuron, tailored to the specific task. Network optimization is commonly achieved using Stochastic Gradient Descent (SGD) in conjunction with objective functions such as mean square error and cross-entropy loss. To handle varying input sizes, image trimming or resizing techniques can be employed.

CNNs offer several benefits compared to traditional approaches:

- **Enhanced Expressiveness:** Deep neural networks, including CNNs, have greater expressive capacity than traditional methods.
- **Automated Feature Learning:** CNNs can learn feature representations directly from data, eliminating the need for manual feature engineering.
- **Superior Performance:** CNNs have consistently demonstrated significant improvements in various computer vision tasks, such as classification and object localization, as exemplified by the Fast R-CNN architecture (Girshick, 2015b).

3 OBJECT DETECTION

Object detection, a cornerstone of computer vision, involves identifying and locating objects within images, enabling comprehensive visual understanding. Traditional methods relied on shallow architectures and handcrafted features, often facing limitations. Deep learning has transformed object detection by enabling automated learning of deep and semantic features. Extracting detailed semantic information from images and videos is a fundamental computer vision task. Generic object detection has broad applications in pedestrian detection (Dollar, Wojek, Schiele, & Perona, 2011; Mateus, Ribeiro, Miraldo, & Nascimento, 2019), skeleton detection (N. Jiang et al., 2019), text recognition (Namysl & Konya, 2019), remote sensing detection (Ma et al., 2019), human behavior analysis (Cao, Simon, Wei, & Sheikh, 2017), face recognition (Yang & Nevatia, 2016), image classification (Jia et al., 2014), medical diagnosis, and autonomous driving (C. Chen, Seff, Kornhauser, & Xiao, 2015; X.

Chen, Ma, Wan, Li, & Xia, 2017). The importance of object detection has fueled significant research interest in recent years (Girshick et al., 2014; Ren et al., 2015).

Object detection, a fundamental task in computer vision, involves pinpointing and locating objects within images or videos. This process facilitates precise object localization, tracking, and counting. However, challenges like occlusion, varying perspectives, scales, orientations, and lighting conditions can impede accurate localization. Traditional object detection approaches typically consist of three main stages: region selection, feature extraction, and classification. Region selection involves identifying potential object locations within the image, often employing techniques such as multi-scale sliding windows, which can be computationally costly and generate redundant regions.

Feature extraction aims to extract robust and semantic visual characteristics of objects. Representative features include SIFT (Lowe, 2004), HOG(Dalal & Triggs, 2005a), and Haar-like features(Lienhart & Maydt, 2002). Manually designing effective feature descriptors can be challenging, especially considering the diverse lighting conditions, variations in appearance, and complex backgrounds.

Classification categorizes the target object among other possibilities. The classification model should be designed to be semantically informative and hierarchical for effective visual recognition. Common classifiers include AdaBoost (Freund & Schapire, 1997), Support Vector Machines (SVM) (Cortes & Vapnik, 1995), and the Deformable Part-Based Model (DPM) (Ren, He, Girshick, Zhang, & Sun, 2016).

The emergence of deep neural networks (DNNs) marked a significant breakthrough in computer vision. R-CNN (LeCun et al., 2015), a pioneering deep learning model, demonstrated the power of CNNs for object detection. Deep neural networks offer several advantages over traditional methods, including deeper architectures, the ability to learn robust features, and various training strategies. These models can automatically learn descriptive representations of objects without manual feature design.

Building upon the foundation of R-CNN, numerous advanced architectures have been developed, including Fast R-CNN (Girshick, 2015b), Faster R-CNN (Ren et al., 2015), and YOLO (Joseph Redmon, Divvala, Girshick, & Farhadi, 2016). These models offer efficient and accurate real-time object detection. Object detection has applications across various domains, including salient object detection (J. Chen et al., 2019; N. Liu, Han, Zhang, Wen, & Liu, 2015),, face detection (D. Chen, Ren, Wei, Cao, & Sun, 2014; H. Jiang & Learned-Miller, 2017), generic object detection (Girshick, 2015b; Girshick et al., 2014; Ren et al., 2015), and pedestrian detection. Salient object detection often employs techniques like local contrast enhancement and pixel-level segmentation. In contrast, generic object detection typically utilizes bounding box regression. While face and pedestrian detection share common geometric features, they present challenges due to complex layouts and variations in appearance. Multi-scale and multi-level feature fusion can effectively address these challenges in generic object detection.

3.1 One Stage /Two-Stage Detector

The sliding window technique has a long history, dating back to the early days of convolutional neural networks for handwritten digit recognition (LeCun et al., 1989; Vaillant, Monrocq, & Le Cun, 1994). While traditional sliding window approaches were effective for tasks such as face and pedestrian detection (Dalal & Triggs, 2005b; Dollár, Tu, Perona, & Belongie, 2009; Viola & Jones, 2001), the resurgence of deep learning has reinvigorated this technique in the field of computer vision. Deep learning-based object detectors can be broadly classified into two main categories: two-stage detectors and one-stage detectors. Figure 2 illustrates key milestones in the field of generic object detection since 2012, showcasing the profound impact of deep learning on this area.

Figure 1. Everyday Applications of Object Detection. Object detection encompasses two primary subfields: generic object detection and salient object detection. These subfields further branch into pedestrian and face recognition. Salient object detection focuses on identifying visually prominent objects within an image, often inspired by human visual attention. Pedestrian detection is crucial for surveillance systems, while face detection is widely used for security applications

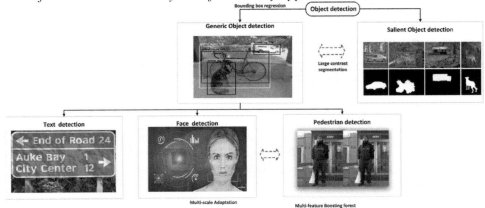

3.1.1 Two-stage detector

Two-stage object detection methods have been a dominant approach in the field. Selective Search (Uijlings, Van De Sande, Gevers, & Smeulders, 2013) pioneered this approach, which comprises two distinct stages: region proposal generation and classification. The region proposal stage seeks to identify a set of candidate regions that enclose potential objects, filtering out negative locations. In the subsequent classification stage, these regions are evaluated to differentiate foreground objects from the background. R-CNN (Girshick et al., 2014) introduced the use of convolutional networks as classifiers in the second stage, leading to substantial accuracy improvements. Subsequent advancements, such as R-CNN variants (Erhan, Szegedy, Toshev, & Anguelov, 2014; Pinheiro, Collobert, & Dollár, 2015; Ren et al., 2015) and learned object proposals [9, 60, 61], further enhanced the speed and accuracy of two-stage detectors. Faster R-CNN (Ren et al., 2015) integrated the region proposal and classification stages into a single convolutional network, known as Region Proposal Networks (RPNs). This approach has inspired numerous extensions and variations (K. He, Gkioxari, Dollár, & Girshick, 2017; K. He et al., 2016; T.-Y. Lin, Dollár, et al., 2017; Shrivastava, Gupta, & Girshick, 2016; Vaillant et al., 1994).

While two-stage detectors have achieved impressive results on various benchmark datasets, they often suffer from slower inference speeds. Notable region proposal models include R-CNN (Girshick et al., 2014), SPP-net (K. He et al., 2015), Fast R-CNN (Girshick, 2015b), Faster R-CNN (Ren et al., 2015), R-FCN (Dai, Li, He, & Sun, 2016), FPN (T.-Y. Lin, Dollár, et al., 2017), and Mask R-CNN (K. He et al., 2017).

Figure 2. Important milestone in field of computer vision, especially generic object detection based on deep learning since 2012. The detector based on region suggestions and the detector based on regression / classification are two main categories of the generic object detector. A list of the two-stage detectors in terms of their time span is displayed in the upper branch, while the lower branch contains the list of single-stage detectors

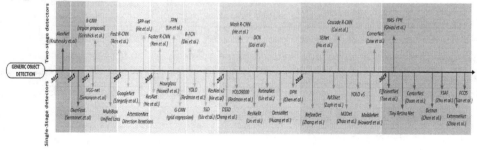

3.1.2 One-stage detector

Single-stage detectors frame object detection as a regression problem, directly predicting bounding box coordinates and class probabilities. Unlike two-stage detectors, they eliminate the separate region proposal step. By analyzing the entire image and classifying each region of interest as either an object or background, single-stage detectors offer a more streamlined approach. . OverFeat (Sermanet et al., 2013) was a pioneering deep network-based single-stage detector. More recently, SSD (Fu, Liu, Ranga, Tyagi, & Berg, 2017; W. Liu et al., 2016) and YOLO (Joseph Redmon et al., 2016; Joseph Redmon & Farhadi, 2017) have gained significant attention due to their speed advantages. Single-stage detectors are particularly attractive for real-time applications, although they may sacrifice some accuracy compared to two-stage detectors.

While two-stage detectors have demonstrated the potential for speed improvements through techniques like reducing input image resolution and the number of proposals [6], single-stage detectors still lag behind in terms of accuracy, despite their computational efficiency. State-of-the-art single-stage detectors include Multibox (Erhan et al., 2014), AttentionNet (Yoo, Park, Lee, Paek, & So Kweon, 2015), G-CNN (Najibi, Rastegari, & Davis, 2016), YOLO (Joseph Redmon et al., 2016), SSD (W. Liu et al., 2016), YOLOv2 (Joseph Redmon & Farhadi, 2017), DSSD (Fu et al., 2017), DSOD (Shen et al., 2017), M2Det (Zhao et al., 2019), RetinaNet (T.-Y. Lin, Goyal, Girshick, He, & Dollár, 2017), Refine-Net (G. Lin, Liu, Milan, Shen, & Reid, 2019). Table 1 provides an overview of key milestones in deep learning-based generic object detection.

4 THE EVOLUTION OF YOLO

4.1 YOLOv1

YOLOv1, a groundbreaking object detection model introduced in 2016 by Joseph Redmon and colleagues, marked a significant advancement in real-time object detection (J Redmon, 2016). Presented at CVPR, YOLOv1 was the first to propose an end-to-end neural network architecture, streamlining the detection process and improving both speed and accuracy. Unlike traditional two-stage methods like Faster R-CNN, YOLOv1 employs a single-shot approach, predicting bounding boxes and class probabilities simultaneously in a single pass. This eliminates the iterative process required by Faster R-CNN, resulting in a more efficient and faster detection pipeline.

YOLOv1, a convolutional neural network (CNN)-based object detector, was evaluated on the PASCAL VOC dataset (Mark Everingham et al., 2015b; J Redmon, 2016). The model extracted features from the input image using convolutional layers and predicted bounding box coordinates and class probabilities using fully connected layers. YOLOv1 employed 24 convolutional layers, each followed by max pooling, and incorporated two fully connected layers. To improve speed, a variant named **Fast YOLO** was introduced. This variant utilized a reduced number of convolutional layers and filters, inspired by GoogleNet's inception module. By employing 1x1 convolutions to reduce the number of channels before 3x3 and 5x5 convolutions, Fast YOLO significantly decreased computational cost and mitigated overfitting. The bounding box coordinates were defined by five components: width (w), height (h), center x-coordinate, center y-coordinate, and confidence score. The confidence score, calculated using Equation, represented the Intersection over Union (IoU) between the predicted bounding box and the ground truth.

$$Confideence\ score = predicted\ (obj) * IoU^{truth}_{predicted}$$

Figure 3. Architecture of YOLOv1 (Vijayakumar, Vairavasundaram, & Applications, 2024)

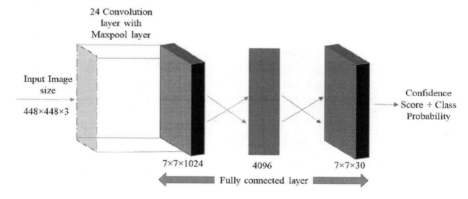

Non-Maximal Suppression (NMS) is utilized in YOLOv1 to tackle the problem of multiple bounding boxes being predicted for the same object. This method optimizes the predictions by retaining only the bounding box with the highest confidence score for each detected object.

The formula for YOLOv1 is expressed as:

$$s * s * (b * 5 + c)$$

In the evaluation on the Pascal VOC dataset, YOLOv1 was tested with specific parameters: b=2b = 2b=2, s=8s = 8s=8, and c=20c = 20c=20. These values are used in the equation:

$$8 * 8 * (2 * 5 + 20) = 8 * 8 * 30$$

Where:

- s is the size of the input image after passing through the convolutional layers.
- b is the number of bounding boxes predicted for each grid cell (which, in this case, is 2).
- c represents the number of object classes, which is 20 in the Pascal VOC dataset.

4.2 YOLO v2

YOLOv2, an enhanced version of YOLOv1, was introduced in 2016 by Joseph Redmon and his team with the aim of improving both speed and accuracy. Initially known as YOLOv2, it was subsequently renamed YOLO9000, reflecting its expanded ability to recognize more than 9,000 object categories (Joseph Redmon & Farhadi, 2017).

YOLOv2 employed a CNN backbone called Darknet-19, which was a more efficient and faster alternative to VGGNet. Darknet-19 primarily utilized 3x3 convolutional layers along with pooling layers, supplemented by 1x1 convolutional layers to compress features. This architecture made Darknet-19 well-suited for the needs of YOLOv2.

In contrast to YOLOv1, which used a 224x224 input size for training and later upsampled to 448x448 for detection, YOLOv2 adopted a 448x448 input size for both training and detection. This adjustment resulted in a 4% improvement in mean Average Precision (mAP) on the ImageNet dataset.

Enhancements in YOLOv2

- **Anchor Boxes**: YOLOv2 introduced the concept of anchor boxes, which are predefined bounding boxes used as templates for detecting objects. By adjusting these anchor boxes through predicted offsets, YOLOv2 can accurately detect objects of different sizes and aspect ratios, adding flexibility to the model.

- **Batch Normalization**: To improve the stability and accuracy of the model, batch normalization was applied across all convolutional layers in YOLOv2. This method acts as a regularization technique, helping to prevent overfitting, especially during multi-scale training, and enhancing the aggregated predictions.
- **Cost Function**: The YOLOv2 cost function integrates three main loss components: localization loss for refining bounding box coordinates, confidence loss for determining the presence or absence of objects, and classification loss to ensure correct categorization of detected objects.
- **Multi-Scale Detection**: YOLOv2 also utilized multi-scale training to increase robustness, where images were resized to various scales during training. The final predictions were made by combining outputs from these different scales.

Figure 4. Anchor Box representation (Vijayakumar et al., 2024)

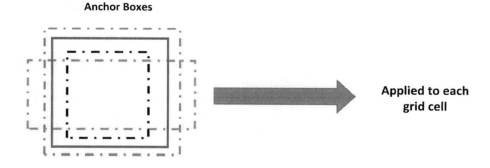

4.3 YOLO v3

YOLOv3, designed as an enhancement over YOLOv2, further improved both speed and accuracy in real-time object detection. A significant advancement in YOLOv3 was its ability to detect smaller objects, achieved through the introduction of skip connections (Furusho, Ikeda, & Processing, 2020),, inspired by ResNet. These connections help mitigate the vanishing gradient issue, allowing the model to capture detailed features more effectively (J. J. a. p. a. Redmon, 2018).

- **Feature Pyramid Network (FPN)**: YOLOv3 incorporated an FPN, which allowed the detection of objects at different scales by merging features from multiple convolutional layers.

- **Bounding Box Prediction**: Like YOLOv2, YOLOv3 predicted bounding box coordinates (tx, ty, tw, th). However, it improved accuracy by applying logistic regression to predict objectness scores for each bounding box.
- **Anchor Box Clustering**: To enhance multi-scale detection, YOLOv3 employed anchor box clustering, optimizing the sizes and aspect ratios of the anchor boxes.

YOLOv3's architecture is structured into three primary components: the backbone, the neck, and the head.

- **Backbone**: The backbone, which typically consists of a convolutional neural network (CNN) with multiple layers, is responsible for extracting key features from the input image or video. It captures a range of features, from simple elements such as edges and textures to more complex features like object parts and semantic details.
- **Neck**: Acting as a bridge between the backbone and the head, the neck integrates a Feature Pyramid Network (FPN) to refine and combine features from the backbone, enhancing the semantic representation of objects at different scales.
- **Head**: The head serves as the final detection layer. It generates the detection results by using the processed features from the backbone and the enhancements made by the neck. To eliminate overlapping bounding box predictions, Non-Maximal Suppression (NMS) is used, ensuring only the most confident detections are kept.

YOLOv3 relies on the Darknet-53 architecture for its backbone. This backbone is composed of 53 convolutional layers, doing away with the pooling layers seen in previous YOLO models. Each layer is followed by batch normalization and a Leaky ReLU activation function to boost performance. Additionally, the detection head adds 53 more layers, bringing the total number of convolutional layers in YOLOv3 to 106.

Figure 5. Configuration of skip connection (Vijayakumar et al., 2024)

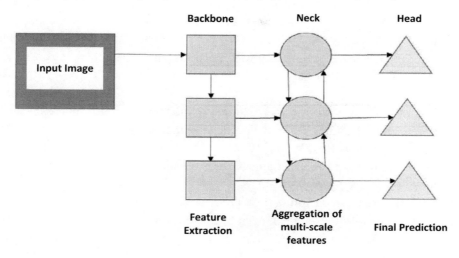

Figure 6. Modern object detection architecture (Vijayakumar et al., 2024)

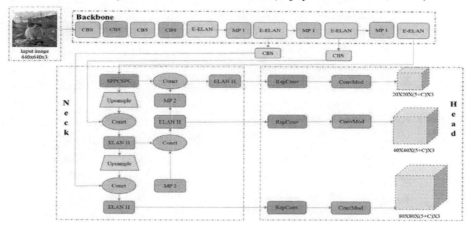

4.4 YOLO v4

YOLOv4, a significant advancement in the YOLO series, was introduced in 2020 by Alexey Bochkovskiy et al. This marked the first update to the YOLO architecture since YOLOv3 (J. J. a. p. a. Redmon, 2018), focusing on enhancing speed and accuracy while preserving the core YOLO principles.

- **Bag of Specials (BoS):** This technique refined the inference process, leading to improved accuracy without significantly increasing computational cost.
- **Bag of Freebies (BoF):** BoF concentrated on data augmentation strategies, exploring different training approaches to enhance performance without affecting inference speed.
- **Self-Adversarial Training (SAT):** SAT involved introducing adversarial perturbations to the input images to make the model more robust to variations and improve its ability to correctly identify objects under challenging conditions.

YOLOv4 Architecture:

- **Backbone:** YOLOv4 (Bochkovskiy, Wang, & Liao, 2020) employed the CSPDarknet-53 architecture as its backbone. Various feature extraction models, such as EfficientNet-B3, CSPDarknet-53, and CSPResNext-50, were experimented with to address the vanishing gradient problem and improve feature representation.
- **Neck:** The neck part of the architecture focused on feature aggregation. The authors explored different techniques, including Path Aggregation Network (PANet) and FPN. PANet, an enhanced version of FPN, utilizes a bottom-up data augmentation path to create fine-grained features. The modified PANet, as shown in Figure 7, employs concatenation instead of addition, leading to improved prediction accuracy.
- **Head:** The head incorporated the CIoU loss function (Zheng et al., 2020), which focuses on the overlap between ground truth and predicted bounding boxes. CIoU emphasizes the importance of overlap while considering the aspect ratio factor.75

YOLOv4 was evaluated on the MS COCO 2017 dataset, achieving an AP_{50} of 65.7% and AP_{75} of 46.6% while maintaining a speed of 50 FPS on a NVIDIA V100 GPU.

Figure 7. Original and Modified version of PANet (Vijayakumar et al., 2024)

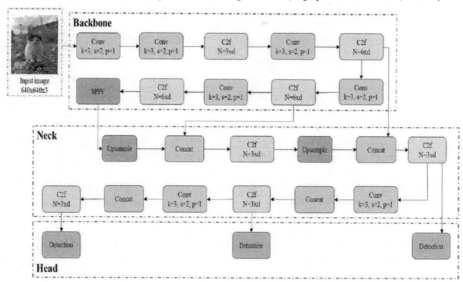

4.5 YOLO v5

YOLOv5, released in 2020, is a significant improvement over YOLOv4. It employs a PyTorch-based architecture, deviating from the Darknet framework used in previous YOLO versions. A key innovation in YOLOv5 is the use of AutoAnchor, an algorithm that optimizes anchor boxes through genetic evolution.

YOLOv5's architecture incorporates SPPF (Spatial Pyramid Pooling Fast), a feature that processes input features at multiple scales. This enhances computational efficiency but also increases the overall network complexity. To maintain feature resolution, upsampling is employed.

The backbone of YOLOv5 utilizes CSPDarknet53, a modified version of the Darknet53 architecture. It incorporates strided convolution with larger window sizes to reduce computational cost. The neck and head components of YOLOv5 incorporate modified CSP-PAN and SPPF, respectively.

To augment the dataset, YOLOv5 leverages various techniques such as mosaic, copy-paste, affine transformations, flipping, HSV augmentation, and mixup (H. J. a. p. a. Zhang, 2017). Each convolutional layer in YOLOv5 includes SiLU activation and batch normalization.

YOLOv5 offers five different versions: YOLOv5n, YOLOv5s, YOLOv5m, YOLOv5l, and YOLOv5x, varying in depth and width. These versions cater to different computational budgets and accuracy requirements.

Developed and maintained by Ultralytics, YOLOv5 is widely used due to its speed and efficiency, particularly compared to previous YOLO versions. Common applications of YOLOv5 include defect detection, vehicle detection, and pedestrian detection.

4.6 YOLO v6

YOLOv6 (H. J. a. p. a.Zhang, 2017), a state-of-the-art object detection model, was introduced by Meituan in September 2022. Designed to meet the demands of real-world applications, YOLOv6 prioritizes high speed and accuracy across various hardware platforms.

The network's architecture comprises CSPStackRep or RepVGG blocks for the backbone, PAN for the neck, and an efficient decoupled head. This design enables YOLOv6 to significantly outperform previous versions in terms of both speed and accuracy.

Similar to YOLOv5, YOLOv6 offers multiple scaled versions ranging from YOLOv6N with fewer parameters and high speed to YOLOv6L with maximum accuracy. By employing an anchor-free approach, YOLOv6 achieves a speed increase of 51% compared to anchor-based methods.

Innovative techniques, such as Rep-PAN and EfficientRep for the neck and backbone, and a decoupled head, contribute to YOLOv6's exceptional performance. Additionally, the model introduces two loss functions: Varifocal Loss (VFL) (H. Zhang, Wang, Dayoub, & Sunderhauf, 2021) for classification and Distribution Focal Loss (DFL) (X. Li et al., 2020) for regression, incorporating SIoU and GIoU.

To optimize detection speed, YOLOv6 utilizes channel-wise distillation (Shu, Liu, Gao, Yan, & Shen, 2021) and RepOptimizer (Ding et al., 2022) for quantization. The model's effectiveness is demonstrated by its evaluation on the MS COCO 2017 dataset, achieving a mean Average Precision (mAP) of 57.2% at 24 frames per second.

Figure 8. Architecture of YOLOv6 (Vijayakumar et al., 2024)

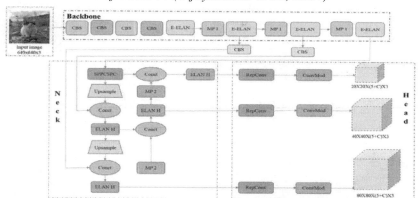

4.7 YOLO v7

YOLOv7 (Ding et al., 2022), a groundbreaking advancement in the realm of real-time object detection, introduces a series of innovative techniques to significantly enhance both speed and accuracy. This paper delves into the architectural enhancements and training strategies that underpin YOLOv7's exceptional performance. By incorporating E-ELAN (H. J. a. p. a. Zhang, 2017) for improved gradient flow, a novel model scaling approach, and a suite of "bag-of-freebies" techniques, YOLOv7 establishes new benchmarks in the field. The demand for efficient and accurate object detection systems has surged in recent years, driving the development of cutting-edge algorithms. YOLOv7, building upon the successes of its predecessors, represents a substantial leap forward in real-time object detection capabilities. This paper provides a comprehensive overview of YOLOv7's architecture and training methodologies, highlighting its key contributions to the field.

YOLOv7 introduces two primary architectural enhancements:

1. **E-ELAN (Extended Efficient Layer Aggregation Network):** E-ELAN builds upon the principles of ELAN, focusing on optimizing gradient flow within the network. By carefully controlling the propagation of information, E-ELAN enables deeper networks to converge more effectively and efficiently. While maintaining the core structure of ELAN, E-ELAN introduces modifications to the computation blocks to enhance model learning without altering the original gradient path.

2. **Model Scaling for Concatenation-Based Models:** YOLOv7 proposes a novel scaling strategy specifically tailored for concatenation-based models. By scaling both depth and width of each block proportionally, this approach preserves the model's structural integrity while reducing computational overhead.

Figure 9. Architecture of YOLOv7 (Vijayakumar et al., 2024)

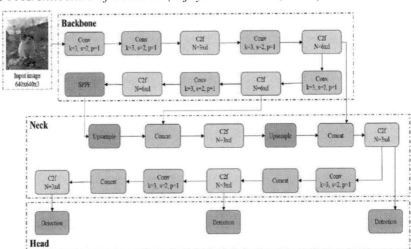

Bag-of-Freebies

YOLOv7 incorporates a collection of training techniques, collectively referred to as "bag-of-freebies," to further boost performance:

1. **Planned Re-parameterized Convolution:** Inspired by re-parameterized convolution (Ding et al., 2021), YOLOv7 introduces a modified approach that avoids the potential negative impact of identity connections on DenseNet and ResNet-like architectures.
2. **Coarse Labels for Auxiliary Head and Fine Labels for Lead Head:** YOLOv7 employs a dual-head architecture, where the auxiliary head provides additional guidance during training while the lead head serves as the final prediction stage.

YOLOv7 demonstrates exceptional performance across various benchmarks, outperforming existing state-of-the-art models in terms of both speed and accuracy. The model's effectiveness is attributed to the synergistic combination of its architectural innovations and training techniques. YOLOv7 represents a significant milestone in real-time object detection. By introducing E-ELAN, a novel model scaling approach, and a suite of "bag-of-freebies," YOLOv7 sets new benchmarks for speed, accuracy, and efficiency. Its contributions have the potential to drive advancements in a wide range of applications, from autonomous vehicles to surveillance systems.

4.8 YOLO v8

YOLOv8, introduced by Ultralytics, represents a cutting-edge model in object detection (**2023, Accessed April 27,2023**). As the successor to YOLOv5, YOLOv8 has gained significant recognition for its outstanding performance and flexibility in various computer vision applications, such as object detection, instance segmentation, and pose estimation. While maintaining the core principles of YOLOv5, YOLOv8 integrates new features, including the C2f module, a convolutional block with cross-stage partial bottlenecks that boosts both feature extraction and computational efficiency (**2023, Accessed April 27,2023**).

In addition to its advancements, YOLOv8 uses an anchor-free detection approach and incorporates a decoupled head architecture, optimizing the processing of classification, localization, and objectness predictions. For bounding box regression, the model utilizes the CIoU loss function (Zheng et al., 2020), and it employs DFL loss for effective classification tasks (X. Li et al., 2020). To further enhance feature extraction and semantic comprehension, YOLOv8 is built on the CSPdarknet53 backbone, leveraging the C2f module to excel in tasks like semantic segmentation.

- **Multiple Backbone Support**: YOLOv8 offers flexibility by providing support for a range of backbone architectures, including CSPDarknet, ResNet, and EfficientNet, enabling users to select the most appropriate model for their specific application requirements.
- **Advanced Data Augmentation**: To improve generalization capabilities, YOLOv8 incorporates sophisticated data augmentation techniques such as CutMix and MixUp, which have been shown to enhance model robustness during training (H. J. a. p. a. Zhang, 2017).
- **Versatile Training Configuration**: YOLOv8 allows for customizable training options, including optimization of learning rates and adjustments to the loss function. These features enable fine-tuning during training, leading to improved performance across various tasks.

In order to assess YOLOv8's real-world applicability, we performed experiments on a dataset of blister tablet packages, consisting of five defect categories: broken tablets, missing tablets, empty pockets, foreign particles, and color mismatch. A subset of 3,529 images was used to train the YOLOv8s model over 50 epochs, utilizing the Stochastic Gradient Descent (SGD) optimizer. Results from these experiments demonstrate the superiority of YOLOv8 in terms of both inference speed and detection accuracy. The normalized confusion matrix, shown in Figure 11, provides insight into the model's performance across the defect classes. In addition, precision, recall, and mAP@0.50 metrics, depicted in Figure 17, underscore the model's high proficiency in accurately detecting and classifying defects. Specifically, YOLOv8s achieved an mAP@0.50 score of 0.97, reflecting its strong ability to localize and identify defects in blister packaging.

4.9 YOLOv9: A Paradigm Shift in Object Detection

YOLOv9 represents a significant advancement in object detection, addressing the limitations of previous approaches (C.-Y. Wang, Yeh, & Liao, 2024). By introducing Programmable Gradient Information (PGI) and the Generalized Efficient Layer Aggregation Network (GELAN), YOLOv9 addresses information bottleneck issues and enhances model efficiency.

PGI provides complete input information for the target task, enabling the calculation of reliable gradient information for network weight updates. This innovative approach mitigates the challenges associated with traditional deep supervision mechanisms, making YOLOv9 applicable to a wider range of architectures, including lightweight models.

GELAN, a novel network architecture, optimizes parameter utilization through its efficient design. By employing conventional convolution operators, GELAN achieves superior performance compared to state-of-the-art depth-wise convolution-based methods. This efficiency, combined with its lightweight nature, makes GELAN well-suited for various inference devices.

The integration of PGI and GELAN in YOLOv9 results in a substantial improvement in object detection performance on the MS COCO dataset. YOLOv9 surpasses existing real-time object detectors in terms of accuracy, while also achieving a significant reduction in parameters and calculations compared to its predecessor, YOLOv8. This demonstrates the effectiveness of YOLOv9's innovative approach and its potential for real-world applications.

Figure 10. Architecture of YOLOv8 (Vijayakumar et al., 2024)

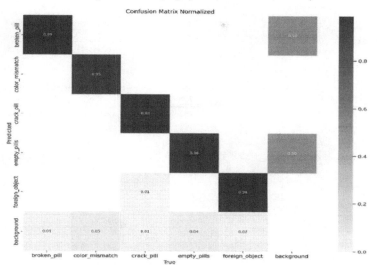

Figure 11. Normalized Confusion matrix (YOLOv8) (Vijayakumar et al., 2024)

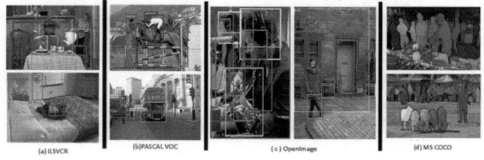

Table 1(a). An outline of the characteristic and performance milestone covered by Generic object detection

Detector	Proposal	Backbone	Input Image	Speed (FPS)	Publish in
R-CNN(Girshick et al., 2014)	Selective search	AlexNet	fixed	<0.1	CVPR-14
SPP-Net(K. He et al., 2015)	EdgeBoxes	ZFNet	Arbitrary	<1	ECCV14
Fast -RCNN(Girshick, 2015b)	Selective Search	AlexNet, VGGM, VGG16	Arbitrary	<1	ICCV15
Faster-RCNN(Ren et al., 2015)	Region proposal Network	ZFNet, VGG	Arbitrary	<5	NIPS15
R- FCN(Dai et al., 2016)	Region proposal Network	ResNet101	Arbitrary	<10	NIPS16
Mask R-CNN(K. He et al., 2017)	Region Proposal Network	ResNet101, ResNeXt101	Arbitrary	<5	ICCV17
FPN(T.-Y. Lin, Dollár, et al., 2017)	Region Proposal Network	--	Arbitrary		
YOLO(Joseph Redmon et al., 2016)	--	GoogLeNet like	Fixed	<25 VGG	CVPR16
SSD(W. Liu et al., 2016)	--	VGG16	Fixed	<60	ECCV16
YOLOv2(Joseph Redmon & Farhadi, 2017)	--	#Darknet	Fixed	<50	CVPR17
DSSD(Fu et al., 2017)		ResNet101	lFixed	<66	---

Table 1(b). An outline of the characteristic and performance milestone covered by Generic object detection

Optimization	Loss Function	Softmax Layer	End- to-end Training	Language	DL/ Plate-form	Remarks
SGD-BP	Hinge loss + BB regression	Yes	X	Matlab	Caffe	**Merits:** region proposal combine with CNN to improved performance **Limitations:** Slow training, sequentially trained multistage pipeline; expensive training phase in term of time and space
SGD	BB regression + Hinge Loss	Yes	X	Matlab	Caffe	**Merits:** SPP based CNN architecture; Convolutional feature map; high in speed as compared to OverFeat; Accelerate RCNN without sacrificing performance **Limitation:** Inherit drawbacks of RCNN; not a significant improve in performance; Conv layer unable to fine-tuning before SPP layer.
SGD	BB regression + ClassLog Loss	Yes	xx	Python	Caffe	**Merits:** improved performance than SPPNet, end-to-end training, Ignoring RP generation; designed RoI pooling layer; No disk storage required. **Limitations:** not feasible for real-time applications; Computation of external RP become a hold-up

continued on following page

Table 1(b). Continued

Optimization	Loss Function	Softmax Layer	End-to-end Training	Language	DL/ Plate-form	Remarks
SGD	Same as above	Yes	Yes	Python/ Matlab	Caffe	**Merits**: Proposed RPN used instead of SS; Introduce multi-scale anchor boxes and translation invariant; CNN layers shared for fast aggregation of RCNN and RPN into a single network; sustain performance and faster than Fast RCNN; with backbone VGG-16 / 5. **Limitation**: complex training; still real-time falls short; not a streamlined process
SGD	Same as above	No	Yes	Matlab	Caffe	**Merits**: Fully Conv detector; a positive set of sensitive score maps are designed using block of specialized CONV layers; faster than Faster RCNN **Limitation**: training phase is not streamlined process and not appropriate for real-time application.
SGD	Semantic Sigmoid loss+ BB regression + ClassLog Loss	Yes	Yes	Matlab/ Python	Tensor-flow/ Keras	**Merits**: Used to generate instance segmentation (additional mask detection branch); boost in performance with FPN. **Limitation**: not suitable for real-time applications.

continued on following page

Table 1(b). Continued

Optimization	Loss Function	Softmax Layer	End- to-end Training	Language	DL/ Plate-form	Remarks
Synchronized SGD	BB Regression + Class Log Loss	Yes	Yes	Python	Tensor-flow	**Merits:** significantly improved over competitive winner and several stable baseline shows in FPN, faster running at 6 to 7 FPS. **Limitation:** Computationally expensive; used of densely sampled image pyramids
SGD	BB regression + (background + object) confidence + Class Sum SquareerrorLoss	Yes	Yes	C	Darknet	**Merits**: improved in speed; primary single stage detector; eliminate RP method; YOLO run at 45 and 155 FPS, respectively. **Limitation:** hardship in detecting tiny objects, compared to other latest detector, its dramatic accuracy fall.
SGD	BB regression + SoftmasLoss	No	Yes	C++/Pythno	Caffe	**Merits:** proposed hybrid approach using multi-scale Conv layers; Faster and significantly more accurate than YOLO; FOS/ 59 FPS. **Limitations:** hardship in detection of small objects

continued on following page

Table 1(b). Continued

Optimization	Loss Function	Softmax Layer	End- to-end Training	Language	DL/ Plate-form	Remarks
SGD	MSE Loss+ BB regression + (object+ background) confidence	No	Yes	C	Darknet	**Merits:** significant improvement in high speed and accuracy; novel DarkNet19 backbone; several existing strategies; YOLO9000 can detect over 9000 object categories in real-time **Limitations:** similar as above
SGD	Combine Softmax loss + localization Loss	No	Yes	Python	Caffe	**Merits:** good in detecting small objects. **Limitation:** computationally expensive

Table 2. Limitations and Performance of YOLO Variants on Object Detection Tasks

Variants of YOLO version	Limitation	Dataset/ mAP	FPS
YOLOv1 (J Redmon, 2016)	- Struggles with detecting small objects in groups. - Limited spatial granularity due to grid and per-cell class restrictions affects detection of densely packed objects. - Poor adaptability to novel aspect ratios and spatial arrangements not covered in training data. - Prone to incorrect localizations.	PASCAL VOC 07/ 63.4%	45
YOLOv2 (Joseph Redmon & Farhadi, 2017)	- YOLO9000's high computational and memory requirements limit its use on resource-constrained devices. - It may struggle with novel or unseen objects not present in its training data, despite covering over 9000 classes. - Performance is highly dependent on hyperparameter choices.	PASCAL VOC 07/ 78.6%	40
YOLOv3 (J. J. a. p. a. Redmon, 2018)	- Increasing the IOU threshold beyond 0.5 makes it difficult for YOLOv3 to align bounding boxes with actual objects. - While using a multi-scale approach with Darknet-53, YOLOv3 struggles with effective cross-scale feature aggregation, limiting fine detail capture. - The logistic loss function in YOLOv3 penalizes only the area difference between predicted and ground truth boxes, not their overlap.	MS COCO / 57.9%	20
YOLOv4 (Bochkovskiy et al., 2020)	- YOLOv4 excels in real-time applications; its accuracy might not be the best for tasks requiring the highest precision - Bag of Freebies (BoF) and Mish activation- These pre-trained weights for the detector training reduces - the accuracy of the detector	MS COCO / 62.8%	38

continued on following page

Table 2. Continued

Variants of YOLO version	Limitation	Dataset/ mAP	FPS
YOLOv5 (G, (2020))	- SPPF loses valuable spatial information compared to SPP, resulting in reduced accuracy, particularly in tasks requiring fine-grained details. - YOLOv5 has limited feature extraction capabilities, suboptimal feature integration, and a restricted receptive field, impacting its target detection performance.	MS COCO / 50.7%	200
YOLOv6 (C. Li et al., 2022)	- SimOTA is used for label assignment, improving training efficiency. - Inference time is faster compared to YOLOv5. - Evaluation is based on the COCO dataset; testing on more diverse, industry-specific objects could highlight generalizability issues.	MS COCO / 43.1%	520
YOLOv7 (H. Zhang et al., 2021)	- The "Trainable bag-of-freebies" approach may risk overfitting, reducing performance on unseen data. - E-ELAN uses group convolutions to boost feature cardinality, potentially adding computational overhead compared to standard convolutions.	MS COCO / 74.4%	36

5 A TRANSFORMER-BASED APPROACH FOR OBJECT DETECTION

5.1 Vision Transformer (ViT)

The success of transformers in natural language processing (NLP) applications (Amjoud & Amrouch, 2021; Rao et al., 2022) has inspired the extension of this architecture to computer vision tasks. In a notable development, Dosovitskiy et al. introduced the Vision Transformer (ViT) (Dosovitskiy, 2020), marking a significant departure from conventional object detection methodologies. Unlike traditional models that combine convolutional neural networks (CNNs) with transformers, ViT employs transformers directly for image processing. The core mechanism of ViT involves partitioning an image into patches, which are linearly embedded and then treated as a sequential input to a transformer encoder. This process is analogous to tokenizing words in NLP, where the patches serve as input tokens. A constant latent vector is used to flatten and map these patches into a fixed-dimensional vector through a learnable projection at each layer of the transformer.

During pre-training, a multi-layer perceptron (MLP) with a single hidden layer is used for classification, which is later replaced by a single-layer classifier during fine-tuning. While the original ViT framework does not explicitly specify a particular loss function (Felzenszwalb, Girshick, McAllester, Ramanan, & intelligence, 2009), the model outputs raw hidden states without a predefined head, making it highly adaptable for a wide range of vision tasks, such as image classification.

5.2 DETR: A Transformer-Based End-to-End Object Detector

The DEtection TRansformer (DETR) (Carion et al., 2020) represents a groundbreaking end-to-end method for object detection, leveraging transformers as its core architecture. DETR combines a pretrained convolutional neural network (CNN) backbone, typically based on ResNet, with a transformer encoder-decoder structure. The CNN backbone extracts low-dimensional image features, which are then augmented with positional encodings before being input into the transformer. Unlike traditional object detectors, DETR eliminates the need for manually designed components such as anchor generation.

In this model, the transformer encoder processes both the image features and positional encodings, while the decoder produces a fixed number of prediction heads. Each head generates a class label and a corresponding bounding box. DETR employs bipartite matching to establish unique correspondences between predicted and ground-truth objects, utilizing a set-based global loss function. This loss consists of both classification and bounding box regression components, ensuring that each object is uniquely identified. By framing object detection as a direct set prediction task, DETR introduces a highly efficient and innovative approach to object detection.

5.3 SMCA: Enhancing DETR Convergence with Spatially Modulated Co-Attention

The Spatially Modulated Co-Attention (SMCA) model (Gao, Zheng, Wang, Dai, & Li, 2021), introduced in 2021, was designed to overcome the slow convergence associated with DETR models, which typically require around 500 training epochs to reach peak performance. SMCA introduced a novel approach to expedite this process by replacing the standard co-attention mechanism in the DETR decoder with a location-aware variant. This modification constrained the co-attention to focus on areas near the initially predicted bounding box locations. The spatial modulation significantly enhanced training efficiency, reducing the number of required epochs to 108, while also delivering superior results. Moreover, SMCA demonstrated the ability to process global information across the image more effectively.

5.4 Swin Transformer: A Shifted Window Approach for Computer Vision

The Swin Transformer (Z. Liu et al., 2021) introduced a novel transformer-based backbone architecture for computer vision tasks. Departing from previous transformer-based models, Swin incorporated the shifted window concept from convolutional neural networks (CNNs). Similar to ViT, Swin initially divides the input image into non-overlapping patches and transforms them into embeddings. However, Swin employs a hierarchical representation, progressively reducing the number of patches across four stages. This contrasts with ViT's single-size patch approach. Swin's key innovation lies in its use of local multi-headed self-attention modules within shifted patch windows. This approach ensures computational efficiency by limiting self-attention calculations to local regions. By alternating shifted windows across blocks, Swin establishes cross-window connections, enhancing feature representation. While Swin utilizes a larger number of parameters compared to convolutional models, its hierarchical structure and efficient attention mechanism contribute to its superior performance in various computer vision tasks.

5.5 Anchor DETR: Enhancing Object Detection with Anchor-Based Queries

Anchor DETR introduced a novel approach to query design in transformer-based object detection by incorporating anchor points (Y. Wang, Zhang, Yang, & Sun, 2021). This innovation addressed the challenge of the lack of explicit physical interpretation in learned object queries, simplifying the optimization process. Inspired by their use in CNN-based detectors, anchor points helped direct object queries toward nearby objects, improving detection accuracy. Anchor DETR also demonstrated the ability to predict multiple objects at a single location. To manage computational complexity, the model employed a Row-Column Decoupled Attention mechanism, reducing memory consumption while maintaining performance. Using ResNet-101 as the backbone, the model achieved an accuracy of 45.1% on the MS-COCO dataset with substantially fewer training epochs compared to DETR.

5.6 DeSTR: Addressing Transformer Limitations for Object Detection

DeSTR (L. He & Todorovic, 2022) introduced a new framework to address several challenges found in existing transformer-based object detection models, particularly in the cross-attention mechanism, self-attention mechanism, and the initialization of decoder content queries. The model proposed the Detection Split Transformer, which separated the content embedding estimation of cross-attention into distinct components for classification and box regression. This specialization enabled each cross-attention module to focus exclusively on its designated task.

For initializing content queries, DeSTR employed a mini-detector designed to learn content embeddings and initialize the positional embeddings for the decoder. This mini-detector included separate heads for classification and regression. Furthermore, to enhance the spatial context in self-attention, DeSTR incorporated spatial information from neighboring queries, thereby improving the overall detection process.

6 BACKBONE CNN NETWORKS

For the first time, the weights of a pre-trained model—initially trained on a large-scale image classification task—were utilized to enhance the performance of an object detector like R-CNN (Girshick et al., 2014), resulting in significantly improved detection accuracy by leveraging higher levels of semantic information. This pre-training strategy has since become a standard practice in most modern object detectors, particularly those employing CNN-based backbone networks. These networks include models such as SENet, VGG-16/19 (Simonyan & Zisserman, 2014), AlexNet (Krizhevsky et al., 2012), ZFNet (Zeiler & Fergus, 2014), GoogLeNet, ResNet (and its variations like ResXNet and ResNet-101), the Inception series (Szegedy, Ioffe, Vanhoucke, & Alemi, 2017), DenseNet, and SENet, as highlighted in Table 3. A detailed survey on the evolution of CNN architectures can be found in (Gu et al., 2018).

Increasing the depth of network layers has become a key factor in achieving robust feature representation, as evidenced by models like AlexNet with eight layers, VGG-16/19 with 16 and 19 layers respectively, and even deeper architectures such as DenseNet and ResNet, which consist of hundreds of layers. While early models like AlexNet (Krizhevsky et al., 2012), ZFNet (Zeiler & Fergus, 2014), and VGG-Net contained large numbers of parameters, most of these originated from fully connected layers despite having fewer layers overall. Recent developments in CNN architectures, such as Inception, ResNet, ResXNet, and DenseNet, have reduced the need for fully connected layers while increasing the overall depth, leading to more efficient models. For instance, the Inception modules in GoogLeNet significantly reduced the number of parameters compared to older models like VGGNet, AlexNet, and ZFNet. ResNet, which won the ILSVRC 2015 classification challenge, introduced residual connections to facilitate the training of very deep networks with hundreds of layers. The Inception-ResNet model (Szegedy et al., 2017) combined these residual connections with the Inception architecture, resulting in a marked improvement in training speed.

Moreover, architectures such as DenseNet, introduced by Huang et al. (Huang, Liu, Van Der Maaten, & Weinberger, 2017), extended the ResNet concept by creating dense connections between layers. Another important advancement is the Squeeze-and-Excitation (SE) block (K. He et al., 2016), designed to enhance existing architectures by recalibrating feature channels in a way that models interdependencies, with minimal computational overhead. This innovation led to winning the ILSVRC 2017 classification task. Research into CNN architectures continues to be a dynamic field, with recent developments including Hourglass (Law & Deng, 2018), Dilated Residual Networks(Yu, Koltun, & Funkhouser, 2017), Xception (Chollet, 2017), DetNet (Z. Li et al., 2018), Dual Path Network (DPN) (Y. Chen et al., 2017), fish-Net (Sun, Pang, Shi, Yi, & Ouyang, 2018), CBNet (Y. Liu et al., 2019), DetNAS (Yukang Chen et al., 2019) and GLoRe(Yunpeng Chen et al., 2019).

Table 3(a). Backbone Framework of DCNN commonly used in Generic object detection

S no	Backbone Framework	No of Parameter $\times 10^6$	CONV+FC (no of layers)
01	AlexNet(Krizhevsky et al., 2012)	57	5+2
02	ZFNet(fast)(Zeiler & Fergus, 2014)	58	5+2
03	OverFeat(Sermanet et al., 2013)	140	6+2
04	VGGNet(Simonyan & Zisserman, 2014)	134	13+2
05	GoogLeNet(Szegedy et al., 2015)	6	22
06	Inception v2(Ioffe & Szegedy, 2015)	12	31
07	Inception v3(Szegedy, Vanhoucke, Ioffe, Shlens, & Wojna, 2016)	22	47
08	YOLONet(Joseph Redmon & Farhadi, 2017)	64	24+1
09	ResNet50(K. He et al., 2016)	23.4	49
10	ResNet101(K. He et al., 2016)	42	100
11	InceptionResNet V1(Szegedy et al., 2017)	21	87
12	InceptionResNet v2(Szegedy et al., 2017)	30	95
13	Inception v4(Szegedy et al., 2017)	41	75
14	ResNeXt(Xie, Girshick, Dollár, Tu, & He, 2017)	23	49
15	DenseNet201(G. Huang et al., 2017)	18	200
16	DarkNet(Joseph Redmon & Farhadi, 2017)	20	19
17	MobileNet(Howard et al., 2017)	3.2	27+1
18	SeResNet(Hu, Shen, & Sun, 2018)	26	50

Table 3(b). Backbone Framework of DCNN commonly used in Generic object detection

Testing Error	First used in	Merits
15.3%	Girshick et al. (Girshick et al., 2014)	First time deep network used for classification; more robust CNN features; win competition the ILSVRC2012.
14.8%	He et al. (K. He et al., 2015)	Different filter size, convolution stride and number of filters like AlexNet
13.6%	Sermanet et al. (Sermanet et al., 2013)	Different filter sizes, no of stride, and number of filters like AlexNet
6.8%	Girshick et al.(Ren et al., 2015)	Stacking of conv filter 3×3 (increase depth)
6.7%	Szegedy et al. (Ioffe & Szegedy, 2015)	First time concatenate the produce feature maps in inception module. Inclusion and global averaging bottleneck.
4.8%	Howard et al.(Howard et al., 2017)	Fast training using Batch normalization
3.6%	--	Inclusion of Separable convolution ad spatial resolution reduction
--	Redmon et al. (Joseph Redmon et al., 2016)	stimulated from GoogLeNet
3.6%	(ResNets) He et al. (K. He et al., 2016)	identity mapping learning
--	He et al.(K. He et al., 2016)	Required fewer parameter as compared to VGG-16; Global average pooling.
3.1%(Ensemble)	--	Faster training process but with computational cost as Inception v3
--	Huang et al. (J. Huang et al., 2017)	Inception version of residual network, significant performance improvement
--	--	No residual connections: A slow Inception-ResNet v2
3.0%	Xie et al(Xie et al., 2017)	Asset of transformation is aggregated in repeated block with the same topology
--	Zhou et al(Y. Zhou, Liu, Shao, & Mellor, 2016)	Feed forward coonection. Parameters reduction, improve the vanishing gradient problem, encourage reuse features.
--	Redmon and Farhadi et al. (Joseph Redmon & Farhadi, 2017)	Lesser no of parameters inspired by VGGNet
--	Howard et al. (Howard et al., 2017)	Lightweight deep CNN (Depth-wise separable convolutions)
2.3%	Hu et al.(Hu et al., 2018)	Squeeze and Excitation block, channel-wise attention

The latest deep architecture of backbone models used in object detection is described in Table 3. Architectural layers, advantages, and properties such as the number of parameters and the test time are explained here.

7 BENCHMARK DATASET

The object recognition application is advancing rapidly with the recent development of the deep learning-based computer vision task. In addition, the need for large amounts of data is controlled in current approaches with a significant improvement in performance. Real-time transaction performance is improved using end-to-end pipelines in modern development techniques. In addition, data is very important, whether it is used to solve complex or challenging problems, or to compare and measure performance against other algorithms. The success of using deep learning techniques in object recognition relies primarily on the availability of large, annotated data. The Internet take part an important role in structuring an inclusive dataset to allow admittance in a variety of images that cover the expanse and variety of objects.

The entire era of deep learning-based generic object recognition includes five famous benchmark data sets such as PASCAL VOC 2007 (Mark Everingham, Van Gool, Williams, Winn, & Zisserman, 2007), PASCAL VOC2012(M Everingham, Van Gool, Williams, Winn, & Zisserman, 2011), ImageNet (J. Deng et al., 2009), Microsoft COCO (T.-Y. Lin et al., 2014) and OpenImages(Krasin et al., 2017). Some specific images from the standard dataset shown in Figure 12 and Table 4 outline the attributes and the measurement of these datasets, while Figure 13 shows the categories of benchmark dataset. A large amount of financial support is required to create a massively interpreted data set. Firstly, define the categories of target objects, secondly, the internet source is used to collect series of images with different dimensions of categories, and finally to comment on the collected images. Each dataset has its own identification challenges, including the interpretation of generally available datasets, standardized assessment software, a yearly competition, and workshops. Statistical details such as image set, training pattern, validation and test set of this data set are explained in Table 5.

Table 4(a). Benchmark Generic Object Detection Databases

S/ no	Benchmark Dataset	Ref	Image quantity	Size
1	PASCAL VOC (2007/ 2012)	(M Everingham et al., 2011; Mark Everingham et al., 2007)	11,540	470x380
2	ImageNet (2015)	(J. Deng et al., 2009)	14,197,122	500x400
3	MS COCO (2014)	(T.-Y. Lin et al., 2014)	328,000+	640 x 480
4	Place (2017)	(B. Zhou, Lapedriza, Khosla, Oliva, & Torralba, 2017)	10 million+	256 x 256
5	Open Images (2019)	(Kuznetsova et al., 2018)	9 million+	Varying

Table 4(b). Benchmark Generic Object Detection Databases

Class Category	Images per category	Objects / image	Begin	Remarks
20	303-4087	2.4	2005	20 categories (Daily life); real- world training images; single image with multiple objects; scene images; Intra-class variations and complex sample
21,841	—	1.5	2010	WordNet hierarchy; single image with more instance and objects; ILSVRC challenged benchmark; Object- centric images
91	--	7.3	2014	Real-world scenes with multiple objects in each image, fully annotated; objects segmentation
434	_--_	—	2014	Scenes recognition annotated dataset with standards 365 places and 365 challenging places; four subsets
6000+	—	8.3	2017	Open Images v5; visual relationship detection and instance segmentation

Computer vision task uses four benchmark dataset such as MS COCO, PASCAL, OpenImage, and ILSVRC that are demonstrated in Table 4.

Table 5. Object detection datasets statistics

challenge	Object categories	Total images			Annotated objects		Training + Val set		
		Train set	Val set	Test set	Train- set	Val-set	Instance	Boxes	Per image boxes
Object detection challenge PASCAL VOC:									
VOC07		2501	2501	4952	6301	6307	5011	12608	2.5
VOC08		2111	2221	4133	5082	5281	4332	10364	2.4
VOC09	20	3473	3581	6650	8505	8713	7054	17218	2.3
VOC10		4998	5105	9637	11577	11797	10103	23374	2.4
VOC11		5717	5823	10,994	13609	13841	11540	27450	2.4
VOC12		5717	5823	10,991	13609	13841	11540	27450	2.4
Object detection challenge ILSVRC:									
ILSVRC13		395909		40152	345854		416030	401356	1
ILSVRC14		456567		40152	478807		476668	534309	1.1
ILSVRC15	200	456567	20121	51294	478807	55502	476668	534309	1.1
ILSVRC16		456567		60000	478807		476668	534309	1.1
ILSVRC17		456567		65500	478807		476668	534309	1.1
Object detection challenge MSCOCO:									

continued on following page

Table 5. Continued

challenge	Object categories	Total images			Annotated objects		Training + Val set		
		Train set	Val set	Test set	Train- set	Val-set	Instance	Boxes	Per image boxes
Object detection challenge PASCAL VOC:									
MSCOCO15		82783	40504	81343	604907	291875			
MSCOCO16	80	82783	40504	81434	604907	291875	123287	896782	7.3
MSCOCO17		118287	5000	40670	860001	36781			
MSCOCO18		118287	5000	40670	860001	36781			
Open images challenge object detection(OICOD):									
OICOD18	500	1643042	100000	99999	11498734	696410	1743042	12195144	7

7.1 PASCAL VOC 2007/2012

The field of object classification and recognition has witnessed a steady progression, marked by the introduction of numerous datasets and annual competitions to evaluate algorithm performance (Mark Everingham et al., 2015a; Mark Everingham et al., 2010). Initiated in 2005 with five object categories, these datasets have expanded to encompass twenty everyday object categories by 2009. The number of images within these datasets has consistently grown since then, facilitating year-over-year result comparisons. While these datasets played a pivotal role in driving advancements, the emergence of larger and more comprehensive benchmarks like MS COCO, ImageNet, and OpenImage has gradually diminished their popularity. The performance of object recognition algorithms is typically evaluated using Average Accuracy (AP) for each category, with mean average accuracy (mAP) serving as a comprehensive metric across all twenty classes.

7.2 ILSVRC (ImageNet Large Scale Visual Recognition Challenge)

Russakovsky et al. introduced ImageNet (J. Deng et al., 2009), a comprehensive dataset designed specifically for object detection tasks. Building upon the PASCAL VOC 07/12 dataset, ImageNet expanded the number of object categories to 1000, encompassing a diverse range of everyday objects. With over 1.2 million images, ImageNet 1000 provides a substantial resource for training and evaluating object detection algorithms. The dataset adheres to the same standards as the ILSVRC image classification challenge, ensuring consistency and comparability of results.

7.3 Microsoft COCO

Lin et al. (T.-Y. Lin et al., 2014) introduced the MS COCO (Microsoft Common Objects in COntext) dataset, designed to facilitate a deeper understanding of natural images through object recognition. To evaluate recognition performance, objects within the dataset are meticulously annotated with fully segmented instances. MS COCO comprises 300,000 fully segmented images, encompassing 80 object categories with an average of seven objects per image. The dataset's complexity stems from the inclusion of less iconic objects, challenging occlusions, and diverse scaling and rotation variations, demanding accurate object localization (Singh & Davis, 2018). To assess the performance of object detectors, average precision is calculated at different Intersection over Union (IoU) thresholds and for varying object sizes. This comprehensive evaluation approach ensures a thorough assessment of detector cap labilities.

7.4 The Open Image Challenge Object Detection (OICOD)

OICOD, derived from OpenImage v4 (currently version 5 in 2019) (Kuznetsova et al., 2018), stands as the largest publicly accessible dataset in this domain. It surpasses previous benchmarks like MS COCO and ILSVRC in terms of image quantity, class categories, bounding boxes, and segmentation masks. OICOD's unique approach involves human review of annotations, ensuring high-quality labels. This distinguishes it from other datasets that rely solely on fully annotated records. In contrast to MS COCO and ILSVRC, OICOD only considers human-confirmed positive annotations.

Figure 12. The illustration shows images from PASCAL VOC 07/12, MS COCO, OpenImages and ILSVCR. In contrast to MS COCO with JSON file, PASCAL VOC has an XML file. A separate file is generated for each image in PASCAL VOC. While developing single file for training, testing and validation in MS COCO. Both datasets have a different format for BB data. The OpenImages dataset contains approximately 9 million images that are annotated at the image level

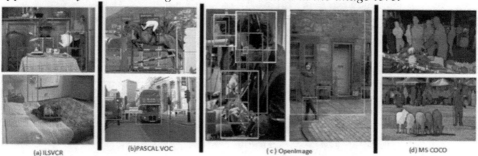

Figure 13. Object Detection challenge with the most frequent object classes. The frequency of each class in the training data set is reflected in the font size of the class name

(a) PACSAL VOC (20 classes)   (b) MS COCO (80 classes)

(c) ILSVRC (200 classes)

(d) Open Images Detection Challenge (500 classes)

218

8 CHALLENGES FACES IN GENERIC OBJECT DETECTION

Ideal generic object recognition systems strive to achieve two primary objectives: high efficiency and high accuracy. Efficiency demands minimal storage and memory requirements to enable real-time operation. Simultaneously, high accuracy necessitates precise localization and recognition of objects within images or videos.

8.1 Intra-Class Variations and Imaging Conditions

Object recognition faces two primary challenges: intra-class variations and the diversity of object categories. Intra-class variations arise from intrinsic factors and imaging conditions. Intrinsic factors encompass differences in material types, color, texture, poses, shapes, sizes, and non-rigid deformations within object categories. Imaging conditions are influenced by external factors like lighting, atmospheric conditions, physical positioning, camera models, viewing distance, illumination, occlusion, and background. Several intra-class factors, including movement, occlusion, shading, lighting, blurring, clutter, scaling, and pose, contribute to variations in object appearance. Additionally, low resolution, noise, digitization artifacts, and filter distortion can hinder detection tasks, as depicted in Figure 14. Current object detectors primarily concentrate on structured object categories, such as the 20 categories in PASCAL VOC (Mark Everingham et al., 2010), the 200 types in ILSVRC (Russakovsky et al., 2015), and the 91 classes in MS COCO (T.-Y. Lin et al., 2014, (Hosni et al., 2018; Anwar et al., 2018; Hosni et al., 2019; Anwar et al., 2024; Ahmad et al., 2022; Akhtar et al., 2022; Ahmad et al., 2018; Abdullah et al., 2022; Anwar et al., 2023; Akhtar et al., 2022)).

8.2 Efficiency Considerations for Object Recognition

The increasing prevalence of mobile and wearable devices, coupled with the growing demand for visual data analysis, has underscored the need for efficient object recognition on resource-constrained platforms. Limited computing power and storage capacity necessitate optimization for portable devices. Challenges such as distractions in individual images, variations in object positions and categories, and the need for high data rate processing in dynamic environments demand advanced object detectors. The growth of images and categories has rendered manual annotation impractical, necessitating automated and scalable annotation schemes.

Figure 14. There are significant differences in image status because of variations in appearance of the same class (a, h) such as atmospheric conditions, lighting effect, occlusion, camera models, physical locations and viewing distance. other challenges arise from variations in pose, shading, blur, clutter, movement, shading, occlusion, and scale. The intra-class variation instances are shown in (i). In contrast, the cases in (j) have some examples of intermediate classes - most of the images from ImageNet (Russakovsky et al., 2015) and MS COCO (T.-Y. Lin et al., 2014)

REFERENCES

Abdullah, F. B., Iqbal, R., Ahmad, S., El-Affendi, M. A., & Abdullah, M. (2022). An empirical analysis of sustainable energy security for energy policy recommendations. *Sustainability*, *14*(10), 6099.

Ahmad, S., El-Affendi, M. A., Anwar, M. S., & Iqbal, R. (2022). Potential future directions in optimization of students' performance prediction system. *Computational Intelligence and Neuroscience*, *2022*(1), 6864955.

Ahmad, S., Li, K., Eddine, H. A. I., & Khan, M. I. (2018). A biologically inspired cognitive skills measurement approach. Biologically inspired cognitive architectures, 24, 35-46.

Akhtar, S., Ali, A., Ahmad, S., Khan, M. I., Shah, S., & Hassan, F. (2022). The prevalence of foot ulcers in diabetic patients in Pakistan: A systematic review and meta-analysis. *Frontiers in Public Health*, *10*, 1017201. DOI: 10.3389/fpubh.2022.1017201 PMID: 36388315

Akhtar, S., Ramzan, M., Shah, S., Ahmad, I., Khan, M. I., Ahmad, S., & Qureshi, H. (2022). Forecasting exchange rate of Pakistan using time series analysis. *Mathematical Problems in Engineering*, *2022*(1), 9108580.

Amjoud, A. B., & Amrouch, M. (2021). *Automatic generation of chest x-ray reports using a transformer-based deep learning model.* Paper presented at the 2021 Fifth International Conference On Intelligent Computing in Data Sciences (ICDS). DOI: 10.1109/ICDS53782.2021.9626725

Anwar, M. S., Choi, A., Ahmad, S., Aurangzeb, K., Laghari, A. A., Gadekallu, T. R., & Hines, A. (2024). A Moving Metaverse: QoE challenges and standards requirements for immersive media consumption in autonomous vehicles. *Applied Soft Computing*, *159*, 111577. DOI: 10.1016/j.asoc.2024.111577

Anwar, M. S., Ullah, I., Ahmad, S., Choi, A., Ahmad, S., Wang, J., & Aurangzeb, K. (2023). Immersive learning and AR/VR-based education: cybersecurity measures and risk management. In *Cybersecurity management in education technologies* (pp. 1–22). CRC Press.

Anwar, M. S., Wang, J., Ullah, A., Khan, W., Li, Z., & Ahmad, S. (2018, October). User profile analysis for enhancing QoE of 360 panoramic video in virtual reality environment. In *2018 International Conference on Virtual Reality and Visualization (ICVRV)* (pp. 106-111). IEEE.

Bochkovskiy, A., Wang, C.-Y., & Liao, H.-Y. M. J. a. p. a. (2020). Yolov4: Optimal speed and accuracy of object detection.

Cao, Z., Simon, T., Wei, S.-E., & Sheikh, Y. (2017). *Realtime multi-person 2d pose estimation using part affinity fields.* Paper presented at the Proceedings of the IEEE Conference on Computer Vision and Pattern Recognition. DOI: 10.1109/CVPR.2017.143

Carion, N., Massa, F., Synnaeve, G., Usunier, N., Kirillov, A., & Zagoruyko, S. (2020). *End-to-end object detection with transformers.* Paper presented at the European conference on computer vision.

Chen, C., Seff, A., Kornhauser, A., & Xiao, J. (2015). *Deepdriving: Learning affordance for direct perception in autonomous driving.* Paper presented at the Proceedings of the IEEE International Conference on Computer Vision. DOI: 10.1109/ICCV.2015.312

Chen, D., Ren, S., Wei, Y., Cao, X., & Sun, J. (2014). *Joint cascade face detection and alignment.* Paper presented at the European Conference on Computer Vision.

Chen, J., Li, Q., Wu, W., Ling, H., Wu, L., Zhang, B., & Li, P. (2019). *Saliency Detection via Topological Feature Modulated Deep Learning.* Paper presented at the 2019 IEEE International Conference on Image Processing (ICIP). DOI: 10.1109/ICIP.2019.8802611

Chen, X., Ma, H., Wan, J., Li, B., & Xia, T. (2017). *Multi-view 3d object detection network for autonomous driving.* Paper presented at the Proceedings of the IEEE Conference on Computer Vision and Pattern Recognition. DOI: 10.1109/CVPR.2017.691

Chen, Y., Li, J., Xiao, H., Jin, X., Yan, S., & Feng, J. (2017). *Dual path networks.* Paper presented at the Advances in neural information processing systems.

Chen, Y., Rohrbach, M., Yan, Z., Shuicheng, Y., Feng, J., & Kalantidis, Y. (2019). *Graph-based global reasoning networks.* Paper presented at the Proceedings of the IEEE Conference on Computer Vision and Pattern Recognition.

Chen, Y., Yang, T., Zhang, X., Meng, G., Xiao, X., & Sun, J. (2019). *DetNAS: Backbone search for object detection.* Paper presented at the Advances in neural information processing systems.

Chollet, F. (2017). *Xception: Deep learning with depthwise separable convolutions.* Paper presented at the Proceedings of the IEEE conference on computer vision and pattern recognition. DOI: 10.1109/CVPR.2017.195

Cortes, C., & Vapnik, V. (1995). Support vector machine. *Machine Learning*, *20*(3), 273–297. DOI: 10.1007/BF00994018

Dai, J., Li, Y., He, K., & Sun, J. (2016). *R-fcn: Object detection via region-based fully convolutional networks.* Paper presented at the Advances in neural information processing systems.

Dalal, N., & Triggs, B. (2005a). *Histograms of oriented gradients for human detection.*

Dalal, N., & Triggs, B. (2005b). *Histograms of oriented gradients for human detection.* Paper presented at the 2005 IEEE computer society conference on computer vision and pattern recognition (CVPR'05). DOI: 10.1109/CVPR.2005.177

Deng, J., Dong, W., Socher, R., Li, L.-J., Li, K., & Fei-Fei, L. (2009). *Imagenet: A large-scale hierarchical image database.* Paper presented at the 2009 IEEE conference on computer vision and pattern recognition. DOI: 10.1109/CVPR.2009.5206848

Deng, L., Seltzer, M. L., Yu, D., Acero, A., Mohamed, A.-r., & Hinton, G. (2010). *Binary coding of speech spectrograms using a deep auto-encoder.* Paper presented at the Eleventh Annual Conference of the International Speech Communication Association. DOI: 10.21437/Interspeech.2010-487

Ding, X., Chen, H., Zhang, X., Huang, K., Han, J., & Ding, G. J. a. p. a. (2022). Re-parameterizing your optimizers rather than architectures.

Ding, X., Zhang, X., Ma, N., Han, J., Ding, G., & Sun, J. (2021). *Repvgg: Making vgg-style convnets great again.* Paper presented at the Proceedings of the IEEE/CVF conference on computer vision and pattern recognition.

Dollár, P., Tu, Z., Perona, P., & Belongie, S. (2009). Integral channel features.

Dollar, P., Wojek, C., Schiele, B., & Perona, P. (2011). Pedestrian detection: An evaluation of the state of the art. *IEEE Transactions on Pattern Analysis and Machine Intelligence*, *34*(4), 743–761. DOI: 10.1109/TPAMI.2011.155 PMID: 21808091

Dosovitskiy, A. J. a. p. a. (2020). An image is worth 16x16 words: Transformers for image recognition at scale.

Erhan, D., Szegedy, C., Toshev, A., & Anguelov, D. (2014). *Scalable object detection using deep neural networks.* Paper presented at the Proceedings of the IEEE conference on computer vision and pattern recognition. DOI: 10.1109/CVPR.2014.276

Everingham, M., Eslami, S. A., Van Gool, L., Williams, C. K., Winn, J., & Zisserman, A. (2015a). The pascal visual object classes challenge: A retrospective. *International Journal of Computer Vision*, *111*(1), 98–136. DOI: 10.1007/s11263-014-0733-5

Everingham, M., Eslami, S. A., Van Gool, L., Williams, C. K., Winn, J., & Zisserman, A. J. I. j. o. c. v. (2015b). The pascal visual object classes challenge: A retrospective. *111*, 98-136.

Everingham, M., Van Gool, L., Williams, C., Winn, J., & Zisserman, A. (2011). *The pascal visual object classes challenge 2012 (voc2012) results (2012).* Paper presented at the URL http://www. pascal-network. org/challenges/VOC/voc2011/ workshop/index. html

Everingham, M., Van Gool, L., Williams, C. K., Winn, J., & Zisserman, A. (2007). The PASCAL visual object classes challenge 2007 (VOC2007) results.

Everingham, M., Van Gool, L., Williams, C. K., Winn, J., & Zisserman, A. (2010). The pascal visual object classes (voc) challenge. *International Journal of Computer Vision, 88*(2), 303–338. DOI: 10.1007/s11263-009-0275-4

Felzenszwalb, P. F., Girshick, R. B., McAllester, D., Ramanan, D. J. I. t. o. p. a., & intelligence, m. (2009). Object detection with discriminatively trained part-based models. *32*(9), 1627-1645.

Freund, Y., & Schapire, R. E. (1997). A decision-theoretic generalization of on-line learning and an application to boosting. *Journal of Computer and System Sciences, 55*(1), 119–139. DOI: 10.1006/jcss.1997.1504

Fu, C.-Y., Liu, W., Ranga, A., Tyagi, A., & Berg, A. C. (2017). Dssd: Deconvolutional single shot detector. *arXiv preprint arXiv:1701.06659.*

Furusho, Y., Ikeda, K. J. A. T. o. S., & Processing, I. (2020). Theoretical analysis of skip connections and batch normalization from generalization and optimization perspectives. *9*, e9.

Gao, P., Zheng, M., Wang, X., Dai, J., & Li, H. (2021). *Fast convergence of detr with spatially modulated co-attention.* Paper presented at the Proceedings of the IEEE/CVF international conference on computer vision. DOI: 10.1109/ICCV48922.2021.00360

Girshick, R. (2015a). *Fast r-cnn.* Paper presented at the Proceedings of the IEEE international conference on computer vision.

Girshick, R. (2015b). *Fast R-CNN ICCV.* Paper presented at the 15Proceedings of the 2015 IEEE International Conference on Computer Vision (ICCV).

Girshick, R., Donahue, J., Darrell, T., & Malik, J. (2014). *Rich feature hierarchies for accurate object detection and semantic segmentation.* Paper presented at the Proceedings of the IEEE conference on computer vision and pattern recognition. DOI: 10.1109/CVPR.2014.81

Grauman, K., & Leibe, B. (2011). Visual object recognition. *Synthesis lectures on artificial intelligence and machine learning, 5*(2), 1-181.

Gu, J., Wang, Z., Kuen, J., Ma, L., Shahroudy, A., Shuai, B., & Cai, J. (2018). Recent advances in convolutional neural networks. *Pattern Recognition, 77,* 354–377. DOI: 10.1016/j.patcog.2017.10.013

He, K., Gkioxari, G., Dollár, P., & Girshick, R. (2017). *Mask r-cnn.* Paper presented at the Proceedings of the IEEE international conference on computer vision.

He, K., Zhang, X., Ren, S., & Sun, J. (2015). Spatial pyramid pooling in deep convolutional networks for visual recognition. *IEEE Transactions on Pattern Analysis and Machine Intelligence, 37*(9), 1904–1916. DOI: 10.1109/TPAMI.2015.2389824 PMID: 26353135

He, K., Zhang, X., Ren, S., & Sun, J. (2016). *Deep residual learning for image recognition.* Paper presented at the Proceedings of the IEEE conference on computer vision and pattern recognition.

He, L., & Todorovic, S. (2022). *Destr: Object detection with split transformer.* Paper presented at the Proceedings of the IEEE/CVF conference on computer vision and pattern recognition.

Hinton, G., Deng, L., Yu, D., Dahl, G., Mohamed, A.-r., Jaitly, N., & Kingsbury, B. (2012). Deep neural networks for acoustic modeling in speech recognition. *IEEE Signal Processing Magazine,* ●●●, 29.

Hinton, G. E., & Salakhutdinov, R. R. (2006). Reducing the dimensionality of data with neural networks. *Science, 313*(5786), 504–507. DOI: 10.1126/science.1127647 PMID: 16873662

Hosni, A. I. E.. "Least cost rumor influence minimization in multiplex social networks." *International Conference on Neural Information Processing.* Cham: Springer International Publishing, 2018. DOI: 10.1007/978-3-030-04224-0_9

Hosni, A. I. E., Li, K., & Ahmad, S. "DARIM: Dynamic approach for rumor influence minimization in online social networks." *International Conference on Neural Information Processing.* Cham: Springer International Publishing, 2019. DOI: 10.1007/978-3-030-36711-4_52

Howard, A. G., Zhu, M., Chen, B., Kalenichenko, D., Wang, W., Weyand, T., . . . Adam, H. (2017). Mobilenets: Efficient convolutional neural networks for mobile vision applications. *arXiv preprint arXiv:1704.04861.*

Hu, J., Shen, L., & Sun, G. (2018). *Squeeze-and-excitation networks.* Paper presented at the Proceedings of the IEEE conference on computer vision and pattern recognition.

Huang, G., Liu, Z., Van Der Maaten, L., & Weinberger, K. Q. (2017). *Densely connected convolutional networks.* Paper presented at the Proceedings of the IEEE conference on computer vision and pattern recognition.

Huang, J., Rathod, V., Sun, C., Zhu, M., Korattikara, A., Fathi, A., . . . Guadarrama, S. (2017). *Speed/accuracy trade-offs for modern convolutional object detectors.* Paper presented at the Proceedings of the IEEE conference on computer vision and pattern recognition. DOI: 10.1109/CVPR.2017.351

Ioffe, S., & Szegedy, C. (2015). Batch normalization: Accelerating deep network training by reducing internal covariate shift. *arXiv preprint arXiv:1502.03167.*

Jia, Y., Shelhamer, E., Donahue, J., Karayev, S., Long, J., Girshick, R., . . . Darrell, T. (2014). *Caffe: Convolutional architecture for fast feature embedding.* Paper presented at the Proceedings of the 22nd ACM international conference on Multimedia. DOI: 10.1145/2647868.2654889

Jiang, H., & Learned-Miller, E. (2017). *Face detection with the faster R-CNN.* Paper presented at the 2017 12th IEEE International Conference on Automatic Face & Gesture Recognition (FG 2017). DOI: 10.1109/FG.2017.82

Jiang, N., Zhang, Y., Luo, D., Liu, C., Zhou, Y., & Han, Z. (2019). *Feature hourglass network for skeleton detection.* Paper presented at the Proceedings of the IEEE Conference on Computer Vision and Pattern Recognition Workshops.

Kavukcuoglu, K., Ranzato, M. A., Fergus, R., & LeCun, Y. (2009). *Learning invariant features through topographic filter maps.* Paper presented at the 2009 IEEE Conference on Computer Vision and Pattern Recognition. DOI: 10.1109/CVPR.2009.5206545

Krasin, I., Duerig, T., Alldrin, N., Ferrari, V., Abu-El-Haija, S., Kuznetsova, A., . . . Veit, A. (2017). Openimages: A public dataset for large-scale multi-label and multi-class image classification. *Dataset available from https://github. com/open-images, 2,* 3.

Krizhevsky, A., Sutskever, I., & Hinton, G. E. (2012). *Imagenet classification with deep convolutional neural networks.* Paper presented at the Advances in neural information processing systems.

Krizhevsky, A., Sutskever, I., & Hinton, G. E. (2017). Imagenet classification with deep convolutional neural networks. *Communications of the ACM, 60*(6), 84–90. DOI: 10.1145/3065386

Kuznetsova, A., Rom, H., Alldrin, N., Uijlings, J., Krasin, I., Pont-Tuset, J., . . . Duerig, T. (2018). The open images dataset v4: Unified image classification, object detection, and visual relationship detection at scale. *arXiv preprint arXiv:1811.00982.*

Law, H., & Deng, J. (2018). *Cornernet: Detecting objects as paired keypoints.* Paper presented at the Proceedings of the European Conference on Computer Vision (ECCV).

LeCun, Y., Bengio, Y., & Hinton, G. (2015). Deep learning. *Nature, 521*(7553), 436–444. DOI: 10.1038/nature14539 PMID: 26017442

LeCun, Y., Boser, B., Denker, J. S., Henderson, D., Howard, R. E., Hubbard, W., & Jackel, L. D. (1989). Backpropagation applied to handwritten zip code recognition. *Neural Computation, 1*(4), 541–551. DOI: 10.1162/neco.1989.1.4.541

Li, C., Li, L., Jiang, H., Weng, K., Geng, Y., Li, L., . . . Nie, W. J. a. p. a. (2022). YOLOv6: A single-stage object detection framework for industrial applications.

Li, X., Wang, W., Wu, L., Chen, S., Hu, X., Li, J., . . . Yang, J. J. A. i. N. I. P. S. (2020). Generalized focal loss: Learning qualified and distributed bounding boxes for dense object detection. *33*, 21002-21012.

Li, Z., Peng, C., Yu, G., Zhang, X., Deng, Y., & Sun, J. (2018). Detnet: A backbone network for object detection. *arXiv preprint arXiv:1804.06215.*

Lienhart, R., & Maydt, J. (2002). *An extended set of haar-like features for rapid object detection.* Paper presented at the Proceedings. international conference on image processing. DOI: 10.1109/ICIP.2002.1038171

Lin, G., Liu, F., Milan, A., Shen, C., & Reid, I. (2019). Refinenet: Multi-path refinement networks for dense prediction. *IEEE Transactions on Pattern Analysis and Machine Intelligence, 42*(5), 1228–1242. DOI: 10.1109/TPAMI.2019.2893630 PMID: 30668461

Lin, T.-Y., Dollár, P., Girshick, R., He, K., Hariharan, B., & Belongie, S. (2017). *Feature pyramid networks for object detection.* Paper presented at the Proceedings of the IEEE conference on computer vision and pattern recognition.

Lin, T.-Y., Goyal, P., Girshick, R., He, K., & Dollár, P. (2017). *Focal loss for dense object detection.* Paper presented at the Proceedings of the IEEE international conference on computer vision.

Lin, T.-Y., Maire, M., Belongie, S., Hays, J., Perona, P., Ramanan, D., . . . Zitnick, C. L. (2014). *Microsoft coco: Common objects in context.* Paper presented at the European conference on computer vision.

Liu, N., Han, J., Zhang, D., Wen, S., & Liu, T. (2015). *Predicting eye fixations using convolutional neural networks.* Paper presented at the Proceedings of the IEEE Conference on Computer Vision and Pattern Recognition.

Liu, W., Anguelov, D., Erhan, D., Szegedy, C., Reed, S., Fu, C.-Y., & Berg, A. C. (2016). *Ssd: Single shot multibox detector.* Paper presented at the European conference on computer vision.

Liu, Y., Wang, Y., Wang, S., Liang, T., Zhao, Q., Tang, Z., & Ling, H. (2019). Cbnet: A novel composite backbone network architecture for object detection. *arXiv preprint arXiv:1909.03625.*

Liu, Z., Lin, Y., Cao, Y., Hu, H., Wei, Y., Zhang, Z., . . . Guo, B. (2021). *Swin transformer: Hierarchical vision transformer using shifted windows.* Paper presented at the Proceedings of the IEEE/CVF international conference on computer vision. DOI: 10.1109/ICCV48922.2021.00986

Lowe, D. G. (2004). Distinctive image features from scale-invariant keypoints. *International Journal of Computer Vision, 60*(2), 91–110. DOI: 10.1023/B:VISI.0000029664.99615.94

Ma, L., Liu, Y., Zhang, X., Ye, Y., Yin, G., & Johnson, B. A. (2019). Deep learning in remote sensing applications: A meta-analysis and review. *ISPRS Journal of Photogrammetry and Remote Sensing, 152,* 166–177. DOI: 10.1016/j.isprsjprs.2019.04.015

Mateus, A., Ribeiro, D., Miraldo, P., & Nascimento, J. C. (2019). Efficient and robust pedestrian detection using deep learning for human-aware navigation. *Robotics and Autonomous Systems, 113,* 23–37. DOI: 10.1016/j.robot.2018.12.007

Najibi, M., Rastegari, M., & Davis, L. S. (2016). *G-cnn: an iterative grid based object detector.* Paper presented at the Proceedings of the IEEE conference on computer vision and pattern recognition. DOI: 10.1109/CVPR.2016.260

Namysl, M., & Konya, I. (2019). *Efficient, lexicon-free OCR using deep learning.* Paper presented at the 2019 International Conference on Document Analysis and Recognition (ICDAR). DOI: 10.1109/ICDAR.2019.00055

Oquab, M., Bottou, L., Laptev, I., & Sivic, J. (2014). *Learning and transferring mid-level image representations using convolutional neural networks.* Paper presented at the Proceedings of the IEEE conference on computer vision and pattern recognition. DOI: 10.1109/CVPR.2014.222

Oquab, M., Bottou, L., Laptev, I., & Sivic, J. (2014). *Weakly supervised object recognition with convolutional neural networks.* Paper presented at the Proc. of NIPS.

Pinheiro, P. O., Collobert, R., & Dollár, P. (2015). *Learning to segment object candidates.* Paper presented at the Advances in neural information processing systems.

Pitts, W., & McCulloch, W. S. (1947). How we know universals the perception of auditory and visual forms. *The Bulletin of Mathematical Biophysics, 9*(3), 127–147. DOI: 10.1007/BF02478291 PMID: 20262674

Rao, S., Li, Y., Ramakrishnan, R., Hassaine, A., Canoy, D., Cleland, J., . . . informatics, h. (2022). An explainable transformer-based deep learning model for the prediction of incident heart failure. *26*(7), 3362-3372.

Redmon, J. (2016). *You only look once: Unified, real-time object detection.* Paper presented at the Proceedings of the IEEE conference on computer vision and pattern recognition. DOI: 10.1109/CVPR.2016.91

Redmon, J., Divvala, S., Girshick, R., & Farhadi, A. (2016). *You only look once: Unified, real-time object detection.* Paper presented at the Proceedings of the IEEE conference on computer vision and pattern recognition. DOI: 10.1109/CVPR.2016.91

Redmon, J., & Farhadi, A. (2017). *YOLO9000: better, faster, stronger.* Paper presented at the Proceedings of the IEEE conference on computer vision and pattern recognition.

Redmon, J. J. a. p. a. (2018). Yolov3: An incremental improvement.

Ren, S., He, K., Girshick, R., & Sun, J. (2015). *Faster r-cnn: Towards real-time object detection with region proposal networks.* Paper presented at the Advances in neural information processing systems.

Ren, S., He, K., Girshick, R., Zhang, X., & Sun, J. (2016). Object detection networks on convolutional feature maps. *IEEE Transactions on Pattern Analysis and Machine Intelligence, 39*(7), 1476–1481. DOI: 10.1109/TPAMI.2016.2601099 PMID: 27541490

Rumelhart, D. E., Hinton, G. E., & Williams, R. J. (1988). Learning representations by back-propagating errors. *Cognitive modeling, 5*(3), 1.

Russakovsky, O., Deng, J., Su, H., Krause, J., Satheesh, S., Ma, S., & Bernstein, M. (2015). Imagenet large scale visual recognition challenge. *International Journal of Computer Vision, 115*(3), 211–252. DOI: 10.1007/s11263-015-0816-y

Sermanet, P., Eigen, D., Zhang, X., Mathieu, M., Fergus, R., & LeCun, Y. (2013). Overfeat: Integrated recognition, localization and detection using convolutional networks. *arXiv preprint arXiv:1312.6229.*

Shen, Z., Liu, Z., Li, J., Jiang, Y.-G., Chen, Y., & Xue, X. (2017). *Dsod: Learning deeply supervised object detectors from scratch.* Paper presented at the Proceedings of the IEEE International Conference on Computer Vision. DOI: 10.1109/ICCV.2017.212

Shrivastava, A., Gupta, A., & Girshick, R. (2016). *Training region-based object detectors with online hard example mining.* Paper presented at the Proceedings of the IEEE conference on computer vision and pattern recognition. DOI: 10.1109/CVPR.2016.89

Shu, C., Liu, Y., Gao, J., Yan, Z., & Shen, C. (2021). *Channel-wise knowledge distillation for dense prediction.* Paper presented at the Proceedings of the IEEE/CVF International Conference on Computer Vision.

Simonyan, K., & Zisserman, A. (2014). Very deep convolutional networks for large-scale image recognition. *arXiv preprint arXiv:1409.1556.*

Singh, B., & Davis, L. S. (2018). *An analysis of scale invariance in object detection snip.* Paper presented at the Proceedings of the IEEE conference on computer vision and pattern recognition. DOI: 10.1109/CVPR.2018.00377

Sun, S., Pang, J., Shi, J., Yi, S., & Ouyang, W. (2018). *Fishnet: A versatile backbone for image, region, and pixel level prediction.* Paper presented at the Advances in neural information processing systems.

Szegedy, C., Ioffe, S., Vanhoucke, V., & Alemi, A. A. (2017). *Inception-v4, inception-resnet and the impact of residual connections on learning.* Paper presented at the Thirty-First AAAI Conference on Artificial Intelligence. DOI: 10.1609/aaai.v31i1.11231

Szegedy, C., Liu, W., Jia, Y., Sermanet, P., Reed, S., Anguelov, D., . . . Rabinovich, A. (2015). *Going deeper with convolutions.* Paper presented at the Proceedings of the IEEE conference on computer vision and pattern recognition.

Szegedy, C., Vanhoucke, V., Ioffe, S., Shlens, J., & Wojna, Z. (2016). *Rethinking the inception architecture for computer vision.* Paper presented at the Proceedings of the IEEE conference on computer vision and pattern recognition. DOI: 10.1109/CVPR.2016.308

Uijlings, J. R., Van De Sande, K. E., Gevers, T., & Smeulders, A. W. (2013). Selective search for object recognition. *International Journal of Computer Vision, 104*(2), 154–171. DOI: 10.1007/s11263-013-0620-5

Vaillant, R., Monrocq, C., & Le Cun, Y. (1994). Original approach for the localisation of objects in images. *IEE Proceedings. Vision Image and Signal Processing, 141*(4), 245–250. DOI: 10.1049/ip-vis:19941301

Viola, P., & Jones, M. (2001). *Rapid object detection using a boosted cascade of simple features.* Paper presented at the Proceedings of the 2001 IEEE computer society conference on computer vision and pattern recognition. CVPR 2001. DOI: 10.1109/CVPR.2001.990517

Wadley, F. (1952). Probit Analysis: A Statistical Treatment of the Sigmoid Response Curve. DJ Finney. New York-London: Cambridge Univ. Press, 1952. 318 pp. $7.00. In: American Association for the Advancement of Science.

Wang, C.-Y., Yeh, I.-H., & Liao, H.-Y. M. J. a. p. a. (2024). Yolov9: Learning what you want to learn using programmable gradient information.

Wang, Y., Zhang, X., Yang, T., & Sun, J. J. a. p. a. (2021). Anchor DETR: Query design for transformer-based object detection. *3*(6).

Xie, S., Girshick, R., Dollár, P., Tu, Z., & He, K. (2017). *Aggregated residual transformations for deep neural networks.* Paper presented at the Proceedings of the IEEE conference on computer vision and pattern recognition. DOI: 10.1109/CVPR.2017.634

Yang, Z., & Nevatia, R. (2016). *A multi-scale cascade fully convolutional network face detector.* Paper presented at the 2016 23rd International Conference on Pattern Recognition (ICPR).

Yoo, D., Park, S., Lee, J.-Y., Paek, A. S., & So Kweon, I. (2015). *Attentionnet: Aggregating weak directions for accurate object detection.* Paper presented at the Proceedings of the IEEE International Conference on Computer Vision. DOI: 10.1109/ICCV.2015.305

Yu, F., Koltun, V., & Funkhouser, T. (2017). *Dilated residual networks.* Paper presented at the Proceedings of the IEEE conference on computer vision and pattern recognition.

Zeiler, M. D., & Fergus, R. (2014). *Visualizing and understanding convolutional networks.* Paper presented at the European conference on computer vision.

Zhang, H., Wang, Y., Dayoub, F., & Sunderhauf, N. (2021). *Varifocalnet: An iou-aware dense object detector.* Paper presented at the Proceedings of the IEEE/CVF conference on computer vision and pattern recognition.

Zhang, H. J. a. p. a. (2017). mixup: Beyond empirical risk minimization.

Zhang, X., Yang, Y.-H., Han, Z., Wang, H., & Gao, C. (2013). Object class detection: A survey. *ACM Computing Surveys*, *46*(1), 1–53. DOI: 10.1145/2522968.2522978

Zhao, Q., Sheng, T., Wang, Y., Tang, Z., Chen, Y., Cai, L., & Ling, H. (2019). *M2det: A single-shot object detector based on multi-level feature pyramid network.* Paper presented at the Proceedings of the AAAI Conference on Artificial Intelligence. DOI: 10.1609/aaai.v33i01.33019259

Zheng, Z., Wang, P., Liu, W., Li, J., Ye, R., & Ren, D. (2020). *Distance-IoU loss: Faster and better learning for bounding box regression.* Paper presented at the Proceedings of the AAAI conference on artificial intelligence. DOI: 10.1609/aaai.v34i07.6999

Zhou, B., Lapedriza, A., Khosla, A., Oliva, A., & Torralba, A. (2017). Places: A 10 million image database for scene recognition. *IEEE Transactions on Pattern Analysis and Machine Intelligence*, *40*(6), 1452–1464. DOI: 10.1109/TPAMI.2017.2723009 PMID: 28692961

Zhou, Y., Liu, L., Shao, L., & Mellor, M. (2016). *DAVE: A unified framework for fast vehicle detection and annotation.* Paper presented at the European Conference on Computer Vision. DOI: 10.1007/978-3-319-46475-6_18

Chapter 8
Speech Emotion Recognition–Based Music Recommender

Yasir Hafeez
https://orcid.org/0000-0002-1206-3792
The University of Nottingham Malaysia, Malaysia

Syed Hasan Adil
AI Society of Pakistan, Pakistan

Mansoor Ebrahim
https://orcid.org/0000-0002-2000-8398
Iqra University, Karachi, Pakistan

Mirzan Izzfitri Bin Mahadir
https://orcid.org/0009-0008-4085-3661
The University of Nottingham Malaysia, Malaysia

ABSTRACT

The objective of this chapter is to provide details implementation of a research project; song recommendations based on speech emotions through Speech Emotion Recognition (SER). This involves developing a Speech Emotion Recognition model utilizing neural network algorithms or deep learning techniques. The selected algorithms include a Convolutional Neural Network (CNN), a Long Short-Term Memory (LSTM) network, a Dense Neural Network (DNN), and a custom hybrid algorithm combining CNN and LSTM. A PyQT5 application framework was implemented to facilitate song recommendations. Users can record their voices, which are processed to predict emotions, and then songs are recommended using the Spotify API, showcasing how SER can enhance personalized content delivery.

DOI: 10.4018/979-8-3693-9057-3.ch008

Copyright © 2025, IGI Global Scientific Publishing. Copying or distributing in print or electronic forms without written permission of IGI Global Scientific Publishing is prohibited.

INTRODUCTION

Music is an essential part of everyday life for most people, whether we are doing our everyday tasks, studying, or even just purely listening to music without doing a single thing. For some, music gives them an emotional impact. It helps with releasing tension, augmenting our current mood, and describing and expressing the emotions that we are going through (Song et al., 2024). However, current music that has been released throughout the decade expresses multiple emotions at once, and some listeners do not like how it is being portrayed. Different listeners have different tastes in music so this should not be a problem when searching for songs to tune in with but there is also a problem where sometimes songs do not fit in with the current mood. So, listeners have to keep skipping to the next song until they have found a song that speaks their soul. As a result, an automatic music recommendation system has been introduced. Where it allows people to discover new music based on their tastes.

But these recommender systems have their drawbacks which is recommending music is complicated due to different genres and the social factors that could influence the preference of people. Most recommender systems rely on usage patterns where the combination of items that people consume or the information of users' preferences information and how both are related to each other. This has sparked an inspiration in developing a system that can recommend music based on people's emotions.

The central focus of this chapter revolves around how individuals express their emotions and moods through speech. Speech plays a vital role in human communication, as it conveys both linguistic and paralinguistic information (Nambiar & Palaniswamy, 2022). Emotion recognition used to be done using only facial recognition where it detects the facial expression of people. But along the way, speech emotion recognition emerges that uses speech signals to recognize emotions. Therefore, this has led to the creation of a Speech Emotion Recognition (SER) based music recommender that uses deep learning methods for the model and Spotify API.

The benefit of using deep learning is that it can give accurate predictions in tasks like speech recognition. It can also recognize complex data patterns such as signals. Speech signals are unstructured data that cannot be understood by the naked eye. Therefore, deep learning can help in unravelling those data and extracting the features correlated to the data.

However, it also has its limitations such as acquiring the dataset. To create deep learning models, a bigger and larger dataset is required but to obtain these datasets could be challenging. In this context, getting datasets on emotion is difficult, especially when finding datasets besides English. The reason for having another dataset in English, acquiring different language datasets is important because there are different ways in which other language speakers display their emotions, especially in their tones. Overfitting can potentially occur when creating the model. Sometimes the model memorizes the training data instead of generalizing the patterns, which can reduce the performance on unseen data.

This chapter focuses to discuss the example of SER, which can be helpful to find music based on current emotions by using the music recommender. By doing so, people can get the music to cater to their emotions and also indirectly help people discover other or new artists outside their comfort zone.

Speech Emotion Recognition

Speech is the primary method of communicating and sharing information with others. It contains a variety of information and also portrays emotions, and it can be visualized through its response towards scenes or events. In other words, every word being uttered contains a certain level of emotions based on the emotional state of the speaker. The principal role of affective speech includes prosodic features such as frequency, speech rate, intensity, and voice quality (Singh et al., 2023). As artificial intelligence (AI) evolved, researchers have increasingly focused on exploring the field of Speech Emotion Recognition (SER).

There have been several attempts where researchers are trying to develop models for SER systems so that they can be used in real-time applications such as song recommendation systems, call centres for customer satisfaction, and security system activation in cars based on driver emotional state. All these are related to monitoring the emotional and mental well-being of people. These kinds of systems can benefit the emotional state of people by keeping their emotions in check. On that note, several studies have suggested using some deep learning techniques in creating a SER model. This approach has started to gain popularity and makes up most of the new literature regarding SER as the accuracies for the models went up from around 70% up to around 90% or more (Abbaschian et al., 2021). Before deep learning was implemented, researchers used machine learning techniques such as support vector machines, Gaussian mixture models, and hidden Markov machines as an approach to making SER models.

RAVDESS Dataset

The Ryerson Audio-Visual Database of Emotional Speech and Song (RAVDESS) is a certified multimodal dataset comprising emotional speech and song. It includes 7,356 audio and video clips and provides samples for both speech and songs, enabling researchers to develop models for analysing emotions in musical recordings. For Speech Emotion Recognition (SER), only the audio samples from the dataset will be utilized. The audio recording contains 1440 speech samples which are recorded by voice actors that consist of 12 men and 12 women. These actors read two neutral English phrases while showing eight emotions which are neutral, calm, happiness, sadness, anger, fear, disgust, and surprise. These actors will say 2 phrases, "Kids are talking by the door" and "Dogs are sitting by the door" while portraying different emotional states. These two phrases are selected according to the length of the syllables, word frequency, and familiarity. The format of the audio files is a lossless wave format provided at 48 kHz to avoid the usual artifacts. This dataset has been extensively use by researchers due to it being one of the most complete data. Deep learning approaches such as Convolutional Neural Networks (CNN) and LSTM have been tested by using this dataset (de Lope & Graña, 2023).

Music Recommender System

In the modern digital era, music stands as a widely embraced form of entertainment and artistic expression. It represents a fusion of human creativity, delivering emotions and thoughts through the intricate blend of melody, harmony, and rhythm. Music encompasses various genres such as pop, rock, jazz, blues, and folk, catering to diverse preferences. With smartphones enabling easy online and offline music playback, accessing songs has become incredibly convenient. However, the immense volume of digital music available has led to information overload, making navigating vast libraries time-consuming (Adiyansjah et al., 2019).

To address this challenge, the development of music recommender systems has gained significant importance. Leading streaming platforms like Spotify and Pandora integrate recommendation features, assisting users in discovering music aligned with their listening history. These systems are crucial for the sustainability of the music streaming industry. They operate by detecting connections between songs or understanding user preferences. Yet, creating an effective music recommender system poses challenges. The primary aim is to consistently present appealing new music while accurately grasping and adapting to user preferences. This requires a personalized approach that comprehensively considers diverse user needs. Such complexity distinguishes a personalized music recommender system from a general one, demanding a deeper understanding of user preferences. Therefore, an effective personalized system entails a thorough analysis of user requirements, integrating music feature recognition and audio processing technologies to extract crucial music features.

Features

Features are one of the aspects that are needed when creating an SER model. Various types of features are used but there is no general set of features that need to be followed when doing feature extraction. This project utilizes features such as Mel-frequency cepstral coefficients (MFCC), Mel-spectrograms, spectral contrasts, chromagrams, and Tonnetz. Both MFCC and Mel-spectrograms are commonly used when building a SER model. This is because these features are capable of mimicking a certain degree of the intrinsic human sound pattern (https://beei.org/index.php/EEI/article/view/4287/2995). The MFCC creates a Mel-frequency spectrum that can be a representation of the short-term sound power spectrum.

When it comes to accurately representing distinct pitch classes and harmony, these qualities often fall short. However, these qualities do a decent job of identifying and tracking the tone changes that occur within a sound file. As a result, chromagrams and Tonnetz are included in order to deal with these kinds of circumstances. When it comes to describing harmony and speech classes, both concepts are comparable to one another. By comparing the peak energy and valley energy in bands converted from spectrogram features, we compute the energy contrast, also known as spectral contrast. This comparison is utilized in order to determine the energy contrast.

Deep Learning Models

Neural networks have emerged as a major focal point within the disciplines of Machine Learning (ML) and Artificial Intelligence (AI) thanks to the development of various extremely efficient learning methodologies and network topologies. Although neural networks have been successfully applied in numerous applications, there has been a waning interest in further research on this topic in recent times. Deep learning was then introduced based on the concept of artificial neural networks (ANN). Nowadays, Deep Learning holds a position as one of the most significant and sought-after topics in machine learning, artificial intelligence, data science, and analytics due to its exceptional learning capabilities derived from processing vast amounts of data. In creating the SER model, various types of deep learning methods have been used.

Convolutional Neural Network(CNN)

Between the many different types of deep learning models, the Convolutional Neural Network (CNN) method is one of the most well-known and widely used. In the realm of computer vision tasks, voice processing, and face recognition, this particular class of artificial neural networks is the most prominent participant. One of the positive aspects of CNN is that it can automatically identify significant characteristics without any human supervision (Alzubaidi et al., 2021). It is the neurons that are found in both human and animal brains that served as the inspiration for the construction of the CNN model. Additionally, it allows for equivalent representations, sparse interaction, and parameter sharing, which are three of its fundamental advantages. A common type of convolutional neural network (CNN) is characterized by the presence of several convolution layers in front of sub-sampling (pooling) layers, and FC layers at the end. This structure is analogous to the multi-layer perceptron (MLP). The following is an illustration of a CNN architecture (Figure 1).

Figure 1. A CNN architecture

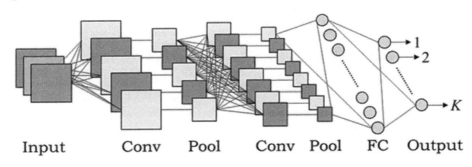

Long Short-Term Memory

The flexible architecture of the long-short-term memory (LSTM) neural network allows for customization to specific forms according to its intended application. The advantage of LSTM is its output, which remains independent of the input length due to its sequential processing of the input. LSTMs demonstrate a strong capability in capturing long-term temporal dependencies. Sub-networks, or memory blocks, connected recurrently, compose the LSTM architecture. The concept of a memory block involves preserving its state over time and managing the flow of information (Van Houdt et al., 2020). LSTMs are commonly used in language modelling, acoustic modelling of speech, and audio and video analysis. The architecture of a LSTM model is presented in Figure 2.

Figure 2. LSTM architecture

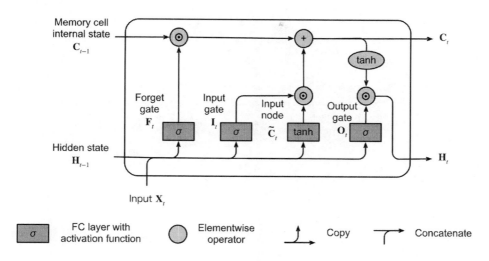

Dense Neural Network

Dense neural networks (DNNs) are one of the simplest forms of neural network architecture. DNNs are biologically inspired computational models which are designed to simulate a human brain in processing information (Nazari & Yan, 2022). A typical DNN is composed of neurons that can be self-optimized during the learning process. The layers of a DNN model are densely connected, meaning that each neuron in a layer will receive all the input from all the neurons in the previous layer. This also works the other way around where all the current neurons in a layer will be the input for the following layers. DNN model can be used to analyse a complex data pattern and be employed in various ranges of applications, whether it is regression analysis, classification or clustering. Figure 3 shows the architecture of a DNN model.

Figure 3. A DNN architecture

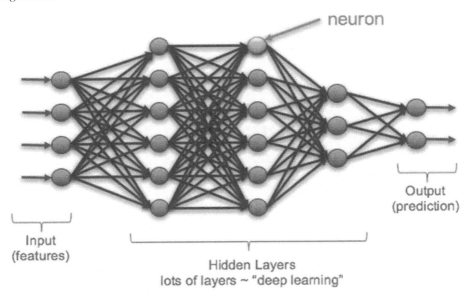

Related Work

This section highlights several studies that utilize neural network algorithms to develop Speech Emotion Recognition (SER) models and music recommendation systems. Only a few related research were included.

Jo and Kwak in (Jo & Kwak, 2023), developed a dual-stream emotion recognition model utilising a Bi-LSTM and a CNN-based transfer learning framework. The utilised dataset was the Korean speech emotion database. This dataset has eight categories of emotion: happiness, neutrality, anger, sadness, chagrin, contempt, and fear. To develop an emotion recognition model, a two-stream architecture was employed, integrating two deep learning models: Bi-LSTM and YAMNet, a CNN-based transfer learning model. The experiment employs diverse feature extraction and deep learning models, and their performance was evaluated comparatively.

A system is proposed by Ullah et al. (Ullah et al., 2023) that employs a Convolutional Neural Network (CNN) and a Multi-Head Convolution Transformer in the model development. Their research delineates the integration of spatial and temporal feature representations of speech emotions using the parallelisation of CNNs and a Transformer encoder utilising the MFCC spectrum. As a greyscale image, they have used MFCC, where the width represents the time scale and the height the frequency scale. Their models achieved impressive results, with benchmark accuracies of 79.80% and 82.31% overall.

A deep learning-based feature fusion technique was proposed by (Liu et al., 2018) to improve SER system performance. Hyperparameter statistical features are extracted from prosodic features in the process of extracting hyper prosodic features (EHPF). The raw voice data is processed to generate two-dimensional spectrogram characteristics, which are then fed into the CNN network to train it. Additionally, the CNN network is utilized to extract the spectra-based feature vectors, and a deep neural network (DNN) is used to fuse the EHPF feature vectors to recognize emotions. The suggested model significantly increased the SER accuracy, as demonstrated by the experiment.

(Wang et al., 2020) have demonstrated the effectiveness of combining MFCC features, and mel-spectrograms produced by audio signals. They have introduced a novel LSTM architecture that can process two mel-spectrograms simultaneously. Their model outperforms the baseline models and current best unimodal models, which only rely on audio signals, by showing that the unimodal model has not reached their full potential.

During the process of developing the model, Harar et al. (Harar et al., 2017) utilised a Deep Neural Network (DNN) approach in their research. A brief audio recording that was divided into chunks of twenty milliseconds was used in their experiment with the intention of determining whether or not it was possible to forecast the emotional state of a person. With an average confidence level of 69.55%, their method was able to attain an accuracy of 96.97% on the testing data. Because their method is context-independent, it is possible to classify the audio segments in a manner that is independent of the context.

Li et al. (Li et al., 2023) did a study in which they developed a voice graph based on feature similarity and proposed an innovative architecture for graph neural networks that incorporates an LSTM aggregator and weighted pooling. The IEMOCAP dataset yielded unweighted and weighted accuracies of 65.39% and 71.83%, respectively, demonstrating performance that is equivalent to or surpasses established baselines. They encountered several deficiencies, including intricate linkages, an excessive amount of redundant features in the graph, unreliable processing and analysis of tiny datasets, and the disregard for the speaker's knowledge. Their research focusses on adult speech and omits the recognition of emotional expression in children's speech.

Xu et al. (Xu et al., 2021) developed a mechanism including the implementation of an ACNN model and conducted experiments utilising the IEMOCAP and RAVDES datasets. It was determined that including noisy data serves as a remedy when there is a lack of high-quality data for SER study (18-25). This also enhances the model's robustness. They attain the best accuracy by incorporating D-S noise, whereas the inclusion of C-L noise results in the lowest accuracy (26-37).

Functional and Non-Functional Requirements

The following section discusses some of the functional and non-functional requirements for the SER.

Functional Requirements

a. Programming Language:
   i. Jupyter Notebook is used for the model development, as it facilitates prototyping, experimentation, and easier debugging during the training process.
   ii. Python is employed to build the music recommender system, leveraging its libraries for retrieving song lists and creating the system's interface.
b. Speech Recognition:
   i. The system should be able to receive audio inputs, such as speech to be able to predict the outcome of emotion.
   ii. The system should be able to detect the audio that is covered within a range of selected emotions, in this case, it's happy, calm, sad, angry, and surprised.
c. Recommender:

The recommender should display songs based on the predicted emotion detected by the model.

d. User Interface:
   i. The interface have a button that the user can press to start recording their audio.
   ii. The interface shall be able to recommend one song every time a result is fetched.
   iii. The emotion detected would be shown above the song list.

Non-functional requirements

a. OS Support: The system should be compatible with multiple operating systems, including Windows, Linux, and Mac.
b. Performance: The system's performance should be efficient, as it only involves recognizing speech-based emotions and displaying the corresponding song recommendations.

c. Usability: The system should be user-friendly, featuring intuitive, self-explanatory buttons. An information button will provide first-time users with simple instructions on how to get started. This simplicity can be achieved by minimizing the number of buttons and focusing only on the essential functionalities of the system.
d. Documentation: For first-time users, the system would include brief, straightforward instructions within the interface. As outlined under usability, this documentation would consist of concise sentences explaining how to use the system.
e. Availability: An Internet connection is required for the system to function, as the recommender fetches songs from an online source using an API.

Methodology

This section outlines the experimental methodology. A ranking approach is employed to evaluate the performance of various neural network models, with the best-performing model selected for integration into the music recommender system.

The programming language used is mainly Python. The SER models are created using Jupyter Notebook which supports Python because it is easy to use and easy to debug. The music recommender system is created using Python on PyCharm.

Pre-processing

This section discusses the pre-processing of data techniques which are being used in SER.

Feature Extraction.

Five features are discussed in the following and would be extracted from the speech signals provided by the audio files to facilitate emotion recognition. The feature types are:

a. MFCC – This feature is widely used in speech recognition tasks due to its ability to capture the spectral characteristics of speech signals.
b. Chroma – This feature represents the distribution of energy across pitch classes that is useful for speech analysis.
c. Mel-Spectrogram – This feature provides a perceptually relevant frequency representation of audio signals.
d. Contrast – This feature encapsulates the spectral contrast of audio signals that can help in differentiating emotions.

e. Tonnetz - This feature represents the tonal content of audio signals which can be beneficial in emotion recognition.

Label encoding

Each audio sample is categorized by assigning an emotion label using a label encoder. This encoder translates categorical labels into numerical values, making the data suitable for machine learning or deep learning algorithms. The encoder is also capable of reversing this process, transforming numerical categories back into their original emotional labels. Thus, the audio files are tagged with diverse emotional classifications.

Data Split Technique

The split technique that is used for this project is the Train-Test-Validation split. This is a common data-splitting technique used in a classification task. The dataset is split into three which are train, test, and validation sets.

a. For the training dataset, the data is used for the models to learn its patterns when making classifications.
b. For the test dataset, it is used to evaluate the trained model in an unbiased format. This is because the testing data are unseen data which are separate from training and validation sets.
c. For the validation dataset, it is used to evaluate the performance of the model during training. It helps in generalizing unseen data and tuning the hyperparameters.

Neural Network Algorithm

This section discusses the Neural Network algorithms employed and the computational methods they use to generate predictions.

Convolutional Neural Network (CNN)

CNN is one of the artificial neural networks used in this research. Figure 1 illustrates that the input data consists of pre-processed training data. This data then goes through a succession of convolutional and pooling layers. Each layer may or may not include an activation function. It would then go to the final layer where it outputs the predictions for K kind of objects.

Each layer of a CNN may utilise a specific activation function that regulates the output value transmitted to the subsequent layer. In intermediate layers, the rectified linear unit (ReLU),

$$f(a_i^l) = \max(0, a_i^l) \tag{1}$$

where $a_i^l \in R$ is a sum of signals received in the i-th unit in the l-th intermediate layer (Vakalopoulou et al., 2023).

For the last layer, the soft-max function is used to obtain the probabilistic outputs.

$$fk(z) = \frac{\exp(zk)}{\sum_{k=1}^{k}\exp(zk)} \tag{2}$$

Where z is a K dimensional vector where z_k is the sum signals received by the k-th unit in the last layer.

Long-Short Term Memory (LSTM)

This project also utilises the LSTM neural network method. An LSTM unit comprises a cell, an input gate x_t, an output gate h_t, and a forget gate. The LSTM architecture comprises a series of recurrently linked sub-networks known as memory blocks. The function of memory blocks is to preserve their state over time and control the flow of information.

The block input initiates the process of updating the component by integrating the current input x_t with the output h_t from the preceding iteration, as delineated in the formula below:

$$z^t = g(Z_{\widetilde{C}}x_t + R_{\widetilde{C}}h_{t-1} + b_{\widetilde{C}})(3)$$

Where $Z_{\widetilde{C}}$ and $R_{\widetilde{C}}$ are weight associated with x_i and h_{t-1} with $b_{\widetilde{C}}$ being the bias weight vector.

Next is the input gate. Every update of the input gate combines the current input gate x_t, the output h_{t-1} and the memory cell c_{t-1} from the last iteration using this formula:

$$I^t = \sigma(Z_I x_t + R_I h_{t-1} + p_I \odot c^{t-1} + b_I)(4)$$

Here $\odot$ represents the element-wise multiplication of two vectors, Z_I and R_I, where p_I specifies the corresponding weights for x_t, h_{t-1} and c^{t-1}, with b_I being the related bias weight vector.

Forget gate; In this gate, the LSTM ascertains which information should be excluded from the preceding cell c^{t-1}.

In time step t, the activation values for forget gates f_t are calculated using the current input values, outputs and memory cells from the previous time step t $-$ 1 including the bias terms b_f using the equation below:

$$f^t = \sigma\left(Z_f x_t + R_f h_{t-1} + p_f \odot c^{t-1} + b_f\right) (5)$$

Where Z_f, R_f and p_f are associated weights for x_t, h_{t-1} and c^{t-1}, while b_f is the associated bias weight vector.

The memory cell computes its value by combining the values of the block input $\bar{c}_t$, the input gate I^t and the forget gate f^t from the previous cell value by using the equation below:

$$c^t = \bar{c}_t \odot I^t + c^{t-1} \odot f^t (6)$$

The output gate combines the current input, the output and the memory cell from the last iteration using the equation below:

$$o^t = \sigma\left(Z_o x_t + R_o h_{t-1} + p_o \odot c^{t-1} + o\right) (7)$$

Where Z_o, R_o and p_o are associated weights for x_t, h_{t-1} and c^{t-1}, while b_o is the associated bias weight vector.

And lastly, the block output is calculated using the equation below:

$$h^t = tanh(c^t) \odot o^t \qquad (8)$$

For tanh and σ, these are denoted as activation functions where $\sigma(x) = \dfrac{1}{1+e^{1-x}}$ is a logistic sigmoid whereas tanh (x) is a hyperbolic tangent that is often used as the block input and output activation function.

Dense Neural Network (DNN)

DNN is an additional algorithm employed in this project. A DNN model is an algorithm characterised by densely connected layers. A DNN model can also be referred to as a Fully Connected Neural Network. A DNN algorithm comprises three types of layers: the input layer, hidden layers, and the output layer.

In the input layer, pre-processed data is used as the initial input of the algorithm. Then it would be transformed when connecting to the next layer which is the hidden layer. The transformation can be depicted as below:

$$z_j = \sum_{i=1}^{n} w_{ij} x_i + b_j \tag{9}$$

where x_i is the input layer, w_{ij} are the weights for the input features, b_j is the bias vector for the layer and z_j is the sum. After getting the sum, it will transform using the activation function ReLU which can be depicted using the formula (1).

This step will be repeated until all of the hidden layers are accounted for with each transformed feature used as the input for the next hidden layer. For the final layer, the output layer will use the soft-max function which can be depicted from formula (2) and compute the probability of the prediction.

Experimentation

This section covers the experimentation in creating the model and also the music recommendation system. All of the codes will be running on a Windows 11 Home 64-bit Operating System with Intel Core i7-10750H CPU @ 2.60GHz, a GPU NVIDIA GeForce GTX 1650 and 16GB RAM.

Dataset

The dataset utilised for this model was sourced from RAVDESS. This dataset contains audio and video clips. In my situation, I exclusively utilise the audio dataset. There are two types of datasets: music and speech. I opted to utilise both datasets as they exhibit distinct tones for the same emotion, hence enhancing accuracy substantially. The files contain audio samples representing eight distinct emotions: neutral, calm, happy, sadness, anger, contempt, surprise, and terror. This project necessitates only five emotions, hence extraneous emotions would be eliminated during the model's development.

Figure 4. Selected Emotions

```
12  # Only Need These Emotions
13  UseEmotions = {
14      "neutral",
15      "calm",
16      "happy",
17      "sad",
18      "angry",
19  }
```

Feature Extraction

Feature extraction will be performed on the audio files utilised in this research. Five features will be extracted: MFCC, chroma, contrast, Mel-spectrogram, and Tonnetz. Only MFCC will be utilised as the chosen feature for model training, owing to its relevance to speech emotion identification tasks. The emotion labels were subsequently converted to numerical values with a label encoder.

The datasets are divided into three categories: training, validation, and testing, with proportions of 55%, 15%, and 30%, respectively. Owing to the disparate input requirements of CNN and DNN, the segmented data are restructured to align with these variations. In CNN, the data is formatted as a three-dimensional array, while in DNN, it is organised into a two-dimensional array.

Model Algorithm

During the course of this investigation, a number of neural network algorithms were chosen, and these algorithms were taken into consideration when trying to design a SER model for a music recommendation system. This was followed by the sorting of these algorithms in order to discover which one performed the best, and then the method that was determined to be the most effective was selected to be used as the SER model. There were three different algorithms that were utilised: CNN, LSTM, and DNN. A hybrid algorithm that mixes CNN and LSTM is also utilised for the aim of establishing whether or not there is a difference in performance between the four algorithms. This is done in order to determine whether or not there is a discrepancy.

All of the models were created in Jupyter Notebook. The algorithms will have a standardised environment shown in Table 1 below.

Table 1. Algorithms environments

Algorithms	Input/Hidden activation	Output activation	Kernel regularizer	Loss	Optimizer	Batch size	epochs
CNN	ReLU	Softmax	L2 = 0.01	Categorical Cross-entropy	Adam	32	100
LSTM	ReLU	Softmax	-	Categorical Cross-entropy	Adam	32	100
DNN	ReLU	Softmax	L2 = 0.01	Categorical Cross-entropy	Adam	32	100
CNN-LSTM	ReLU	Softmax	L2 = 0.01	Categorical Cross-entropy	Adam	32	100

CNN Algorithm

The CNN algorithm development process employed a multi-dimensional input CNN architecture. We developed this technique to learn features from sequential data, where each sample is a sequence of forty samples. The datasets are sequential in nature. This process has developed three convolutional layers. All sixteen neurones in the first layer will have a kernel size of five. These neurones will divide the input sequence into windows consisting of five consecutive features. This assures that the output feature maps will have the same length as the input sequence because the padding is set to "same," which is the default setting. We will use the ReLU algorithm as the activation function, allowing it to learn intricate patterns. Furthermore, we employed L2 regularisation to mitigate the effects of large parameter values and prevent overfitting.

Next, we added a MaxPooling layer with a pooling size of 2. This layer has the ability to lower the spatial dimensions of the feature maps, contribute to the reduction of computational complexity, and also prevent overfitting while maintaining the essential features. Additionally, we added dropout, which operates at a rate of 0.1 and randomly deactivates a portion of neurones during practice.

We have increased the number of neurones to 32 and 64, respectively, and added two additional layers. Every aspect of the kernel, including its size, padding, activation, and regularization, remains unchanged. We implemented the batch normalisation algorithm between these two layers to standardise the activations and stabilise the learning process. After the third layer completes, a dense layer utilising the softmax activation function transforms the output into a one-dimensional vector. This layer then transforms the output into a probability score.

The algorithm was then compiled using categorical cross-entropy as the loss function and Adam optimizer. The model is trained using the training and validation data with a batch size of 32 and for 100 epochs.

LSTM Algorithm

There exists a singular layer for LSTM. The LSTM layer will consist of 50 neurones to handle data sequences. We will employ ReLU as the activation function, and each input sample will consist of a sequence of 40 features.

Following the LSTM layer, we append a dense layer with 5 units and a softmax activation function. This layer functions as the output layer that generates probability scores. We subsequently construct the model using the same loss function and optimiser. We train the model using the same training and validation datasets as the CNN, ensuring a batch size of 32 across 100 epochs.

DNN Algorithm

The architecture of DNN will include a number of fully connected layers. The dense layers first flatten the input data into a single-dimensional vector before processing it. Within the framework of this concept, there are seven levels that are dense. Each layer employs the same activation function, which is ReLU, but its number of units varies from layer to layer. One hundred and twenty-eight neurones make up the first layer, and the second and third levels each have sixty-four neurones. The final two levels each include sixteen neurones, whereas the fourth layer makes use of thirty-two neurones, respectively.

Each layer uses L2 regularisation to prevent overfitting. The last layer makes use of five neurones, which is equivalent to the number of classes that are required for this project. The activation function that it employs is softmax. We use the categorical cross-entropy as the loss function and the Adam optimiser to assemble the model. In this particular model, the training process makes use of a distinct train and validation set shape, with the batch size being 32 for a total of one hundred epochs.

CNN-LSTM Algorithm

This hybrid algorithm integrates convolutional neural networks (CNN) with long short-term memory (LSTM) architectures. The process begins with a one-dimensional convolutional layer that consists of 16 neurones and employs a kernel size of 5. The activation functions, padding, and regularisation techniques used are the same as those implemented in the CNN algorithm. Next, we configure the LSTM layer with 50 neurones and enable the return sequences parameter. A dropout layer is subsequently incorporated to mitigate the risk of overfitting. Max pooling is implemented using a pooling size of 2. A subsequent convolutional layer is incorporated with 32 units, maintaining the same configurations as the initial layer. Batch normalisation is implemented following this layer to standardise the activations obtained from the previous layers.

A dense layer comprising 5 neurones will transform the data into a one-dimensional vector and process it, using softmax as the activation function. The model utilises the same loss function and optimiser as those used in the previous models. The model is trained using the CNN training and validation dataset, with a batch size set to 32 and a total duration of 100 epochs.

Evaluation Metrics

Five indicators are selected to assess these models. The metrics include accuracy, validation accuracy, recall, precision, and F1-score. Accuracy and validation accuracy measure the correct predictions, namely True Positives (TP) and True Negatives (TN), in relation to the total number of predictions executed. Validation accuracy differs from standard accuracy in that it uses a distinct dataset to assess the model's performance. The following formula illustrates this concept:

$$Accuracy = \frac{TP + TN}{TP + TN + FP + FN} \tag{10}$$

Where FP and FN are False Positive and False Negative.

Recall is to measure the sensitivity of a model or the ability of a model to correctly identify positive instances. The formula below depicts how to recall:

$$Recall = \frac{TP}{TP + FN} \tag{11}$$

Precision measures the accuracy of correct predictions made by a model. Below is the depiction of precision:

$$Precision = \frac{TP}{TP + FP} \tag{12}$$

Lastly, F1-score. F1-score is the harmonic mean between precision and recall metrics. This can be depicted using the formula below:

$$Precision = \frac{2 * Precision * Recall}{Precision + Recall} \qquad (13)$$

Music Recommender System

The music recommendation system was developed in Python. The system's principles include the capability to capture audio, preprocess the recorded audio for emotion prediction, then utilise this prediction to identify a song that aligns with the identified feeling.

The system will be developed on the Python GUI framework package known as PyQt5. This library facilitates the development of a desktop application. We developed four pages for this application: the main window housing the homepage, the information page, the loading page, and the music recommendation page.

On the homepage, users have the option to record their audio and receive forecasts of their feelings. Additionally, users can access the information page that presents instructions and details about the system. Once the recording is complete, the loading page will appear. The purpose of this page is to preprocess audio output and use the SER model to predict emotions.

After that, the tab that provides song recommendations will display the forecast. We utilised an application programming interface (API) for Spotify to obtain the song to display. Spotipy is a Python package that has the power to enable access to the Spotify application programming interface (API). Creating a client ID and a client secret for the Spotify service is required in order to acquire song data from Spotify. This is a prerequisite for obtaining song data from Spotify. It is possible to extract a significant number of information from Spotify by utilising the application programming interface (API). However, the information that was necessary was the name of the artist, the title of the song, an image of the song, and the URL of the song. The following is an illustration of what the user interface would look like in Figure 5, Figure 6, Figure 7, and Figure 8.

Figure 5. Home page

Figure 6. Information Page

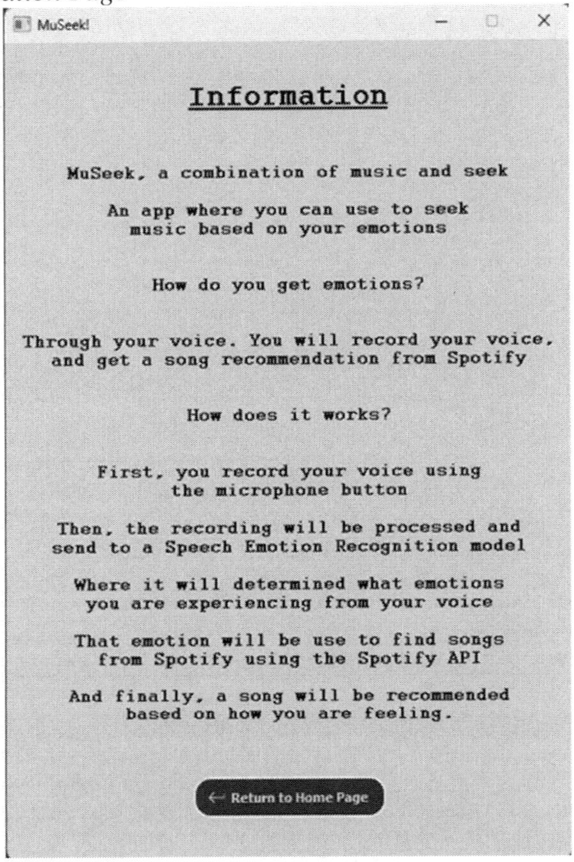

Information

MuSeek, a combination of music and seek

An app where you can use to seek
music based on your emotions

How do you get emotions?

Through your voice. You will record your voice,
and get a song recommendation from Spotify

How does it works?

First, you record your voice using
the microphone button

Then, the recording will be processed and
send to a Speech Emotion Recognition model

Where it will determined what emotions
you are experiencing from your voice

That emotion will be use to find songs
from Spotify using the Spotify API

And finally, a song will be recommended
based on how you are feeling.

← Return to Home Page

Figure 7. Loading Page

Figure 8. Song Page

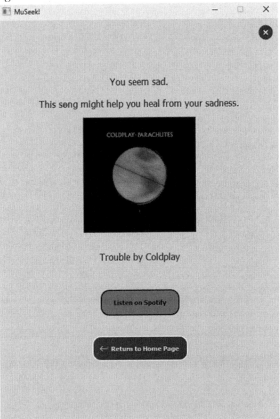

Evaluation

In this section, we will examine the outcomes of all of the models, employ a rating mechanism to identify the algorithm that has the highest level of performance, and then apply that algorithm as the SER model for this individual project. The following Table 2 provides a tabular representation of the results for each of the evaluation metrics:

Table 2. Evaluation Results

Algorithms	Accuracy	Validation Accuracy	Precision	Recall	F1-Score
CNN	83.95%	72.05%	74.96%	74.41%	74.15%
LSTM	82.94%	70.08%	70.43%	70.08%	70.06%
DNN	69.34%	68.50%	68.18%	66.14%	64.49%
CNN-LSTM	97.97%	77.36%	82.22%	80.71%	81.00%

The table presents a comparative analysis of the performance of four distinct algorithms: CNN, LSTM, DNN, and CNN-LSTM.

The CNN-LSTM model exhibited superior overall accuracy, achieving a performance level of 97.97% and a validation accuracy of 77.36%. This indicates that the integration of convolutional and recurrent neural networks proficiently captures both temporal and spatial characteristics in the audio data.

The CNN model demonstrated commendable performance, attaining an accuracy of 85.57% alongside a validation accuracy of 79.92%.

Nonetheless, the LSTM and DNN models demonstrated reduced performance, achieving accuracies that fell short of 83%. This suggests that, although LSTM is proficient at capturing temporal dependencies, it might face challenges with intricate audio features. Conversely, DNN might not possess the capability to efficiently extract pertinent features from the audio data.

The findings indicate that the integration of CNN and LSTM architectures can notably enhance the effectiveness of emotion recognition models.

On the basis of the table, we are able to identify two possible algorithms that have the potential to serve as the SER model. However, the validation accuracy of the CNN-LSTM algorithm is lower than that of the CNN algorithm. The CNN algorithm has the best accuracy among all options. In addition, CNN has the top score in terms of precision, recall, and F1-Score scoring. After implementing a ranking system, the CNN model emerged as the top performer, followed by CNN-LSTM in second place, based on the criteria. Last but not least, LSTM and DNN came in third and fourth, respectively.

CONCLUSION

The primary objective of this study is to develop a Speech Emotion Recognition (SER) model that is able to make predictions about the emotions the speaker is experiencing. A deep learning approach will be utilised in order to successfully attain this goal. In order to implement all of the methods, we utilised neural networks. Convolutional Neural Networks (CNN), Long-Short Term Memory (LSTM),

Dense Neural Networks (DNN), and a hybrid model that includes both CNN and LSTM were the types of neural networks that were utilised in this study. To be more specific, we made use of the RAVDESS collection, which not only contains audio and video data but also data that has been combined with music and audio. For the purpose of this experiment, just one type of data was collected, and that was of an audio nature. During the course of working on this project, there was only one model that performed much better than the others. CNN outscored the CNN-LSTM hybrid in every additional measure, despite the fact that the hybrid achieved the highest accuracy. After that, we exported the model, and then we used it in the process of developing the music recommendation system at a later time. Through the use of Spotify's application programming interface (API), we succeeded in obtaining the songs that were shown.

For the goal of training models in the future, it is recommended to make use of a wider variety of datasets. When it comes to efficiently distinguishing between various states of mind, this can be of use in situations when datasets are available for a wide variety of languages and dialects with the goal of achieving differentiation. Fine-tuning the hyperparameters of the models is something that may be done in order to optimise the performance of the models even further. The modification of the learning rates, the use of a wide range of activation functions, and the optimisation of the model structure are some of the realistic tactics that are available for the accomplished goal of this purpose. Incorporating a greater number of hybrid models into the model is yet another viable method towards the creation of a model that performs better.

REFERENCES

Abbaschian, B. J., Sierra-Sosa, D., & Elmaghraby, A. (2021). Deep learning techniques for speech emotion recognition, from databases to models. *Sensors (Basel)*, *21*(4), 1–27. DOI: 10.3390/s21041249 PMID: 33578714

Abdullah, F. B., Iqbal, R., Ahmad, S., El-Affendi, M. A., & Abdullah, M. (2022). An empirical analysis of sustainable energy security for energy policy recommendations. *Sustainability*, *14*(10), 6099.

Abdullah, F. B., Iqbal, R., Ahmad, S., El-Affendi, M. A., & Kumar, P. (2022). Optimization of multidimensional energy security: An index based assessment. *Energies*, *15*(11), 3929.

Adiyansjah, G., Gunawan, A. A. S., & Suhartono, D. (2019). Music recommender system based on genre using convolutional recurrent neural networks. *Procedia Computer Science*, *157*, 99–109. DOI: 10.1016/j.procs.2019.08.146

Ahmad, S., Anwar, M. S., Ebrahim, M., Khan, W., Raza, K., Adil, S. H., & Amin, A. (2020). Deep network for the iterative estimations of students' cognitive skills. *IEEE Access : Practical Innovations, Open Solutions*, *8*, 103100–103113. DOI: 10.1109/ACCESS.2020.2999064

Ahmad, S., Anwar, M. S., Khan, M. A., Shahzad, M., Ebrahim, M., & Memon, I. (2021, November). Deep Frustration Severity Network for the Prediction of Declined Students' Cognitive Skills. In 2021 4th international conference on Computing & Information Sciences (ICCIS) (pp. 1-6). IEEE.

Ahmad, S., El-Affendi, M. A., Anwar, M. S., & Iqbal, R. (2022). Potential future directions in optimization of students' performance prediction system. *Computational Intelligence and Neuroscience*, *2022*(1), 6864955.

Ahmad, S., Li, K., Amin, A., & Khan, S. (2018). A novel technique for the evaluation of posterior probabilities of student cognitive skills. *IEEE Access : Practical Innovations, Open Solutions*, *6*, 53153–53167. DOI: 10.1109/ACCESS.2018.2870877

Ahmad, S., Li, K., Eddine, H. A. I., & Khan, M. I. (2018). A biologically inspired cognitive skills measurement approach. Biologically inspired cognitive architectures, 24, 35-46.

Akhtar, M., Rahim, M., Alanzi, A. M., Ahmad, S., Fatlane, J. M., Aphane, M., & Khalifa, H. A. E.-W. (2023). Dombi Aggregation Operators for p, qr–Spherica Fuzzy Sets: Application in the Stability Assessment of Cryptocurrencies. *IEEE Access : Practical Innovations, Open Solutions*, *12*, 10366–10382. DOI: 10.1109/ACCESS.2023.3346916

Akhtar, S., Ali, A., Ahmad, S., Khan, M. I., Shah, S., & Hassan, F. (2022). The prevalence of foot ulcers in diabetic patients in Pakistan: A systematic review and meta-analysis. *Frontiers in Public Health*, *10*, 1017201. DOI: 10.3389/fpubh.2022.1017201 PMID: 36388315

Akhtar, S., Ramzan, M., Shah, S., Ahmad, I., Khan, M. I., Ahmad, S., & Qureshi, H. (2022). Forecasting exchange rate of Pakistan using time series analysis. *Mathematical Problems in Engineering*, *2022*(1), 9108580.

Alzubaidi, L., Zhang, J., Humaidi, A. J., Al-Dujaili, A., Duan, Y., Al-Shamma, O., Santamaría, J., Fadhel, M. A., Al-Amidie, M., & Farhan, L. (2021). Review of deep learning: Concepts, CNN architectures, challenges, applications, future directions. *Journal of Big Data*, *8*(1), 53. DOI: 10.1186/s40537-021-00444-8 PMID: 33816053

Anwar, M. S.. (2023). *"Immersive learning and AR/VR-based education: cybersecurity measures and risk management." Cybersecurity Management in Education Technologies*. CRC Press. DOI: 10.1201/9781003369042-1

Anwar, M. S., Choi, A., Ahmad, S., Aurangzeb, K., Laghari, A. A., Gadekallu, T. R., & Hines, A. (2024). A Moving Metaverse: QoE challenges and standards requirements for immersive media consumption in autonomous vehicles. *Applied Soft Computing*, *159*, 111577. DOI: 10.1016/j.asoc.2024.111577

Anwar, M. S., Wang, J., Ullah, A., Khan, W., Ahmad, S., & Li, Z. (2019, December). Impact of stalling on QoE for 360-degree virtual reality videos. In *2019 IEEE International Conference on Signal, Information and Data Processing (ICSIDP)* (pp. 1-6). IEEE.

Anwar, M. S., Wang, J., Ullah, A., Khan, W., Li, Z., & Ahmad, S. (2018, October). User profile analysis for enhancing QoE of 360 panoramic video in virtual reality environment. In *2018 International Conference on Virtual Reality and Visualization (ICVRV)* (pp. 106-111). IEEE.

de Lope, J., & Graña, M. (2023). An ongoing review of speech emotion recognition. *Neurocomputing*, *528*, 1–11. DOI: 10.1016/j.neucom.2023.01.002

Haq, M. U., Sethi, M. A. J., Ahmad, S., ELAffendi, M. A., & Asim, M. (2024). Automatic Player Face Detection and Recognition for Players in Cricket Games. *IEEE Access : Practical Innovations, Open Solutions, 12*, 41219–41233. DOI: 10.1109/ACCESS.2024.3377564

Harar, P., Burget, R., & Dutta, M. K. (2017). Speech emotion recognition with deep learning. *2017 4th International Conference on Signal Processing and Integrated Networks, SPIN 2017*, 137–140. DOI: 10.1109/SPIN.2017.8049931

Hosni, A. I. E., Li, K., & Ahmad, S. (2019, December). DARIM: Dynamic approach for rumor influence minimization in online social networks. In *International Conference on Neural Information Processing* (pp. 619-630). Cham: Springer International Publishing.

Hosni, A. I. E., Li, K., Ding, C., & Ahmed, S. (2018, November). Least cost rumor influence minimization in multiplex social networks. In *International Conference on Neural Information Processing* (pp. 93-105). Cham: Springer International Publishing.

Jo, A.-H., & Kwak, K.-C. (2023). Speech Emotion Recognition Based on Two-Stream Deep Learning Model Using Korean Audio Information. *Applied Sciences (Basel, Switzerland), 13*(4), 2167. DOI: 10.3390/app13042167

Khan, S., Zhang, Z., Zhu, L., Rahim, M. A., Ahmad, S., & Chen, R. (2020). SCM: Secure and accountable TLS certificate management. *International Journal of Communication Systems, 33*(15), e4503.

Li, Y., Wang, Y., Yang, X., & Im, S. K. (2023). Speech emotion recognition based on Graph-LSTM neural network. *EURASIP Journal on Audio, Speech, and Music Processing, 2023*(1), 40. DOI: 10.1186/s13636-023-00303-9

Liu, G., He, W., & Jin, B. (2018). Feature Fusion of Speech Emotion Recognition Based on Deep Learning. *Proceedings of 2018 6th IEEE International Conference on Network Infrastructure and Digital Content, IC-NIDC 2018*, 193–197. DOI: 10.1109/ICNIDC.2018.8525706

Memon, F. S., Abdullah, F. B., Iqbal, R., Ahmad, S., Hussain, I., & Abdullah, M. (2023). Addressing women's climate change awareness in Sindh, Pakistan: An empirical study of rural and urban women. *Climate and Development, 15*(7), 565–577. DOI: 10.1080/17565529.2022.2125784

Nambiar, K. R., & Palaniswamy, S. (2022). Speech Emotion Based Music Recommendation. *2022 3rd International Conference for Emerging Technology, INCET 2022*, 1–6. DOI: 10.1109/INCET54531.2022.9824457

Nazari, F., & Yan, W. (2022). Convolutional versus Dense Neural Networks: Comparing the Two Neural Networks' Performance in Predicting Building Operational Energy Use Based on the Building Shape. *Building Simulation Conference Proceedings*, 495–502. DOI: 10.26868/25222708.2021.30735

Rahim, M., Amin, F., Tag Eldin, E. M., Khalifa, A. E. W., & Ahmad, S. (2024). p, q-Spherical fuzzy sets and their aggregation operators with application to third-party logistic provider selection. *Journal of Intelligent & Fuzzy Systems*, *46*(1), 505–528.

Singh, J., Saheer, L. B., & Faust, O. (2023). Speech Emotion Recognition Using Attention Model. *International Journal of Environmental Research and Public Health*, *20*(6), 5140. DOI: 10.3390/ijerph20065140 PMID: 36982048

Song, Y., Ali, N., & Nater, U. M. (2024). The effect of music on stress recovery. *Psychoneuroendocrinology*, *168*, 107137. DOI: 10.1016/j.psyneuen.2024.107137 PMID: 39024851

Ullah, R., Asif, M., Shah, W. A., Anjam, F., Ullah, I., Khurshaid, T., Wuttisittikulkij, L., Shah, S., Ali, S. M., & Alibakhshikenari, M. (2023). Speech Emotion Recognition Using Convolution Neural Networks and Multi-Head Convolutional Transformer. *Sensors (Basel)*, *23*(13), 6212. DOI: 10.3390/s23136212 PMID: 37448062

Vakalopoulou, M., Christodoulidis, S., Burgos, N., Colliot, O., & Lepetit, V. (2023). *Deep Learning: Basics and Convolutional Neural Networks (CNNs)* (pp. 77–115). DOI: 10.1007/978-1-0716-3195-9_3

Van Houdt, G., Mosquera, C., & Nápoles, G. (2020). A review on the long short-term memory model. *Artificial Intelligence Review*, *53*(8), 5929–5955. DOI: 10.1007/s10462-020-09838-1

Wang, J., Xue, M., Culhane, R., Diao, E., Ding, J., & Tarokh, V. (2020). Speech emotion recognition with dual-sequence LSTM architecture. *ICASSP, IEEE International Conference on Acoustics, Speech and Signal Processing - Proceedings*, *2020-May*, 6474–6478. DOI: 10.1109/ICASSP40776.2020.9054629

Xu, M., Zhang, F., & Zhang, W. (2021). Head Fusion: Improving the Accuracy and Robustness of Speech Emotion Recognition on the IEMOCAP and RAVDESS Dataset. *IEEE Access : Practical Innovations, Open Solutions*, *9*, 74539–74549. DOI: 10.1109/ACCESS.2021.3067460

Chapter 9
Smart Processing Line for Automobile Sector Based on Computer Vision

Muhammad Atif Saeed

Shaheed Zulfikar Ali Bhutto Institute of Science and Technology, Pakistan

Faraz Junejo

Shaheed Zulfikar Ali Bhutto Institute of Science and Technology, Pakistan

Imran Amin

Shaheed Zulfikar Ali Bhutto Institute of Science and Technology, Pakistan

Irfan Khan Tanoli

https://orcid.org/0000-0002-3863-5824

Universidade da Beira Interior, Portugal

ABSTRACT

The paper discusses the need for Industrial Automation in Pakistan's automobile and manufacturing industrial sectors. And what are the reasons which hold up this idea factors are controlling its implementation. The work proposes a Smart Painting Machine, a parts painting robot that can be placed in the production line of automobile and manufacturing industries to paint various geometrical parts simultaneously. The factors that stop Pakistani Industries from adopting Industrial Automation are initial high capital investment and maintenance of the machine, efficiency, and productivity, and painting various geometrical parts on the same machine with one program. Also, the machine targets reducing human health risks by promoting automatic painting and welding. The painting mechanism of the machine is a CNC mechanism including a 3-axis (X, Y, and Z) and the program is based on

DOI: 10.4018/979-8-3693-9057-3.ch009

Copyright © 2025, IGI Global Scientific Publishing. Copying or distributing in print or electronic forms without written permission of IGI Global Scientific Publishing is prohibited.

Image Processing which identifies the part geometry and painting real-time, which eradicates the issue of having multiple programs to paint a variety of geometrical parts at a particular time.

I. INTRODUCTION

Today, the Modern Industrial Revolution is on its way towards advancements. The industrial revolution is taking over the entire world at a glance. One of the major goals of today's industrial revolution is to adopt automation. Almost in every sector such as military, agriculture, automobile, manufacturing and design and development etc. Presently, automation is widely being implemented and used in the industrial sector all over the world, this is done in order to increase the efficiency and productivity of the manufactured goods. The automobile sector is also using automation to perform various tasks in the cars body manufacturing, assembly and paint shops in order to increase their per day productivity and efficiency of the cars. But however, the industrial automation is not implemented and used in Pakistan at its maximum pace. Thus, a lot of tasks are done manually, this affects the efficiency and productivity of the produced parts. In Pakistan, especially in the automobile sector, painting procedures are not fully carried out by robots, instead paid labors (humans) are also employed in painting small parts such as mirror covers, mud flaps, door handles, spoiler and fog lamps etc. And also, automatic painting is adopted only by factories and industries which produce large lot sizes of same type/variant of parts.

This paper discusses the possible feasible solution which will help shift the small-scale industries and the automobile industries to implement modern industrial automation by placing robots in their production line in order to increase their productivity and efficiency of produced goods.

Currently, Pakistan is not able to completely not able to adopt the industrial revolution along with the modern automation as because the initial capital cost is way too much for which small industries can't invest in it. The other major reason is that most of the robots are able to paint only one part variant at a time, thus industries not producing large lot sizes of same part variant are unable to get automatic painting being carried out in their industry. Another problem caused by this is the human health issues, as the painting process contains the release of harmful chemical fumes which ultimately affects human health. Also, human painted parts are sometimes not up to the mark as the paint coatings are uneven, thus the parts are not passed from quality check departments which results in reducing the productivity as well as efficiency of the parts produced by the industry. Thus, all these reasons affect the productivity and efficiency of the industrial produced goods.

Our idea is to introduce a Smart Painting Machine which will be capable of painting various geometry parts at a time. By this our aim is to introduce the concept of automatic painting in small-scale industries who cannot afford costly automatic painting machines within their vicinity. We basically derived the idea of automatic painting from the automobile industries where small parts such as mud flaps, door handles, spoilers, fog lamps etc. are painted by labors.

The key feature of this machine is basically its programming part which waves off the requirement to burn/run different programs for different geometrical parts. The programming embedded with the smart painting machine is basically based on image processing. A camera is mounted in the workspace of the painting machine which takes the real-time image of the part and then the image is processed. After processing the image, its geometry is detected by applying edge detection and contour detection. This results in identifying the object geometry by which the object coordinated are detected. Thus, the part is painted as per its geometry. This feature allows small lots of various geometrical parts to be painted with a single machine and single program. Thus, it's very beneficial for industries as it saves a lot of capital investment.

As far as human health is concerned, this machine follows all the safety protocols. The painting workspace is enclosed by a glass/acrylic frame house to eliminate the chances of spilling out paint particles as well as escape any painting chemical fumes. Thus, a lot of health issues like coughing, sneezing, nausea and breathing issues are eradicated.

II. LITERATURE REVIEW

The author in this paper plans to introduce a process for advance mechanizing spray painting of unknown parts. The machine made by this experiment will be very useful for painting unknown shapes. The time consumed by this machine is very less as compared to manual painting. It will, save expenditure such as labor cost and the total cost of painting any jobs. (Swarakar et al., 2018)

The author (Dhaval Thakar) in this paper gives essential knowledge about mini and large scaled industries manufacturing parts are painted for protecting from rust, so the spray method consumes large amount of time and paint which required the workers who are skilled emerge with the application. Robotic painting techniques is not applicable for large efficiency so the rise in such method have to be made which is affordable, have accuracy and precision, consumes minimum time for the coating of the part so objective has to developed in such a manner that the mechanism which coat the part with the dipping and baking process having semi-automated techniques which is up to the required mark and which can be valuable for mini and large scale factories. (Thakar & Vora, 2014)

Author in this research highlights some key features through the system test, it is fact that the design of intelligent robot have many advantage not only has good painting effect but also has high efficiency which can only at least 2-6 minutes to draw the simple cartoon images and also take no more than 15 minutes to draw complex portrait images. We also provided an illustrative example to show our required results. (Feng, Chen, Zhou, & Huang, 2017)

Author (Mohamed Abdellatif) in his research describes the design, construction and working of an Automatic wall painting robotic machine. This visionary and remarkable design of a robot which is movable to be used for painting interior walls of residential buildings or offices has been described. Robot has a roller that is fed with liquid paint and keeps contact with the wall surfaces. The robot has advanced options that helps the roller to scan vertically as well as horizontally to the painted walls. The robot has advance technology that can adjust itself in front of the wall. (Abdellatif, 2014)

The author (Berardo Naticchia) in his research shows that mechanical painting can be not only be done to upgrade production and also allows quality checking. The robotic arm application with high precision and accuracy is required. An automatic system to convert to the normal coordinates of the liquid colors to reproduce the moveable speed of the robot's end tool and valve opening and closing end of the mixing board. The maximum work shall be probably required to get high resolution (Naticchia, Giretti, & Carbonari, 2007)

The author in his research presents his work on articulated robots like these robots are widely re-known by basically automobile company commercials and robot dance applications. SCARA (Selective-Compliance-Articulated-Robot-Arm) robots are also re-known for their usage and proliferate in industries from 1970's. Two kind of robot articulated and SCARA robot's combination to gather linear and rotary motion accomplishing in formation for complex tasks (Eleyan, 2017)

In this research paper, the goal was to learn the system for coating and painting tasks carried out in automobile repair and then change manual painting by robot painting. So, the most important study was for skilled spray gun handling for automobile repair painting which were observed and compared with those with little or no experience. The spray gun movements of the experts were characterized by longer length, longer time, higher speed, and narrower swing range, compared with the non-experts. The results were collected and accordingly the spray gun movement was set. (Ikemoto et al., 2015)

The author of this paper presents research on (Image Processing) that can be directed to (Machine Learning) and the process of computing can identify pattern of high diverse parts. (Machine learning) is very close and similar to computing statistics that consist of spam filter optical character identification search engines and computer vision. Their extensive arrays of knowledge observed (algorithms) to reduce destruction noise such linear filter of (Gaussian-based) algorithm. Algorithms can remove certain kinds of grain noise destruction from a picture. Because every pixel of picture in setting to mean values in its environment the normal variations tested by the grain are reduced. (Wiley & Lucas, 2018)(Hosni, Li, & Ahmad, 2019)(Hosni et al., 2018)(Anwar et al., 2020)(Khan et al., 2023)(Hosni, Li, & Ahmad, 2018)(Ahmad et al., 2018)(Fatima et al., 2022)(Hosni, Li, & Ahmad, 2020)(Anwar et al., 2024)(Anwar et al., 2019)(Ahmad et al., 2020)

Author in this project through his studies, successfully identified the part from the background picture used for color process is required to remove the background by 1st filer grayscale filtering is the second step and finally by Circular Hough Transform (CHT) and binary testing for part that is in circular object detection. Using color processing is used as a powerful process to identify the part as it is in normal color process it has a lot of information as human eyes are capable of doing. For the grayscale filter it filters the (pixel and smoothness) the picture to the edge clear. In last CHT is required to detect the parts which are circular and total number is displayed. (Hussin, Juhari, Kang, Ismail, & Kamarudin, 2012)

Author In this research paper formulates that it is not possible to consider a single process for all types of images, nor can all process perform well for particular types of images. The background subtraction process identifies parts with noise destruction and output is not accurate and precise. The object behind the object is not recognized. During identification of part when any other thing comes before the part problem occurs. The image cannot be recognized if the position of camera is not accurate & object in picture is not snapped properly. (Jain & Chadokar, 2015)

Author In this paper through his knowledge and work proposes an algorithm that has been proved to meet the requirement of object detection without using the color feature in an automatic robot. The proposed algorithm especially relies on two main processes that emphasize shape identification and feature extraction that follows. The first method is edge detection and line-oriented method to perform contour extraction, which results in object detection in very less or no time. Next, the second method is a geometric moment that captures and computes the global features of the objects. Both the process is well assured in image processing, however, a mixture of both is a novel method in this study and has been proven to precisely detect static and moving object under illumination variety. (Dewi, Sundararajan, Prabuwono, & Cheng, 2019)

III. METHODOLOGY

A. Designing Phase

i. Hardware Designing

So initially, it is not recommended to go towards hardware fabrication directly. It is more desirable to first virtually design the hardware on a CADCAM Software, such as SolidWorks. Mostly, the thinking and fabricating part does not go hand to hand simultaneously as it's necessary that what we think can be implemented and fabricated practically, this leads to loss of time and capital. So, in order to check our design ideas and their practical fabrication feasibility, we will do the design work first.

So, in the designing phase, we first started with our conveyor. First the conveyor frame structure of dimensions 70in x 20in x 3in was made. To understand it, it is basically like a table structure. Now, in order to run to make the conveyor bed, we attached 2 rollers at each end of the conveyor frame. By attaching two rollers, it was observed that the conveyor belt be stable while moving as when the part comes in the middle of the conveyor belt while travelling, the belt will sag downwards due to no roller in the middle and this will cause irregular movement of the conveyor belt. Thus, we added a third roller in the middle of the conveyor frame. We now added a white rubber belt of 2mm thickness over the rollers to form a conveyor bed. Three double slotted pulleys were mounted on each of the three rollers in order to inter-connect the rollers with each other so that movement of the rollers is in sync. These pulleys are interconnected 2 rubber V-Belt, and the third belt of size is connected with a pulley and with a D.C Geared Motor of 30Nm torque (24V-3A) in order to drive the conveyor. The part to be painted will be placed on the conveyor, which will help in transporting the part to and from the painting work area. The conveyor design is given below in Figure 1.

Figure 1. Conveyor Design

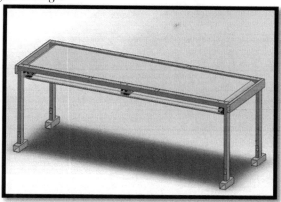

After the completion of the Conveyor Design or the Part Transporting Mechanism, we started to design the CNC Mechanism which is the Painting Mechanism of our Machine. The overall size of the CNC mechanism is 24in x 20in x 24in. Each of the 3 axis of the CNC machine is made of square shaped 2.5"x1" mild steel pipe. The main axis mechanism is formed of a ball screw of length 500mm and 8mm size of double threads. Each of the two ends of the ball screw is connected in the 8mm bearing which is mounted inside bearing housing. Now we will screw an 8mm double threaded nut over which an aluminum cube is fixed which acts as a traveler. All these things are fixed to form a single axis structure. We replicate this structure four times to form X, Y and Z axis individually (X axis is made from 2 of these structures). We mount individual Stepper Motor on each axis in order to rotate the ball screw so that the aluminum cube mounted over a nut move linearly back and forth. Each axis motion is limited/restricted by attaching a limit switch at both ends. This helps in restricting the axis motion in a forward or backward direction, so all the 3-axis does not collide with each other. The painting spray gun is mounted on the Z-axis of the CNC Mechanism. The Design of CNC Mechanism is given below in Figure 2.

Figure 2. CNC Mechanism Design

This CNC Mechanism is mounted on the conveyor in the middle, thus the area under the CNC mechanism is the painting working area. Ball screws are used to move the 3-axis of the CNC mechanism. These ball screws are rotated with the help of stepper motor and stepper drives are also used. The painting spray gun is mounted on the Z-axis of the CNC Mechanism.

Figure 3. Smart Painting Machine Complete Hardware Design

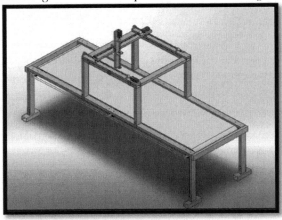

ii. Electronic Circuitry Designing

Apart from the hardware of the machine, the Brain which will help in driving the functionality of this machine is the Electronic Circuitry. Basically, the electronic Circuit of this machine needs to be designed exclusively for itself. The readily available circuits can't be integrated with one another to drive this painting machine, instead its circuit needs to be designed. The main task required by the circuitry is to:

1. Drive and control the motion of the Conveyor.
2. Drive and control the motion of the Painting Mechanism (i.e. 3-axis CNC Mechanism).
3. Assist the Image Processing Program in execution so that the part Geometry can be identified, and it's coordinated can be extracted in order to move the painting mechanism to perform the painting task.

Thus, in order to accomplish this task, we chose Raspberry Pi Microcontroller which will control the entire circuitry. Raspberry Pi will be powered by a 5V supply input which is fed from a 24V Power Supply after connected to a buck converter in series in order to step down the voltage. Also, the conveyor motor will be powered by this power supply and its programmable controlling will be handled by the switching of a relay which is connected to the raspberry pi microcontroller. The Raspberry Pi Camera Module will be connected to the microcontroller which through its assistance will capture the image of the part which will enter the workspace to be painted. Also, the Image Processing Software, which is developed on OpenCV to detect the part, identify it and calculate its geometrical coordinates, will also be executed by this microcontroller. Also, after the extraction of the parts center coordinates, these coordinates will be via Encoder and TTL IC will be fed to Arduino. The Arduino Microcontroller will take in the centroid coordinates of the part (X, Y, Z) and then drive the painting mechanism motors in order to paint the part. The motion of the axis is limited by Limit Switches.

The Designed Circuit for Smart Painting Machine is given in Figure 4 and Figure 5 below.

Figure 4. Design of Circuit 1

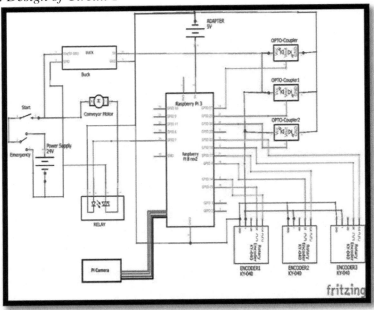

Figure 5. Design of Circuit 2

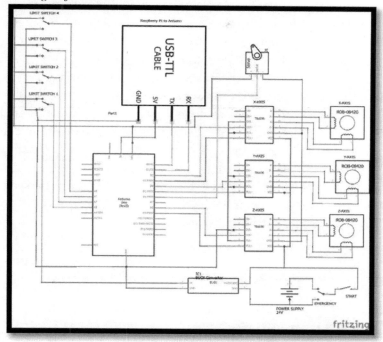

iii. Software Designing

The heart of this Smart Painting Machine is its Software. The software is basically termed as heart because the sole purpose which makes this machine smart is the image processing program. We thought of applying image processing in this machine as to get rid of uploading new programing from every new part and also forbid the idea of keeping/placing the part to be painted in a fixed place or to be fixed in its respective jigs. Image processing will help in determining the part orientation on the conveyor bed and also will calculate the part coordinates and will command the motor to move the axis respectively in order to paint it. To implement this idea, we had to first check whether his idea is working or is practically feasible to implement on a machine to calculate the part coordinates on real-time basis. Thus, for developing, testing and final implementation of this program, we chose to do this task using Python. The camera which will be taking the part image will be mounted over the workspace. Once the part enters the workspace, the IR sensor will indicate the microcontroller to stop the conveyor and then the part image will be taken and processed and then the part will get painted and then the conveyor will move, and the part will depart the workstation. So, to implement the software idea, we made a program which works as follows:

First the part image is read by the program. After reading the image, filters of erosion (processes which remove pixel from boundary of the object in an image) and Dilation (processes which add pixel to boundary of the object in an image) are implemented. Then the object in the image is subtracted from its background and then thresholding is applied on the image. After this Canny Edge Algorithm (which detects edges of the object with noises suppressed at the same time) is applied and then the Counter detection is applied (which joins the curve of all the continuous points along with boundaries of same pixel intensity). This enables the program to calculate the center of the object and its dimension. After this the coordination of the image is found. Then the motor steps are calculated, and this is passed on to the XYZ Algorithm which then controls the motor movement of the CNC axis. The below Figure 6 shows the Software design flowchart.

Figure 6. Software Flowchart

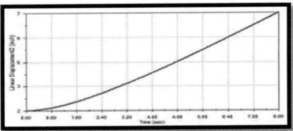

B. Implementation Via Virtual Simulation of the Painting Machine

i. SolidWorks Design Simulation and Analysis of The Hardware

As the Hardware was not able to get complete due to the pandemic situation, what we did that we designed and made a complete CAD Model of our hardware (which was to be fabricated) with exact configurations so that the hardware can be tested with respect to its structural properties and working principle. SolidWorks Software was used to make the CAD Model of the Hardware, and its Tools were used to obtain graphical results of the Structural Rigidity Tests which include Stress and Strain graphs of the critical hardware element. Also, Motion Analysis was performed of the working hardware and respective graphical results were calculated and portrayed in order to confirm the smooth working of the hardware and its motor while on full loading conditions. This will not only confirm the proper hardware working but will also help in analyzing the motor selection done in our project based on the interrupted working of the motors under loading conditions. Also, the speed of the CNC mechanism, i.e. the speed with which its axis moves can also be obtained.

ii. Image Processing Programming Simulation Using Jupyter

As briefed before, the Image Processing Program is used to detect the part geometry (i.e. the part which will be placed on a conveyor and enter the workspace) so that part can be painted as per its geometrical figure. This image processing programming was done on Python. This task was to be performed on real-time basis that as the part would enter the workspace, the camera mounted on the workspace would capture the image of the part placed on the conveyor and then image processing program would process this image and compare it with original part image in the directory and would classify the part and detect its geometry and center coordinates so that the part could be painted as per its geometry. However, due to unavailability of the hardware of this project, the testing of this image processing programming was performed on Jupyter. The testing results were perfect (as predicted) and the part was classified, its geometry was identified, and its center coordinates were perfectly calculated. This data found by Image Processing Program is useful to paint the part as per its geometry.

iii. Simulation Of Electronic Circuits and Painting Mechanism Using Arduino and Proteus:

At first, Raspberry Pi was to be used as a Controller in order to run the entire Painting Machine and its Electronics. As we moved towards Simulation, due to unavailability of the raspberry pi simulator, we used Proteus and Arduino in order to simulate the painting mechanism and other electronics of our project. The Part Coordinates obtained from the Image Processing is now fed into Arduino Programming (used to drive the Painting Mechanism as per the part geometry in order to perform Painting). This Arduino coding was interfaced to Proteus on which we had made the entire Electronic Circuitry of the Painting Machine. As we ran the Arduino coding, the part coordinates interpreted by the coding was used in the simulation of the circuitry in Proteus. The Smart Painting Machine Circuitry in the Proteus Simulation worked sequentially. As the part is placed on the conveyor, Sensor 1 detects the part presence, and the Conveyor Motor starts. Now as the part enters the workspace, Sensor 2 detects the part and stops the Conveyor Motor and after getting the part coordinates via image processing the Painting Mechanism starts moving as per the geometry and the part is painted. After the painting process is completed, the conveyor starts again and the part starts to move along the conveyor until it reaches the end of the conveyor where Sensor 3 detects the parts and stops the conveyor motor so that the painted part can be picked up by the human operator/labor.

C. Smart Painting Machine Working Principle

Initially, the conveyor will be stationary i.e. it won't be moving. There is an IR sensor mounted on the input side of the conveyor frame. The task of this IR sensor is to signal the conveyor's motor driver circuit that the part is placed at the input side of the conveyor. As the part is placed the conveyor, motor starts, and the belt begins to rotate over the conveyor rollers and the part moves forward towards the workspace i.e. Painting Mechanism. Now as the part moves inside the workspace, I.R sensor mounted inside the workspace signals the conveyor motor driver circuit to stop its motion and simultaneously it also informs the Main Controller of the Painting Machine (i.e. Raspberry Pi) that the part is now present inside the workspace. As now the part is stationary inside the workspace, the camera mounted in the workspace captures the image of the part and sends it to the main controller where further the part geometry is calculated by the program. As soon as the part geometry is calculated the main controller dispatches X Y Z Algorithm to the motor driving circuit of CNC mechanism. The CNC mechanism has a Painting Spray gun mounted on its z-axis. CNC mechanism or the painting mechanism moves as per the X Y Z Algorithm and the paint gun paints the part as per its geometry by moving about the coordinates of the part edges. Here the Limit Switches which is connected to each, and every axis of the CNC machine restricts the extra axis motion and helps in avoiding axis collision, thus there is no chance of distortion occurrence during the painting procedure. Also, the Encoder Sensors mounted on the motors shaft keeps the stepper motor control drive updated about motors' direction of rotation, position and speed. After the completion of part painting or we can say that after the complete execution of the X Y Z Algorithm, the painting mechanism moves at its home position and the camera captures a photo of the part and sends it to the main controller to check the painting work. After this machine controller sends a signal to the motor driver circuit of the conveyor motor to start its motion which in turn takes the path outside of the workspace and the part keeps on moving and until it reaches the end of the conveyor bed where IR sensor detects the part arrival and inform the motor driver circuit of the conveyor to stop its motion so that the part can be picked up by the user. As the part is picked up, the sensor signals the motor driver circuit of the conveyor that it can start its motion and thus the cycle of painting the next part continues. Also, for Safety purposes, Human/Obstacle Detection Sensors are mounted outside the workspace which signal the main controller stops all the operations at once if any human detection is made near the workspace. This promotes human safety.

Figure 7. Standard Operating Procedure of Smart Painting Machine

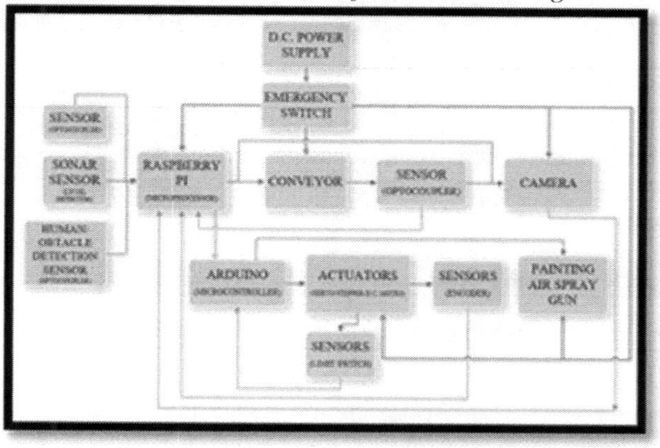

IV. RESULTS AND DISCUSSION

A. Hardware Simulation Results

Smart Painting Machine's Hardware was designed and simulated on SolidWorks. The hardware was fabricated asper the designed model. During the designing phase the material used for fabrications of the machine, ball-screw material and design configurations, driving motors, conveyor belt material and other things were all kept the same which we were going to use for the real hardware fabrications. This was done so to check the proper working of hardware during the simulation phase and rectify and error/problem (if any) so that it can be tackled during the designing phase only and no problems are caused during fabrications. To further ensure the hardware structural rigidity reliability, the critical element of the hardware (the component which bears maximum load during operation) was checked for its maximum stress it can handle, and its factor of safety (FOS) was checked. It was found out that the Yield Stress of ball screw is 350MPa and due to the load exertion, the Stress caused on ball screw is not more than 66.04MPa. Also, the Factor of Safety is 2.7 which means that the ball screw is very far away from fracture.

Figure 8. Ball Screw Stress Analysis

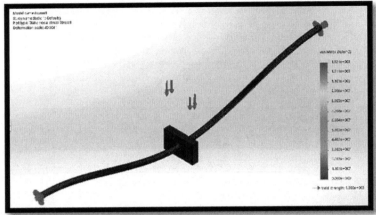

Figure 9. Ball Screw Factor of Safety

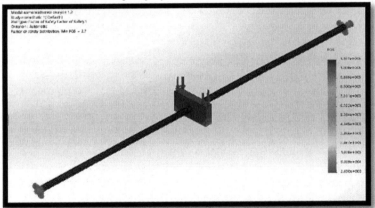

Also, to ensure the smooth working and motion of the Painting Mechanism (CNC Mechanism) we used the Motion Simulation Tool to check and calculate the graph of the Linear Displacement of the Motors which are used in driving the CNC Mechanism. The Results obtained shows a smooth homogenous curve free of distortion which shows that the motors driving the CNC Mechanism are working smoothly under the loading conditions without any jerks.

Figure 10. Linear Displacement of X-Axis Motor

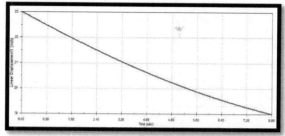

Figure 11. Linear Displacement of Y-Axis Motor

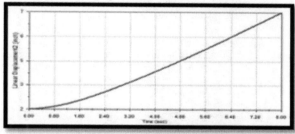

Figure 12. Linear Displacement of Z-Axis Motor

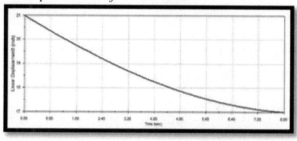

B. Image Processing Program Simulation Results

After successfully making the Image Processing Program of Object Detection and Classification and Simulating the Program on Jupyter, the desired results were obtained. The Resulting Images of the Parts show perfect geometry detection of the part which is to be painted and also its center coordinates are given. Almost 11 different parts were tested, result of some parts are given below.

Figure 13. Indicator Back cover- Object Detection

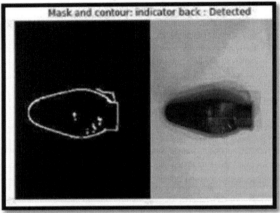

Figure 14. Indicator Back cover- Object Classification

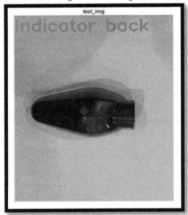

Figure 15. Indicator Back cover- Object Center Coordinates

```
Image Dimension    : (705, 531, 3)
Image Height       : 705
Image Width        : 531
Number of Channels : 3
0.6845390070921986 0.9088512241054615
centre in mm is   214.4888888888889 250.5412765957447
```

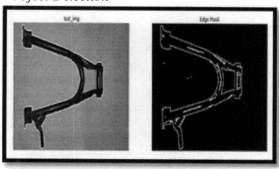

Figure 16. Stand- Object Detection

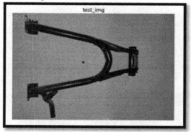

Figure 17. Stand- Object Classification

Figure 18. Stand- Object Center Coordinates

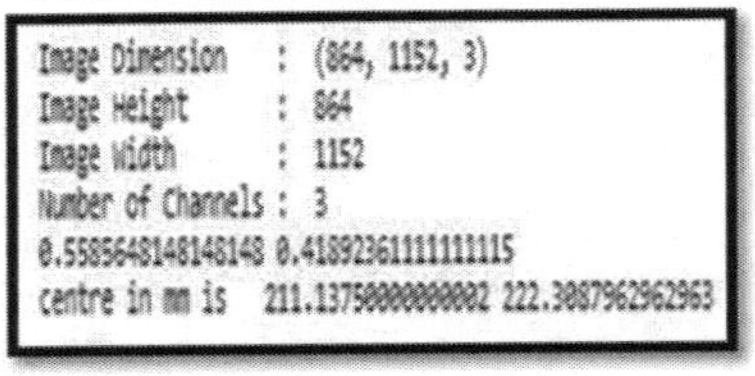

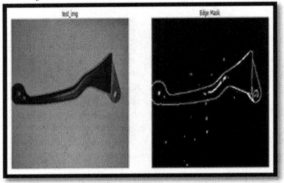

Figure 19. Handle- Object Detection

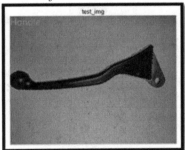

Figure 20. Handle- Object Classification

Figure 21. Handle- Object Center Coordinates

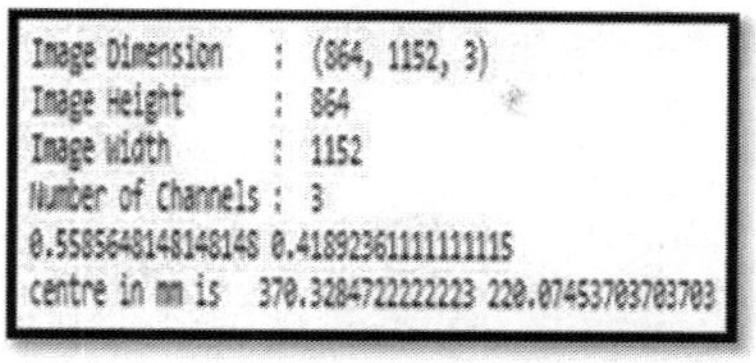

```
Image Dimension   : (864, 1152, 3)
Image Height      : 864
Image Width       : 1152
Number of Channels: 3
0.5585648148148148 0.4189236111111115
centre in mm is   370.3284722222223 220.07453703703703
```

C. Electronic Circuitry Simulation Result

The simulation of entire Electronic Circuitry which Drives and controls the Smart Painting Machine is done On Proteus. This simulation includes the whole sequential working of Smart Painting. Also, Arduino is interfaced with Proteus in this simulation in order control the motion of the Painting Mechanism (CNC Mechanism) as per the geometry of the part. The geometrical data of the part to be painted is extracted using the Image Processing Program and fed into the Arduino code. This allows the CNC Mechanism to move the Spray Paint Gun as per the part geometry. Circuit Simulated is given in Figure 16 below.

Figure 22. Proteus Simulated Circuit

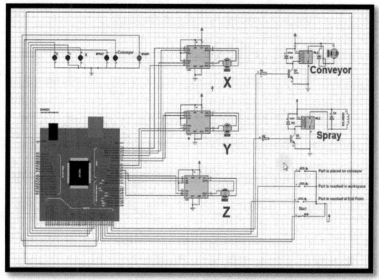

V. CONCLUSION AND RECOMMENDATIONS

A. Conclusion

By analyzing and observing the simulated results we can conclude that the Smart Painting Machine works as per the requirement and is performing the desired job efficiently. The Simulated Results of the hardware the shows feasibility of functionality and robustness of the machine itself. The designing part helps us determine whether the components that are to be incorporated in the machine structure will work as per the requirement and also how the maximum loading conditions will affect the working of the painting mechanism. The results obtained from the testing of the Hardware CAD Model further prove that Hardware Design is up to the mark in all aspects of robustness and functionality.

Also, by observing the simulation results of the Image Processing Program, we can conclude that the objects which will be placed on the conveyor will be correctly identified by the Developed Program using Image Processing. We have developed this program using Python OpenCV. The results obtained are very much accurate to that of the objects in the sample/saved images of the parts in the directory. We have also identified that whatever the orientation of the part on the conveyor, still the program will be able to identify the part correctly. Also, we during testing of this program also observed that the size of the real-time captured image of the part (zoomed-in or zoomed-out photograph) but still the program will detect and classify the part. However, there is a limitation that the angle of capturing the image of the sample and test image should be same.

The simulation of the Electronic Circuitry of the Smart Painting Machine was executed very well. This is because the Designed Circuitry of the Painting Machine fulfills all the requirements of which assists in smooth operation of the painting machine.

B. Recommendation And Future Works

As our FYP i.e., the Smart Painting Machine, which is designed and fabricated to be used in Automobile and Manufacturing Industries to Paint Various Geometrical Parts belonging to different families in a Single Batch by Painting the Part on the basis of its Geometry Detection. Thus, Image Processing Program (which is the heart of this machine) can be used to detect various geometrical parts and paint them as per their extracted contour and dimensions. Also, as currently static images are captured of the part that is to be painted as soon as it enters the workspace, and the conveyor movement is stopped. However, the programming can be further improved by implementing some algorithms which enable the program to still identify the part geometry efficiently even if the conveyor motion prolongs for a millisecond although Proximity Sensor 2 detects the part presence inside the workspace. If in this instance the camera captures the part image so there might be errors in detecting the part geometry of a slightly distorted image. Using effective image enhancement algorithms can help in overcoming this shortcoming.

For the Simulation of Image Processing Program, the participation of the images was captured by a phone camera. Thus, the angle capturing the part photo was not always the same thus this produced a slight error in marking the Center Point of the part in the image (Although the part is Detected and Classified correctly). So, when we run this programming by using the machine hardware, then the camera must be mounted at a fixed angle so that the Camera (For Capturing Part Image) at a Fixed Position and Orientation so that the captured image is properly aligned.

Also, this The Image Processing Program developed for Smart Painting Machine can be used in Following Applications:

- This Program can be used for sorting the objects with Pick and Place Robot.
- It can be used in Smart Welding Robot.
- This system can be used for the Identification of Currency Papers.

REFERENCES

Abdellatif, M. (2012, August). Design of an autonomous wall painting robot. In *First International Symposium on Socially and Technically Symbiotic Systems.* Okayama, Japan.

Abdullah, F. B., Iqbal, R., Ahmad, S., El-Affendi, M. A., & Abdullah, M. (2022). An empirical analysis of sustainable energy security for energy policy recommendations. *Sustainability, 14*(10), 6099.

Abdullah, F. B., Iqbal, R., Ahmad, S., El-Affendi, M. A., & Kumar, P. (2022). Optimization of multidimensional energy security: An index based assessment. *Energies, 15*(11), 3929.

Ahmad, S., Anwar, M. S., Ebrahim, M., Khan, W., Raza, K., Adil, S. H., & Amin, A. (2020). Deep network for the iterative estimations of students' cognitive skills. *IEEE Access : Practical Innovations, Open Solutions, 8*, 103100–103113. DOI: 10.1109/ACCESS.2020.2999064

Ahmad, S., El-Affendi, M. A., Anwar, M. S., & Iqbal, R. (2022). Potential future directions in optimization of students' performance prediction system. *Computational Intelligence and Neuroscience, 2022*(1), 6864955.

Ahmad, S., Li, K., Amin, A., Anwar, M. S., & Khan, W. (2018). A multilayer prediction approach for the student cognitive skills measurement. *IEEE Access : Practical Innovations, Open Solutions, 6*, 57470–57484. DOI: 10.1109/ACCESS.2018.2873608

Ahmad, S., Li, K., Eddine, H. A. I., & Khan, M. I. (2018). A biologically inspired cognitive skills measurement approach. Biologically inspired cognitive architectures, 24, 35-46.

Akhtar, S., Ali, A., Ahmad, S., Khan, M. I., Shah, S., & Hassan, F. (2022). The prevalence of foot ulcers in diabetic patients in Pakistan: A systematic review and meta-analysis. *Frontiers in Public Health, 10*, 1017201. DOI: 10.3389/fpubh.2022.1017201 PMID: 36388315

Akhtar, S., Ramzan, M., Shah, S., Ahmad, I., Khan, M. I., Ahmad, S., & Qureshi, H. (2022). Forecasting exchange rate of Pakistan using time series analysis. *Mathematical Problems in Engineering, 2022*(1), 9108580.

Anwar, M. S., Choi, A., Ahmad, S., Aurangzeb, K., Laghari, A. A., Gadekallu, T. R., & Hines, A. (2024). A Moving Metaverse: QoE challenges and standards requirements for immersive media consumption in autonomous vehicles. *Applied Soft Computing, 159*, 111577. DOI: 10.1016/j.asoc.2024.111577

Anwar, M. S., Ullah, I., Ahmad, S., Choi, A., Ahmad, S., Wang, J., & Aurangzeb, K. (2023). Immersive learning and AR/VR-based education: cybersecurity measures and risk management. In *Cybersecurity management in education technologies* (pp. 1–22). CRC Press.

Anwar, M. S., Wang, J., Ahmad, S., Khan, W., Ullah, A., Shah, M., & Fei, Z. (2020). Impact of the impairment in 360-degree videos on users VR involvement and machine learning-based QoE predictions. *IEEE Access : Practical Innovations, Open Solutions*, 8, 204585–204596. DOI: 10.1109/ACCESS.2020.3037253

Anwar, M. S., Wang, J., Ullah, A., Khan, W., Ahmad, S., & Li, Z. (2019, December). Impact of stalling on QoE for 360-degree virtual reality videos. In *2019 IEEE International Conference on Signal, Information and Data Processing (ICSIDP)* (pp. 1-6). IEEE.

Anwar, M. S., Wang, J., Ullah, A., Khan, W., Li, Z., & Ahmad, S. (2018, October). User profile analysis for enhancing QoE of 360 panoramic video in virtual reality environment. In *2018 International Conference on Virtual Reality and Visualization (ICVRV)* (pp. 106-111). IEEE.

Dewi, D. A., Sundararajan, E., Prabuwono, A. S., & Cheng, L. M. (2019). Object detection without color feature: Case study Autonomous Robot. *International Journal of Mechanical Engineering and Robotics Research*, 8(4), 646–650. DOI: 10.18178/ijmerr.8.4.646-650

Eleyan, A. (2017)... *An Autonomous Robotic Cell for Painting Applications*, (April). Advance online publication. DOI: 10.2316/P.2017.848-014

Fatima, R., Samad Shaikh, N., Riaz, A., Ahmad, S., El-Affendi, M. A., Alyamani, K. A., & Latif, R. M. A. (2022). A natural language processing (NLP) evaluation on COVID-19 rumour dataset using deep learning techniques. *Computational Intelligence and Neuroscience*, 2022(1), 6561622.

Feng, X., Chen, L., Zhou, W., & Huang, Z. (2017). Research on the Design of Smart Paint Robot. DEStech Transactions on Materials Science and Engineering, c, 1-5.

Hosni, A. I. E., Li, K., & Ahmad, S. (2019, December). DARIM: Dynamic approach for rumor influence minimization in online social networks. In *International Conference on Neural Information Processing* (pp. 619-630). Cham: Springer International Publishing.

Hosni, A. I. E., Li, K., & Ahmad, S. (2020). Analysis of the impact of online social networks addiction on the propagation of rumors. *Physica A*, *542*, 123456. DOI: 10.1016/j.physa.2019.123456

Hosni, A. I. E., Li, K., & Ahmed, S. (2018). HISBmodel: A rumor diffusion model based on human individual and social behaviors in online social networks. In Neural Information Processing: 25th International Conference, ICONIP 2018, Siem Reap, Cambodia, December 13–16, 2018 [Springer International Publishing.]. *Proceedings*, *25*(Part II), 14–27.

Hosni, A. I. E., Li, K., Ding, C., & Ahmed, S. (2018, November). Least cost rumor influence minimization in multiplex social networks. In *International Conference on Neural Information Processing* (pp. 93-105). Cham: Springer International Publishing.

Hussin, R., Juhari, M. R., Kang, N. W., Ismail, R. C., & Kamarudin, A. (2012). Digital image processing techniques for object detection from complex background image. *Procedia Engineering*, *41*, 340–344.

Ikemoto, S., Liao, M., Takai, Y., Goto, A., Nishimoto, H., & Hamada, H. (2015). RETRACTED: Impact of Operator Experience on Spray Gun Handling for Automobile Repair.

Jain, S., & Chadokar, S. (2015). A Object Detection in Image Processing: A Review. International Journal of Electrical. *Electronics and Computer Engineering*, *4*(2), 26.

Khan, M. I., Qureshi, H., Bae, S. J., Khattak, A. A., Anwar, M. S., Ahmad, S., Hassan, F., & Ahmad, S. (2023). Malaria prevalence in Pakistan: A systematic review and meta-analysis (2006–2021). *Heliyon*, *9*(4), 4. DOI: 10.1016/j.heliyon.2023. e15373 PMID: 37123939

Khan, S., Zhang, Z., Zhu, L., Rahim, M. A., Ahmad, S., & Chen, R. (2020). SCM: Secure and accountable TLS certificate management. *International Journal of Communication Systems*, *33*(15), e4503.

Naticchia, B., Giretti, A., & Carbonari, A. (2007). Set up of an automated multi-colour system for interior wall painting. *International Journal of Advanced Robotic Systems*, *4*(4), 407–416. DOI: 10.5772/5666

Rahim, M., Amin, F., Tag Eldin, E. M., Khalifa, A. E. W., & Ahmad, S. (2024). p, q-Spherical fuzzy sets and their aggregation operators with application to third-party logistic provider selection. *Journal of Intelligent & Fuzzy Systems*, *46*(1), 505–528.

Swarakar, J. R.. (2018).. . *Design and Fabrication of Automatic Spray Painting Machine*, (2), 1388–1394.

Thakar, D., & Vora, C. P. (2014). A Review on Design & Development of Semi-Automated Colour Painting Machine [Online] [. Available: www.ijera.com.]. *J. Eng. Res. Appl.*, *4*(4), 58–61. www.ijera.com

Wiley, V., & Lucas, T. (2018). Computer Vision and Image Processing: A Paper Review. *Int. J. Artif. Intell. Res.*, 2(1), 22. DOI: 10.29099/ijair.v2i1.42

Compilation of References

. Abd El-Rahiem, B., & Hammad, M. (2022). A multi-fusion IoT authentication system based on internal deep fusion of ECG signals. *Security and Privacy Preserving for IoT and 5G Networks: Techniques, Challenges, and New Directions*, 53-79.

. Chopra, A., Prashar, A., & Sain, C. (2013). Natural language processing. International journal of technology enhancements and emerging engineering research, 1(4), 131-134.

. Roiger, R. J. (2017). Data mining: a tutorial-based primer.

Abbaschian, B. J., Sierra-Sosa, D., & Elmaghraby, A. (2021). Deep learning techniques for speech emotion recognition, from databases to models. *Sensors (Basel)*, *21*(4), 1–27. DOI: 10.3390/s21041249 PMID: 33578714

Abbas, K., Tawalbeh, L. A. A., Rafiq, A., Muthanna, A., Elgendy, I. A., & Abd El-Latif, A. A. (2021). Convergence of blockchain and IoT for secure transportation systems in smart cities. *Security and Communication Networks*, *2021*, 1–13. DOI: 10.1155/2021/5597679

Abd El-Latif, A. A., Maleh, Y., El-Affendi, M. A., & Ahmad, S. (Eds.). (2023). *Cybersecurity Management in Education Technologies: Risks and Countermeasures for Advancements in E-learning*. CRC Press. DOI: 10.1201/9781003369042

Abd-El-Atty, B., Iliyasu, A. M., Alanezi, A., & Abd El-latif, A. A. (2021). Optical image encryption based on quantum walks. *Optics and Lasers in Engineering*, *138*, 106403. DOI: 10.1016/j.optlaseng.2020.106403

Abdellatif, M. (2012, August). Design of an autonomous wall painting robot. In *First International Symposium on Socially and Technically Symbiotic Systems*. Okayama, Japan.

Abdullah, F. B., Iqbal, R., Ahmad, S., El-Affendi, M. A., & Abdullah, M. (2022). An empirical analysis of sustainable energy security for energy policy recommendations. *Sustainability*, *14*(10), 6099.

Abdullah, F. B., Iqbal, R., Ahmad, S., El-Affendi, M. A., & Kumar, P. (2022). Optimization of multidimensional energy security: An index based assessment. *Energies*, *15*(11), 3929.

Abdullah, T., & Ahmet, A. (2022). Deep learning in sentiment analysis: Recent architectures. *ACM Computing Surveys*, *55*(8), 1–37. DOI: 10.1145/3548772

Abdullayev, S. (2023). The evolving landscape of translation. *Philological issues are in the eyes of young researchers, 1*[1].

Adiyansjah, G., Gunawan, A. A. S., & Suhartono, D. (2019). Music recommender system based on genre using convolutional recurrent neural networks. *Procedia Computer Science*, *157*, 99–109. DOI: 10.1016/j.procs.2019.08.146

Agrawal, A. V., Magulur, L. P., Priya, S. G., Kaur, A., Singh, G., & Boopathi, S. (2023). Smart Precision Agriculture Using IoT and WSN. In *Handbook of Research on Data Science and Cybersecurity Innovations in Industry 4.0 Technologies* (pp. 524–541). IGI Global. DOI: 10.4018/978-1-6684-8145-5.ch026

Ahmad, S., & Adnan, A. (2015, July). Machine learning based cognitive skills calculations for different emotional conditions. In *2015 IEEE 14th International Conference on Cognitive Informatics & Cognitive Computing (ICCI* CC)* (pp. 162-168). IEEE. DOI: 10.1109/ICCI-CC.2015.7259381

Ahmad, S., Anwar, M. S., Khan, M. A., Shahzad, M., Ebrahim, M., & Memon, I. (2021, November). Deep Frustration Severity Network for the Prediction of Declined Students' Cognitive Skills. In *2021 4th international conference on Computing & Information Sciences (ICCIS)* (pp. 1-6). IEEE.

Ahmad, S., Li, K., Amin, A., & Faheem, M. Y. (2018, July). Simulation of student skills: The novel technique based on quantization of cognitive skills outcomes. In *2018 IEEE 17th International Conference on Cognitive Informatics & Cognitive Computing (ICCI* CC)* (pp. 97-102). IEEE.

Ahmad, S., Li, K., Eddine, H. A. I., & Khan, M. I. (2018). A biologically inspired cognitive skills measurement approach. *Biologically inspired cognitive architectures, 24*, 35-46.

Ahmad, S., Li, K., Li, Y., Qureshi, H., & Khan, S. (2017, July). Formulation of Cognitive Skills: A theoretical model based on psychological and neurosciences studies. In *2017 IEEE 16th International Conference on Cognitive Informatics & Cognitive Computing (ICCI*CC)* (pp. 167-174). IEEE. DOI: 10.1109/ICCI-CC.2017.8109746

Ahmad, T., Ahmad, S., Rahim, A., & Shah, N. (2023). Development of a Novel Deep Convolutional Neural Network Model for Early Detection of Brain Stroke Using CT Scan Images. In *Recent Advancements in Multimedia Data Processing and Security: Issues, Challenges, and Techniques* (pp. 197-229). IGI Global. DOI: 10.4018/978-1-6684-7216-3.ch010

Ahmad, P. N., Guo, J., AboElenein, N. M., Haq, Q. M. U., Ahmad, S., Algarni, A. D., & Ateya, A. (1827). A. (2025). Hierarchical graph-based integration network for propaganda detection in textual news articles on social media. *Scientific Reports*, *15*(1).

Ahmad, P. N., Liu, Y., Ali, G., Wani, M. A., & ElAffendi, M. (2023). Robust Benchmark for Propagandist Text Detection and Mining High-Quality Data. *Mathematics*, *11*(12), 2668. Advance online publication. DOI: 10.3390/math11122668

Ahmad, S., Adnan, A., Khan, G., & Mehmood, N. (2015). Emotions, age, and gender based cognitive skills calculations. *International Journal of Computer Theory and Engineering*, *7*(1), 76–80. DOI: 10.7763/IJCTE.2015.V7.934

Ahmad, S., Anwar, M. S., Ebrahim, M., Khan, W., Raza, K., Adil, S. H., & Amin, A. (2020). Deep network for the iterative estimations of students' cognitive skills. *IEEE Access : Practical Innovations, Open Solutions*, 8, 103100–103113. DOI: 10.1109/ACCESS.2020.2999064

Ahmad, S., Aoun, N. B., Ali, G., El-Affendi, M. A., & Anwar, M. S. (2023). Multi-Clustered Mathematical Model for Student Cognitive Skills Prediction Optimization. *IEEE Access : Practical Innovations, Open Solutions*, *11*, 65371–65381. DOI: 10.1109/ACCESS.2023.3285612

Ahmad, S., Ben Aoun, N., Affendi, M. A. E., Anwar, M. S., Abbas, S., & Latif, A. A. A. E. (2022). Optimization of Students' Performance Prediction through an Iterative Model of Frustration Severity. *Computational Intelligence and Neuroscience*, *2022*(1), 3183492. DOI: 10.1155/2022/3183492 PMID: 36017453

Ahmad, S., El-Affendi, M. A., Anwar, M. S., & Iqbal, R. (2022). Potential future directions in optimization of students' performance prediction system. *Computational Intelligence and Neuroscience*, *2022*(1), 6864955. DOI: 10.1155/2022/6864955 PMID: 35619762

Ahmad, S., Li, K., Amin, A., Anwar, M. S., & Khan, W. (2018). A multilayer prediction approach for the student cognitive skills measurement. *IEEE Access : Practical Innovations, Open Solutions, 6*, 57470–57484. DOI: 10.1109/ACCESS.2018.2873608

Ahmad, S., Li, K., Amin, A., & Khan, S. (2018). A novel technique for the evaluation of posterior probabilities of student cognitive skills. *IEEE Access : Practical Innovations, Open Solutions, 6*, 53153–53167. DOI: 10.1109/ACCESS.2018.2870877

Ahmed, J., & Ahmed, M. (2023). Classification, detection and sentiment analysis using machine learning over next generation communication platforms. *Microprocessors and Microsystems, 98*, 104795. DOI: 10.1016/j.micpro.2023.104795

Ahmed, M. T., Antar, A. H., Rahman, M., Islam, A. Z. M. T., Das, D., & Rashed, M. G. (2023). Social media cyberbullying detection on political violence from Bangla texts using machine learning algorithm. *Journal of Intelligent Learning Systems and Applications, 15*(4), 108–122. DOI: 10.4236/jilsa.2023.154008

Ahmed, W., Semary, N. A., Amin, K., & Hammad, M. (2025). Hyperparameter Optimization of Machine Learning Models Using Grid Search for Twitter Sentiment Analysis. In *Humanizing Technology With Emotional Intelligence* [pp. 419-432]. IGI Global Scientific Publishing.

Airlangga, G. (2024). Comparative Analysis of Machine Learning Models for Real-Time Disaster Tweet Classification: Enhancing Emergency Response with Social Media Analytics. *Brilliance: Research of Artificial Intelligence, 4*(1), 25–31. DOI: 10.47709/brilliance.v4i1.3669

Akhtar, M., Rahim, M., Alanzi, A. M., Ahmad, S., Fatlane, J. M., Aphane, M., & Khalifa, H. A. E.-W. (2023). Dombi Aggregation Operators for p, qr–Spherica Fuzzy Sets: Application in the Stability Assessment of Cryptocurrencies. *IEEE Access : Practical Innovations, Open Solutions, 12*, 10366–10382. DOI: 10.1109/ACCESS.2023.3346916

Akhtar, S., Ali, A., Ahmad, S., Khan, M. I., Shah, S., & Hassan, F. (2022). The prevalence of foot ulcers in diabetic patients in Pakistan: A systematic review and meta-analysis. *Frontiers in Public Health, 10*, 1017201. DOI: 10.3389/fpubh.2022.1017201 PMID: 36388315

Akhtar, S., Ramzan, M., Shah, S., Ahmad, I., Khan, M. I., Ahmad, S., & Qureshi, H. (2022). Forecasting exchange rate of Pakistan using time series analysis. *Mathematical Problems in Engineering, 2022*(1), 9108580.

Al-Dabagh, M. Z. N., Hussein, H. I., Raheem, S. A., Ahmed, M. I., & Othman, N. A. (2024). Enhancing Face Recognition for Security Systems: An Approach Using Gabor Wavelet, t-SNE, and SVM. In *ITM Web of Conferences* (Vol. 64, p. 01008). EDP Sciences.

Ali, K. M., Ahmed Khan, T., Ali, S. M., Aziz, A., Khan, S. A., & Ahmad, S. (2024). An Exhaustive Comparative Study of Machine Learning Algorithms for Natural Language Processing Applications. *Engineering Proceedings*, *76*(1), 79.

Ali, M. N., Senthil, T., Ilakkiya, T., Hasan, D. S., Ganapathy, N. B. S., & Boopathi, S. (2024). IoT's Role in Smart Manufacturing Transformation for Enhanced Household Product Quality. In *Advanced Applications in Osmotic Computing* (pp. 252–289). IGI Global. DOI: 10.4018/979-8-3693-1694-8.ch014

Ali, S., Kayani, U., & Yousaf, I. (2024). Time-frequency comovements between news sentiments, Non-fungible tokens, and DeFi assets: Evidence from the wavelet analysis. *Applied Economics*, *0*(0), 1–20. DOI: 10.1080/00036846.2024.2405659

Almeshekah, M. H., & Spafford, E. H. (2014, September). Planning and integrating deception into computer security defenses. In *Proceedings of the 2014 New Security Paradigms Workshop* (pp. 127-138). DOI: 10.1145/2683467.2683482

Al-Tameemi, I. K. S., Feizi-Derakhshi, M. R., Pashazadeh, S., & Asadpour, M. (2024). A comprehensive review of visual–textual sentiment analysis from social media networks. *Journal of Computational Social Science*, *7*(3), 2767–2838. DOI: 10.1007/s42001-024-00326-y

Alzubaidi, L., Zhang, J., Humaidi, A. J., Al-Dujaili, A., Duan, Y., Al-Shamma, O., Santamaría, J., Fadhel, M. A., Al-Amidie, M., & Farhan, L. (2021). Review of deep learning: Concepts, CNN architectures, challenges, applications, future directions. *Journal of Big Data*, *8*(1), 53. DOI: 10.1186/s40537-021-00444-8 PMID: 33816053

Amjoud, A. B., & Amrouch, M. (2021). *Automatic generation of chest x-ray reports using a transformer-based deep learning model.* Paper presented at the 2021 Fifth International Conference On Intelligent Computing in Data Sciences (ICDS). DOI: 10.1109/ICDS53782.2021.9626725

Anand, R., Sindhwani, N., & Juneja, S. (2022). *"Cognitive Internet of Things, Its Applications, and Its Challenges: A Survey." Harnessing the Internet of Things (IoT) for a Hyper-Connected Smart World.* Apple Academic Press. DOI: 10.1201/9781003277347-5

Androutsopoulos, J. (2011). Language change and digital media: A review of conceptions and evidence. *Standard languages and language standards in a changing. Europe, 1*, 145–159.

Anwar, M. S.. (2023). *"Immersive learning and AR/VR-based education: cybersecurity measures and risk management." Cybersecurity Management in Education Technologies.* CRC Press. DOI: 10.1201/9781003369042-1

Anwar, M. S., Choi, A., Ahmad, S., Aurangzeb, K., Laghari, A. A., Gadekallu, T. R., & Hines, A. (2024). A Moving Metaverse: QoE challenges and standards requirements for immersive media consumption in autonomous vehicles. *Applied Soft Computing, 159*, 111577. DOI: 10.1016/j.asoc.2024.111577

Anwar, M. S., Ullah, I., Ahmad, S., Choi, A., Ahmad, S., Wang, J., & Aurangzeb, K. (2023). Immersive learning and AR/VR-based education: cybersecurity measures and risk management. In *Cybersecurity management in education technologies* (pp. 1–22). CRC Press.

Anwar, M. S., Wang, J., Ahmad, S., Khan, W., Ullah, A., Shah, M., & Fei, Z. (2020). Impact of the impairment in 360-degree videos on users VR involvement and machine learning-based QoE predictions. *IEEE Access : Practical Innovations, Open Solutions, 8*, 204585–204596. DOI: 10.1109/ACCESS.2020.3037253

Anwar, M. S., Wang, J., Ullah, A., Khan, W., Ahmad, S., & Li, Z. (2019, December). Impact of stalling on QoE for 360-degree virtual reality videos. In *2019 IEEE International Conference on Signal, Information and Data Processing (ICSIDP)* (pp. 1-6). IEEE.

Anwar, M. S., Wang, J., Ullah, A., Khan, W., Li, Z., & Ahmad, S. (2018, October). User profile analysis for enhancing QoE of 360 panoramic video in virtual reality environment. In *2018 International Conference on Virtual Reality and Visualization (ICVRV)* (pp. 106-111). IEEE.

Apicella, A., Arpaia, P., Frosolone, M., Improta, G., Moccaldi, N., & Pollastro, A. (2022). Eeg-based measurement system for monitoring student engagement in learning 4.0. *Scientific Reports, 12*(1), 12. DOI: 10.1038/s41598-022-09578-y PMID: 35393470

Arabian, H., Wagner-Hartl, V., & Moeller, K. (2021). Traditional versus neural network classification methods for facial emotion recognition. *Current Directions in Biomedical Engineering, 7*(2), 203–206. DOI: 10.1515/cdbme-2021-2052

Araque, O., Corcuera-Platas, I., Sánchez-Rada, J. F., & Iglesias, C. A. (2017). Enhancing deep learning sentiment analysis with ensemble techniques in social applications. *Expert Systems with Applications*, *77*, 236–246. DOI: 10.1016/j. eswa.2017.02.002

Arif, F., Khan, N. A., ul Haq, Q. M., Asim, M., & Ahmad, S. (2024). An SDN-AI-Based Approach for Detecting Anomalies in Imbalance Data within a Network of Smart Medical Devices. *IEEE Consumer Electronics Magazine*.

Arshad, M., Khan, B., Ahmad, S., & Asim, M. (2024). Predicting Age and Gender in Author Profiling: A Multi-Feature Exploration. *Computers, Materials & Continua*, *79*(2), 3333–3353. DOI: 10.32604/cmc.2024.049254

Arshad, M., Khan, B., Khan, K., Qamar, A. M., & Khan, R. U. (2024). ABMRF: An Ensemble Model for Author Profiling Based on Stylistic Features Using Roman Urdu. *Intelligent Automation & Soft Computing*, *39*(2), 301–317. DOI: 10.32604/iasc.2024.045402

Asharf, J., Moustafa, N., Khurshid, H., Debie, E., Haider, W., & Wahab, A. (2020). A review of intrusion detection systems using machine and deep learning in internet of things: Challenges, solutions and future directions. *Electronics (Basel)*, *9*(7), 1177. DOI: 10.3390/electronics9071177

Ateya, A. A., Mahmoud, M., Zaghloul, A., Soliman, N. F., & Muthanna, A. (2022). Empowering the Internet of Things Using Light Communication and Distributed Edge Computing. *Electronics (Basel)*, *11*(9), 1511. DOI: 10.3390/electronics11091511

Ateya, A. A., Muthanna, A., Koucheryavy, A., Maleh, Y., & El-Latif, A. A. A. (2023). Energy efficient offloading scheme for MEC-based augmented reality system. *Cluster Computing*, *26*(1), 1–18. DOI: 10.1007/s10586-022-03914-7

Ateya, A. A., Soliman, N. F., Alkanhel, R., Alhussan, A. A., Muthanna, A., & Koucheryavy, A. (2022). Lightweight Deep Learning-Based Model for Traffic Prediction in Fog-Enabled Dense Deployed IoT Networks. *Journal of Electrical Engineering & Technology*, ●●●, 1–11.

Avital, M., & Te'Eni, D. (2009). From generative fit to generative capacity: Exploring an emerging dimension of information systems design and task performance. *Information Systems Journal*, *19*(4), 345–367. DOI: 10.1111/j.1365-2575.2007.00291.x

Balovsyak, S., Derevyanchuk, O., Kovalchuk, V., Kravchenko, H., & Kozhokar, M. (2024). Face Mask Recognition by the Viola-Jones Method Using Fuzzy Logic. *International Journal of Image* [IJIGSP]. *Graphics and Signal Processing*, *16*(3), 39–51. DOI: 10.5815/ijigsp.2024.03.04

Beigi, G., Hu, X., Maciejewski, R., & Liu, H. (2016). An overview of sentiment analysis in social media and its applications in disaster relief. *Sentiment analysis and ontology engineering: An environment of computational intelligence*, 313-340.

Bhavani, S. A., & Karthikeyan, C. (2024). Robust 3D face recognition in unconstrained environment using distance based ternary search siamese network. *Multimedia Tools and Applications*, *83*(17), 51925–51953. DOI: 10.1007/s11042-023-17545-6

Bochkovskiy, A., Wang, C.-Y., & Liao, H.-Y. M. J. a. p. a. (2020). Yolov4: Optimal speed and accuracy of object detection.

Boopathi, S. (2024). Advancements in Optimizing Smart Energy Systems Through Smart Grid Integration, Machine Learning, and IoT. In Optimization Techniques for Hybrid Power Systems: Renewable Energy, Electric Vehicles, and Smart Grid (pp. 33-61). IGI Global.

Boopathi, S. (2024). Sustainable Development Using IoT and AI Techniques for Water Utilization in Agriculture. In *Sustainable Development in AI, Blockchain, and E-Governance Applications* (pp. 204–228). IGI Global. DOI: 10.4018/979-8-3693-1722-8.ch012

Boopathi, S. (2023). Internet of Things-Integrated Remote Patient Monitoring System: Healthcare Application. In *Dynamics of Swarm Intelligence Health Analysis for the Next Generation* (pp. 137–161). IGI Global. DOI: 10.4018/978-1-6684-6894-4.ch008

Boopathi, S. (2024). Advancements in Machine Learning and AI for Intelligent Systems in Drone Applications for Smart City Developments. In *Futuristic e-Governance Security With Deep Learning Applications* (pp. 15–45). IGI Global. DOI: 10.4018/978-1-6684-9596-4.ch002

Bushelenkov, S., Paramonov, A., Muthanna, A., El-Latif, A. A. A., Koucheryavy, A., Alfarraj, O., Pławiak, P., & Ateya, A. A. (2023). Multi-Story Building Model for Efficient IoT Network Design. *Mathematics*, *11*(6), 1403. DOI: 10.3390/math11061403

Calo, S. B., Touna, M., Verma, D. C., & Cullen, A. (2017, December). Edge computing architecture for applying AI to IoT. In 2017 IEEE International Conference on Big Data (Big Data) (pp. 3012-3016). IEEE. DOI: 10.1109/BigData.2017.8258272

Cambria, E., & White, B. (2014). Jumping NLP curves: A review of natural language processing research. *IEEE Computational Intelligence Magazine*, *9*(2), 48–57. DOI: 10.1109/MCI.2014.2307227

Canchila, S., Meneses-Eraso, C., Casanoves-Boix, J., Cortés-Pellicer, P., & Castelló-Sirvent, F. (2024). Natural language processing: An overview of models, transformers and applied practices. *Computer Science and Information Systems*, *21*(00), 31–31. DOI: 10.2298/CSIS230217031C

Cao, Z., Simon, T., Wei, S.-E., & Sheikh, Y. (2017). *Realtime multi-person 2d pose estimation using part affinity fields.* Paper presented at the Proceedings of the IEEE Conference on Computer Vision and Pattern Recognition. DOI: 10.1109/CVPR.2017.143

Carion, N., Massa, F., Synnaeve, G., Usunier, N., Kirillov, A., & Zagoruyko, S. (2020). *End-to-end object detection with transformers.* Paper presented at the European conference on computer vision.

Chang, R. M., Kauffman, R. J., & Kwon, Y. (2014). Understanding the paradigm shift to computational social science in the presence of big data. *Decision Support Systems*, *63*, 67–80. DOI: 10.1016/j.dss.2013.08.008

Chen, C., Seff, A., Kornhauser, A., & Xiao, J. (2015). *Deepdriving: Learning affordance for direct perception in autonomous driving.* Paper presented at the Proceedings of the IEEE International Conference on Computer Vision. DOI: 10.1109/ICCV.2015.312

Chen, D., Ren, S., Wei, Y., Cao, X., & Sun, J. (2014). *Joint cascade face detection and alignment.* Paper presented at the European Conference on Computer Vision.

Chen, J., Li, Q., Wu, W., Ling, H., Wu, L., Zhang, B., & Li, P. (2019). *Saliency Detection via Topological Feature Modulated Deep Learning.* Paper presented at the 2019 IEEE International Conference on Image Processing (ICIP). DOI: 10.1109/ICIP.2019.8802611

Chen, X., Ma, H., Wan, J., Li, B., & Xia, T. (2017). *Multi-view 3d object detection network for autonomous driving.* Paper presented at the Proceedings of the IEEE Conference on Computer Vision and Pattern Recognition. DOI: 10.1109/CVPR.2017.691

Chen, Y., Li, J., Xiao, H., Jin, X., Yan, S., & Feng, J. (2017). *Dual path networks.* Paper presented at the Advances in neural information processing systems.

Chen, Y., Rohrbach, M., Yan, Z., Shuicheng, Y., Feng, J., & Kalantidis, Y. (2019). *Graph-based global reasoning networks.* Paper presented at the Proceedings of the IEEE Conference on Computer Vision and Pattern Recognition.

Chen, Y., Yang, T., Zhang, X., Meng, G., Xiao, X., & Sun, J. (2019). *DetNAS: Backbone search for object detection.* Paper presented at the Advances in neural information processing systems.

Chen, M. S., Han, J., & Yu, P. S. (1996). Data mining: An overview from a database perspective. *IEEE Transactions on Knowledge and Data Engineering, 8*(6), 866–883. DOI: 10.1109/69.553155

Chen, M., Herrera, F., & Hwang, K. (2018). Cognitive computing: Architecture, technologies and intelligent applications. *IEEE Access: Practical Innovations, Open Solutions, 6,* 19774–19783. DOI: 10.1109/ACCESS.2018.2791469

Chen, M., Li, W., Fortino, G., Hao, Y., Hu, L., & Humar, I. (2019). A dynamic service migration mechanism in edge cognitive computing. *ACM Transactions on Internet Technology, 19*(2), 1–15. DOI: 10.1145/3239565

Chen, M., Wang, H., Mehrotra, S., Leung, V. C., & Humar, I. (2019). Intelligent networks assisted by cognitive computing and machine learning. *IEEE Network, 33*(3), 6–8. DOI: 10.1109/MNET.2019.8726065

Chen, Q. (2023). *Summary of research on facial expression recognition.* Highlights in Science, Engineering and Technology. DOI: 10.54097/hset.v44i.7200

Chen, T., Gao, T., Li, S., Zhang, X., Cao, J., Yao, D., & Li, Y. (2021). A novel face recognition method based on fusion of LBP and HOG. *IET Image Processing, 15*(14), 3559–3572. DOI: 10.1049/ipr2.12192

Chollet, F. (2017). *Xception: Deep learning with depthwise separable convolutions.* Paper presented at the Proceedings of the IEEE conference on computer vision and pattern recognition. DOI: 10.1109/CVPR.2017.195

Chowdhury, N. M. K., & Boutaba, R. (2009). Network virtualization: State of the art and research challenges. *IEEE Communications Magazine, 47*(7), 20–26. DOI: 10.1109/MCOM.2009.5183468

Chowdhury, N. M. K., & Boutaba, R. (2010). A survey of network virtualization. *Computer Networks, 54*(5), 862–876. DOI: 10.1016/j.comnet.2009.10.017

Clavel, C., & Callejas, Z. (2015). Sentiment analysis: From opinion mining to human-agent interaction. *IEEE Transactions on Affective Computing, 7*(1), 74–93. DOI: 10.1109/TAFFC.2015.2444846

Cortes, C., & Vapnik, V. (1995). Support vector machine. *Machine Learning, 20*(3), 273–297. DOI: 10.1007/BF00994018

Costa, E. (2018). Affordances-in-practice: An ethnographic critique of social media logic and context collapse. *New Media & Society, 20*(10), 3641–3656. DOI: 10.1177/1461444818756290 PMID: 30581356

Dai, J., Li, Y., He, K., & Sun, J. (2016). *R-fcn: Object detection via region-based fully convolutional networks.* Paper presented at the Advances in neural information processing systems.

Dalal, N., & Triggs, B. (2005a). *Histograms of oriented gradients for human detection.*

Dalal, N., & Triggs, B. (2005b). *Histograms of oriented gradients for human detection.* Paper presented at the 2005 IEEE computer society conference on computer vision and pattern recognition (CVPR'05). DOI: 10.1109/CVPR.2005.177

Dang, N. C., Moreno-García, M. N., & De la Prieta, F. (2020). Sentiment analysis based on deep learning: A comparative study. *Electronics (Basel), 9*(3), 483. DOI: 10.3390/electronics9030483

Daniyal, S. M., Masood, A., Ebrahim, M., Adil, S. H., & Raza, K. (2024). An Improved Face Recognition Method Based on Convolutional Neural Network. *Journal of Independent Studies and Research Computing, 22*(1), 103–110. DOI: 10.31645/JISRC.24.22.1.10

Dawoud, A., Shahristani, S., & Raun, C. (2018). Deep learning and software-defined networks: Towards secure IoT architecture. *Internet of Things : Engineering Cyber Physical Human Systems, 3*, 82–89. DOI: 10.1016/j.iot.2018.09.003

De Chiffre, L., Carmignato, S., Kruth, J. P., Schmitt, R., & Weckenmann, A. (2014). Industrial applications of computed tomography. *CIRP Annals, 63*(2), 655–677. DOI: 10.1016/j.cirp.2014.05.011

de Lope, J., & Graña, M. (2023). An ongoing review of speech emotion recognition. *Neurocomputing, 528*, 1–11. DOI: 10.1016/j.neucom.2023.01.002

Deng, J., Dong, W., Socher, R., Li, L.-J., Li, K., & Fei-Fei, L. (2009). *Imagenet: A large-scale hierarchical image database.* Paper presented at the 2009 IEEE conference on computer vision and pattern recognition. DOI: 10.1109/CVPR.2009.5206848

Deng, L., Seltzer, M. L., Yu, D., Acero, A., Mohamed, A.-r., & Hinton, G. (2010). *Binary coding of speech spectrograms using a deep auto-encoder.* Paper presented at the Eleventh Annual Conference of the International Speech Communication Association. DOI: 10.21437/Interspeech.2010-487

Deng, J., Xuan, X., Wang, W., Li, Z., Yao, H., & Wang, Z. (2020). A review of research on object detection based on deep learning. *Journal of Physics: Conference Series, 1684*(1), 012028. DOI: 10.1088/1742-6596/1684/1/012028

Deng, L., & Li, X. (2013). Machine learning paradigms for speech recognition: An overview. *IEEE Transactions on Audio, Speech, and Language Processing, 21*(5), 1060–1089. DOI: 10.1109/TASL.2013.2244083

Dewi, D. A., Sundararajan, E., Prabuwono, A. S., & Cheng, L. M. (2019). Object detection without color feature: Case study Autonomous Robot. *International Journal of Mechanical Engineering and Robotics Research, 8*(4), 646–650. DOI: 10.18178/ijmerr.8.4.646-650

Dimililer, K., Dindar, H., & Al-Turjman, F. (2021). Deep learning, machine learning and internet of things in geophysical engineering applications: An overview. *Microprocessors and Microsystems, 80*, 103613. DOI: 10.1016/j.micpro.2020.103613

Dina, M. (2022). Abdulhussien and Laith Jasim Saud. Evaluation study of face detection by viola-jones algorithm. *International Journal of Health Sciences*.

Ding, X., Chen, H., Zhang, X., Huang, K., Han, J., & Ding, G. J. a. p. a. (2022). Re-parameterizing your optimizers rather than architectures.

Ding, X., Zhang, X., Ma, N., Han, J., Ding, G., & Sun, J. (2021). *Repvgg: Making vgg-style convnets great again.* Paper presented at the Proceedings of the IEEE/CVF conference on computer vision and pattern recognition.

Dollár, P., Tu, Z., Perona, P., & Belongie, S. (2009). Integral channel features.

Dollar, P., Wojek, C., Schiele, B., & Perona, P. (2011). Pedestrian detection: An evaluation of the state of the art. *IEEE Transactions on Pattern Analysis and Machine Intelligence, 34*(4), 743–761. DOI: 10.1109/TPAMI.2011.155 PMID: 21808091

Dosovitskiy, A. J. a. p. a. (2020). An image is worth 16x16 words: Transformers for image recognition at scale.

Dwivedi, Y. K., Ismagilova, E., Hughes, D. L., Carlson, J., Filieri, R., Jacobson, J., Jain, V., Karjaluoto, H., Kefi, H., Krishen, A. S., Kumar, V., Rahman, M. M., Raman, R., Rauschnabel, P. A., Rowley, J., Salo, J., Tran, G. A., & Wang, Y. (2021). Setting the future of digital and social media marketing research: Perspectives and research propositions. *International Journal of Information Management, 59*, 102168. DOI: 10.1016/j.ijinfomgt.2020.102168

Eckhoff, D., & Wagner, I. (2017). Privacy in the smart city—Applications, technologies, challenges, and solutions. *IEEE Communications Surveys and Tutorials, 20*(1), 489–516. DOI: 10.1109/COMST.2017.2748998

Eisenlauer, V. (2013). A critical hypertext analysis of social media. *A Critical Hypertext Analysis of Social Media*, 1-256.

Eleyan, A. (2017)... *An Autonomous Robotic Cell for Painting Applications*, (April). Advance online publication. DOI: 10.2316/P.2017.848-014

Elgendy, I. A., Meshoul, S., & Hammad, M. (2023). Joint Task Offloading, Resource Allocation, and Load-Balancing Optimization in Multi-UAV-Aided MEC Systems. *Applied Sciences (Basel, Switzerland), 13*(4), 2625. DOI: 10.3390/app13042625

Elhanashi, A., Dini, P., Saponara, S., & Zheng, Q. (2023). Integration of deep learning into the iot: A survey of techniques and challenges for real-world applications. *Electronics (Basel), 12*(24), 4925. DOI: 10.3390/electronics12244925

El-Latif, A. A. A., Chelloug, S. A., Alabdulhafith, M., & Hammad, M. (2023). Accurate Detection of Alzheimer's Disease Using Lightweight Deep Learning Model on MRI Data. *Diagnostics (Basel), 13*(7), 1216. DOI: 10.3390/diagnostics13071216 PMID: 37046434

Erhan, D., Szegedy, C., Toshev, A., & Anguelov, D. (2014). *Scalable object detection using deep neural networks.* Paper presented at the Proceedings of the IEEE conference on computer vision and pattern recognition. DOI: 10.1109/CVPR.2014.276

Everingham, M., Eslami, S. A., Van Gool, L., Williams, C. K., Winn, J., & Zisserman, A. J. I. j. o. c. v. (2015b). The pascal visual object classes challenge: A retrospective. *111*, 98-136.

Everingham, M., Van Gool, L., Williams, C. K., Winn, J., & Zisserman, A. (2007). The PASCAL visual object classes challenge 2007 (VOC2007) results.

Everingham, M., Van Gool, L., Williams, C., Winn, J., & Zisserman, A. (2011). *The pascal visual object classes challenge 2012 (voc2012) results (2012).* Paper presented at the URL http://www. pascal-network. org/challenges/VOC/voc2011/ workshop/index. html

Everingham, M., Eslami, S. A., Van Gool, L., Williams, C. K., Winn, J., & Zisserman, A. (2015a). The pascal visual object classes challenge: A retrospective. *International Journal of Computer Vision, 111*(1), 98–136. DOI: 10.1007/s11263-014-0733-5

Everingham, M., Van Gool, L., Williams, C. K., Winn, J., & Zisserman, A. (2010). The pascal visual object classes (voc) challenge. *International Journal of Computer Vision, 88*(2), 303–338. DOI: 10.1007/s11263-009-0275-4

Fatima, R., Samad Shaikh, N., Riaz, A., Ahmad, S., El-Affendi, M. A., Alyamani, K. A., & Latif, R. M. A. (2022). A natural language processing (NLP) evaluation on COVID-19 rumour dataset using deep learning techniques. *Computational Intelligence and Neuroscience, 2022*(1), 6561622.

Feisheng, L. [2024, April]. Systematic Review of Sentiment Analysis: Insights Through CNN-LSTM Networks. In *20245th International Conference on Industrial Engineering and Artificial Intelligence [IEAI]* [pp. 102-109]. IEEE.

Felzenszwalb, P. F., Girshick, R. B., McAllester, D., Ramanan, D. J. I. t. o. p. a., & intelligence, m. (2009). Object detection with discriminatively trained part-based models. *32*(9), 1627-1645.

Feng, X., Chen, L., Zhou, W., & Huang, Z. (2017). Research on the Design of Smart Paint Robot. DEStech Transactions on Materials Science and Engineering, c, 1-5.

Feng, S., Setoodeh, P., & Haykin, S. (2017). Smart home: Cognitive interactive people-centric Internet of Things. *IEEE Communications Magazine, 55*(2), 34–39. DOI: 10.1109/MCOM.2017.1600682CM

Freund, Y., & Schapire, R. E. (1997). A decision-theoretic generalization of on-line learning and an application to boosting. *Journal of Computer and System Sciences, 55*(1), 119–139. DOI: 10.1006/jcss.1997.1504

Fu, C.-Y., Liu, W., Ranga, A., Tyagi, A., & Berg, A. C. (2017). Dssd: Deconvolutional single shot detector. *arXiv preprint arXiv:1701.06659.*

Furusho, Y., Ikeda, K. J. A. T. o. S., & Processing, I. (2020). Theoretical analysis of skip connections and batch normalization from generalization and optimization perspectives. *9*, e9.

Gann, D. M., & Salter, A. J. (2000). Innovation in project-based, service-enhanced firms: The construction of complex products and systems. *Research Policy, 29*(7-8), 955–972. DOI: 10.1016/S0048-7333(00)00114-1

Gao, P., Zheng, M., Wang, X., Dai, J., & Li, H. (2021). *Fast convergence of detr with spatially modulated co-attention.* Paper presented at the Proceedings of the IEEE/CVF international conference on computer vision. DOI: 10.1109/ICCV48922.2021.00360

Gasco, L., Clavel, C., Asensio, C., & de Arcas, G. (2019). Beyond sound level monitoring: Exploitation of social media to gather citizens subjective response to noise. *The Science of the Total Environment, 658,* 69–79. DOI: 10.1016/j.scitotenv.2018.12.071 PMID: 30572215

Ge, H., Zhu, Z., Dai, Y., Wang, B., & Wu, X. (2022). Facial expression recognition based on deep learning. *Computer Methods and Programs in Biomedicine, 215,* 106621. DOI: 10.1016/j.cmpb.2022.106621 PMID: 35164903

George, A. S., & Baskar, T. (2024). Leveraging Big Data and Sentiment Analysis for Actionable Insights: A Review of Data Mining Approaches for Social Media. *Partners Universal International Innovation Journal, 2*(4), 39–59.

Georgescu, T. M. (2020). Natural language processing model for automatic analysis of cybersecurity-related documents. *Symmetry, 12*(3), 354. DOI: 10.3390/sym12030354

Ghasemi, Y., Jeong, H., Choi, S. H., Park, K.-B., & Lee, J. Y. (2022). Deep learning-based object detection in augmented reality: A systematic review. *Computers in Industry, 139,* 103661. DOI: 10.1016/j.compind.2022.103661

Girshick, R. (2015a). *Fast r-cnn.* Paper presented at the Proceedings of the IEEE international conference on computer vision.

Girshick, R. (2015b). *Fast R-CNN ICCV.* Paper presented at the 15Proceedings of the 2015 IEEE International Conference on Computer Vision (ICCV).

Girshick, R., Donahue, J., Darrell, T., & Malik, J. (2014). *Rich feature hierarchies for accurate object detection and semantic segmentation.* Paper presented at the Proceedings of the IEEE conference on computer vision and pattern recognition. DOI: 10.1109/CVPR.2014.81

Goldberg, Y. (2017). *Neural network methods in natural language processing.* Morgan & Claypool Publishers. DOI: 10.1007/978-3-031-02165-7

Grauman, K., & Leibe, B. (2011). Visual object recognition. *Synthesis lectures on artificial intelligence and machine learning, 5*(2), 1-181.

Gu, J., Wang, Z., Kuen, J., Ma, L., Shahroudy, A., Shuai, B., & Cai, J. (2018). Recent advances in convolutional neural networks. *Pattern Recognition, 77,* 354–377. DOI: 10.1016/j.patcog.2017.10.013

Gupta, R., & Kumar, S. (2023). Facial expression recognition using deep learning. *International Journal of Computer Vision.*

Gupta, S., Kar, A. K., Baabdullah, A., & Al-Khowaiter, W. A. (2018). Big data with cognitive computing: A review for the future. *International Journal of Information Management, 42*, 78–89. DOI: 10.1016/j.ijinfomgt.2018.06.005

Hammad, M., Abd El-Latif, A. A., Hussain, A., Abd El-Samie, F. E., Gupta, B. B., Ugail, H., & Sedik, A. (2022). Deep learning models for arrhythmia detection in IoT healthcare applications. *Computers & Electrical Engineering, 100*, 108011. DOI: 10.1016/j.compeleceng.2022.108011

Hammad, M., Bakrey, M., Bakhiet, A., Tadeusiewicz, R., Abd El-Latif, A. A., & Pławiak, P. (2022). A novel end-to-end deep learning approach for cancer detection based on microscopic medical images. *Biocybernetics and Biomedical Engineering, 42*(3), 737–748. DOI: 10.1016/j.bbe.2022.05.009

Hammad, M., Iliyasu, A. M., Elgendy, I. A., & Abd El-Latif, A. A. (2022). End-to-end data authentication deep learning model for securing IoT configurations. *Hum. Cent. Comput. Inf. Sci, 12*(4).

Hammad, M., Kandala, R. N., Abdelatey, A., Abdar, M., Zomorodi-Moghadam, M., San Tan, R., & Pławiak, P. (2021). Automated detection of Shockable ECG signals: A Review. *Information Sciences, 571*, 580–604. DOI: 10.1016/j.ins.2021.05.035

Hammad, M., Tawalbeh, L. A., Iliyasu, A. M., Sedik, A., Abd El-Samie, F. E., Alkinani, M. H., & Abd El-Latif, A. A. (2022). Efficient multimodal deep-learning-based COVID-19 diagnostic system for noisy and corrupted images. *Journal of King Saud University. Science, 34*(3), 101898. DOI: 10.1016/j.jksus.2022.101898 PMID: 35185304

Haq, M. U., Sethi, M. A. J., Ahmad, S., ELAffendi, M. A., & Asim, M. (2024). Automatic Player Face Detection and Recognition for Players in Cricket Games. *IEEE Access : Practical Innovations, Open Solutions, 12*, 41219–41233. DOI: 10.1109/ACCESS.2024.3377564

Harar, P., Burget, R., & Dutta, M. K. (2017). Speech emotion recognition with deep learning. *2017 4th International Conference on Signal Processing and Integrated Networks, SPIN 2017*, 137–140. DOI: 10.1109/SPIN.2017.8049931

Hartmann, J., Huppertz, J., Schamp, C., & Heitmann, M. (2019). Comparing automated text classification methods. *International Journal of Research in Marketing, 36*(1), 20–38. DOI: 10.1016/j.ijresmar.2018.09.009

He, K., Gkioxari, G., Dollár, P., & Girshick, R. (2017). *Mask r-cnn.* Paper presented at the Proceedings of the IEEE international conference on computer vision.

He, K., Zhang, X., Ren, S., & Sun, J. (2016). *Deep residual learning for image recognition.* Paper presented at the Proceedings of the IEEE conference on computer vision and pattern recognition.

He, L., & Todorovic, S. (2022). *Destr: Object detection with split transformer.* Paper presented at the Proceedings of the IEEE/CVF conference on computer vision and pattern recognition.

He, K., Zhang, X., Ren, S., & Sun, J. (2015). Spatial pyramid pooling in deep convolutional networks for visual recognition. *IEEE Transactions on Pattern Analysis and Machine Intelligence, 37*(9), 1904–1916. DOI: 10.1109/TPAMI.2015.2389824 PMID: 26353135

Hema, N., Krishnamoorthy, N., Chavan, S. M., Kumar, N., Sabarimuthu, M., & Boopathi, S. (2023). A Study on an Internet of Things (IoT)-Enabled Smart Solar Grid System. In *Handbook of Research on Deep Learning Techniques for Cloud-Based Industrial IoT* (pp. 290–308). IGI Global. DOI: 10.4018/978-1-6684-8098-4.ch017

Hinton, G. E., & Salakhutdinov, R. R. (2006). Reducing the dimensionality of data with neural networks. *Science, 313*(5786), 504–507. DOI: 10.1126/science.1127647 PMID: 16873662

Hinton, G., Deng, L., Yu, D., Dahl, G., Mohamed, A.-r., Jaitly, N., & Kingsbury, B. (2012). Deep neural networks for acoustic modeling in speech recognition. *IEEE Signal Processing Magazine,* ●●●, 29.

Hirschberg, J., & Manning, C. D. (2015). Advances in natural language processing. *Science, 349*(6245), 261–266. DOI: 10.1126/science.aaa8685 PMID: 26185244

Hosni, A. I. E., Li, K., & Ahmad, S. (2019, December). DARIM: Dynamic approach for rumor influence minimization in online social networks. In *International Conference on Neural Information Processing* (pp. 619-630). Cham: Springer International Publishing.

Hosni, A. I. E., Li, K., & Ahmad, S. (2020). Analysis of the impact of online social networks addiction on the propagation of rumors. *Physica A, 542,* 123456. DOI: 10.1016/j.physa.2019.123456

Hosni, A. I. E., Li, K., & Ahmed, S. (2018). HISBmodel: A rumor diffusion model based on human individual and social behaviors in online social networks. In Neural Information Processing: 25th International Conference, ICONIP 2018, Siem Reap, Cambodia, December 13–16, 2018 [Springer International Publishing.]. *Proceedings, 25*(Part II), 14–27.

Hosni, A. I. E., Li, K., Ding, C., & Ahmed, S. (2018, November). Least cost rumor influence minimization in multiplex social networks. In *International Conference on Neural Information Processing* (pp. 93-105). Cham: Springer International Publishing.

Howard, A. G., Zhu, M., Chen, B., Kalenichenko, D., Wang, W., Weyand, T., . . . Adam, H. (2017). Mobilenets: Efficient convolutional neural networks for mobile vision applications. *arXiv preprint arXiv:1704.04861.*

Hu, J., Shen, L., & Sun, G. (2018). *Squeeze-and-excitation networks.* Paper presented at the Proceedings of the IEEE conference on computer vision and pattern recognition.

Huang, G., Liu, Z., Van Der Maaten, L., & Weinberger, K. Q. (2017). *Densely connected convolutional networks.* Paper presented at the Proceedings of the IEEE conference on computer vision and pattern recognition.

Huang, J., Rathod, V., Sun, C., Zhu, M., Korattikara, A., Fathi, A., . . . Guadarrama, S. (2017). *Speed/accuracy trade-offs for modern convolutional object detectors.* Paper presented at the Proceedings of the IEEE conference on computer vision and pattern recognition. DOI: 10.1109/CVPR.2017.351

Hu, B., & Zhang, Z. (2022). Evaluation of Big Data Analytics and cognitive computing in smart health systems. *Journal of Commercial Biotechnology, 27*(2), 2. DOI: 10.5912/jcb1088

Hung, B. T. (2021). Face recognition using hybrid HOG-CNN approach. In *Research in Intelligent and Computing in Engineering: Select Proceedings of RICE 2020* (pp. 715-723). Springer Singapore. DOI: 10.1007/978-981-15-7527-3_67

Hurwitz, J., Kaufman, M., Bowles, A., Nugent, A., Kobielus, J. G., & Kowolenko, M. D. (2015). *Cognitive computing and big data analytics* [Vol. 288]. Wiley.

Hussain, T., Yu, L., Asim, M., Ahmed, A., & Wani, M. A. (2024). Enhancing E-Learning Adaptability with Automated Learning Style Identification and Sentiment Analysis: A Hybrid Deep Learning Approach for Smart Education. *Information (Basel), 15*(5), 277. Advance online publication. DOI: 10.3390/info15050277

Hussein, H. I., Dino, H. I., Mstafa, R. J., & Hassan, M. M. (2022). Person-independent facial expression recognition based on the fusion of HOG descriptor and cuttlefish algorithm. *Multimedia Tools and Applications, 81*(8), 11563–11586. DOI: 10.1007/s11042-022-12438-6

Hussin, R., Juhari, M. R., Kang, N. W., Ismail, R. C., & Kamarudin, A. (2012). Digital image processing techniques for object detection from complex background image. *Procedia Engineering, 41*, 340–344.

Ikemoto, S., Liao, M., Takai, Y., Goto, A., Nishimoto, H., & Hamada, H. (2015). RETRACTED: Impact of Operator Experience on Spray Gun Handling for Automobile Repair.

Ikram, S., Ahmad, H., Mahmood, N., Faisal, C. M. N., Abbas, Q., Qureshi, I., & Hussain, A. (2023). C. M. Nadeem Faisal, Qaisar Abbas, Imran Qureshi, and Ayyaz Hussain. Recognition of student engagement state in a classroom environment using a deep and efficient transfer learning algorithm. *Applied Sciences (Basel, Switzerland), 13*(15), 8637. DOI: 10.3390/app13158637

Ilieva, R. T., & McPhearson, T. (2018). Social-media data for urban sustainability. *Nature Sustainability, 1*(10), 553–565. DOI: 10.1038/s41893-018-0153-6

Ioffe, S., & Szegedy, C. (2015). Batch normalization: Accelerating deep network training by reducing internal covariate shift. *arXiv preprint arXiv:1502.03167*.

Irshad, M. H., Ebrahim, M., Abro, A. A., Raza, K., & Adil, S. H. (2024). Detecting Shadows in Computer Vision: A MATLAB-Based Approach. *The Asian Bulletin of Big Data Management, 4*(1). *Science*, ●●●, 4.

Jain, D. K., Boyapati, P., Venkatesh, J., & Prakash, M. (2022). An intelligent cognitive-inspired computing with big data analytics framework for sentiment analysis and classification. *Information Processing & Management, 59*(1), 102758.

Jain, S., & Chadokar, S. (2015). A Object Detection in Image Processing: A Review. International Journal of Electrical. *Electronics and Computer Engineering, 4*(2), 26.

Jeevanantham, Y. A., Saravanan, A., Vanitha, V., Boopathi, S., & Kumar, D. P. (2022). Implementation of Internet-of Things (IoT) in Soil Irrigation System. *IEEE Explore*, 1–5.

Jeong, B., & Lee, K. J. (2024). NLP-based Recommendation Approach for Diverse Service Generation. *IEEE Access : Practical Innovations, Open Solutions, 12*, 14260–14274. DOI: 10.1109/ACCESS.2024.3355546

Jia, Y., Shelhamer, E., Donahue, J., Karayev, S., Long, J., Girshick, R., . . . Darrell, T. (2014). *Caffe: Convolutional architecture for fast feature embedding*. Paper presented at the Proceedings of the 22nd ACM international conference on Multimedia. DOI: 10.1145/2647868.2654889

Jiang, H., & Learned-Miller, E. (2017). *Face detection with the faster R-CNN*. Paper presented at the 2017 12th IEEE International Conference on Automatic Face & Gesture Recognition (FG 2017). DOI: 10.1109/FG.2017.82

Jiang, N., Zhang, Y., Luo, D., Liu, C., Zhou, Y., & Han, Z. (2019). *Feature hourglass network for skeleton detection.* Paper presented at the Proceedings of the IEEE Conference on Computer Vision and Pattern Recognition Workshops.

Jiang, X., Hadid, A., Pang, Y., Granger, E., & Feng, X. (2019). *Deep learning in object detection and recognition.*

Jiao, L., Zhang, F., Liu, F., Yang, S., Li, L., Feng, Z., & Qu, R. (2019). A survey of deep learning-based object detection. *IEEE Access : Practical Innovations, Open Solutions*, 7, 128837–128868. DOI: 10.1109/ACCESS.2019.2939201

Jiao, L., Zhang, R., Liu, F., Yang, S., Hou, B., Li, L., & Tang, X. (2021). New generation deep learning for video object detection: A survey. *IEEE Transactions on Neural Networks and Learning Systems*, 33(8), 3195–3215. DOI: 10.1109/TNLS.2021.3053249 PMID: 33534715

Jo, A.-H., & Kwak, K.-C. (2023). Speech Emotion Recognition Based on Two-Stream Deep Learning Model Using Korean Audio Information. *Applied Sciences (Basel, Switzerland)*, 13(4), 2167. DOI: 10.3390/app13042167

Kang, Y., Cai, Z., Tan, C. W., Huang, Q., & Liu, H. (2020). Natural language processing (NLP) in management research: A literature review. *Journal of Management Analytics*, 7(2), 139–172. DOI: 10.1080/23270012.2020.1756939

Karimah, S. N., & Hasegawa, S. (2022). Automatic engagement estimation in smart education/learning settings: A systematic review of engagement definitions, datasets, and methods. *Smart Learning Environments*, 9(1), 31.

Karthik, S., Hemalatha, R., Aruna, R., Deivakani, M., Reddy, R. V. K., & Boopathi, S. (2023). Study on Healthcare Security System-Integrated Internet of Things (IoT). In *Perspectives and Considerations on the Evolution of Smart Systems* (pp. 342–362). IGI Global.

KAV. R. P., Pandraju, T. K. S., Boopathi, S., Saravanan, P., Rathan, S. K., & Sathish, T. (2023, November). Hybrid Deep Learning Technique for Optimal Wind Mill Speed Estimation. In 2023 7th International Conference on Electronics, Communication and Aerospace Technology (ICECA) (pp. 181-186). IEEE.

Kavitha, C., Varalatchoumy, M., Mithuna, H., Bharathi, K., Geethalakshmi, N., & Boopathi, S. (2023). Energy Monitoring and Control in the Smart Grid: Integrated Intelligent IoT and ANFIS. In *Applications of Synthetic Biology in Health, Energy, and Environment* (pp. 290–316). IGI Global.

Kavukcuoglu, K., Ranzato, M. A., Fergus, R., & LeCun, Y. (2009). *Learning invariant features through topographic filter maps.* Paper presented at the 2009 IEEE Conference on Computer Vision and Pattern Recognition. DOI: 10.1109/CVPR.2009.5206545

Khabibullaevna, N. A. (2023). Unveiling the labyrinth of internet phraseology: navigating the linguistic landscape of the digital era. *qo 'qon universiteti xabarnomasi, 7*, 78-81.

Khan, S., Vohra, S., Siddique, S. A., Abro, A. A., & Ebrahim, M. (2024, January). A Computer Vision-Based Vehicle Detection System Leveraging Deep Learning. In *2024 IEEE 1st Karachi Section Humanitarian Technology Conference (KHI-HTC)* (pp. 1-7). IEEE. DOI: 10.1109/KHI-HTC60760.2024.10482163

Khan, A. R. (2022). Facial emotion recognition using conventional machine learning and deep learning methods: Current achievements, analysis and remaining challenges. *Information (Basel), 13*(6), 268.

Khan, B., Naseem, R., Muhammad, F., Abbas, G., & Kim, S. (2020). An empirical evaluation of machine learning techniques for chronic kidney disease prophecy. *IEEE Access : Practical Innovations, Open Solutions, 8*, 55012–55022. DOI: 10.1109/ACCESS.2020.2981689

Khanday, A. M. U. D., Wani, M. A., Rabani, S. T., Khan, Q. R., & Abd El-Latif, A. A. (2024). HAPI: An efficient Hybrid Feature Engineering-based Approach for Propaganda Identification in social media. *PLoS One, 19*(7), e0302583. DOI: 10.1371/journal.pone.0302583 PMID: 38985703

Khan, M. I., Qureshi, H., Bae, S. J., Khattak, A. A., Anwar, M. S., Ahmad, S., Hassan, F., & Ahmad, S. (2023). Malaria prevalence in Pakistan: A systematic review and meta-analysis (2006–2021). *Heliyon, 9*(4), 4. DOI: 10.1016/j.heliyon.2023.e15373 PMID: 37123939

Khan, M. T., Durrani, M., Ali, A., Inayat, I., Khalid, S., & Khan, K. H. (2016). Sentiment analysis and the complex natural language. *Complex Adaptive Systems Modeling, 4*(1), 1–19. DOI: 10.1186/s40294-016-0016-9

Khan, S., Zhang, Z., Zhu, L., Rahim, M. A., Ahmad, S., & Chen, R. (2020). SCM: Secure and accountable TLS certificate management. *International Journal of Communication Systems, 33*(15), e4503.

Khuda, I. E., Aftab, A., Hasan, S., Ikram, S., Ahmad, S., Ateya, A. A., & Asim, M. (2024). Trends of Social Anxiety in University Students of Pakistan Post-COVID-19 Lockdown: A Healthcare Analytics Perspective. *Information (Basel)*, *15*(7), 373. DOI: 10.3390/info15070373

Khuda, I. E., Ahmed, S., & Ateya, A. A. (2024). STEM-Based Bayesian Computational Leaning Model-BCLM for Effective Learning of Bayesian Statistics. *IEEE Access : Practical Innovations, Open Solutions*, *12*, 91217–91228. DOI: 10.1109/ACCESS.2024.3420731

Kleyko, D., Rachkovskij, D., Osipov, E., & Rahimi, A. (2023). A survey on hyper-dimensional computing aka vector symbolic architectures, part ii: Applications, cognitive models, and challenges. *ACM Computing Surveys*, *55*(9), 1–52. DOI: 10.1145/3558000

Kopalidis, T., Solachidis, V., Vretos, N., & Daras, P. (2024). Advances in facial expression recognition: A survey of methods, benchmarks, models, and datasets. *Information (Basel)*, *15*(3), 135. DOI: 10.3390/info15030135

Kovács, E. A., Ország, A., Pfeifer, D., & Benczúr, A. (2024). Generalized Naive Bayes. arXiv preprint arXiv:2408.15923.

Krasin, I., Duerig, T., Alldrin, N., Ferrari, V., Abu-El-Haija, S., Kuznetsova, A., . . . Veit, A. (2017). Openimages: A public dataset for large-scale multi-label and multi-class image classification. *Dataset available fromhttps://github. com/open-images, 2, 3.*

Krizhevsky, A., Sutskever, I., & Hinton, G. E. (2012). *Imagenet classification with deep convolutional neural networks*. Paper presented at the Advances in neural information processing systems.

Krizhevsky, A., Sutskever, I., & Hinton, G. E. (2017). Imagenet classification with deep convolutional neural networks. *Communications of the ACM*, *60*(6), 84–90. DOI: 10.1145/3065386

KS. K. K., Isaac, J. S., Pratheep, V. G., Jasmin, M., Kistan, A., & Boopathi, S. (2025). Smart Food Quality Monitoring by Integrating IoT and Deep Learning for Enhanced Safety and Freshness. In Edible Electronics for Smart Technology Solutions (pp. 79-110). IGI Global.

Kubara, M., & Kopczewska, K. (2024). Akaike information criterion in choosing the optimal k-nearest neighbours of the spatial weight matrix. *Spatial Economic Analysis*, *19*(1), 73–91. DOI: 10.1080/17421772.2023.2176539

Kumar, H., Soh, P. J., & Ismail, M. A. (2022). Big data streaming platforms: A review. *Iraqi Journal for Computer Science and Mathematics*, *3*(2), 95–100. DOI: 10.52866/ijcsm.2022.02.01.010

Kumar, M., Khan, L., & Chang, H. T. (2025). Evolving techniques in sentiment analysis: A comprehensive review. *PeerJ. Computer Science*, *11*, e2592. DOI: 10.7717/peerj-cs.2592 PMID: 39957863

Kuznetsova, A., Rom, H., Alldrin, N., Uijlings, J., Krasin, I., Pont-Tuset, J., . . . Duerig, T. (2018). The open images dataset v4: Unified image classification, object detection, and visual relationship detection at scale. *arXiv preprint arXiv:1811.00982*.

Lakshmanna, K., Kaluri, R., Gundluru, N., Alzamil, Z. S., Rajput, D. S., Khan, A. A., Haq, M. A., & Alhussen, A. (2022). A review on deep learning techniques for IoT data. *Electronics (Basel)*, *11*(10), 1604. DOI: 10.3390/electronics11101604

Lauriola, I., Lavelli, A., & Aiolli, F. (2022). An introduction to deep learning in natural language processing: Models, techniques, and tools. *Neurocomputing*, *470*, 443–456. DOI: 10.1016/j.neucom.2021.05.103

Law, H., & Deng, J. (2018). *Cornernet: Detecting objects as paired keypoints*. Paper presented at the Proceedings of the European Conference on Computer Vision (ECCV).

LeCun, Y., Bengio, Y., & Hinton, G. (2015). Deep learning. *Nature*, *521*(7553), 436–444. DOI: 10.1038/nature14539 PMID: 26017442

LeCun, Y., Boser, B., Denker, J. S., Henderson, D., Howard, R. E., Hubbard, W., & Jackel, L. D. (1989). Backpropagation applied to handwritten zip code recognition. *Neural Computation*, *1*(4), 541–551. DOI: 10.1162/neco.1989.1.4.541

Li, C., Li, L., Jiang, H., Weng, K., Geng, Y., Li, L., . . . Nie, W. J. a. p. a. (2022). YOLOv6: A single-stage object detection framework for industrial applications.

Li, X., Wang, W., Wu, L., Chen, S., Hu, X., Li, J., . . . Yang, J. J. A. i. N. I. P. S. (2020). Generalized focal loss: Learning qualified and distributed bounding boxes for dense object detection. *33*, 21002-21012.

Li, Z., Peng, C., Yu, G., Zhang, X., Deng, Y., & Sun, J. (2018). Detnet: A backbone network for object detection. *arXiv preprint arXiv:1804.06215*.

Lienhart, R., & Maydt, J. (2002). *An extended set of haar-like features for rapid object detection*. Paper presented at the Proceedings. international conference on image processing. DOI: 10.1109/ICIP.2002.1038171

Li, H., Luo, Y., Gu, T., & Chang, L. (2024). BFFN: A novel balanced feature fusion network for fair facial expression recognition. *Engineering Applications of Artificial Intelligence*, *138*, 109277. DOI: 10.1016/j.engappai.2024.109277

Li, L., Goh, T. T., & Jin, D. (2020). How textual quality of online reviews affect classification performance: A case of deep learning sentiment analysis. *Neural Computing & Applications*, *32*(9), 4387–4415. DOI: 10.1007/s00521-018-3865-7

Lin, T.-Y., Dollár, P., Girshick, R., He, K., Hariharan, B., & Belongie, S. (2017). *Feature pyramid networks for object detection.* Paper presented at the Proceedings of the IEEE conference on computer vision and pattern recognition.

Lin, T.-Y., Goyal, P., Girshick, R., He, K., & Dollár, P. (2017). *Focal loss for dense object detection.* Paper presented at the Proceedings of the IEEE international conference on computer vision.

Lin, T.-Y., Maire, M., Belongie, S., Hays, J., Perona, P., Ramanan, D., . . . Zitnick, C. L. (2014). *Microsoft coco: Common objects in context.* Paper presented at the European conference on computer vision.

Lin, G., Liu, F., Milan, A., Shen, C., & Reid, I. (2019). Refinenet: Multi-path refinement networks for dense prediction. *IEEE Transactions on Pattern Analysis and Machine Intelligence*, *42*(5), 1228–1242. DOI: 10.1109/TPAMI.2019.2893630 PMID: 30668461

Lin, J., Nogueira, R., & Yates, A. (2022). *Pretrained transformers for text ranking: Bert and beyond.* Springer Nature. DOI: 10.1007/978-3-031-02181-7

Lin, Y. T., Hung, T. W., & Huang, L. T. L. (2021). Engineering equity: How AI can help reduce the harm of implicit bias. *Philosophy & Technology*, *34*(S1, Suppl 1), 65–90. DOI: 10.1007/s13347-020-00406-7

Liu, N., Han, J., Zhang, D., Wen, S., & Liu, T. (2015). *Predicting eye fixations using convolutional neural networks.* Paper presented at the Proceedings of the IEEE Conference on Computer Vision and Pattern Recognition.

Liu, W., Anguelov, D., Erhan, D., Szegedy, C., Reed, S., Fu, C.-Y., & Berg, A. C. (2016). *Ssd: Single shot multibox detector.* Paper presented at the European conference on computer vision.

Liu, Y., Wang, Y., Wang, S., Liang, T., Zhao, Q., Tang, Z., & Ling, H. (2019). Cbnet: A novel composite backbone network architecture for object detection. *arXiv preprint arXiv:1909.03625.*

Liu, Z., Lin, Y., Cao, Y., Hu, H., Wei, Y., Zhang, Z., . . . Guo, B. (2021). *Swin transformer: Hierarchical vision transformer using shifted windows*. Paper presented at the Proceedings of the IEEE/CVF international conference on computer vision. DOI: 10.1109/ICCV48922.2021.00986

Liu, B. (2010). Sentiment analysis: A multi-faceted problem. *IEEE Intelligent Systems*, *25*(3), 76–80. DOI: 10.1109/MIS.2022.3145503

Liu, G., He, W., & Jin, B. (2018). Feature Fusion of Speech Emotion Recognition Based on Deep Learning. *Proceedings of 2018 6th IEEE International Conference on Network Infrastructure and Digital Content, IC-NIDC 2018*, 193–197. DOI: 10.1109/ICNIDC.2018.8525706

Liu, L., Ouyang, W., Wang, X., Fieguth, P., Chen, J., Liu, X., & Pietikäinen, M. (2020). Deep learning for generic object detection: A survey. *International Journal of Computer Vision*, *128*(2), 261–318. DOI: 10.1007/s11263-019-01247-4

Liu, Y., Sun, P., Wergeles, N., & Shang, Y. (2021). A survey and performance evaluation of deep learning methods for small object detection. *Expert Systems with Applications*, *172*, 114602. DOI: 10.1016/j.eswa.2021.114602

Li, Y., Wang, Y., Yang, X., & Im, S. K. (2023). Speech emotion recognition based on Graph-LSTM neural network. *EURASIP Journal on Audio, Speech, and Music Processing*, *2023*(1), 40. DOI: 10.1186/s13636-023-00303-9

Li, Z., Wang, Y., Zhang, N., Zhang, Y., Zhao, Z., Xu, D., Ben, G., & Gao, Y. (2022). Deep learning-based object detection techniques for remote sensing images: A survey. *Remote Sensing (Basel)*, *14*(10), 2385. DOI: 10.3390/rs14102385

Lowe, D. G. (2004). Distinctive image features from scale-invariant keypoints. *International Journal of Computer Vision*, *60*(2), 91–110. DOI: 10.1023/B:VISI.0000029664.99615.94

Lytras, M., Visvizi, A., Zhang, X., & Aljohani, N. R. (2020). Cognitive computing, Big Data Analytics and data driven industrial marketing. *Industrial Marketing Management*, *90*, 663–666. DOI: 10.1016/j.indmarman.2020.03.024

Maguluri, L. P., Arularasan, A., & Boopathi, S. (2023). Assessing Security Concerns for AI-Based Drones in Smart Cities. In *Effective AI, Blockchain, and E-Governance Applications for Knowledge Discovery and Management* (pp. 27–47). IGI Global. DOI: 10.4018/978-1-6684-9151-5.ch002

Maheswari, B. U., Imambi, S. S., Hasan, D., Meenakshi, S., Pratheep, V., & Boopathi, S. (2023). Internet of things and machine learning-integrated smart robotics. In *Global Perspectives on Robotics and Autonomous Systems: Development and Applications* (pp. 240–258). IGI Global. DOI: 10.4018/978-1-6684-7791-5.ch010

Maheswari, V. U., & Priya, R. (2024). Optimized deep learning framework for analyzing offensive content on social media with bilstm and dual attention mechanisms. In *Computer Science Engineering* [pp. 360-370]. CRC Press.

Ma, L., Liu, Y., Zhang, X., Ye, Y., Yin, G., & Johnson, B. A. (2019). Deep learning in remote sensing applications: A meta-analysis and review. *ISPRS Journal of Photogrammetry and Remote Sensing, 152*, 166–177. DOI: 10.1016/j.isprsjprs.2019.04.015

Ma, L., & Sun, B. (2020). Machine learning and AI in marketing–Connecting computing power to human insights. *International Journal of Research in Marketing, 37*(3), 481–504. DOI: 10.1016/j.ijresmar.2020.04.005

Maritza Bustos-Lo'pez. (2022). Nicandro Cruz-Ram'ırez, Alejandro Guerra-Herna'ndez, Laura Nely Sa'nchez-Morales, Nancy Aracely Cruz-Ramos, and Giner Alor- Herna'ndez. Wearables for engagement detection in learning environments: A review. *Biosensors (Basel)*, ●●●, 12.

Masita, K. L., Hasan, A. N., & Shongwe, T. (2020). Deep learning in object detection: A review. *2020 International Conference on Artificial Intelligence, Big Data, Computing and Data Communication Systems (icABCD)*, 1–11. DOI: 10.1109/icABCD49160.2020.9183866

Mateus, A., Ribeiro, D., Miraldo, P., & Nascimento, J. C. (2019). Efficient and robust pedestrian detection using deep learning for human-aware navigation. *Robotics and Autonomous Systems, 113*, 23–37. DOI: 10.1016/j.robot.2018.12.007

Ma, X., Yao, T., Hu, M., Dong, Y., Liu, W., Wang, F., & Liu, J. (2019). A survey on deep learning empowered IoT applications. *IEEE Access : Practical Innovations, Open Solutions, 7*, 181721–181732. DOI: 10.1109/ACCESS.2019.2958962

Maynard, D., Roberts, I., Greenwood, M. A., Rout, D., & Bontcheva, K. (2017). A framework for real-time semantic social media analysis. *Journal of Web Semantics, 44*, 75–88. DOI: 10.1016/j.websem.2017.05.002

Medhat, N., Moussa, S. M., Badr, N. L., & Tolba, M. F. (2020). A framework for continuous regression and integration testing in iot systems based on deep learning and search-based techniques. *IEEE Access : Practical Innovations, Open Solutions, 8*, 215716–215726. DOI: 10.1109/ACCESS.2020.3039931

Medhat, W., Hassan, A., & Korashy, H. (2014). Sentiment analysis algorithms and applications: A survey. *Ain Shams Engineering Journal, 5*(4), 1093–1113. DOI: 10.1016/j.asej.2014.04.011

Mehrabinezhad, A., Teshnehlab, M., & Sharifi, A. (2024). A comparative study to examine principal component analysis and kernel principal component analysis-based weighting layer for convolutional neural networks. *Computer Methods in Biomechanics and Biomedical Engineering. Imaging & Visualization, 12*(1), 2379526. DOI: 10.1080/21681163.2024.2379526

Memon, F. S., Abdullah, F. B., Iqbal, R., Ahmad, S., Hussain, I., & Abdullah, M. (2023). Addressing women's climate change awareness in Sindh, Pakistan: An empirical study of rural and urban women. *Climate and Development, 15*(7), 565–577. DOI: 10.1080/17565529.2022.2125784

Mishra, A. K., Raghuvanshi, C. S., Soni, H. K., & Goswami, P. (2025). Analytics of Text and Social Media for Challenges of Hateful and Offensive Speech Detection. In *Text and Social Media Analytics for Fake News and Hate Speech Detection* [pp. 75-91]. Chapman and Hall/CRC.

Mishra, N., & Silakari, S. (2012). Predictive analytics: A survey, trends, applications, oppurtunities & challenges. *International Journal of Computer Science and Information Technologies, 3*(3), 4434–4438.

Mohanraj, G., Krishna, K. S., Lakshmi, B. S., Vijayalakshmi, A., Pramila, P. V., & Boopathi, S. (2024). Optimizing Trust and Security in Healthcare 4.0: Human Factors in Lightweight Secured IoMT Ecosystems. In *Lightweight Digital Trust Architectures in the Internet of Medical Things (IoMT)* (pp. 52–72). IGI Global. DOI: 10.4018/979-8-3693-2109-6.ch004

Mohibullah, M., Ahammad, M. K., Muzammel, C. S., Hosen, M. S., & Islam, M. R. (2022). Face Detection and Recognition from Real Time Video or Recoded Video using Haar Features with Viola Jones Algorithm and Eigenface Approach with PCA. *International Journal of Research Publications, 93*(1), 122–133. DOI: 10.47119/IJRP1009311120222769

Monroe, W., Hawkins, R. X., Goodman, N. D., & Potts, C. (2017). Colors in context: A pragmatic neural model for grounded language understanding. *Transactions of the Association for Computational Linguistics, 5*, 325–338. DOI: 10.1162/tacl_a_00064

Montoyo, A., Martínez-Barco, P., & Balahur, A. (2012). Subjectivity and sentiment analysis: An overview of the current state of the area and envisaged developments. *Decision Support Systems, 53*(4), 675–679. DOI: 10.1016/j.dss.2012.05.022

Moshagen, S. N., Pirinen, F., Antonsen, L., Gaup, B., Mikkelsen, I., Trosterud, T., ... & Hiovain-Asikainen, K. The GiellaLT infrastructure: A multilingual infrastructure for rule-based NLP1. *Rule-Based Language Technology*, 70.

Mukesh, K., Jayaprakash, S. L., & Kumar, R. P. (2024). QViLa: Quantum Infused Vision-Language Model for Enhanced Multimodal Understanding. *SN Computer Science*, 5(8), 1–12. DOI: 10.1007/s42979-024-03398-9

Muliyah, T. P., Aminatun, D., Nasution, S. S., Hastomo, T., & Setiana, S. W. S. (2020). No Title No Title No Title. *J. GEEJ*, 7(2).

Nadeau, S. E. (2015). Neural Network Mechanisms of Adult Language. In *Routledge handbook of communication disorders* [pp. 22-33]. Routledge.

Naeem, M. (2019). Uncovering the role of social media and cross-platform applications as tools for knowledge sharing. *VINE Journal of Information and Knowledge Management Systems*, 49(3), 257–276. DOI: 10.1108/VJIKMS-01-2019-0001

Najibi, M., Rastegari, M., & Davis, L. S. (2016). *G-cnn: an iterative grid based object detector*. Paper presented at the Proceedings of the IEEE conference on computer vision and pattern recognition. DOI: 10.1109/CVPR.2016.260

Nambiar, K. R., & Palaniswamy, S. (2022). Speech Emotion Based Music Recommendation. *2022 3rd International Conference for Emerging Technology, INCET 2022*, 1–6. DOI: 10.1109/INCET54531.2022.9824457

Namysl, M., & Konya, I. (2019). *Efficient, lexicon-free OCR using deep learning*. Paper presented at the 2019 International Conference on Document Analysis and Recognition (ICDAR). DOI: 10.1109/ICDAR.2019.00055

Naticchia, B., Giretti, A., & Carbonari, A. (2007). Set up of an automated multi-colour system for interior wall painting. *International Journal of Advanced Robotic Systems*, 4(4), 407–416. DOI: 10.5772/5666

Nazari, F., & Yan, W. (2022). Convolutional versus Dense Neural Networks: Comparing the Two Neural Networks' Performance in Predicting Building Operational Energy Use Based on the Building Shape. *Building Simulation Conference Proceedings*, 495–502. DOI: 10.26868/25222708.2021.30735

Nguyen, N.-D., Do, T., Ngo, T. D., & Le, D.-D. (2020). An evaluation of deep learning methods for small object detection. *Journal of Electrical and Computer Engineering*, 2020(1), 3189691. DOI: 10.1155/2020/3189691

Nieminen, M. (2023). The Transformer Model and Its Impact on the Field of Natural Language Processing.

Nithya, S., Presskila, X. A., Sakthivel, B., Krishnan, R. S., Narayanan, K. L., & Sundararajan, S. (2023, September). Enhancing Sentiment Analysis of Twitter Data Using Recurrent Neural Networks with Attention Mechanism. In 2023 4th International Conference on Smart Electronics and Communication (ICOSEC) (pp. 1348-1354). IEEE.

Novielli, N., Calefato, F., Dongiovanni, D., Girardi, D., & Lanubile, F. (2020, June). Can we use se-specific sentiment analysis tools in a cross-platform setting? In *Proceedings of the 17th International Conference on Mining Software Repositories* (pp. 158-168).

Onyedum, A. (2012). *Social media Neologisms: A morpho-semantic analysis*. University of Lagos.

Onyema, E. M., Shukla, P. K., Dalal, S., Mathur, M. N., Zakariah, M., & Tiwari, B. (2021). Enhancement of patient facial recognition through deep learning algorithm: ConvNet. *Journal of Healthcare Engineering*, *2021*(1), 5196000. DOI: 10.1155/2021/5196000 PMID: 34912534

Oquab, M., Bottou, L., Laptev, I., & Sivic, J. (2014). *Learning and transferring mid-level image representations using convolutional neural networks*. Paper presented at the Proceedings of the IEEE conference on computer vision and pattern recognition. DOI: 10.1109/CVPR.2014.222

Oquab, M., Bottou, L., Laptev, I., & Sivic, J. (2014). *Weakly supervised object recognition with convolutional neural networks*. Paper presented at the Proc. of NIPS.

Pabba, C., & Kumar, P. (2022). An intelligent system for monitoring students' engagement in large classroom teaching through facial expression recognition. *Expert Systems: International Journal of Knowledge Engineering and Neural Networks*, *39*(1), e12839. DOI: 10.1111/exsy.12839

Pal, S. K., Pramanik, A., Maiti, J., & Mitra, P. (2021). Deep learning in multi-object detection and tracking: State of the art. *Applied Intelligence*, *51*(9), 6400–6429. DOI: 10.1007/s10489-021-02293-7

Pathak, A. R., Pandey, M., & Rautaray, S. (2018). Application of deep learning for object detection. *Procedia Computer Science*, *132*, 1706–1717. DOI: 10.1016/j.procs.2018.05.144

Patil, S. M., Raut, C. M., Pande, A. P., Yeruva, A. R., & Morwani, H. (2022). An efficient approach for object detection using deep learning. *Journal of Pharmaceutical Negative Results*, ●●●, 563–572. DOI: 10.47750/pnr.2022.13.S09.062

Patro, K. K., Prakash, A. J., Neelapu, B. C., Tadeusiewicz, R., Acharya, U. R., Hammad, M., & Pławiak, P. (2023). Application of Kronecker convolutions in deep learning technique for automated detection of kidney stones with coronal CT images. *Information Sciences*, *640*, 119005. DOI: 10.1016/j.ins.2023.119005

Pinheiro, P. O., Collobert, R., & Dollár, P. (2015). *Learning to segment object candidates*. Paper presented at the Advances in neural information processing systems.

Pitts, W., & McCulloch, W. S. (1947). How we know universals the perception of auditory and visual forms. *The Bulletin of Mathematical Biophysics*, *9*(3), 127–147. DOI: 10.1007/BF02478291 PMID: 20262674

Popescu, A., & Vaľko, M. (2023). Social Media Sentiment Analysis in the Age of Big Data: Understanding User Behavior and Predicting Trends. *International Journal of Business Intelligence and Big Data Analytics*, *6*(1), 31–39.

Poria, S., Cambria, E., Winterstein, G., & Huang, G. B. (2014). Sentic patterns: Dependency-based rules for concept-level sentiment analysis. *Knowledge-Based Systems*, *69*, 45–63. DOI: 10.1016/j.knosys.2014.05.005

Prakash, A. J., Patro, K. K., Hammad, M., Tadeusiewicz, R., & Pławiak, P. (2022). BAED: A secured biometric authentication system using ECG signal based on deep learning techniques. *Biocybernetics and Biomedical Engineering*, *42*(4), 1081–1093. DOI: 10.1016/j.bbe.2022.08.004

Prusa, J. D., & Khoshgoftaar, T. M. (2017). Improving deep neural network design with new text data representations. *Journal of Big Data*, *4*(1), 1–16. DOI: 10.1186/s40537-017-0065-8

Qian, Y., Xu, W., Liu, X., Ling, H., Jiang, Y., Chai, Y., & Liu, Y. (2022). Popularity prediction for marketer-generated content: A text-guided attention neural network for multi-modal feature fusion. *Information Processing & Management*, *59*(4), 102984. DOI: 10.1016/j.ipm.2022.102984

Raees, M., & Fazilat, S. (2024). Lexicon-based sentiment analysis on text polarities with evaluation of classification models. arXiv preprint arXiv:2409.12840.

Raghavan, V. V., Gudivada, V. N., Govindaraju, V., & Rao, C. R. (2016). *Cognitive computing: Theory and applications*. Elsevier.

Rahamathunnisa, U., Sudhakar, K., Padhi, S., Bhattacharya, S., Shashibhushan, G., & Boopathi, S. (2024). Sustainable Energy Generation From Waste Water: IoT Integrated Technologies. In *Adoption and Use of Technology Tools and Services by Economically Disadvantaged Communities: Implications for Growth and Sustainability* (pp. 225–256). IGI Global.

Rahim, A., Zhong, Y., Ahmad, T., Ahmad, S., Pławiak, P., & Hammad, M. (2023). Enhancing smart home security: Anomaly detection and face recognition in smart home IoT devices using logit-boosted CNN models. *Sensors (Basel), 23*(15), 6979. DOI: 10.3390/s23156979 PMID: 37571762

Rahim, M., Amin, F., Tag Eldin, E. M., Khalifa, A. E. W., & Ahmad, S. (2024). p, q-Spherical fuzzy sets and their aggregation operators with application to third-party logistic provider selection. *Journal of Intelligent & Fuzzy Systems, 46*(1), 505–528.

Rangayya, V., Virupakshappa, , & Patil, N. (2024). Improved face recognition method using SVM-MRF with KTBD based KCM segmentation approach. *International Journal of System Assurance Engineering and Management, 15*(1), 1–12. DOI: 10.1007/s13198-021-01483-3

Rao, S., Li, Y., Ramakrishnan, R., Hassaine, A., Canoy, D., Cleland, J., . . . informatics, h. (2022). An explainable transformer-based deep learning model for the prediction of incident heart failure. *26*(7), 3362-3372.

Reddy, P., & Nithya, R. (2024, May). Comparative analysis of detection rate in real-time novel facial recognition using k-nearest neighbor algorithm with linear discriminant analysis algorithm. In *AIP Conference Proceedings* (Vol. 2853, No. 1). AIP Publishing. DOI: 10.1063/5.0203740

Reddy, M. A., Reddy, B. M., Mukund, C., Venneti, K., Preethi, D., & Boopathi, S. (2023). Social Health Protection During the COVID-Pandemic Using IoT. In *The COVID-19 Pandemic and the Digitalization of Diplomacy* (pp. 204–235). IGI Global. DOI: 10.4018/978-1-7998-8394-4.ch009

Redmon, J. (2016). *You only look once: Unified, real-time object detection.* Paper presented at the Proceedings of the IEEE conference on computer vision and pattern recognition. DOI: 10.1109/CVPR.2016.91

Redmon, J. J. a. p. a. (2018). Yolov3: An incremental improvement.

Redmon, J., & Farhadi, A. (2017). *YOLO9000: better, faster, stronger.* Paper presented at the Proceedings of the IEEE conference on computer vision and pattern recognition.

Ren, S., He, K., Girshick, R., & Sun, J. (2015). *Faster r-cnn: Towards real-time object detection with region proposal networks.* Paper presented at the Advances in neural information processing systems.

Ren, J., Zhang, D., He, S., Zhang, Y., & Li, T. (2019). A survey on end-edge-cloud orchestrated network computing paradigms: Transparent computing, mobile edge computing, fog computing, and cloudlet. *ACM Computing Surveys*, *52*(6), 1–36. DOI: 10.1145/3362031

Ren, S., He, K., Girshick, R., Zhang, X., & Sun, J. (2016). Object detection networks on convolutional feature maps. *IEEE Transactions on Pattern Analysis and Machine Intelligence*, *39*(7), 1476–1481. DOI: 10.1109/TPAMI.2016.2601099 PMID: 27541490

Rosenfeld, A. (1988). Computer vision: Basic principles. *Proceedings of the IEEE*, *76*(8), 863–868. DOI: 10.1109/5.5961

Rumelhart, D. E., Hinton, G. E., & Williams, R. J. (1988). Learning representations by back-propagating errors. *Cognitive modeling, 5*(3), 1.

Russakovsky, O., Deng, J., Su, H., Krause, J., Satheesh, S., Ma, S., & Bernstein, M. (2015). Imagenet large scale visual recognition challenge. *International Journal of Computer Vision*, *115*(3), 211–252. DOI: 10.1007/s11263-015-0816-y

Sakr, A. S., Pławiak, P., Tadeusiewicz, R., & Hammad, M. (2022). Cancelable ECG biometric based on combination of deep transfer learning with DNA and amino acid approaches for human authentication. *Information Sciences*, *585*, 127–143. DOI: 10.1016/j.ins.2021.11.066

Sakr, A. S., Soliman, N. F., Al-Gaashani, M. S., Pławiak, P., Ateya, A. A., & Hammad, M. (2022). An efficient deep learning approach for colon cancer detection. *Applied Sciences (Basel, Switzerland)*, *12*(17), 8450. DOI: 10.3390/app12178450

Salankar, N., Qaisar, S. M., Pławiak, P., Tadeusiewicz, R., & Hammad, M. (2022). EEG based alcoholism detection by oscillatory modes decomposition second order difference plots and machine learning. *Biocybernetics and Biomedical Engineering*, *42*(1), 173–186. DOI: 10.1016/j.bbe.2021.12.009

Samikannu, R., Koshariya, A. K., Poornima, E., Ramesh, S., Kumar, A., & Boopathi, S. (2022). Sustainable Development in Modern Aquaponics Cultivation Systems Using IoT Technologies. In *Human Agro-Energy Optimization for Business and Industry* (pp. 105–127). IGI Global.

Sánchez-Rada, J. F., & Iglesias, C. A. (2019). Social context in sentiment analysis: Formal definition, overview of current trends and framework for comparison. *Information Fusion*, *52*, 344–356. DOI: 10.1016/j.inffus.2019.05.003

Saravanan, S., Khare, R., Umamaheswari, K., Khare, S., Krishne Gowda, B. S., & Boopathi, S. (2024). AI and ML Adaptive Smart-Grid Energy Management Systems: Exploring Advanced Innovations. In *Principles and Applications in Speed Sensing and Energy Harvesting for Smart Roads* (pp. 166–196). IGI Global. DOI: 10.4018/978-1-6684-9214-7.ch006

Sarro, F., Moussa, R., Petrozziello, A., & Harman, M. (2020). Learning from mistakes: Machine learning enhanced human expert effort estimates. *IEEE Transactions on Software Engineering*, *48*(6), 1868–1882. DOI: 10.1109/TSE.2020.3040793

Sattar, T., Ullah, M. I., & Ahmad, B. (2022). The role of stakeholders participation, goal directness and learning context in determining student academic performance: Student engagement as a mediator. *Frontiers in Psychology*, *13*, 13. DOI: 10.3389/fpsyg.2022.875174 PMID: 35928408

Saurav, S., Saini, R., & Singh, S. (2023). Fast facial expression recognition using boosted histogram of oriented gradient (BHOG) features. *Pattern Analysis & Applications*, *26*(1), 381–402. DOI: 10.1007/s10044-022-01112-0

Schneider, S., Taylor, G. W., & Kremer, S. (2018). Deep learning object detection methods for ecological camera trap data. *2018 15th Conference on Computer and Robot Vision (CRV)*, 321–328.

Sedik, A., Hammad, M., Abd El-Latif, A. A., El-Banby, G. M., Khalaf, A. A., Abd El-Samie, F. E., & Iliyasu, A. M. (2021). Deep learning modalities for biometric alteration detection in 5G networks-based secure smart cities. *IEEE Access : Practical Innovations, Open Solutions*, *9*, 94780–94788. DOI: 10.1109/ACCESS.2021.3088341

Semary, N. A., Ahmed, W., Amin, K., Pławiak, P., & Hammad, M. (2023). Improving sentiment classification using a RoBERTa-based hybrid model. *Frontiers in Human Neuroscience*, *17*, 1292010. DOI: 10.3389/fnhum.2023.1292010 PMID: 38130432

Semary, N. A., Ahmed, W., Amin, K., Pławiak, P., & Hammad, M. (2024, February). Enhancing machine learning-based sentiment analysis through feature extraction techniques. *PLoS One*, *19*(2). Advance online publication. DOI: 10.1371/journal.pone.0294968 PMID: 38354193

Semary, N., Ahmed, W., Amin, K., Pławiak, P., & Hammad, M. (2024). Enhancing machine learning-based sentiment analysis through feature extraction techniques. *PLoS One*, *19*(2), e0294968.

Sermanet, P., Eigen, D., Zhang, X., Mathieu, M., Fergus, R., & LeCun, Y. (2013). Overfeat: Integrated recognition, localization and detection using convolutional networks. *arXiv preprint arXiv:1312.6229*.

Sfärlea, A., Buhl, C., Lukas, L., & Schulte-Körne, G. (2024). Superior facial emotion recognition in adolescents with anorexia nervosa–A replication study. *European Eating Disorders Review*, *32*(5), 943–951. DOI: 10.1002/erv.3103 PMID: 38733271

Shamsan, A. H., & Faridi, A. R. (2019, March). Network softwarization for IoT: A survey. In 2019 6th International Conference on Computing for Sustainable Global Development (INDIACom) (pp. 1163-1168). IEEE.

Sharma, N. A., Ali, A. S., & Kabir, M. A. (2024). A review of sentiment analysis: Tasks, applications, and deep learning techniques. *International Journal of Data Science and Analytics*, ●●●, 1–38. DOI: 10.1007/s41060-024-00594-x

Shen, Z., Liu, Z., Li, J., Jiang, Y.-G., Chen, Y., & Xue, X. (2017). *Dsod: Learning deeply supervised object detectors from scratch*. Paper presented at the Proceedings of the IEEE International Conference on Computer Vision. DOI: 10.1109/ICCV.2017.212

Shrivastava, A., Gupta, A., & Girshick, R. (2016). *Training region-based object detectors with online hard example mining*. Paper presented at the Proceedings of the IEEE conference on computer vision and pattern recognition. DOI: 10.1109/CVPR.2016.89

Shu, C., Liu, Y., Gao, J., Yan, Z., & Shen, C. (2021). *Channel-wise knowledge distillation for dense prediction*. Paper presented at the Proceedings of the IEEE/CVF International Conference on Computer Vision.

Shukla, K., Vashishtha, E., Sandhu, M., & Choubey, P. R. (2023). *Natural Language Processing: Unlocking the Power of Text and Speech Data*. Xoffencerpublication.

Sikha, O. K., & Bharath, B. (2022). VGG16-random Fourier hybrid model for masked face recognition. *Soft Computing*, *26*(22), 12795–12810. DOI: 10.1007/s00500-022-07289-0 PMID: 35844262

Simonyan, K., & Zisserman, A. (2014). Very deep convolutional networks for large-scale image recognition. *arXiv preprint arXiv:1409.1556*.

Singh, B., & Davis, L. S. (2018). *An analysis of scale invariance in object detection snip*. Paper presented at the Proceedings of the IEEE conference on computer vision and pattern recognition. DOI: 10.1109/CVPR.2018.00377

Singh, J., Saheer, L. B., & Faust, O. (2023). Speech Emotion Recognition Using Attention Model. *International Journal of Environmental Research and Public Health*, *20*(6), 5140. DOI: 10.3390/ijerph20065140 PMID: 36982048

Singh, P., Kansal, M., Singh, R., Kumar, S., & Sen, C. (2024). A Hybrid Approach based on Haar Cascade, Softmax, and CNN for Human Face Recognition: A HYBRID APPROACH FOR HUMAN FACE RECOGNITION. [JSIR]. *Journal of Scientific and Industrial Research*, *83*(4), 414–423.

Song, Y., Ali, N., & Nater, U. M. (2024). The effect of music on stress recovery. *Psychoneuroendocrinology*, *168*, 107137. DOI: 10.1016/j.psyneuen.2024.107137 PMID: 39024851

Sonia, R., Gupta, N., Manikandan, K., Hemalatha, R., Kumar, M. J., & Boopathi, S. (2024). Strengthening Security, Privacy, and Trust in Artificial Intelligence Drones for Smart Cities. In *Analyzing and Mitigating Security Risks in Cloud Computing* (pp. 214–242). IGI Global. DOI: 10.4018/979-8-3693-3249-8.ch011

Sreedevi, A. G., Harshitha, T. N., Sugumaran, V., & Shankar, P. (2022). Application of cognitive computing in healthcare, cybersecurity, big data and IoT: A literature review. *Information Processing & Management*, *59*(2), 102888.

Sreedevi, A. G., Nitya Harshitha, T., Sugumaran, V., & Shankar, P. (2022). Vijayan Sugumaran, and P. Shankar. "Application of cognitive computing in healthcare, cybersecurity, big data and IoT: A literature review.". *Information Processing & Management*, *59*(2), 102888. DOI: 10.1016/j.ipm.2022.102888

Sriman, K. P., Kumar, P. R., Naveen, A., & Kumar, R. S. (2021, March). Comparison of Paul Viola–Michael Jones algorithm and HOG algorithm for face detection. [). IOP Publishing.]. *IOP Conference Series. Materials Science and Engineering*, *1084*(1), 012014.

Stieglitz, S., Dang-Xuan, L., Bruns, A., & Neuberger, C. (2014). Social media analytics: An interdisciplinary approach and its implications for information systems. *Business & Information Systems Engineering*, *6*(2), 89–96. DOI: 10.1007/s12599-014-0315-7

Subbaiah, B., Murugesan, K., Saravanan, P., & Marudhamuthu, K. (2024). An efficient multimodal sentiment analysis in social media using hybrid optimal multi-scale residual attention network. *Artificial Intelligence Review*, *57*(2), 34. DOI: 10.1007/s10462-023-10645-7

Suman, C., Chaudhary, R. S., Saha, S., & Bhattacharyya, P. (2022). An attention based multi-modal gender identification system for social media users. *Multimedia Tools and Applications*, *81*(19), 1–23. DOI: 10.1007/s11042-021-11256-6

Sun, S., Pang, J., Shi, J., Yi, S., & Ouyang, W. (2018). *Fishnet: A versatile backbone for image, region, and pixel level prediction.* Paper presented at the Advances in neural information processing systems.

Sundar, R., Srikaanth, P. B., Naik, D. A., Murugan, V. P., Karumudi, M., & Boopathi, S. (2024). Achieving Balance Between Innovation and Security in the Cloud With Artificial Intelligence of Things: Semantic Web Control Models. In *Advances in Web Technologies and Engineering* (pp. 1–26). IGI Global. DOI: 10.4018/979-8-3693-1487-6.ch001

Sun, Z., Wang, G., Li, P., Wang, H., Zhang, M., & Liang, X. (2024). An improved random forest based on the classification accuracy and correlation measurement of decision trees. *Expert Systems with Applications*, *237*, 121549. DOI: 10.1016/j. eswa.2023.121549

Swarakar, J. R.. (2018).. . *Design and Fabrication of Automatic Spray Painting Machine*, (2), 1388–1394.

Szegedy, C., Ioffe, S., Vanhoucke, V., & Alemi, A. A. (2017). *Inception-v4, inception-resnet and the impact of residual connections on learning.* Paper presented at the Thirty-First AAAI Conference on Artificial Intelligence. DOI: 10.1609/aaai. v31i1.11231

Szegedy, C., Liu, W., Jia, Y., Sermanet, P., Reed, S., Anguelov, D., . . . Rabinovich, A. (2015). *Going deeper with convolutions.* Paper presented at the Proceedings of the IEEE conference on computer vision and pattern recognition.

Szegedy, C., Vanhoucke, V., Ioffe, S., Shlens, J., & Wojna, Z. (2016). *Rethinking the inception architecture for computer vision.* Paper presented at the Proceedings of the IEEE conference on computer vision and pattern recognition. DOI: 10.1109/ CVPR.2016.308

Tang, C., Feng, Y., Yang, X., Zheng, C., & Zhou, Y. (2017). The object detection based on deep learning. *2017 4th International Conference on Information Science and Control Engineering (ICISCE)*, 723–728.

Thakar, D., & Vora, C. P. (2014). A Review on Design & Development of Semi-Automated Colour Painting Machine [Online] [. Available: www.ijera.com.]. *J. Eng. Res. Appl.*, *4*(4), 58–61. www.ijera.com

Thakkar, A., & Lohiya, R. (2021). A review on machine learning and deep learning perspectives of IDS for IoT: Recent updates, security issues, and challenges. *Archives of Computational Methods in Engineering*, *28*(4), 3211–3243. DOI: 10.1007/ s11831-020-09496-0

Thakur, D., Saini, J. K., & Srinivasan, S. (2023). DeepThink IoT: The strength of deep learning in internet of things. *Artificial Intelligence Review*, *56*(12), 14663–14730. DOI: 10.1007/s10462-023-10513-4

Thatere, A., Meshram, A., Verma, P., & Jirapure, A. (2024, March). Face Recognition under Occlusion: An efficient Handcrafted Feature & SVM based Approach. In *2024 IEEE International Conference on Interdisciplinary Approaches in Technology and Management for Social Innovation (IATMSI)* (Vol. 2, pp. 1-5). IEEE. DOI: 10.1109/ IATMSI60426.2024.10502484

Thilagavathi, B., Suthendran, K., & Srujanraju, K. (2021). Evaluating the AdaBoost algorithm for biometric-based face recognition. In *Data Engineering and Communication Technology* [Springer Singapore.]. *Proceedings of ICDECT*, *2020*, 669–678.

Tirlangi, S., Teotia, S., Padmapriya, G., Senthil Kumar, S., Dhotre, S., & Boopathi, S. (2024). Cloud Computing and Machine Learning in the Green Power Sector: Data Management and Analysis for Sustainable Energy. In *Developments Towards Next Generation Intelligent Systems for Sustainable Development* (pp. 148–179). IGI Global. DOI: 10.4018/979-8-3693-5643-2.ch006

Toivonen, T., Heikinheimo, V., Fink, C., Hausmann, A., Hiippala, T., Järv, O., Tenkanen, H., & Di Minin, E. (2019). Social media data for conservation science: A methodological overview. *Biological Conservation*, *233*, 298–315. DOI: 10.1016/j. biocon.2019.01.023

Tong, K., Wu, Y., & Zhou, F. (2020). Recent advances in small object detection based on deep learning: A review. *Image and Vision Computing*, *97*, 103910. DOI: 10.1016/j.imavis.2020.103910

Tripathi, R. K., & Jalal, A. S. (2021, May). A Local Descriptor for Age Invariant Face Recognition under Uncontrolled Environment. In *2021 2nd International Conference on Secure Cyber Computing and Communications (ICSCCC)* (pp. 513-517). IEEE. DOI: 10.1109/ICSCCC51823.2021.9478154

Tripathy, J. K., Sethuraman, S. C., Cruz, M. V., Namburu, A., Mangalraj, P., & Vijayakumar, V. (2021). Comprehensive analysis of embeddings and pre-training in NLP. *Computer Science Review*, *42*, 100433. DOI: 10.1016/j.cosrev.2021.100433

Tsimenidis, S., Lagkas, T., & Rantos, K. (2022). Deep learning in IoT intrusion detection. *Journal of Network and Systems Management*, *30*(1), 8. DOI: 10.1007/ s10922-021-09621-9

Ugandar, R., Rahamathunnisa, U., Sajithra, S., Christiana, M. B. V., Palai, B. K., & Boopathi, S. (2023). Hospital Waste Management Using Internet of Things and Deep Learning: Enhanced Efficiency and Sustainability. In *Applications of Synthetic Biology in Health, Energy, and Environment* (pp. 317–343). IGI Global.

Uijlings, J. R., Van De Sande, K. E., Gevers, T., & Smeulders, A. W. (2013). Selective search for object recognition. *International Journal of Computer Vision, 104*(2), 154–171. DOI: 10.1007/s11263-013-0620-5

Ullah, R., Asif, M., Shah, W. A., Anjam, F., Ullah, I., Khurshaid, T., Wuttisittikulkij, L., Shah, S., Ali, S. M., & Alibakhshikenari, M. (2023). Speech Emotion Recognition Using Convolution Neural Networks and Multi-Head Convolutional Transformer. *Sensors (Basel), 23*(13), 6212. DOI: 10.3390/s23136212 PMID: 37448062

Vaillant, R., Monrocq, C., & Le Cun, Y. (1994). Original approach for the localisation of objects in images. *IEE Proceedings. Vision Image and Signal Processing, 141*(4), 245–250. DOI: 10.1049/ip-vis:19941301

Vakalopoulou, M., Christodoulidis, S., Burgos, N., Colliot, O., & Lepetit, V. (2023). *Deep Learning: Basics and Convolutional Neural Networks (CNNs)* (pp. 77–115). DOI: 10.1007/978-1-0716-3195-9_3

Van Houdt, G., Mosquera, C., & Nápoles, G. (2020). A review on the long short-term memory model. *Artificial Intelligence Review, 53*(8), 5929–5955. DOI: 10.1007/s10462-020-09838-1

Vassakis, K., Petrakis, E., & Kopanakis, I. (2018). Big data analytics: applications, prospects and challenges. Mobile big data: A roadmap from models to technologies, 3-20.

Veeranjaneyulu, R., Boopathi, S., Kumari, R. K., Vidyarthi, A., Isaac, J. S., & Jaiganesh, V. (2023). Air Quality Improvement and Optimisation Using Machine Learning Technique. *IEEE- Explore*, 1–6.

Velickovski, F., Ceccaroni, L., Roca, J., Burgos, F., Galdiz, J. B., Marina, N., & Lluch-Ariet, M. (2014). Clinical Decision Support Systems (CDSS) for preventive management of COPD patients. *Journal of Translational Medicine, 12*(Suppl 2), 1–10. DOI: 10.1186/1479-5876-12-S2-S9 PMID: 25471545

Venkatasubramanian, V., Chitra, M., Sudha, R., Singh, V. P., Jefferson, K., & Boopathi, S. (2024). Examining the Impacts of Course Outcome Analysis in Indian Higher Education: Enhancing Educational Quality. In *Challenges of Globalization and Inclusivity in Academic Research* (pp. 124–145). IGI Global.

Venkateswaran, N., Kiran Kumar, K., Maheswari, K., Kumar Reddy, R. V., & Boopathi, S. (2024). Optimizing IoT Data Aggregation: Hybrid Firefly-Artificial Bee Colony Algorithm for Enhanced Efficiency in Agriculture. *AGRIS On-Line Papers in Economics and Informatics, 16*(1), 117–130. DOI: 10.7160/aol.2024.160110

Viola, P., & Jones, M. (2001). *Rapid object detection using a boosted cascade of simple features.* Paper presented at the Proceedings of the 2001 IEEE computer society conference on computer vision and pattern recognition. CVPR 2001. DOI: 10.1109/CVPR.2001.990517

von Eschenbach, W. J. (2021). Transparency and the black box problem: Why we do not trust AI. *Philosophy & Technology, 34*(4), 1607–1622. DOI: 10.1007/s13347-021-00477-0

Wadley, F. (1952). Probit Analysis: A Statistical Treatment of the Sigmoid Response Curve. DJ Finney. New York-London: Cambridge Univ. Press, 1952. 318 pp. $7.00. In: American Association for the Advancement of Science.

Wang, C.-Y., Yeh, I.-H., & Liao, H.-Y. M. J. a. p. a. (2024). Yolov9: Learning what you want to learn using programmable gradient information.

Wang, J., Xue, M., Culhane, R., Diao, E., Ding, J., & Tarokh, V. (2020). Speech emotion recognition with dual-sequence LSTM architecture. *ICASSP, IEEE International Conference on Acoustics, Speech and Signal Processing - Proceedings, 2020-May*, 6474–6478. DOI: 10.1109/ICASSP40776.2020.9054629

Wang, X. & others. (2016). Deep learning in object recognition, detection, and segmentation. *Foundations and Trends® in Signal Processing, 8*(4), 217–382.

Wang, Y., Zhang, X., Yang, T., & Sun, J. J. a. p. a. (2021). Anchor DETR: Query design for transformer-based object detection. *3*(6).

Wang, F. Y., Yang, L., Cheng, X., Han, S., & Yang, J. (2016). Network softwarization and parallel networks: Beyond software-defined networks. *IEEE Network, 30*(4), 60–65. DOI: 10.1109/MNET.2016.7513865

Wang, Y., Kung, L., & Byrd, T. A. (2018). Big data analytics: Understanding its capabilities and potential benefits for healthcare organizations. *Technological Forecasting and Social Change, 126*, 3–13. DOI: 10.1016/j.techfore.2015.12.019

Wan, S., Gu, Z., & Ni, Q. (2020). Cognitive computing and wireless communications on the edge for healthcare service robots. *Computer Communications, 149*, 99–106. DOI: 10.1016/j.comcom.2019.10.012

Webb, B. (2000). What does robotics offer animal behaviour? *Animal Behaviour, 60*(5), 545–558. DOI: 10.1006/anbe.2000.1514 PMID: 11082225

Weiss, M., Jacob, F., & Duveiller, G. (2020). Remote sensing for agricultural applications: A meta-review. *Remote Sensing of Environment, 236,* 111402. DOI: 10.1016/j.rse.2019.111402

Wen, K. C. S., Markom, M. A., Tan, E. S. M. M., Adom, A. H., & Markom, A. M. (2024, February). Multi faces recognition using deep learning approach. In *AIP Conference Proceedings* (Vol. 2898, No. 1). AIP Publishing. DOI: 10.1063/5.0192131

Wiley, V., & Lucas, T. (2018). Computer Vision and Image Processing: A Paper Review. *Int. J. Artif. Intell. Res., 2*(1), 22. DOI: 10.29099/ijair.v2i1.42

Wu, D., Qiang, J., Hong, W., Du, H., Yang, H., Zhu, H., Pan, H., Shen, Z., & Chen, S. (2024). Artificial intelligence facial recognition system for diagnosis of endocrine and metabolic syndromes based on a facial image database. *Diabetes & Metabolic Syndrome, 18*(4), 103003. DOI: 10.1016/j.dsx.2024.103003 PMID: 38615568

Wu, X., Sahoo, D., & Hoi, S. C. (2020). Recent advances in deep learning for object detection. *Neurocomputing, 396,* 39–64. DOI: 10.1016/j.neucom.2020.01.085

Xiao, B., & Kang, S.-C. (2021). Development of an image data set of construction machines for deep learning object detection. *Journal of Computing in Civil Engineering, 35*(2), 05020005. DOI: 10.1061/(ASCE)CP.1943-5487.0000945

Xiao, Y., Tian, Z., Yu, J., Zhang, Y., Liu, S., Du, S., & Lan, X. (2020). A review of object detection based on deep learning. *Multimedia Tools and Applications, 79*(33-34), 23729–23791. DOI: 10.1007/s11042-020-08976-6

Xie, S., Girshick, R., Dollár, P., Tu, Z., & He, K. (2017). *Aggregated residual transformations for deep neural networks.* Paper presented at the Proceedings of the IEEE conference on computer vision and pattern recognition. DOI: 10.1109/CVPR.2017.634

Xu, M., Zhang, F., & Zhang, W. (2021). Head Fusion: Improving the Accuracy and Robustness of Speech Emotion Recognition on the IEMOCAP and RAVDESS Dataset. *IEEE Access : Practical Innovations, Open Solutions, 9,* 74539–74549. DOI: 10.1109/ACCESS.2021.3067460

Xun, G., Jia, X., Gopalakrishnan, V., & Zhang, A. (2016). A survey on context learning. *IEEE Transactions on Knowledge and Data Engineering, 29*(1), 38–56. DOI: 10.1109/TKDE.2016.2614508

Xu, Q. A., Chang, V., & Jayne, C. (2022). A systematic review of social media-based sentiment analysis: Emerging trends and challenges. *Decision Analytics Journal*, *3*, 100073. DOI: 10.1016/j.dajour.2022.100073

Xu, Z., Liu, W., Huang, J., Yang, C., Lu, J., & Tan, H. (2020). Artificial intelligence for securing IoT services in edge computing: A survey. *Security and Communication Networks*, *2020*, 1–13. DOI: 10.1155/2020/8872586

Yadav, A., & Vishwakarma, D. K. (2020). Sentiment analysis using deep learning architectures: A review. *Artificial Intelligence Review*, *53*(6), 4335–4385. DOI: 10.1007/s10462-019-09794-5

Yang, Z., & Nevatia, R. (2016). *A multi-scale cascade fully convolutional network face detector.* Paper presented at the 2016 23rd International Conference on Pattern Recognition (ICPR).

Yıldırım, S., & Asgari-Chenaghlu, M. (2024). *Mastering Transformers: The Journey from BERT to Large Language Models and Stable Diffusion.* Packt Publishing Ltd.

Yoo, D., Park, S., Lee, J.-Y., Paek, A. S., & So Kweon, I. (2015). *Attentionnet: Aggregating weak directions for accurate object detection.* Paper presented at the Proceedings of the IEEE International Conference on Computer Vision. DOI: 10.1109/ICCV.2015.305

Yousefpour, A., Fung, C., Nguyen, T., Kadiyala, K., Jalali, F., Niakanlahiji, A., Kong, J., & Jue, J. P. (2019). All one needs to know about fog computing and related edge computing paradigms: A complete survey. *Journal of Systems Architecture*, *98*, 289–330. DOI: 10.1016/j.sysarc.2019.02.009

Yousif, A., Niu, Z., Tarus, J. K., & Ahmad, A. (2019). A survey on sentiment analysis of scientific citations. *Artificial Intelligence Review*, *52*(3), 1805–1838. DOI: 10.1007/s10462-017-9597-8

Yousuf, W. B., Talha, U., Abro, A. A., Ahmad, S., Daniyal, S. M., Ahmad, N., & Ateya, A. A. (2024). Novel Prognostic Methods for System Degradation Using LSTM. *IEEE Access : Practical Innovations, Open Solutions*.

Yu, F., Koltun, V., & Funkhouser, T. (2017). *Dilated residual networks.* Paper presented at the Proceedings of the IEEE conference on computer vision and pattern recognition.

Zaidi, S. S. A., Ansari, M. S., Aslam, A., Kanwal, N., Asghar, M., & Lee, B. (2022). A survey of modern deep learning based object detection models. *Digital Signal Processing*, *126*, 103514. DOI: 10.1016/j.dsp.2022.103514

Zeiler, M. D., & Fergus, R. (2014). *Visualizing and understanding convolutional networks*. Paper presented at the European conference on computer vision.

Zhang, H. J. a. p. a. (2017). mixup: Beyond empirical risk minimization.

Zhang, H., Wang, Y., Dayoub, F., & Sunderhauf, N. (2021). *Varifocalnet: An iou-aware dense object detector*. Paper presented at the Proceedings of the IEEE/CVF conference on computer vision and pattern recognition.

Zhang, K., Ni, J., Yang, K., Liang, X., Ren, J., & Shen, X. S. (2017). Security and privacy in smart city applications: Challenges and solutions. *IEEE Communications Magazine, 55*(1), 122–129. DOI: 10.1109/MCOM.2017.1600267CM

Zhang, Q., Gong, Y., Wu, J., Huang, H., & Huang, X. (2016, October). Retweet prediction with attention-based deep neural network. In *Proceedings of the 25th ACM international on conference on information and knowledge management* (pp. 75-84).

Zhang, W. Z., Elgendy, I. A., Hammad, M., Iliyasu, A. M., Du, X., Guizani, M., & Abd El-Latif, A. A. (2020). Secure and optimized load balancing for multitier IoT and edge-cloud computing systems. *IEEE Internet of Things Journal, 8*(10), 8119–8132. DOI: 10.1109/JIOT.2020.3042433

Zhang, X., Yang, Y.-H., Han, Z., Wang, H., & Gao, C. (2013). Object class detection: A survey. *ACM Computing Surveys, 46*(1), 1–53. DOI: 10.1145/2522968.2522978

Zhang, Y., Wu, C., Qiao, C., Sadek, A., & Hulme, K. F. (2022). A cognitive computational model of driver warning response performance in connected vehicle systems. *IEEE Transactions on Intelligent Transportation Systems, 23*(9), 14790–14805. DOI: 10.1109/TITS.2021.3134058

Zhao, Q., Sheng, T., Wang, Y., Tang, Z., Chen, Y., Cai, L., & Ling, H. (2019). *M2det: A single-shot object detector based on multi-level feature pyramid network*. Paper presented at the Proceedings of the AAAI Conference on Artificial Intelligence. DOI: 10.1609/aaai.v33i01.33019259

Zhao, Z.-Q., Zheng, P., Xu, S., & Wu, X. (2019). Object detection with deep learning: A review. *IEEE Transactions on Neural Networks and Learning Systems, 30*(11), 3212–3232. DOI: 10.1109/TNNLS.2018.2876865 PMID: 30703038

Zheng, Z., Wang, P., Liu, W., Li, J., Ye, R., & Ren, D. (2020). *Distance-IoU loss: Faster and better learning for bounding box regression*. Paper presented at the Proceedings of the AAAI conference on artificial intelligence. DOI: 10.1609/aaai.v34i07.6999

Zhou, Y., Liu, L., Shao, L., & Mellor, M. (2016). *DAVE: A unified framework for fast vehicle detection and annotation.* Paper presented at the European Conference on Computer Vision. DOI: 10.1007/978-3-319-46475-6_18

Zhou, B., Lapedriza, A., Khosla, A., Oliva, A., & Torralba, A. (2017). Places: A 10 million image database for scene recognition. *IEEE Transactions on Pattern Analysis and Machine Intelligence, 40*(6), 1452–1464. DOI: 10.1109/TPAMI.2017.2723009 PMID: 28692961

Zhou, J., Zhang, Q., Zeng, S., Zhang, B., & Fang, L. (2024). Latent linear discriminant analysis for feature extraction via isometric structural learning. *Pattern Recognition, 149*, 110218. DOI: 10.1016/j.patcog.2023.110218

About the Contributors

Sadique Ahmad has achieved over 70 research articles in peer-reviewed journals and conferences. Also, over 5 research articles are under review in top journals such as Information Sciences (Elsevier), Expert Systems with Application, Scientific Report, and Applied Soft Computing (Elsevier). Currently, I am focusing on Deep Cognitive Modeling for Multiple Goals, such as Cognitive Modelling in Image Segmentation, Image Analysis, Trust Management in Social Cybersecurity, and IoT. Previously, I worked on Cognitive Computing, Deep Cognitive Modeling for Students' Performance Prediction, and Cognitive Modeling in Object Detection using remote sensing images.

Mansoor Ebrahim received the Ph.D. degree from Sunway University, Malaysia, in 2017. He is currently the Head of the Department of Software Engineering, Iqra University. His current research interests include image processing, network security, and VSN.

Mohamed A. ElAffendi is currently a Professor of computer science with the Department of Computer Science, Prince Sultan University, the Former Dean of CCIS, AIDE, the Rector, the Founder, and the Director of the Data Science Laboratory (EIAS), and the Founder and the Director of the Center of Excellence in CyberSecurity. His current research interests include data science, intelligent and cognitive systems, machine learning, and natural language processing.

Mohamed Hammad Received my Ph.D. degree in 2019, at the School of Computer Science and Technology, Harbin Institute of Technology, Harbin, China. I'm an assistant professor in the Faculty of Computers and Information, Menoufia University, Egypt. I'm currently a researcher in the EIAS Data Science Lab, College of Computer and Information Sciences, Prince Sultan University. My research interests include Biomedical Imaging, Bioinformatics, Cyber Security, IoT, Computer Vision, Machine Learning, Deep Learning, Pattern Recognition, and

Biometrics. I have published more than 50 papers in international SCI-IF journals. Furthermore, I have served as an Editor Board member in PLOS ONE journal, an Editor Board member in BMC Bioinformatics journal, an Associate Editor in IJISP, a Topics Board editor in Forensic Sciences (MPDI) journal, a guest editor in many international journals such as IJDCF, Sensors (MDPI) and Information (MDPI). Reviewer of more than 500 papers for many prestigious journals and listed in the top 2% of scientists worldwide (According to the recently released list by Stanford University USA in 2022 and 2023.

***

Faiza Abbasi holds a Bachelor's degree in Computer Science from Karachi University and is currently pursuing her Master's degree at Iqra University. She is also working in the FEST department at Iqra University.

Abdul Ahad Abro received the Ph.D. degree in computer engineering from Ege University, Turkiye, with a focus on artificial intelligence, deep learning, computer vision, and machine learning. In his studies, he is working on conceptualizing, designing, and implementing artificial intelligence products. He is currently an Assistant Professor at the Faculty of Engineering Science and Technology, Computer Science Department, Iqra University.

Lubna Aziz is a dedicated and accomplished researcher and educator in the field of Artificial Intelligence (AI). With a Ph.D. in Computer Science from Universiti Teknologi Malaysia and a strong publication record, Dr. Aziz specializes in applying AI techniques to healthcare and environmental monitoring. Her expertise includes deep learning, explainable AI, and generative AI models. Currently, she serves as the Head of the Artificial Intelligence Department at Iqra University, Karachi, where she leads research and teaching initiatives. Dr. Aziz's commitment to academic excellence is evident in her numerous awards and recognitions, including Gold Medals for her undergraduate and graduate studies. Her passion for AI and her dedication to her students make her a valuable asset to the academic community.

J.S.S.L. Bharani, Department of S.R.K.R. Engineering College, Bhimavaram, Andhra Pradesh 534204, India.

|Mirzan Bin Mahadir - Contributing Author|I'm a graduate in Bachelor of Science with Honours in Computer Science with Artificial Intelligence. I am eager to learn and create projects revolves around machine learning, deep learning and GenAI that can be implemented in real life use cases.

Dhanya D, Department of Artificial Intelligence and Data Science,Mar Ephraem College of Engineering and Technology,Kanyakumari, Tamil Nadu 629171, India.

Syed Muhammad Daniyal received the M.S. degree in Computer Science from Iqra University, Pakistan, with a focus on artificial intelligence, medical imaging, computer vision, and machine learning. He is currently a Junior Lecturer at the Faculty of Engineering Science and Technology, Computer Science Department, Iqra University.

N Divya, Department of Civil Engineering, Prince Shri Venkateshwara Padmavathy Engineering College, Chennai, Tamil Nadu 600127, India.

Sakthivel M, Assistant Professor Department of Electronics and Communication Engineering, Velammal College of Engineering and Technology Madurai, Tamil Nadu 625014, India.

Nellore Manoj Kumar, Department of Saveetha School of Engineering,Saveetha Institute of Medical and Technical Sciences (SIMATS),Thandalam, Chennai, Tamil Nadu 602105, India.

Pydikalva Padmavathi, Department of Electrical and Electronics Engineering, Srinivasa Ramanujan Institute of Technology, Rotarypuramu Village, BKS Mandal Anantapuramu Andhra Pradesh 515701, India.

Lakshmana Phanendra Magulur, Department of Computer Science and Engineering, Koneru Lakshmaiah Education Foundation, 'Vaddeswaram, Andhra Pradesh 522302 India.

R. Rajitha Jasmine, Department of Information Technology, R.M.K. Engineering College, Tamil Nadu 601206, India.

Muhammad Atif Saeed is an Assistant Professor in the Department of Mechatronics Engineering at SZABIST University, where he has been serving for the past five years. His research focuses on promoting sustainability in design and manufacturing, as well as process optimization and effective decision-making. With a strong passion for innovation and education, Mr. Saeed continues to contribute to the academic and research community, inspiring future generations of engineers and researchers.

M L Sworna Kokila, Department of Computing Technologies, School of Computing, Faculty of Engineering and Technology, SRM Institute of Science and Technology, Kattankulathur, Tamil Nadu 603203, India.

V.Thrimurthulu Department of Computer Science Engineering, MLR Institute of Technology, Hyderabad, Telangana 500043, India.

Sailaja V, Department of Electronics and Communication and Engineering, Pragati Engineering College, Surampalem, Andhra Pradesh 533437, India.

Ilyas Younus is a Senior Lecturer at Iqra University, where he has been contributing to academic excellence for several years. He holds a Master's degree in Telecommunication from Iqra University, specializing in advanced communication technologies. With a passion for teaching and a deep understanding of his field, Ilyas plays a key role in shaping the next generation of professionals in telecommunications and related disciplines.

Index

A

Automation 20, 97, 98, 100, 101, 103, 105, 110, 111, 112, 113, 115, 116, 119, 126, 128, 129, 131, 132, 142, 150, 151, 152, 177, 263, 264

B

Backbone Networks 181, 210
Benchmark Datasets 181, 187
big data 1, 2, 3, 4, 13, 14, 17, 18, 19, 20, 21, 22, 26, 27, 28, 29, 30, 31, 56, 57, 59, 92, 122, 147, 260

C

CNN 29, 57, 63, 66, 67, 68, 69, 81, 85, 86, 87, 88, 92, 94, 97, 99, 102, 103, 104, 105, 106, 108, 109, 110, 118, 139, 183, 184, 185, 187, 188, 189, 190, 192, 202, 203, 204, 208, 209, 210, 211, 212, 224, 225, 226, 228, 229, 233, 236, 237, 238, 240, 241, 244, 245, 248, 249, 250, 251, 257, 258, 260
Cognitive computation 2
Cognitive Computing 1, 2, 3, 4, 5, 6, 7, 8, 9, 10, 12, 13, 15, 16, 17, 18, 19, 20, 21, 22, 23, 24, 26, 27, 28, 29, 30, 31, 57, 159
Computer Vision 11, 12, 30, 64, 65, 66, 70, 73, 77, 80, 92, 93, 98, 122, 136, 144, 181, 182, 184, 185, 186, 199, 207, 209, 212, 214, 222, 223, 224, 225, 226, 227, 228, 229, 230, 231, 232, 237, 263, 267, 289
Convolutional Neural Networks 35, 65, 66, 67, 68, 70, 80, 85, 93, 101, 102, 104, 108, 127, 130, 139, 146, 182, 183, 186, 207, 209, 225, 226, 228, 236, 250, 257, 262
cybersecurity 1, 2, 3, 4, 15, 16, 17, 19, 20, 21, 22, 23, 27, 30, 90, 121, 154, 177, 221, 260, 287

D

deep learning 25, 27, 29, 30, 35, 36, 43, 54, 55, 56, 58, 60, 61, 63, 64, 65, 66, 67, 68, 69, 71, 72, 81, 86, 92, 93, 95, 97, 98, 99, 100, 101, 102, 103, 104, 106, 108, 110, 111, 114, 115, 116, 117, 118, 120, 121, 122, 123, 124, 125, 126, 127, 128, 129, 130, 131, 132, 133, 134, 135, 138, 139, 140, 141, 142, 143, 144, 145, 146, 147, 148, 149, 150, 151, 152, 153, 155, 156, 157, 158, 174, 175, 178, 181, 182, 183, 184, 185, 186, 188, 212, 213, 221, 222, 227, 228, 229, 233, 234, 235, 236, 237, 240, 241, 244, 257, 259, 260, 261, 262, 287
DNN 233, 239, 241, 247, 248, 249, 250, 257, 258

E

Emotion Detection 63, 67, 77, 81, 82
Energy Management 105, 123, 126, 127, 128, 145, 146, 152, 157
Environmental Monitoring 7, 126, 127, 128, 145, 146

F

Face Expression Recognition 75, 78
Faster R-CNN 68, 99, 102, 108, 109, 110, 185, 187, 188, 189, 226, 229
Feature Extraction 42, 60, 63, 64, 65, 66, 67, 68, 69, 70, 74, 76, 77, 79, 95, 98, 108, 109, 126, 127, 130, 137, 140, 163, 164, 179, 185, 194, 199, 207, 237, 240, 243, 248, 267

H

healthcare 1, 2, 3, 4, 6, 9, 10, 11, 12, 13, 14, 17, 18, 19, 20, 21, 22, 27, 28, 30, 31, 71, 88, 89, 93, 105, 106, 111, 113, 122, 150, 151, 155, 156

I

Industrial Automation 103, 111, 119, 126, 131, 132, 142, 150, 263, 264

Integration Strategies 128

Internet of Things 1, 4, 17, 25, 27, 31, 121, 122, 126, 128, 132, 155, 156, 157, 158

IoT 1, 2, 3, 4, 5, 6, 7, 8, 9, 17, 19, 20, 21, 22, 23, 25, 26, 27, 29, 30, 31, 97, 98, 99, 100, 102, 103, 105, 106, 109, 111, 112, 113, 114, 115, 116, 117, 118, 119, 120, 121, 122, 123, 125, 126, 127, 128, 129, 130, 131, 132, 133, 134, 135, 136, 138, 139, 140, 141, 142, 143, 144, 145, 146, 147, 148, 149, 150, 151, 152, 153, 154, 155, 156, 157, 158

L

LSTM 57, 61, 66, 71, 127, 139, 140, 233, 236, 238, 240, 241, 245, 246, 248, 249, 250, 251, 257, 258, 261, 262

M

machine learning 2, 9, 11, 15, 23, 26, 29, 30, 34, 55, 56, 60, 65, 66, 71, 93, 98, 118, 121, 123, 126, 130, 134, 135, 137, 142, 144, 150, 155, 156, 157, 158, 160, 161, 162, 163, 164, 167, 169, 176, 177, 178, 179, 183, 223, 225, 235, 237, 244, 266, 287

Multi-modal Content 46

N

Natural Language Processing 2, 5, 9, 11, 13, 15, 20, 26, 27, 28, 29, 33, 34, 55, 56, 57, 59, 60, 66, 140, 152, 165, 166, 178, 207, 287

O

Object Detection 68, 72, 97, 98, 99, 100, 101, 102, 103, 105, 108, 109, 110, 111, 112, 113, 114, 115, 116, 117, 118, 119, 120, 121, 122, 123, 124, 131, 139, 181, 182, 184, 185, 186, 187, 188, 191, 196, 197, 198, 199, 200, 202, 203, 206, 207, 208, 209, 211, 212, 214, 215, 216, 219, 222, 223, 224, 225, 227, 228, 229, 230, 231, 267, 280, 287, 288

P

Performance Metrics 48, 143, 181

Predictive Maintenance 105, 116, 117, 126, 128, 143, 144, 146, 147, 152

R

R-CNN 68, 99, 102, 108, 109, 110, 184, 185, 187, 188, 189, 202, 210, 224, 225, 226, 229

Real-time Analysis 175

Recommendation System 234, 247, 248, 252, 258

S

Sentiment Analysis 15, 28, 29, 33, 34, 35, 36, 40, 41, 42, 43, 44, 45, 46, 47, 48, 49, 51, 52, 53, 54, 55, 56, 57, 58, 59, 60, 61, 159, 160, 161, 162, 163, 164, 165, 167, 169, 170, 171, 172, 173, 174, 175, 176, 178, 179

Smart Engineering 125, 126, 128, 143, 146, 149, 150, 151, 152, 153

Smart Environments 97, 100, 101, 103, 105, 106, 109, 110, 112, 115

Smart Manufacturing 8, 98, 126, 127, 128, 131, 144, 146, 152, 154

Smart Painting 263, 265, 271, 273, 275, 276, 277, 283, 284, 285

Social Media 14, 15, 20, 33, 34, 35, 36, 37, 38, 39, 40, 41, 42, 43, 44, 45, 46, 47, 48, 49, 51, 52, 53, 54, 55, 56, 57, 58, 59, 60, 61, 63, 159, 160, 161, 162, 163, 164, 177

Speech 52, 56, 58, 60, 89, 183, 223, 225, 233, 234, 235, 236, 237, 238, 240, 241, 242, 243, 247, 248, 257, 259,

260, 261, 262

SSD 188, 202, 228

T

Text Processing 40, 52

Transformer Models 35, 66

Y

YOLO 97, 99, 100, 102, 103, 111, 112, 113, 114, 115, 120, 181, 185, 188, 189, 190, 191, 192, 194, 195, 196, 197, 199, 202, 205, 206

Printed in the United States
by Baker & Taylor Publisher Services